INTEREST GROUP POLITICS

INTEREST GROUP POLITICS

Eighth Edition

Edited by

Allan J. Cigler
Burdett A. Loomis
University of Kansas

Los Angeles | London | New Delhi
Singapore | Washington DC

CQ Press
2300 N Street, NW, Suite 800
Washington, DC 20037

Phone: 202-729-1900; toll-free, 1-866-4CQ-PRESS (1-866-427-7737)

Web: www.cqpress.com

Cover design: Anne C. Kerns, Anne Likes Red, Inc.
Composition: C&M Digitals (P) Ltd.

♾ The paper used in this publication exceeds the requirements of the American
National Standard for Information Sciences—Permanence of Paper for Printed Library
Materials, ANSI Z39.48-1992.

Printed and bound in the United States of America

15   14   13   12   11   1   2   3   4   5

Library of Congress Cataloging-in-Publication Data

Interest group politics / edited by Allan J. Cigler, Burdett A. Loomis. — 8th ed.
   p. cm.
  Includes bibliographical references and index.
  ISBN 978-1-60426-637-5 (pbk. : alk. paper) 1. Pressure groups—United States.
I. Cigler, Allan J. II. Loomis, Burdett A.
  JK1118.I565 2011
  322.4'30973—dc23

2011025072

Contents

Preface

Almost thirty years ago, two then-young political science professors at the University of Kansas thought there should be a new collection of original essays on interest groups. They made a few inquiries and decided to work with the fledgling CQ Press. That was the beginning of a most pleasant and rewarding mutual relationship, spanning eight editions and dozens of authors and many first-rate contributions to the literature on organized interests.

This edition, like all those that followed the initial one, seeks to address major scholarly issues while simultaneously providing contemporary perspectives and analyses on a wide range of group-based topics. In this edition we address the classic questions of group survival over time, collective action issues, and the role of groups in financing electoral politics. At the same time, we include new and innovative pieces on the interest group–political party connections within the Congress, the development of organized interests during the eighteenth century, and the potential of groups to teach their members and leaders the skills to participate in civic action.

The most important domestic policy issue of the past several years has been health care reform. We are especially pleased to include three distinct perspectives on how organized interests influenced, and were influenced by, the 2009–2010 battle over health care legislation. Richard L. Hall and Richard Anderson address the growth of issue advertising by groups, while Timothy M. LaPira compares the group politics over the Clinton reform proposals in 1993–1994 with the politicking over the recent legislation, developed in the Congress but often referred to as "Obamacare." And Maryann Barakso provides a distinct perspective by examining the internal struggles within the American Medical Association, a still-significant group but one that has lost power over the past few decades.

Much as in past editions, we seek to provide both breadth and depth in assessing the changing roles of organized interests, even as the contexts of American politics have evolved over the years—especially in the extent to which political parties have gained strength in Capitol Hill decision making. And we continue to wrestle with the question of the centrality of groups within the American political process. In the end, we have come to believe that, while groups are indeed significant, using organized interests to develop comprehensive explanations about American politics is a losing proposition. Rather, interest groups must always be considered as part of the political context of representation across society, and their impact can sometimes be decisive.

As with any edited volume, many people deserve thanks for their valuable contributions. As always, we are indebted to our contributors, who once again have produced well-written essays on important topics. At CQ Press over the years we have benefited from two wonderful political science editors—Brenda Carter and Charisse Kiino. We can scarcely give them enough credit, and they've been great fun to work with. Paula Fleming has done a great job with this volume's copyediting, which is par for the course with CQ Press.

As always, Beth Cigler and Michel Loomis have demonstrated tremendous patience with two veteran scholars, who truly enjoy what we do and the modest contributions we may make.

Allan Cigler
Burdett Loomis
Lawrence, Kansas
April 2011

Contributors

Richard Anderson is a PhD candidate in the Department of Political Science at the University of Michigan. His research interests include distributive politics, interest groups, and political representation.

Kenneth T. Andrews is Associate Professor of Sociology at the University of North Carolina at Chapel Hill. He studies social movements, political institutions, and social changes. He has developed a movement infrastructure theory to explain why civil rights organizing had an enduring legacy in some areas but not others. His current projects examine civil rights campaigns in desegregated public facilities, the diffusion of local prohibition laws, and the organization of and leadership in contemporary environmental movements.

Matthew Baggetta is Assistant Professor of Public and Environmental Affairs at Indiana University. His research examines the effects of voluntary associations on civic engagement. He has studied the unintended politicizing effects of participation in recreational arts groups and is developing a new study of youth civic development.

Maryann Barakso earned her PhD at MIT and is currently Assistant Professor in the Department of Political Science at the University of Massachusetts–Amherst. Her research and publications explore the factors influencing the strategic and tactical choices of interest groups and the political and civic implications of those choices. She is the author of *Governing Now: Grassroots Activism in the National Organization for Women* (2004). Her recent research examines the role of dissent in interest groups and social movement organizations. She is president-elect of the Women and Politics Research Section of the American Political Science Association.

Allan J. Cigler is Chancellors Club Teaching Professor of Political Science at the University of Kansas. His research and teaching interests focus upon parties and interest groups in the US context. In recent years his research activity and publications have explored the role and consequences of organized interest money in federal elections, especially money not regulated by the Federal Election Commission.

Beverly A. Cigler is Professor of Public Policy and Administration at Penn State–Harrisburg and is a fellow at the National Academy of Public Administration. She specializes in intermunicipal and state-local relations, service delivery, public finance, and emergency management. Her current research involves state funding mandates, capacity building, and system change related to local governments during times of fiscal stress.

Lee Drutman is an adjunct professor at the University of California, Berkeley and teaches at the University of California, Washington Center. His research focuses on corporate lobbying in American politics.

Michael Franz is Associate Professor of Government and Legal Studies at Bowdoin College. His research interests include campaign finance and political advertising. He is the author or coauthor of three books, including *Choices and Changes: Interest Groups in the Electoral Process* (2008), and is currently codirector of the Wesleyn Media Project, which tracks and codes political ads on television.

Marshall Ganz is Lecturer in Public Policy at the Kennedy School of Government, where he specializes in leadership, organizing, and advocacy in social movements, civic associations, and politics. His work has been published in the *American Journal of Sociology*, *American Political Science Review*, *American Prospect*, *Washington Post*, *Los Angeles Times*, and elsewhere. His newest book, *Why David Sometimes Wins: Leadership, Organization, and Strategy in the California Farm Worker Movement* (2009), earned the Michael J. Harrington Book Award of the American Political Science Association. He was awarded an honorary doctorate in divinity by the Episcopal Divinity School in 2010.

Richard L. Hall is Professor of Political Science and Public Policy at the University of Michigan. He teaches and conducts research on legislative politics and political advocacy. He is currently writing a book on lobbying in US national policy making and starting a project on issue advertising.

Darren R. Halpin is Associate Professor of Political Science at Aarhus University, Denmark. He also holds the post of Visiting Professor at the Robert Gordon University, United Kingdom. He has published widely on interest groups, representation, and public policy, including his most recent book, *Groups, Representation, and Democracy* (2010).

Hahrie C. Han is the Sidney R. Knafel Assistant Professor of Social Sciences at Wellesley College and was a Robert Wood Johnson Health Policy Scholar at Harvard University in 2009–2011. Her research focuses on civic and political participation, civic organizations, and political organizing. Her first book, *Moved to Action: Motivation, Inequality, and Participation in American Politics*, was published in 2009.

Michael T. Heaney is Assistant Professor of Organization Studies and Political Science at the University of Michigan. He studies the interaction of interest groups, political parties, and social movements through political networks. His current research focuses on the interplay between the Democratic Party and the antiwar movement in the United States after 9/11.

Ronald J. Hrebenar is Professor of Political Science and former Director of the Hinckley Institute of Politics at the University of Utah. His books include *Japan's New Party System* (2000), *Interest Group Politics in America* (1997), *Parties, Interest Groups, and Political Campaigns* (2008), and *Lobbying in America* (2009). He is also the author and coauthor of over fifty articles and book chapters on interest groups, lobbying, and political parties.

Timothy M. LaPira is Assistant Professor of Political Science at James Madison University. His current research projects examine the structure and dynamics of new policy domains and interest group agendas.

Chaeyoon Lim is Assistant Professor of Sociology at the University of Wisconsin–Madison. His current research includes the effects of interpersonal behavior on political behavior, the civic and political outcomes of religious involvement, and the civic consequences of economic hard times.

Burdett A. Loomis is professor of political science at the University of Kansas. A former American Political Science Association Congressional Fellow and recipient of a Kemper Teaching Award, he has written extensively on legislatures, political careers, interest groups, and policymaking. His recent publications include the edited volume *The U.S. Senate: From Deliberation to Dysfunction* (2011).

James M. McCormick is Professor and Chair of the Department of Political Science at Iowa State University. He has authored or edited ten books, including the fifth edition of *American Foreign Policy and Process* (2010) and the fifth edition of *The Domestic Sources of American Foreign Policy: Insights and Evidence*, coedited with Eugene R. Wittkopf (2008). In addition, he has published more than sixty book chapters and articles on American foreign policy and international politics in such journals as *World Politics*, *American Political Science Review*, *American Journal of Political Science*, *The Journal of Politics*, *International Studies Quarterly*, and *Legislative Studies Quarterly*.

Anthony J. Nownes is Professor of Political Science at the University of Tennessee–Knoxville. His most recent research focuses on interest group populations, interest group survival, and lobbying. His book *Pressure and Power: Interest Groups in American Politics* will be published by Routledge in 2012.

Clive S. Thomas is a Senior Fellow at the Foley Institute for Public Policy at Washington State University. Previously he taught at the University of Alaska. He has published extensively on interest groups and lobbying, most recently on Latin America as a region and on its individual countries.

Jennifer Nicoll Victor is Assistant Professor of Political Science at the University of Pittsburgh. Her research focuses on legislative politics, primarily in the US Congress, interest group participation in lawmaking, and social network analysis.

1

Introduction

The Changing Nature of Interest Group Politics*

Burdett A. Loomis and Allan J. Cigler

From James Madison to Madison Avenue, political interests have played a central role in American politics. But this great continuity in our political experience has been matched by ambivalence toward interest groups from citizens, politicians, and scholars. James Madison's warnings of the dangers of faction echo in the rhetoric of reformers from Populists and Progressives near the turn of the century to the so-called public interest advocates of today.

If organized special interests are nothing new in American politics, can today's group politics nevertheless be seen as having changed fundamentally? Acknowledging that many important, continuing trends exist, we seek to place in perspective a broad series of changes in modern interest group politics. Among the most substantial of these developments are these:

- A great proliferation of interest groups since the early 1960s
- A centralization of group headquarters in Washington, D.C., rather than New York City or elsewhere
- Major technological developments in information processing that promote more sophisticated, more timely, and more specialized communications strategies, such as grassroots lobbying and the message politics of issue-based campaigns
- The rise of single-issue groups
- Changes in campaign finance laws (1971, 1974) and the ensuing growth of political action committees (PACs) and, more recently, the sharp increases in soft money contributions to parties and issue advocacy campaign advertisements for individual candidates
- The increased formal penetration of political and economic interests into the bureaucracy (advisory committees), the presidency

---

*This overview chapter remains unchanged from its revision circa 2000 of a piece first written in 1983. Thus references to the "health care debate" address the Clinton-era proposals, and some material does not reflect subsequent developments, especially for campaign finance. See Allan Cigler's Chapter 7 for relevant updates.

(White House group representatives), and the Congress (caucuses of members)

- The continuing decline of political parties' ability to perform key electoral and policy-related activities, despite their capacity to funnel soft money to candidates
- The increased number, activity, and visibility of public interest groups, such as Common Cause and the Ralph Nader–inspired public interest research organizations
- The growth of activity and impact of institutions, including corporations, universities, state and local governments, and foreign interests
- A continuing rise in the amount and sophistication of group activity in state capitals, especially given the devolution of some federal programs and substantial increases in state budgets

All these developments have antecedents in earlier eras of American political life; there is little that is genuinely new under the interest group sun. Political action committees have replaced (or complemented) other forms of special interest campaign financing. Group-generated mail directed at Congress has been a tactic since at least the early 1900s.[1] Many organizations have long been centered in Washington, D.C., members of Congress traditionally have represented local interests, and so on.

Still, the level of group activity, coupled with growing numbers of organized interests, distinguishes contemporary group politics from the politics of earlier eras. Group involvement trends lend credence to the fears of scholars such as political scientist Theodore Lowi and economist Mancur Olson, who have viewed interest-based politics as contributing to governmental stalemate and reduced accountability.[2] If accurate, these analyses point to a fundamentally different role for interest groups than those suggested by Madison and group theorists after him.

Only during the past thirty years, in the wake of Olson's pathbreaking research, have scholars begun to examine realistically why people join and become active in groups.[3] It is by no means self-evident that citizens should naturally become group members—quite the contrary in most cases. We are faced, then, with the paradoxical and complex question of why groups have proliferated when it can be economically unwise for people to join them.

Interest Groups in American Politics

Practical politicians and scholars alike generally agree that interest groups (also known as factions, organized interests, pressure groups, and special interests) are natural phenomena in a democratic regime—that is, individuals will band together to protect their interests.[4] In Madison's words, "The causes of faction . . . are sown in the nature of man." But controversy continues as to whether groups and group politics are benign or malignant forces in American politics. "By a faction," Madison wrote, "I understand a number of citizens, whether amounting to a majority or minority of the whole, who are united and actuated by some common impulse of passion, or of interest, adverse to the rights of other citizens, or to the permanent and aggregate interests of the community."[5]

Although Madison rejected the remedy of direct controls over factions as "worse than the disease," he saw the need to limit their negative effects by promoting competition among them and by devising an elaborate system of procedural "checks and balances" to reduce the potential power of any single, strong group, whether that interest represented a majority or minority position.

Hostility toward interest groups became more virulent in industrialized America, where the great concentrations of power far outstripped anything Madison might have imagined. In the early twentieth century many Progressives railed at various monopolistic "trusts" and intimate connections between interests and corrupt politicians. Later, in 1935, Hugo Black, then a senator and later a Supreme Court justice, painted a grim picture of group malevolence: "Contrary to tradition, against the public morals, and hostile to good government, the lobby has reached such a position of power that it threatens government itself. Its size, its power, its capacity for evil, its greed, trickery, deception and fraud condemn it to the death it deserves."[6]

Similar suspicions are expressed today, especially in light of the increased role of money in electoral politics. The impact of groups on elections has grown steadily since the adoption of the Federal Election Campaign Act of 1971 and its 1974 amendments—reform legislation originally intended to limit the impact of organized interests. Instead, such interests accelerated their spending on campaigns. Until the 1990s most concerns focused on PACs; indeed, direct PAC contributions to congressional candidates rose from less than $23 million in 1975–1976 to nearly $260 million in the 1999–2000 election cycle. The number of PACs has leveled off at about 4,000, and only a few are major players in electoral politics. Moreover, PACs encourage large numbers of contributors to pool their funds, a tactic that enhances Americans' political participation.

More worrisome over the past decade have been the growing amount and impact of essentially unregulated money from organized interests. "Soft money" contributions to national political parties totaled nearly $600 million in 2000, almost doubling the amount in the 1996 presidential year. Democrats received 98 percent more, and Republicans upped their totals by 81 percent. Even more troublesome may be issue advocacy advertising by organized interests, which does not fall under the expenditure limits and disclosure requirements of the Federal Election Commission. Thus in the 2000 campaign, the drug industry group called Citizens for Better Medicare spent more than $40 million on advertisements designed to help congressional allies, both past and prospective.[7] At the time, this group and many like it did not need to disclose where their funds came from. Nor was there any limit on the amount of expenditures, as long as they did not "expressly advocate" a preference for a candidate (that is, use the words vote for and similar words) or coordinate efforts with a candidate or party committee.

By focusing on "hard money" activity (largely reported contributions to candidates), "the [Federal Election Commission] . . . could no longer restrain most of the financial activity that takes place in modern elections."[8] Such an environment has renewed calls for additional campaign finance reform. So far, however, Congress has resisted changing laws that regulate group activity in national elections, and public cynicism about special interest influence will likely continue.

Pluralism and Liberalism

Despite popular distrust of interest group politics, political scientists and other observers often have viewed groups in a positive light. This perspective draws on Madison's *Federalist* writings but is tied more closely to the growth of the modern state. Political science scholars such as Arthur Bentley, about 1910, and David Truman, forty years later, placed groups at the heart of politics and policy making in a complex, large, and increasingly specialized governmental system. The interest group becomes an element of continuity in a changing political world. Truman noted the "multiplicity of co-ordinate or nearly co-ordinate points of access to governmental decisions" and concluded that "the significance of these many points of access and of the complicated texture of relationships among them is great. This diversity assures various ways for interest groups to participate in the formation of policy, and this variety is a flexible, stabilizing element."[9]

Derived from Truman's work and that of other group-oriented scholars is the notion of the pluralist state, in which competition among interests, in and out of government, will produce policies roughly responsive to public desires and no single set of interests will dominate.

> Pluralist theory assumes that within the public arena there will be countervailing centers of power within governmental institutions and among outsiders. Competition is implicit in the notion that groups, as surrogates for individuals, will produce products representing the diversity of opinions that might have been possible in the individual decision days of democratic Athens.[10]

In many ways the pluralist vision of American politics corresponds to the realities of policy making and the distribution of policy outcomes, but a host of scholars, politicians, and other observers have roundly criticized this perspective. Two broad (although sometimes contradictory) critiques have special merit.

The first argues that some interests habitually lose in the policy process, while others habitually win. Without endorsing the contentions of elite theorists that a small number of interests and individuals conspire to dominate societal policies, one can make a strong case that interests with more resources (money, access, information, and so forth) usually will obtain better results than interests that possess fewer assets and employ them less effectively. The small, cohesive, well-heeled defense industry, for example, does well year in and year out in policy making; marginal farmers and the urban poor produce a much less successful track record.[11] Based on continuing unequal results, critics of the pluralist model argue that interests are still represented unevenly and unfairly.

The second critique generally agrees that inequality of results remains an important aspect of group politics. But this perspective, most forcefully set out by Theodore Lowi, sees interests as generally succeeding in their goals of influencing government—to the point that government itself, in one form or another, provides a measure of protection to almost all societal interests. Everyone thus retains some vested interest in the structure of government and array of public policies. This does not mean that all interests get exactly what they want from governmental policies; rather, all interests get at least some rewards. From this point of view, the tobacco industry surely wishes to see its crop subsidies maintained, but the small farmer and the urban poor also have pet programs, such as guaranteed loans and food stamps.

Lowi has labeled the proliferation of groups and their growing access to government "interest group liberalism." He argues that this phenomenon is pathological for a democratic government:

> Interest group liberal solutions to the problem of power [who will exercise it] provide the system with stability by spreading a sense of representation at the expense of genuine flexibility, at the expense of democratic forms, and ultimately at the expense of legitimacy.[12]

Interest group liberalism is pluralism, but it is sponsored pluralism, and the government is the chief sponsor. On the surface, it appears that the unequal results and interest group liberalism critiques of pluralism are at odds. Reconciliation, however, is relatively straightforward. Lowi does not suggest that all interests are effectively represented. Rather, there exists in many instances only the appearance of representation. Political scientist Murray Edelman pointed out that a single set of policies can provide two related types of rewards: tangible benefits for the few and symbolic reassurances for the many.[13] Such a combination encourages groups to form, become active, and claim success.

The Climate for Group Proliferation

Substantial cleavages among citizens are essential for interest group development. American culture and the constitutional arrangements of the US government have encouraged the emergence of multiple political interests. In the pre-Revolutionary period, sharp conflicts existed between commercial and landed interests, debtor and creditor classes, coastal residents and those in the hinterlands, and citizens with either Tory or Whig political preferences. As the new nation developed, its vastness, characterized by geographical regions varying in climate, economic potential, culture, and tradition, contributed to a great heterogeneity. Open immigration policies further led to a diverse cultural mix with a wide variety of racial, ethnic, and religious backgrounds represented among the populace. Symbolically, the notion of the United States as a "melting pot," emphasizing group assimilation, has received much attention, but a more appropriate image may be a "tossed salad."[14]

The Constitution also contributes to a favorable environment for group development. Guarantees of free speech, association, and the right to petition the government for redress of grievances are basic to group formation. Because political organization often parallels government structure, federalism and the separation of powers—principles embodied in the Constitution—have greatly influenced large numbers of interest groups in the United States.

The decentralized political power structure in the United States allows important decisions to be made at the national, state, or local levels. Within each level of government there are multiple points of access. For example, business-related policies such as taxes are acted on at each level, and interest groups may affect these policies in the legislative, executive, or judicial arenas. In the case of federated organizations such as the U.S. Chamber of Commerce, state and local affiliates often act independently of the national organization. Numerous business organizations thus focus on the varied channels of access.

In addition, the decentralized political parties found in the United States are less unified and disciplined than parties in many other nations. The resulting power vacuum in the decision-making process offers great potential for alternative political organizations, such as interest groups, to influence policy. Even in an era of strong legislative parties (mid-1980s on), many opportunities for influence remain.

Finally, American cultural values may encourage group development. As Alexis de Tocqueville observed in the 1830s, values such as individualism and the need for personal achievement underlie the propensity of citizens to join groups. Moreover, the large number of access points—local, state, and national—contributes to Americans' strong sense of political efficacy when compared with that expressed by citizens of other nations.[15] Not only do Americans see themselves as joiners, but they tend to belong to more political groups than do people of other countries.[16]

Theories of Group Development

A climate favorable to group proliferation does little to explain how interest groups organize. Whatever interests are latent in society and however favorable the context for group development may be, groups do not arise spontaneously. Farmers and a landed interest existed long before farm organizations first appeared; laborers and craftspeople were on the job before unions. In a simple society, even though distinct interests exist, there is little need for interest group formation. Farmers have no political or economic reason to organize when they work only for their families. Before the industrial revolution, workers were craftspeople who often labored in small family enterprises. Broad-based political organizations were not needed, although local guilds often existed to train apprentices and protect jobs.

David Truman has suggested that increasing societal complexity, characterized by economic specialization and social differentiation, is fundamental to group proliferation.[17] In addition, technological changes and the increasing interdependence of economic sectors often create new interests and redefine old ones. Robert Salisbury's discussion of American farming is instructive:

> The full-scale commercialization of agriculture, beginning largely with the Civil War, led to the differentiation of farmers into specialized interests, each increasingly different from the next. . . . The interdependence that accompanied the specialization process meant potential conflicts of interests or values both across the bargaining encounter and among the competing farmers themselves as each struggled to secure his own position.[18]

Many political scientists assume that an expansion of the interest group universe is a natural consequence of growing societal complexity. According to Truman, however, group formation "tends to occur in waves" and is greater in some periods than in others.[19] Groups organize politically when the existing order is disturbed and certain interests are, in turn, helped or hurt.

It is not surprising, then, that economic interests develop both to improve their position and to protect existing advantages. The National Association of Manufacturers originally was created to further the expansion of business opportunities in foreign trade, but it became a more powerful organization largely in response to the rise of organized labor.[20] Mobilization of business interests since the 1960s often has resulted from threats posed by consumer advocates and environmentalists, as well as requirements imposed by the steadily growing role of the federal government.

Disturbances that trigger group formation need not be strictly economic or technological. Wars, for example, place extreme burdens on society, and lengthy conflicts lead to a growth of groups, whether based on support of (World War II) or opposition to (Vietnam) the conflict. Likewise, broad societal changes may disturb the status quo. The origin of the Ku Klux Klan, for example, was fear that increased numbers of ethnic and racial minorities threatened white, Christian America.

Truman's theory of group proliferation suggests that the interest group universe is inherently unstable. Groups formed from an imbalance of interests in one area induce a subsequent disequilibrium, which acts as a catalyst for individuals to form groups as counterweights to the new perceptions of inequity. Group politics thus is characterized by successive waves of mobilization and countermobilization. The liberalism of one era may prompt the resurgence of conservative groups in the next. Similarly, periods of business domination often are followed by eras of reform group ascendancy. In the 1990s health care reform proposals raised the stakes for almost all segments of society. Interest group politicking reached historic proportions as would-be reformers, the medical community, and business interests sought to influence the direction of change in line with their own preferences. And given the complexity of health care policy making, the struggles among organized interests will surely continue for years.

Personal Motivations and Group Formation

Central to theories of group proliferation are the pluralist notions that elements of society possess common needs and share a group identity or consciousness, and that these are sufficient conditions for the formation of effective political organizations. Although the perception of common needs may be necessary for political organization, whether it is sufficient for group formation and effectiveness is open to question. Historical evidence documents many instances in which groups have not emerged spontaneously, even when circumstances such as poverty or discrimination would seem, in retrospect, to have required it.

Mancur Olson effectively challenged many pluralist tenets in *The Logic of Collective Action*, first published in 1965. Basing his analysis on a model of the "rational economic man," Olson posited that even individuals who have common interests are not inclined to join organizations that attempt to address their concerns. The major barrier to group participation is the "free rider" problem: "rational" individuals choose not to bear the participation costs (time, membership fees) because they can enjoy the group benefits (such as favorable legislation) without joining. Groups that pursue "collective" benefits, which accrue to all members of a class or segment of society regardless of membership status, will have great difficulty forming and surviving. According to Olson, it would be economically irrational for individual farmers to join a group seeking higher farm prices when benefits from price increases would be enjoyed by all farmers, even those who contribute nothing to the group. Similarly, it would be irrational for an individual environmentalist to become part of organized attempts to reduce air pollution, when all citizens, members of environmental groups or not, would reap the benefits of cleaner air. The free rider problem is especially serious for large groups because the larger the group, the less likely an individual will perceive his or her contribution as having any impact on group success.

For Olson, a key to group formation—and especially group survival—is "selective" benefits. These rewards—for example, travel discounts, informative publications, and cheap insurance—go only to members. Organizations in the best positions to offer such benefits are those initially formed for some nonpolitical purpose and that ordinarily provide material benefits to their clientele. In the case of unions, for example, membership may be a condition of employment. For farmers, the American Farm Bureau Federation offers inexpensive insurance, which induces individuals to join even if they disagree with the group's goals. In professional circles, membership in professional societies may be a prerequisite for occupational advancement and opportunity.

Olson's notions have sparked several extensions of the rational man model, and a reasonably coherent body of incentive theory literature now exists.[21] Incentive theorists view individuals as rational decision makers interested in making the most of their time and money by choosing to participate in groups that offer benefits greater than or equal to the costs they incur by participation. Three types of benefits are available. Olson, an economist, emphasized material benefits—tangible rewards of participation, such as income or services that have monetary value. Solidary benefits are the socially derived, intangible rewards created by the act of association, such as fun, camaraderie, status, or prestige. Finally, expressive (also known as purposive) benefits derive from advancing a particular cause or ideology.[22] Groups formed on both sides of issues such as abortion or gun control illustrate the strength of such expressive incentives.

The examination of group members' motivations, and in particular the focus on nonmaterial incentives, allows for some reconciliation between the traditional group theorists' expectations of group development and the recent rational actor studies, which emphasize barriers to group formation. Nonmaterial incentives, such as fellowship and self-satisfaction, may encourage the proliferation of highly politicized groups and "have the potential for producing a more dynamic group context in which politics, political preferences, and group goals are more centrally determining factors than in material associations, linking political considerations more directly to associational size, structure, and internal processes."[23] Indeed, pure political benefits may attract members, and even collective benefits can prove decisive in inducing individuals to join large groups. Like elected officials, groups may find it possible to take credit for widely approved government actions, such as higher farm prices, stronger environmental regulations, or the protection of Social Security.[24]

Finally, several studies indicate that the free rider problem may not be quite the obstacle to participation that it was once thought to be, especially in an affluent society. Albert Hirschman, for example, has argued that the costs and benefits of group activity are not always clear; in fact, some costs of participation for some individuals, such as time and effort expended, might be regarded as benefits (in terms of personal satisfaction) by others.[25] Other researchers have questioned whether individuals even engage in rational, cost-benefit thinking as they make membership decisions. Michael McCann noted that "there seems to be a general threshold level of involvement below which free rider calculations pose few inhibitions for . . . commitment from moderately affluent citizen supporters."[26] In short, individuals may join and participate in groups for reasons beyond narrow economic self-interest or the availability of selective benefits.[27]

Contemporary Interest Group Politics

Several notable developments mark the modern age of interest group politics. Of primary importance is the large and growing number of active groups and other interests. The data here are sketchy, but one major study found that most current groups came into existence after World War II and that group formation has accelerated substantially since the early 1960s.[28] Also, since the 1960s groups have increasingly directed their attention toward the center of power in Washington, D.C., as the scope of federal policy making has grown and groups seeking influence have determined to "hunt where the ducks are." As a result, the 1960s and 1970s marked an explosion in the number of groups lobbying in Washington.

A second key change is evident in the composition of the interest group universe. Beginning in the late 1950s, political participation patterns underwent some significant transformations. Conventional activities such as voting declined, and political parties, the traditional aggregators and articulators of mass interests, became weaker. Yet at all levels of government, evidence of citizen involvement has been apparent, often in the form of new or revived groups. Particularly impressive has been the growth of citizens' groups—those organized around an idea or cause (at times a single issue) with no occupational basis for membership. Fully 30 percent of such groups have formed since 1975, and in 1980 they made up more than one-fifth of all groups represented in Washington.[29]

In fact, a participation revolution occurred in the country as many citizens became active in an increasing number of protest groups, citizens' organizations, and special interest groups. These groups often comprise issue-oriented activists or individuals who seek collective material benefits. The free rider problem has proven not to be an insurmountable barrier to group formation, and many new interest groups do not use selective material benefits to gain support. Still, since the late 1970s, the number of these groups has remained relatively stable, and they are well established in representing consumers, environmentalists, and other public interest organizations.[30]

Third, government itself has profoundly affected the growth and activity of interest groups. Early in this century, workers found organizing difficult because business and industry used government-backed injunctions to prevent strikes. By the 1930s, however, with the prohibition of injunctions in private labor disputes and the rights of collective bargaining established, most governmental actions directly promoted the growth of labor unions. In more recent years, changes in campaign finance laws have led to an explosion in the number of political action committees, especially among business, industry, and issue-oriented groups. Laws facilitating group formation certainly have contributed to group proliferation, but government policy in a broader sense has been equally responsible.

Fourth, not only has the number of membership groups grown in recent decades, but a similar expansion has occurred in the political activity of many other interests, such as individual corporations, universities, churches, governmental units, foundations, and think tanks.[31] Historically, most of these interests have been satisfied with representation by trade or professional associations. Since the mid-1960s, however, many have chosen to employ their own Washington, D.C., representatives. Between 1961 and 1982, for example, the number of corporations with Washington offices increased tenfold.[32] The chief beneficiaries of this trend are Washington-based lawyers, lobbyists, and public relations firms. The number of attorneys in the nation's capital, taken as a rough indicator of lobbyist strength, tripled between 1973 and 1983, and the growth of public relations firms was likewise dramatic. The lobbying community of Washington is large, increasingly diverse, and part of the expansion of policy domain participation, whether in agriculture, the environment, or industrial development. Political scientist James Thurber has calculated that 91,000 lobbyists and people associated with lobbying were employed in the Washington, D.C., area in the early 1990s.[33] As of 2001, the *Encyclopedia of Associations* listed approximately 22,200 organizations, up more than 50 percent since 1980 and almost 400 percent since 1955.[34] And this number does not include hundreds of corporations and other institutions (such as universities) that also are represented in Washington.

The Growth of Government

Although the government prompted the establishment of some agricultural interest groups in the nineteenth century, since the 1930s the federal government has become increasingly active as a spur to group formation. One major New Deal goal was to use government as an agent in balancing the relationships among contending forces in society, particularly between industry and labor. One objective was to create greater equality of opportunity, including the "guarantee of identical liberties to all individuals, especially with regard to their pursuit of economic success."[35] For example, the Wagner Act (1935), which established collective bargaining rights, attempted to equalize workers' rights with those of their employers. Some New Deal programs did have real redistributive qualities, but most, even Social Security, sought only to ensure minimum standards of citizen welfare. Workers were clearly better off, but "the kind of redistribution that took priority in the public philosophy of the New Deal was not of wealth, but a redistribution of power."[36]

The Role of Public Policy.   The expansion of federal programs accelerated between 1960 and 1980; since then, costs have continued to increase, despite resistance to new programs. In what political scientist Hugh Heclo termed an "Age of Improvement," the federal budget has grown rapidly (from nearly $100 billion in 1961 to $2.1 trillion in 2001) and has widened the sweep of federal regulations.[37] Lyndon Johnson's Great Society—a multitude of federal initiatives in education, welfare, health care, civil rights, housing, and urban affairs—created a new array of federal responsibilities and program beneficiaries. The growth of many of these programs has continued, although that growth was slowed markedly by the Reagan and Bush administrations, as well as by the Republican capture of Congress in 1994. In the 1970s the federal government further expanded its activities in consumer affairs, environmental protection, and energy regulation. It also redefined some policies, such as affirmative action, to seek greater equality of results.

Many of the government policies adopted early in the Age of Improvement did not result from interest group activity by potential beneficiaries. Several targeted groups, such as the poor, were not effectively organized during the period of policy development. Initiatives typically came from elected officials responding to a variety of private and public sources, such as task forces of academics and policy professionals.[38]

The proliferation of government activities led to a mushrooming of groups around the affected policy areas. Newly enacted programs provided benefit packages that encouraged interest group formation. Consider group activity in policy toward the aging. The radical Townsend Movement, based on age grievances, received much attention during the 1930s, but organized political activity focused on age-based concerns had virtually no influence in national politics. Social Security legislation won approval without the involvement of age-based interest groups. Four decades later, by 1978, roughly $112 billion (approximately 24 percent of total federal expenditures) went to the elderly population, and it was projected that in fifty years the outlay would amount to 40 percent of the budget.[39] By the early 1990s, however, the elderly population already received one-third of federal outlays, and long-term projections had been revised upward. The existence of such massive benefits has spawned a variety of special interest groups and has encouraged other organizations, often formed for nonpolitical reasons, to redirect their attention to the politics of aging.

Across policy areas, two types of groups develop in response to governmental policy initiatives: recipients and service deliverers. In the sector devoted to policies affecting elderly individuals, recipient groups are mass-based organizations concerned with protecting—and if possible expanding—old-age benefits. The largest of these groups—indeed, the largest voluntary association represented in Washington—is the AARP (formerly the American Association of Retired Persons).

The AARP is well over twice the size of the AFL-CIO and, after the Roman Catholic Church, is the nation's largest organization. In 1998 it counted 33 million members, an increase of 23 million in twenty years.[40] Approximately half of Americans ages fifty or older, or one-fifth of all voters, belong to the group, in part because membership is cheap—$8 a year. Much of the organization's revenue comes from advertising in its bimonthly magazine, *Modern Maturity*. The organization's headquarters in Washington has its own zip code; a legislative/policy staff of 165; 28 registered, in-house lobbyists; and more than 1,200 staff members in the field. Charles Peters, editor of *Washington Monthly*, claimed that the "AARP is becoming the most dangerous lobby in America," given its vigorous defense of the elderly population's interests.[41] At the same time, because the AARP represents such a wide array of individuals, it is often cautious and slow in its actions.

Federal program growth also has generated substantial growth among service delivery groups. In the health care sector, for example, these range from professional associations of doctors and nurses to hospital groups to the insurance industry to suppliers of drugs and medical equipment. Not only is there enhanced group activity, but hundreds of individual corporations have strengthened their lobbying capacities by opening Washington offices or hiring professional representatives from the capital's many lobbying firms.[42]

Federal government policy toward the aging is probably typical of the tendency to "greatly increase the incentives for groups to form around the differential effects of these policies, each refusing to allow any other group to speak in its name."[43] The complexity of government decision making increases under such conditions, and priorities are hard to set. Particularly troublesome for decision makers concerned with national policy is the role played by service delivery groups. In the area of aging, some service groups are largely organizational middlemen concerned with their status as vendors for the elderly population. The trade associations, for example, are most interested in the conditions surrounding the payment of funds to elderly individuals. The major concern of the Gerontological Society, an organization of professionals, is to obtain funds for research on problems of elderly individuals.

Middleman organizations do not usually evaluate government programs according to the criteria used by recipient groups; rather, what is important to them is the relationship between the program and the well-being of their organizations. Because many service delivery groups offer their members vitally important selective material incentives (financial advantages and job opportunities), they are usually far better organized than most recipient groups (the elderly population in this case, the AARP notwithstanding). As a result, service groups sometimes speak for the recipients. This is particularly true when recipient groups represent disadvantaged people, such as poor or mentally ill populations.

Middleman groups have accounted for a large share of total group growth since 1960, and many of them are state and local government organizations. Since the late 1950s the federal government has grown in expenditures and regulations more than in personnel. Employment in the federal government has risen only 20 percent since 1955, whereas that of states and localities has climbed more than 250 percent. Contemporary federal activism largely involves overseeing and regulating state and local governmental units, which seek funding for a wide range of purposes. The intergovernmental lobby, which includes the National League of Cities, the International City Manager Association, the National Association of Counties, the National Governors' Association, the U.S. Conference of Mayors, and more, has grown to become one of the most important lobbies in Washington. In addition, many local officials, such as transportation or public works directors, are represented by groups, and even single cities and state boards of regents have established Washington offices.

Direct Intervention by Government.   Not only do public policies contribute to group proliferation, but government often directly intervenes in group creation. This is not an entirely new activity. In the early twentieth century officials in the Department of Agriculture encouraged the formation of the American Farm Bureau Federation, and officials in the Commerce Department did the same for the U.S. Chamber of Commerce. Since the 1960s the federal government has been especially active in providing start-up funds and in sponsoring groups. One study found that government agencies have concentrated on sponsoring organizations of public service professions:

> Federal agencies have an interest in encouraging coordination among the elements of these complex service delivery systems and in improving the diffusion of new ideas and techniques. Groups like the American Public Transit Association or the American Council on Education . . . serve as centers of professional development and informal channels for administrative coordination in an otherwise unwieldy governmental system.[44]

Government sponsorship also helps explain the recent rise of citizens' groups. Most federal domestic legislation has included provisions requiring some citizen participation, which has spurred the development of various citizen action groups, including grassroots neighborhood associations, environmental action councils, legal defense coalitions, health care organizations, and senior citizens' groups. Such group sponsorship evolved for two reasons:

> First, there is the ever-present danger that administrative agencies may exceed or abuse their discretionary power. In this sense, the regulators need regulating. Although legislatures have responsibility for doing this . . . the administrative bureaucracy has grown too large for them to monitor. Therefore, citizen participation has developed as an alternative means of monitoring government agencies. Second, government agencies are not entirely comfortable with their discretionary power. . . . [T]o reduce the potential of unpopular or questionable decisions, agencies frequently use citizen participation as a means for improving, justifying, and developing support for their decisions.[45]

Citizens' groups thus have two sometimes inconsistent missions: to oversee an agency and to act as an advocate for the groups' programs.

Government funding of citizens' groups takes numerous forms. Several federal agencies—including the Federal Trade Commission, Food and Drug Administration, and Environmental Protection Agency—have reimbursed groups for participation in agency proceedings.[46] At other times the government makes available seed money or outright grants. Interest group scholar Jack Walker found that 89 percent of citizens' groups received outside funding in their initial stages of development.[47] Not all the money was from federal sources, but much did come from government grants or contracts. Government can also take away, however, and the Reagan administration made a major effort to "defund" left-leaning interests, especially citizens' groups. But once established, groups have strong instincts for survival. Indeed, the Reagan administration provided an attractive target for many citizens' groups in their recruiting efforts. This dance of defunding took place again, in 1995, after Republicans won control of the House of Representatives.

Citizens' groups, numbering in the thousands, continually confront the free rider problem because they are largely concerned with collective goods and rarely can offer the selective material incentives so important for expanding and maintaining membership. With government funding, however, the development of a stable group membership is not crucial. Many groups are essentially staff organizations with little or no membership base. In the world of interest group politics, resources are often more important than members.

Unintended Intervention.   Government policies contribute to group formation in many unintended ways as well. Policy failures can impel groups to form, as happened with the rise of the American Agriculture Movement in the wake of the Nixon administration's grain export policies. An important factor in the establishment of the Moral Majority was the perceived harassment of church-run schools by government officials. As for abortion, the 1973 Supreme Court decision in *Roe v. Wade* played a major role in the mobilization of antiabortion rights groups. And the 1989 *Webster* decision, which limited the availability of legal abortions, did the same for abortion rights groups. Even the lack of federal funding can play a role. The rise in the incidence of prostate cancer, coupled with a modest budget for research, helped lead to the formation of the National Prostate Cancer Coalition. This group has pressed the government to increase funding on prostate cancer toward levels that are spent on AIDs and breast cancer, given that the three diseases kill about the same number of individuals each year.

Finally, the expansion of government activity often inadvertently contributes to group development and the resulting complexity of politics. The development of the Bass Anglers Sportsman Society (BASS) is a good example. From the late 1940s through the 1960s the Army Corps of Engineers dammed enough Southern and Midwestern streams to create a host of lakes, thereby providing an inviting habitat for largemouth bass. Anglers arrived in droves to catch their limits, and the fishing industry responded by creating expensive boats filled with specialized and esoteric equipment. The number and affluence of bass aficionados did not escape the attention of Ray Scott, an enterprising soul who began BASS in 1967. In the early 1990s, with its membership approaching 1 million (up from 400,000 in 1982), BASS remained privately organized, offering its members selective benefits such as a slick magazine filled with tips on how to catch their favorite fish, packages of lures and line in return for joining or renewing their memberships, instant information about fishing hot spots, and boat owners' insurance. BASS also provided a number of solidary benefits, such as the camaraderie of fishing with fellow members in specially sanctioned fishing tournaments and the vicarious excitement of fishing with "BASS pros" whose financial livelihood revolved around competitive tournament fishing. The organization is an excellent example of Robert Salisbury's exchange theory approach to interest groups, because it provides benefits to both members and organizers in a "mutually satisfactory exchange."[48]

In fact, "members" may be a misnomer, in that the nominal members have no effective role in group decision making. In 1993 a federal district judge dismissed a $75 million suit filed against Scott by some BASS members. The judge reasoned that the organization was and always had been a for-profit corporation; its "members" thus had no standing to sue.

Although Scott sold the organization to a private corporation in 1986 (the ultimate expression of entrepreneurial success), he remained active in much of its work and wrote a column for the monthly publication, *BassMaster.* Never denying that the organization was anything but a profit-making entity, Scott stated, "Every time I see one of those BASS stickers I get a lump, right in my wallet."[49]

Like most groups, BASS did not originate as a political organization, and for the most part it remains an organization for anglers, with 600,000 members, even in the wake of its 2001 acquisition by the ESPN television network.[50] Yet BASS has entered politics. *BassMaster* has published political commentary, and in 1980, 1988, and 1992 it endorsed George Bush for president. It also has called for easing travel restrictions to Cuba, where world-record catches may lurk.

Most groups claim that access is their major goal within the lobbying process, and here BASS has succeeded beyond its wildest dreams. Former president George Bush has been a life member of BASS since 1978 and has claimed that *BassMaster* is his favorite magazine. Scott used his relationship with Bush to lobby for the fishing community in general and BASS in particular. In March 1989 Scott visited the White House and, during a horseshoe match with President Bush, indicated his concern about rumors that the Office of Management and Budget (OMB) planned to limit the disbursement of $100 million in trust funds for fishery management projects. The next morning Bush informed Scott that "all of our monies are secure from OMB or anyone else."[51]

BASS increased its political activities by sponsoring Voice of the Environment, which lobbies on water quality issues, and filing class-action lawsuits on behalf of anglers against environmental polluters. Although the organization can point to a number of conservation and environmental activities, it is distrusted by much of the mainstream environmental movement. BASS's connections to the boating industry often put it at odds with groups seeking to preserve a pristine natural environment or elite angling organizations whose members fish for trout in free-flowing streams rather than for the bass behind federally funded dams.

Indeed, regardless of Scott's entrepreneurial skills, there would probably be no BASS if it were not for the federal government and the Army Corps of Engineers. Fifty years of dam building by the Corps and the U.S. Bureau of Reclamation have altered the nature of fish populations. Damming of rivers and streams has reduced the quality of fishing for cold-water species such as trout and pike and enhanced the habitat for largemouth bass, a game fish that can tolerate the warmer waters and mud bottoms of man-made lakes. Finally, because many of these lakes are located close to cities, the government has made bass fishing accessible to a large number of anglers.

From angling to air traffic control, the federal government has affected, and sometimes dominated, group formation. But many other forces have contributed to group proliferation, often in concert with increased public sector involvement.

The Decline of Political Parties

In a diverse political culture characterized by divided power, political parties emerged early in our history as instruments to structure conflict and facilitate mass participation. Parties function as intermediaries between the public and formal government institutions, as they reduce and combine citizen demands into a manageable number of issues and enable the system to focus on society's most important problems.

The party performs its mediating function primarily through coalition building—"the process of constructing majorities from the broad sentiments and interests that can be found to bridge the narrower needs and hopes of separate individuals and communities."[52] The New Deal coalition, forged in the 1930s, illustrates how this works. Socioeconomic divisions dominated politics from the 1930s through the 1960s. Less affluent citizens tended to support government provisions for social and economic security and the regulation of private enterprise. Those economically better off usually took the opposite position. The Democratic coalition, by and large, represented disadvantaged urban workers, Catholics, Jews, Italians, Eastern Europeans, and African-Americans. On a variety of issues, southerners joined the coalition, along with a smattering of academics and urban liberals. The Republicans were concentrated in the rural and suburban areas outside the South; the party was made up of established ethnic groups, businesspeople, and farmers and was largely Protestant. Party organizations dominated electoral politics through the New Deal period, and interest group influence was felt primarily through the party apparatus.

Patterns of partisan conflict are never permanent, however, and since the 1940s social forces have contributed to the creation of new interests and the redefinition of old ones. This has destroyed the New Deal coalition without putting a new partisan structure in its place and has provided opportunities for the creation of large numbers of political groups—many that are narrowly focused and opposed to the bargaining and compromise patterns of coalition politics. The changes of recent decades reflect the societal transformation that scholars have labeled the "postindustrial society." Postindustrial society is centered on several interrelated developments:

> affluence, advanced technological development, the central importance of knowledge, national communication processes, the growing prominence and independence of the culture, new occupational structures, and with them new life styles and expectations, which is to say new social classes and new centers of power.[53]

At the base is the role of affluence. Between 1947 and 1972 median family income doubled, even after controlling for the effects of inflation. During that same period the percentage of families earning $10,000 and more, in constant dollars, grew from 15 percent to 60 percent of the population.[54] A large proportion of the population began to enjoy substantial discretionary income and moved beyond subsistence.

The consequences of spreading abundance did not reduce conflict, as some observers had predicted.[55] Instead, conflict heightened, because affluence increased dissatisfaction by contributing to a "mentality of demand, a vastly expanded set of expectations concerning what is one's due, a diminished tolerance of conditions less than ideal."[56] By the 1960s the democratizing impact of affluence had become apparent, as an extraordinary number of people enrolled in institutions of higher education. It is not surprising that the government was under tremendous pressure to satisfy expectations, and it too contributed to increasing demands both in rhetoric and through many of its own Age of Improvement initiatives.

With the rise in individual expectations, class divisions and conflicts were drastically transformed. Political parties scholar Walter Dean Burnham noted that the New Deal's class structure changed, and by the late 1960s the industrial class pattern of upper, middle, and working class had been "supplanted by one which is relevant to a system dominated by advanced postindustrial technology." At the top of the new class structure was a "professional-managerial-technical elite . . . closely connected with the university and research centers and significant parts of it have been drawn—both out of ideology and interest—to the federal government's social activism." This growing group tended to be cosmopolitan and more socially permissive than the rest of society. The spread of affluence in postindustrial society was uneven, however, and certain groups were disadvantaged by the changes. At the bottom of the new class structure were those "whose economic functions had been undermined or terminated by the technical revolution of the past generation . . . people, black and white, who tend to be in hard core poverty areas."[57] The focus of President Lyndon B. Johnson's War on Poverty was to be on this class.

The traditional political party system found it difficult to deal effectively with citizens' high expectations and a changing class structure. The economic, ethnic, and ideological positions that had developed during the New Deal became less relevant to parties, elections, and voter preferences. The strains were particularly evident among working-class Democrats. New Deal policies had been particularly beneficial to the white working class, enabling that group to earn incomes and adopt lifestyles that resembled those of the middle class. And although Age of Improvement policies initiated by Democratic politicians often benefited whites as well as minorities, many white workers viewed these policies as attempts to aid lower-class blacks at the expense of whites. By the late 1960s the white working class had taken on trappings of the middle class and conservatism, both economically and culturally.

At the same time, such New Deal divisions as ethnicity also had lost their cutting edge because of social and geographic mobility.

> It does not seem inaccurate to portray the current situation as one in which the basic coalitions and many of the political symbols and relationships, which were developed around one set of political issues and problems, are confronted with new issues and new cleavages for which these traditional relationships and associations are not particularly relevant. Given these conditions, the widespread confusion, frustration, and mistrust are not surprising.[58]

Various conditions led to the party system's inability to realign—build coalitions of groups to address new concerns to adapt to changing societal divisions. For example, consider the difficulty of building coalitions around the kinds of issues that have emerged over the past fifteen or twenty years.

Valence issues—general evaluations of the goodness or badness of the times—have become important, especially when related to the cost of living. Yet most such issues do not divide the country politically. Everyone is against inflation and crime. A second set of increasingly important issues are those that are highly emotional, cultural, or moral in character, such as abortion, euthanasia, AIDS, the death penalty, and drug laws. These subjects divide the electorate but elicit intense feelings from only a relatively few citizens. Opinion on such issues often is unrelated to traditional group identifications. Moreover, public opinion is generally disorganized or in disarray—that is, opinions often are unrelated or weakly related to one another on major issues, further retarding efforts to build coalitions.

There is some question about whether parties retain the capacity to shape political debate even on issues that lend themselves to coalition building. Although the decline of political parties began well before the 1960s, the weakening of the party organization has accelerated in the postindustrial age. The emergence of a highly educated electorate, less dependent on party as an electoral cue, has produced a body of citizens that seeks out independent sources of information. Technological developments—such as television, computer-based direct mail, and political polling—have enabled candidates to virtually bypass political parties in their quest for public office. The rise of political consultants has reduced even further the need for party expertise in running for office. The recruitment function of parties also has been largely lost to the mass media, as journalists now "act out the part of talent scouts, conveying the judgment that some contenders are promising, while dismissing others as of no real talent."[59]

Considerable evidence suggests that parties have adapted to this new political environment, but party organizations no longer dominate the electoral process. In an era of candidate-centered politics, parties are less mobilizers of a diverse electorate than service vendors to ambitious individual candidates. The weakness of political parties has helped to create a vacuum in electoral politics since 1960, and in recent years interest groups have moved aggressively to fill it. Indeed, in the 2000 election, many interests bypassed the parties—and even the candidates' organizations—to advertise directly on behalf of particular candidates, all the while articulating their own positions on key issues such as Medicare, drug pricing, term limits, Social Security, and gun control. Simultaneously, organized interests such as labor, environmentalists, antiabortion rights groups, and some corporations have worked closely with parties both by contributing soft money and by implicitly coordinating the corporation's campaign activities with those of the parties.

The Growth of Interest Groups

Although it may be premature to formulate a theory that accounts for growth spurts, we can identify several factors fundamental to group proliferation in contemporary politics.[60] Rapid social and economic changes, powerful catalysts for group formation, have created new interests (for example, the recreation industry) and redefined traditional ones (for example, higher education). The spread of affluence and education, coupled with advanced communication technologies, further contributes to the translation of interests into formal group organizations. Postindustrial changes have generated many new interests, particularly among occupational and professional groups in the scientific and technological arenas. For instance, genetic-engineering associations have sprung up in the wake of recent DNA discoveries, to say nothing of the growing clout and sophistication of the computer industry, from Microsoft on down.

Perhaps more important, postindustrial changes have altered the pattern of conflict in society and created an intensely emotional setting in which groups rise or fall in status. Ascending groups, such as members of the new professional-managerial-technical elite, have both benefited from and supported government activism; they represent the new cultural liberalism—politically cosmopolitan and socially permissive. At the same time, rising expectations and feelings of entitlement have increased pressures on government by aspiring groups and the disadvantaged. The 1960s and early 1970s witnessed wave after wave of group mobilization based on causes ranging from civil rights to women's issues to the environment to consumer protection.

Threat as Motivation.   Abrupt changes and alterations in status, however, threaten many citizens. Middle America, perceiving itself as downwardly mobile, has grown alienated from the social, economic, and cultural dominance of the postindustrial elites, on one hand, and resentful of government attempts to aid minorities and other aspiring groups on the other. The conditions of a modern, technologically based culture also are disturbing to more traditional elements in society. Industrialization and urbanization can uproot people, cutting them loose from familiar life patterns and values and depriving them of meaningful personal associations. Fundamentalist elements feel threatened by various technological advances (such as use of fetal tissue for medical research) as well as by the more general secular liberalism and moral permissiveness of contemporary life. In the 1990s the growth of the Christian Coalition, both nationally and locally, profoundly affected both electoral and legislative politics by mobilizing citizens and activists. In addition, the growth of bureaucracy, in and out of government, antagonizes everyone at one time or another.

Elites feel postindustrial threats as well. The nuclear arms race and its potential for mass destruction fostered the revived peace movement of the 1980s and its goal of a freeze on nuclear weapons. In addition, the excesses and errors of technology, such as oil spills and toxic waste disposal, have led to group formation among some of the most advantaged and ascending elements of society.

The growth of the animal rights movement since the mid-1980s illustrates interest groups' potential for enhanced participation and influence. Although traditional animal protection organizations such as the Humane Society have existed for decades, the 1990s spawned a host of pro-animal offspring, such as People for Ethical Treatment of Animals (PETA), Progressive Animal Welfare Society, Committee to Abolish Sport Hunting, and the Animal Rights Network. Reminiscent of the 1960s, there is even the Animal Liberation Front, an extremist group that engages in direct actions that sometimes include violence.[61] Membership in the organizations that make up the animal rights movement increased rapidly; founded in 1980, PETA grew from 20,000 members in 1984 to 370,000 by 1994 and 600,000 in 2001. One 1991 estimate placed the number of animal rights organizations at 400, representing approximately 10 million members.[62]

One major goal of these groups is to stop, or greatly retard, scientific experimentation on animals. Using a mix of protest, lobbying, and litigation, the movement contributed to the closing of several animal labs, including the Defense Department's Wound Laboratory and a University of Pennsylvania facility involved in research on head injuries. In 1988 the animal rights group Trans-Species forced the Cornell University Medical College to give up a $600,000 grant, which left unfinished a fourteen-year research project in which cats were fed barbiturates.[63]

As the most visible of the animal rights groups, PETA embarked on an intensive campaign in the early 1990s to influence children's attitudes and values toward society's treatment of animals. Using a seven-foot mascot, Chris P. Carrot, to spread its message, PETA organizers sought to visit public schools throughout the Midwest. Although some of PETA's message is noncontroversial (for example, children should eat their vegetables), the organization also argues aggressively against consuming meat. Chris P. Carrot thus carries a placard stating, "Eat your veggies, not your friends." More prosaically, PETA produces publications denouncing hunting, trapping, and other practices that abuse animals; PETA's Kids Can Save Animals even encourages students to

> call the toll-free numbers of department stores to protest furs and animal-test cosmetics, to call sponsors and object to rodeos, circulate petitions for "violence-free" schools that do not use frog corpses for biology lab, and to boycott zoos and aquariums, and marine parks.[64]

It is not surprising that PETA protests have spawned countermobilizations, for example, an anti–animal rights movement. In the forefront of such actions are organizations that support hunting as a sport. They must contend with a public that has become increasingly hostile to hunting; a 1993 survey reported that 54 percent of Americans were opposed to hunting, with the youngest respondents (ages eighteen to twenty-nine) expressing the most negative sentiments.[65] In addition, farm and medical groups have mobilized against the animal rights movements, and a number of new organizations have been formed. Such groups range from the incurably ill for Animal Research (iiFAR), representing those who hope for medical breakthroughs in biomedical research, to the Foundation for Animal Health, organized by the American Medical Association in hopes of diverting funds away from animal rights groups.

The most visible group in the animal rights countermobilization, Putting People First (PPF), claimed more than 35,000 members and 100 local chapters within one year of its formation. PPF counted hunting clubs, trapping associations, rodeos, zoos, circuses, veterinary hospitals, kennels and stables, and carriage horse companies among its membership. Taking a page from animal rights' public relations activities, PPF has begun a Hunters for the Hungry campaign that has provided 160,000 pounds of venison to economically disadvantaged families in the South. To PPF, the animal rights movement has declared war on much of America and is "seeking to destroy a way of life—to tell us we can no longer believe in the Judeo-Christian principles this country was founded on. They insist every form of life is equal: humans and dogs and slugs and cockroaches." PPF leaders see the organization as speaking for "the average American who eats meat and drinks milk, benefits from medical research, wears leather, wool, and fur, hunts and fishes, and owns a pet and goes to the zoo."[66]

The intensity of conflict between the animal rights advocates and their opponents typifies the deep cultural divisions of the postindustrial era. Similar differences affect many other key issues, from gun control to education (school choice) to immigration policy. Moreover, many of these conflicts do not lend themselves to compromise, whether because of vast policy differences or group leaders' desire to keep "hot" issues alive as a way to increase membership.

Affluent Members and Sponsors.   Although postindustrial conflicts generate the issues for group development, the spread of affluence also systematically contributes to group formation and maintenance. In fact, affluence creates a large potential for "checkbook" membership. Issue-based groups have done especially well. Membership in such groups as PETA and Common Cause might once have been a luxury, but the growth in discretionary income has placed the cost of modest dues within reach of most citizens. For a $15–25 membership fee, people can make an "expressive" statement without incurring other organizational obligations. Increasing education also has been a factor in that "organizations become more numerous as ideas become more important."[67]

Reform groups and citizens' groups depend heavily on the educated white middle class for their membership and financial base. A Common Cause poll, for example, found that members' mean family income was $17,000 above the national average and that 43 percent of members had an advanced degree.[68] Animal rights groups display a similar membership profile, although they are disproportionately composed of college-educated, urban, professional women.[69] Other expressive groups, including those on the political right, have been aided as well by the increased wealth of constituents and the community activism that result from education and occupational advancement.

Groups can overcome the free rider problem by finding a sponsor who will support the organization and reduce its reliance on membership contributions. During the 1960s and 1970s private sources (often foundations) backed groups. Jeffrey Berry's 1977 study of eighty-three public interest organizations found that at least one-third received more than half their funds from private foundations, and one in ten received more than 90 percent of their operating expenses from such sources.[70] Jack Walker's 1981 study of Washington-based interest groups confirmed many of Berry's earlier findings, indicating that foundation support and individual grants provide 30 percent of all citizens' group funding.[71] Such patterns produce many staff organizations with no members, raising major questions about the representativeness of the new interest group universe. Finally, groups themselves can sponsor other groups. The National Council of Senior Citizens (NCSC), for example, was founded by the AFL-CIO, which helped recruit members from the ranks of organized labor and still pays part of NCSC's expenses.

Patrons often are more than just passive sponsors who respond to group requests for funds. In many cases group mobilization comes from the top down, rather than the reverse. The patron—whether an individual such as General Motors' heir Stewart Mott or the peripatetic conservative Richard Mellon Scaife, an institution, another group, or a government entity—may initiate group development to the point of seeking entrepreneurs and providing a forum for group pronouncements.

Postindustrial affluence and the spread of education also have contributed to group formation and maintenance through the development of a large pool of potential group organizers. This group tends to be young, well educated, from the middle class, and caught up in a movement for change and inspired by ideas or doctrine. The 1960s was a period of opportunity for entrepreneurs, as college enrollments skyrocketed and powerful forces such as civil rights and the antiwar movement contributed to an idea orientation in both education and politics. Communications-based professions—from religion to law to university teaching—attracted social activists, many of whom became involved in forming groups. The government itself became a major source of what James Q. Wilson called "organizing cadres." Government employees of the local Community Action Agencies of the War on Poverty and personnel from Volunteers in Service to America were active in forming voluntary associations, some created to oppose government actions.[72]

Technological Opportunities.   Compounding the effects of the growing number of increasingly active groups are changes in what organizations can do, largely as a result of contemporary technology. On a grand scale, technological change produces new interests, such as cable television and the silicon chip industry, which organize to protect themselves as interests historically have done. Beyond this, communications breakthroughs make group politics much more visible than in the past. Civil rights activists in the South understood this, as did many protesters against the Vietnam War. Of equal importance, however, is the fact that much of what contemporary interest groups do derives directly from developments in information-related technology. Many group activities, whether fund-raising or grassroots lobbying or sampling members' opinions, rely heavily on computer-based operations that can target and send messages and process the responses.

Although satellite television links and survey research are important tools, the technology of direct mail has had by far the greatest impact on interest group politics. With a minimum initial investment and a reasonably good list of potential contributors, any individual can become a group entrepreneur. These activists literally create organizations, often based on emotion-laden appeals about specific issues, from Sarah Brady's Handgun Control to Randall Terry's Operation Rescue.[73] To the extent that an entrepreneur can attract members and continue to pay the costs of direct mail, he or she can claim—with substantial legitimacy—to articulate the organization's positions on the issues, positions probably defined initially by the entrepreneur.

In addition to helping entrepreneurs develop organizations that require few (if any) active members, information technology also allows many organizations to exert considerable pressure on elected officials. Washington-based interests are increasingly turning to grassroots techniques to influence legislators. Indeed, after the mid-1980s these tactics had become the norm in many lobbying efforts, to the point that they were sometimes discounted as routine and "manufactured" by groups and consultants.

Communications technology is widely available but expensive. In the health care debate, most mobilized opinion has come from the best-financed interests, such as insurance companies, the drug industry, and the medical profession. Money remains the mother's milk of politics. Indeed, one of the major impacts of technology may be to inflate the costs of political action, whether for candidates engaged in increasingly expensive election campaigns or in public lobbying efforts that employ specifically targeted advertisements and highly sophisticated grassroots efforts.

Group Impact on Policy and Process

Assessing the policy impact of interest group actions has never been an easy task. We may, however, gain some insights by looking at two different levels of analysis: a broad, societal overview and a middle-range search for relatively specific patterns of influence (for example, the role of direct mail or political action committee funding). Considering impact at the level of individual lobbying efforts is also possible, but here even the best work relies heavily on nuance and individualistic explanations.

Although the public often views lobbying and special interest campaigning with distrust, political scientists have not produced much evidence to support this perspective. Academic studies of interest groups have demonstrated few conclusive links between campaign or lobbying efforts and actual patterns of influence. This does not mean that such patterns or individual instances do not exist. Rather, the question of determining impact is exceedingly difficult to answer. The difficulty is, in fact, compounded by groups' claims of impact and decision makers' equally vociferous claims of freedom from any outside influence.

The major studies of lobbying in the 1960s generated a most benign view of this activity. Lester Milbrath painted a Boy Scout–like picture of Washington lobbyists, depicting them as patient contributors to policy making.[74] Rarely stepping over the limits of propriety, lobbyists had only a marginal impact at best. Similarly, Raymond Bauer, Ithiel de Sola Pool, and Lewis Dexter's lengthy analysis of foreign trade policy, published in 1963, found the business community to be largely incapable of influencing Congress in its lobbying attempts.[75] Given the many internal divisions within the private sector over trade matters, this was not an ideal issue to illustrate business cooperation, but the research stood as the central work on lobbying for more than a decade—ironically, in the very period when groups proliferated and became more sophisticated in their tactics. Lewis Dexter, in his 1969 treatment of Washington representatives as an emerging professional group, suggested that lobbyists would play an increasingly important role in complex policy making, but he provided few details.[76]

The picture of benevolent lobbyists who seek to engender trust and convey information, although accurate in a limited way, does not provide a complete account of the options open to any interest group that seeks to exert influence. Lyndon Johnson's long-term relationship with the Texas-based construction firm of Brown & Root illustrates the depth of some ties between private interests and public officeholders. The Washington representative for Brown & Root claimed that he never went to Capitol Hill for any legislative help because "people would resent political influence."[77] But Johnson, first as a representative and later as a senator, systematically dealt directly with the top management (the Brown family) and aided the firm by passing along crucial information and watching over key government-sponsored construction projects.

> [The link between Johnson and Brown & Root] was, indeed, a partnership, the campaign contributions, the congressional look-out, the contracts, the appropriations, the telegrams, the investment advice, the gifts and the hunts and the free airplane rides—it was an alliance of mutual reinforcement between a politician and a corporation. If Lyndon was Brown & Root's kept politician, Brown & Root was Lyndon's kept corporation. Whether he concluded that they were public-spirited partners or corrupt ones, "political allies" or cooperating predators, in its dimensions and its implications for the structure of society, their arrangement was a new phenomenon on its way to becoming the new pattern for American society.[78]

Entering the twenty-first century, one could legitimately substitute Senator Trent Lott's (R-MS) name for Johnson's and that of defense and shipbuilding giant Northrup Grumman for Brown & Root; the basic set of links were very similar. Any number of events, such as the 1980s savings-and-loan scandal, show that legislators can be easily approached with unethical and illegal propositions; such access is one price of an open system. In addition, the growth of interest representation has raised long-term questions about the ethics of former government officials acting as lobbyists. Despite some modest reforms, many executive branch officials, members of Congress, and high-level bureaucrats leave office and eventually return to lobby their friends and associates. Access is still important, and its price is often high.

Contemporary Practices

Modern lobbying emphasizes information, often on complex and difficult subjects. Determining actual influence is, as one lobbyist noted, "like finding a black cat in the coal bin at midnight," but we can make some assessments about the impact of group proliferation and increased activity.[79]

First, more groups are engaged in more forms of lobbying than ever before—both classic forms, such as offering legislative testimony, and newer forms, such as mounting computer-based direct mail campaigns to stir up grassroots support.[80] As the number of new groups rises and existing groups become more active, the pressure on decision makers—especially legislators—mounts at a corresponding rate. Thus a second general point can be made: congressional reforms that opened up the legislative process during the 1970s have provided a much larger number of access points for today's lobbyists. Most committee (and subcommittee) sessions, including the markups at which legislation is written, remain open to the public, as do many conference committee meetings. More roll call votes are taken, and congressional floor action is televised. Thus interests can monitor individual members of Congress as never before. This does nothing, however, to facilitate disinterested decision making or foster graceful compromises on most issues.

In fact, monitoring the legions of Washington policy actors has become the central activity of many groups. As Robert Salisbury has observed, "Before [organized interests] can advocate a policy, they must determine what position they wish to embrace. Before they do this, they must find out not only what technical policy analysis can tell them but what relevant others, inside and outside the government, are thinking and planning."[81] Given the volume of policy making, just keeping up can be a major undertaking.

The government itself has encouraged many interests to organize and articulate their demands. The rise of group activity thus leads us to another level of analysis: the impact of contemporary interest group politics on society. Harking back to Lowi's description of interest group liberalism, we see the eventual result to be an immobilized society, trapped by its willingness to allow interests to help fashion self-serving policies that embody no firm criteria of success or failure. For example, even in the midst of the savings-and-loan debacle, the government continued to offer guarantees to various sectors, based not on future promise but on past bargains and continuing pressures.

The notion advanced by Olson that some such group-related stagnation affects all stable democracies makes the prognosis all the more serious. In summary form, Olson argued that the longer societies are politically stable, the more interest groups they develop; the more interest groups they develop, the worse they work economically.[82] The United Automobile Workers' protectionist leanings, the American Medical Association's fight against intervention by the Federal Trade Commission into physicians' business affairs, and the insurance industry's successful prevention of FTC investigations all illustrate the possible link between self-centered group action and poor economic performance—that is, higher automobile prices, doctors' fees, and insurance premiums for no better product or service.

In particular, the politics of Social Security demonstrate the difficulties posed by a highly mobilized, highly representative set of interests. Virtually everyone agrees that the Social Security system requires serious reform; at the same time, many groups of elderly citizens (with the AARP being among the most moderate) have resisted changes that might reduce their benefits over time. Moreover, many groups outside the traditional Social Security policy community have argued for the system's privatization, either partial or total. The system will have to be modified to maintain its viability, but groups will continue to frame the debate in ways that benefit their interests, perhaps at the expense of the general good.

Conclusion

The ultimate consequences of the growing number of organized interests, their expanding activities in Washington, D.C., and in state capitals, and the growth of citizens' groups remain unclear. From one perspective, such changes have made politics more representative than ever. Although most occupation-based groups traditionally have been well organized in American politics, many other interests have not been. Population groupings such as African-Americans, Hispanics, and women have mobilized since the 1950s and 1960s. Likewise, animals and the unborn are well represented in the interest group arena, as is the broader "public interest," however defined.

Broadening the base of interest group participation may have opened the political process, thus curbing the influence of special interests. For example, agricultural policy making in the postwar era was largely the prerogative of a tight "iron triangle" composed of congressional committee members from farm states, government officials representing the agriculture bureaucracy, and major agriculture groups such as the American Farm Bureau. Activity in the 1970s by consumer and environmental interest groups changed agricultural politics, making it more visible and lengthening the agenda to consider such questions as how farm subsidies affect consumer purchasing power and how fertilizers, herbicides, and pesticides affect public health.

From another perspective, more interest groups and more openness do not necessarily mean better policies or ones that genuinely represent the national interest. Government may be unable to process demands effectively, and openness may result in complexity. Moreover, the content of demands may be ambiguous and priorities difficult to set.

Finally, elected leaders may find it practically impossible to build the kinds of political coalitions necessary to govern effectively, especially in an era of partisan parity and the unrelenting demands of the permanent campaign, which requires continual fund-raising from organized interests.

This second perspective suggests that the American constitutional system is extraordinarily susceptible to the excesses of minority faction—in an ironic way a potential victim of the Madisonian solution of dealing with the tyranny of the majority. Decentralized government, especially one that wields considerable power, provides no adequate controls over the excessive demands of interest group politics. Decision makers feel obliged to respond to many of these demands, and "the cumulative effect of this pressure has been the relentless and extraordinary rise of government spending and inflationary deficits, as well as the frustration of efforts to enact effective national policies on most major issues."[83]

In sum, the problem of contemporary interest group politics is one of representation. For particular interests, especially those that are well defined and adequately funded, the government is responsive to the issues of their greatest concern. But representation is not just a matter of responding to specific interests or citizens; the government also must respond to the collective needs of a society, and here the success of individual interests reduces the possibility of overall responsiveness. The very vibrancy and success of contemporary groups contribute to a society that finds it increasingly difficult to formulate solutions to complex policy questions.

Notes

1. Kay Lehman Schlozman and John T. Tierney, "More of the Same: Washington Pressure Group Activity in a Decade of Change," *Journal of Politics* 45, no. 2 (1983): 351–377. For an earlier era, see Margaret S. Thompson, *The Spider's Web* (Ithaca, NY: Cornell University, 1985).
2. Theodore J. Lowi, *The End of Liberalism*, 2nd ed. (New York: Norton, 1979); Mancur Olson, *The Rise and Decline of Nations* (New Haven, CT: Yale University, 1982).

3. Mancur Olson, *The Logic of Collective Action*, rev. ed. (Cambridge, MA: Harvard University, 1971); Robert Salisbury, "An Exchange Theory of Interest Groups," *Midwest Journal of Political Science* 13, no. 1 (1969): 1–32; and Terry M. Moe, *The Organization of Interests* (Chicago: University of Chicago, 1980).

4. David Truman's widely used definition of *interest group* is "any group that, on the basis of one or more shared attitudes, makes certain claims upon other groups in the society for the establishment, maintenance, or enhancement of forms of behavior that are implied by the shared attitudes." David B. Truman, *The Governmental Process*, 2nd ed. (New York: Knopf, 1971): 33.

5. James Madison, "Federalist 10," in *The Federalist Papers*, 2nd ed., ed. Roy P. Fairfield (Baltimore: Johns Hopkins University, 1981): 16.

6. Quoted in L. Harmon Ziegler and Wayne Peak, *Interest Groups in American Society*, 2nd ed. (Englewood Cliffs, NJ: Prentice-Hall, 1972): 35.

7. Michael Trister, "The Rise and Reform of Stealth PACs," *The American Prospect* 11 (November 30, 2000): 32–35. Available at http://prospect.org/cs/articles?article= the_rise_and_reform_of_stealth_pacs.

8. Anthony Corrado, "Financing the 2000 Elections," in *The Election of 2000*, ed. Gerald Pomper (New York: Chatham House, 2001): x.

9. Truman, *Governmental Process*, 519.

10. Carole Greenwald, *Group Power* (New York: Praeger, 1977): 305.

11. Leslie Wayne, "800-Pound Guests at the Pentagon," *New York Times*, March 15, 1998.

12. Lowi, *End of Liberalism*, 62.

13. Murray Edelman, *The Politics of Symbolic Action* (Chicago: Markham, 1971).

14. Theodore J. Lowi, *Incomplete Conquest: Governing America* (New York: Holt, Rinehart & Winston, 1976): 47.

15. Gabriel Almond and Sidney Verba, *The Civic Culture* (Boston: Little, Brown, 1963): chaps. 8 and 10.

16. Almond and Verba, *Civic Culture*, 246–47.

17. Truman, *Governmental Process*, 57.

18. Salisbury, "Exchange Theory of Interest Groups," 3–4.

19. Truman, *Governmental Process*, 59.

20. James Q. Wilson, *Political Organizations* (New York: Basic Books, 1973): 154.

21. Major works include Olson, *Logic of Collective Action;* Peter B. Clark and James Q. Wilson, "Incentive Systems: A Theory of Organizations," *Administrative Science Quarterly* 6, no. 2 (1961): 126–66; Wilson, *Political Organizations;* Terry M. Moe, "A Calculus of Group Membership," *American Journal of Political Science* 24, no. 4 (1980): 593–632; and Moe, *Organization of Interests*. The notion of group organizers as political entrepreneurs is best represented by Salisbury, "Exchange Theory of Interest Groups," 1–15.

22. See Clark and Wilson, "Incentive Systems," 129–66; Wilson, *Political Organizations*, 30–51. In recent years researchers have preferred the term *expressive* to *purposive*, because, as Salisbury notes, *purposive* includes what we call collective material benefits. *Material, solidary*, and *expressive* would seem to be mutually exclusive conceptual categories. See Salisbury, "Exchange Theory of Interest Groups," 16–17.

23. Moe, *Organization of Interests*, 144.

24. John Mark Hansen, "The Political Economy of Group Membership," *American Political Science Review* 79, no. 1 (1985): 79–96.

25. Albert O. Hirschman, *Shifting Involvements* (Princeton, NJ: Princeton University, 1982).

26. Michael W. McCann, "Public Interest Liberalism and the Modern Regulatory State," *Polity* 21 (Winter 1988): 385.

27. See, for example, Kenneth Godwin and Robert Cameron Mitchell, "Rational Models, Collective Goods, and Nonelectoral Political Behavior," *Western Political Quarterly* 35, no. 2 (1982): 161–80; Lawrence S. Rothenberg, "Choosing among Public Interest Groups: Membership, Activism and Retention in Political Organizations," *American Political Science Review* 82 (December 1988): 1129–52.

28. Jack L. Walker, "The Origins and Maintenance of Interest Groups in America," *American Political Science Review* 77 (June 1983): 390–406. For a conservative critique of this trend, see James T. Bennett and Thomas DiLorenzo, *Destroying Democracy* (Washington, DC: Cato Institute, 1986). See also many of the articles in Mark P. Petracca, ed., *The Politics of Interests* (Boulder, CO: Westview, 1992).

29. Walker, "Origins and Maintenance of Interest Groups," 395.

30. Robert H. Salisbury, "Interest Representation and the Dominance of Institutions," *American Political Science Review* 78 (March 1984): 64–77.

31. See Jeffrey Berry, *The New Liberalism: The Power of Citizen Groups* (Washington, DC: Brookings Institution, 1999).

32. Gregory Colgate, ed., *National Trade and Professional Associations of the United States, 1982* (Washington, DC: Columbia Books, 1984).

33. Cited in Kevin Phillips, *Arrogant Capital* (Boston: Back Bay/Little, Brown, 1995): 43.

34. Encyclopedia of Associations, http://library.dialog.com/bluesheets/html/bl0114.html, December 5, 2001.

35. Samuel H. Beer, "In Search of a New Public Philosophy," in *The New American Political System*, ed. Anthony King (Washington, DC: American Enterprise Institute, 1978): 12.

36. Beer, "In Search of a New Public Philosophy," 10.

37. Hugh Heclo, "Issue Networks and the Executive Establishment," in *The New American Political System*, ed. Anthony King (Washington, DC: American Enterprise Institute, 1978): 89.

38. Beer, "In Search of a New Public Philosophy," 16.

39. Allan J. Cigler and Cheryl Swanson, "Politics and Older Americans," in *The Dynamics of Aging*, ed. Forrest J. Berghorn, Donna E. Schafer, and Associates (Boulder, CO: Westview, 1981): 171.

40. The AARP offers free memberships to spouses, which artificially enlarges its ranks, but it remains—by any count—a huge group. See John Tierney's articles: "Old Money, New Power," *New York Times Magazine*, October 23, 1988: 17; "The Big Gray Money Machine," *Newsweek*, August 15, 1988: 47.

41. Tierney, "Old Money, New Power," 17; Tierney, "The Big Gray Money Machine," 47.

42. Tierney, "Old Money, New Power."

43. Heclo, "Issue Networks and the Executive Establishment," 96.

44. Walker, "Origins and Maintenance of Interest Groups," 401.

45. Stuart Langton, "Citizen Participation in America: Current Reflections on the State of the Art," in *Citizen Participation in America*, ed. Stuart Langton (Lexington, MA: Lexington Books, 1978): 7.

46. Langton, "Citizen Participation in America," 4.

47. Walker, "Origins and Maintenance of Interest Groups," 398.

48. Salisbury, "Exchange Theory of Interest Groups," 25.

49. Quoted in Ted Williams, "River Retrieval," *Fly Rod and Reel* 15 (January–February 1994): 17.

50. The April 2001 ESPN purchase both enhanced and limited the potential political clout of BASS. It lost much of its independent political identity, but it might well have benefited from its position within the ABC-Disney corporate family.

51. Ray Scott, "Presidential Promises," *BassMaster*, May 1989: 7.

52. David S. Broder, "Introduction," in *Emerging Coalitions in American Politics*, ed. Seymour Martin Lipset (San Francisco, CA: Institute for Contemporary Studies, 1978): 3.

53. Everett Carll Ladd Jr., *Transformations of the American Party System: Political Coalitions from the New Deal to the 1970s*, 2nd ed. With Charles D. Hadley. (New York: Norton, 1978): 182.

54. Ladd Jr., *Transformations of the American Party System*, 196.

55. See, for example, Daniel Bell, *The End of Ideology* (New York: Free Press, 1960).

56. Ladd Jr., *Transformations of the American Party System*, 203.

57. For all three quotes in this paragraph, Walter Dean Burnham, *Critical Elections and the Mainsprings of American Politics* (New York: Norton, 1970): 139.

58. Richard E. Dawson, *Public Opinion and Contemporary Disarray* (New York: Harper and Row, 1973): 194.

59. Everett Carll Ladd Jr., *Where Have All the Voters Gone?* 2nd ed. (New York: Norton, 1982): 57.

60. But see Virginia Gray and David Lowery, *The Population Ecology of Interest Representation* (Ann Arbor: University of Michigan, 1996).

61. Kevin Kasowski, "Showdown on the Hunting Ground," *Outdoor America* 51 (Winter 1986): 9.

62. Lauristan R. King and Kimberly Stephens, "Politics and the Animal Rights Movement" (paper presented at the annual meeting of the Southern Political Science Association, Tampa, FL, November 7–9, 1991).

63. Sara Lyall, "Scientist Gives up Grant to Do Research on Cats," *New York Times*, November 21, 1988.

64. John Balzar, quoted in Kit Harrison, "Animal 'Rightists' Target Children," *Sports Afield* 211 (June 1994): 12.

65. "Americans Divided on Animal Rights," *Los Angeles Times*, December 17, 1993. This national survey of 1,612 adults also found that 50 percent opposed the wearing of fur.

66. Phil McCombs, "Attack of the Omnivore," *Washington Post*, March 27, 1992.

67. Wilson, *Political Organizations*, 201.

68. Andrew S. McFarland, *Common Cause* (Chatham, NJ: Chatham House, 1984): 48–49.

69. King and Stephens, "Politics and the Animal Rights Movement," 15.

70. Jeffrey M. Berry, *Lobbying for the People* (Princeton, NJ: Princeton University, 1977): 72.

71. Walker, "Origins and Maintenance of Interest Groups," 400.

72. Wilson, *Political Organizations*, 203.

73. Sarah Brady, wife of former White House press secretary James Brady, organized Handgun Control after her husband was wounded in John Hinckley's 1981 attack on Ronald Reagan. Randall Terry formed Operation Rescue, which seeks to shut down abortion clinics through direct action (for example, blocking entrances), after concluding that other antiabortion rights groups were not effective in halting abortions.

74. Lester Milbrath, *The Washington Lobbyists* (Chicago: Rand-McNally, 1963).
75. Raymond Bauer, Ithiel de Sola Pool, and Lewis Dexter, *American Business and Public Policy* (New York: Atherton, 1963).
76. Lewis A. Dexter, *How Organizations Are Represented in Washington* (Indianapolis, IN: Bobbs-Merrill, 1969): chap. 9.
77. See Ronnie Dugger, *The Politician* (New York: Norton, 1982): 273; Robert A. Caro, *The Years of Lyndon Johnson: The Path to Power* (New York: Knopf, 1982) and *The Years of Lyndon Johnson: Means of Ascent* (New York: Knopf 1990).
78. Dugger, *Politician,* 286.
79. Quoted in Burdett A. Loomis, "A New Era: Groups and the Grass Roots," in *Interest Group Politics,* 2nd ed., ed. Allan J. Cigler and Burdett A. Loomis (Washington, DC: CQ Press, 1983): 184.
80. Schlozman and Tierney, "More of the Same," 18.
81. Robert H. Salisbury, "The Paradox of Interest Groups in Washington—More Groups and Less Clout," in *The New American Political System,* 2nd ed., ed. Anthony King (Washington, DC: American Enterprise Institute, 1990): 225–26.
82. For an expansion of this argument, see Jonathan Rauch, *Democlerosis* (New York: New York Times Books, 1994).
83. Everett Carll Ladd Jr., "How to Tame the Special Interest Groups," *Fortune,* October 1980: 6.

I. GROUP ORGANIZATION

2

Learning to Lobby

Groups, Venues, and Information in Eighteenth-Century America

Burdett A. Loomis

In 1787, congregational pastor Manasseh Cutler descended upon the Continental Congress to convince that body to grant his sponsors, the Ohio Company, the right to purchase a large tract of the Northwest Territory. In so doing, he may well have pulled off the biggest lobbying coup of his era and thus demonstrated the value of the effective representation of interests at the national level.

Cutler showed how a private interest could change governmental policy to its overwhelming advantage. Historian Jeffrey Pasley states, Cutler "pulled off what is arguably the greatest feat of lobbying in American history, the 1787 purchase of several million acres of public land on behalf of a group of . . . Revolutionary war veterans and land speculators calling themselves the Ohio Company. . . ."[1] The Land Ordinance of 1787 had opened up land ownership to thousands of individuals, but Cutler, acting as agent of the Ohio Company, sought an entire region of the Northwest Territory for the corporation. The government was being asked to sell a huge block of land, mostly on credit; the debt would eventually be paid in Revolutionary War debt certificates, worth pennies on the dollar.

Cutler arrived in New York, then the national capital, on July 5, 1787, and left twenty-two days later, his job complete. By October, he had made the first of eight $500,000 payments, delivering debt certificates accumulated by the group. This down payment permitted the Ohio Company to occupy and develop the initial 750,000 acres without receiving a formal deed. Just as many modern lobbyists do, Cutler continued to work for his clients by monitoring the implementation of the land purchase. Over the next two years, debt certificates rose in value, and the consortium found it increasingly difficult to make its payments. Cutler returned to the capitol in 1790 to press his case for a lower per-acre price and an extended payment deadline. Unfortunately for Cutler and the Ohio Company, Treasury Secretary Hamilton's ambitious financial proposals were dominating the first U.S. Congress's agenda. Like any good lobbyist, Cuter understood the virtue of timing, so he bypassed the executive branch and sought support from individual legislators. He "visited members in their homes, quietly rounding up support for a rather cheeky request that the contract price be knocked down to twenty cents per acre," which would have saved the company $500,000.[2] Cutler ultimately failed in this effort, largely because the Congress simply did not take up his proposal.

He left New York but was back in Philadelphia, the new capital, in March 1792, when the entire deal was at risk of collapsing. Again, the members of Congress disappointed him, as he found it hard to command their attention; either committees could not mount quorums or the legislators had gotten caught up in nonstop "Philadelphia entertainments." Still, Cutler prevailed, working the congressional system as well as any contemporary lobbyist. Drawing on friendships based on geographical or college ties, Cutler helped create a special committee whose members acted quickly on his proposal to reduce the price for the entire 1.5 million acre tract to twenty cents per acre.

Although the final legislative product was not quite as generous, the bill passed both chambers in about six weeks, with Cutler's special lobbying target, Vice President Adams, casting the deciding vote.

What accounted for Cutler's pathbreaking success? Pasley argues that, while some questionable bargaining did occur, Cutler's lobbying victory largely derived from his style or "complaisance," which was part of a genteel culture in which the capacity to make others feel at ease was highly valued, especially given contentious circumstances. Modern lobbyists would recognize such a quality in an instant. Manesseh Cutler, the well-read and personable pastor, knew how to make others feel at ease and highly valued, and none more so than his targets in the American Congress.

Cutler's successes in 1787 and 1792 bookend the writing of the Constitution, its adoption, and the ratification of the first amendment, which guaranteed the rights of citizens to engage in lobbying. In short, as the new nation was emerging in the 1790s, lobbying the government, beyond mere petitioning, had become both a constitutional right and, in nascent form, a fact of political life. This combination of legal guarantees and political practices served as the foundation for the group-based politics observed by Alexis de Tocqueville in the 1830s, embraced by nineteenth-century interests, and institutionalized in the late twentieth century.

By the early 1790s, American interest groups, either existing or potential, possessed the right to lobby the government as well as a host of other targets. In particular, merchants from major cities, bondholders, planters, and religious groups sought specific governmental actions. From the first days of the nation under the Constitution, Madison and other framers fully expected interests to participate in the give-and-take of government at both the state and national levels. With a long history of interacting with the English bureaucracy and Parliament, as well as with colonial governors and assemblies, interest groups in the new nation proved more than ready to take part effectively in politics and policy making, often through lobbying or the stimulation of constituents' support at the grassroots. The institutional developments of the early republic did not occur in a vacuum, and they beg for explanation. What follows will lay out the emergence of group-based politics and early lobbying efforts over the course of the eighteenth century, which essentially laid the groundwork for such political participation over the next two centuries.

Moreover, looking back from the vantage point of contemporary interest group and lobbying scholarship, several trends emerge in the eighteenth century that presage the great importance of information in lobbying, the significance of coalitions, the relevance of institutional forms and venue shopping in framing lobbying efforts, and the significance of grassroots efforts. In sum, Americans learned to organize and lobby in the eighteenth century, and they put that knowledge to work from the earliest days of Republic.

The Politics of American Interests: 1690–1750s: English Connections

Understanding the growing involvement of American interests in policy making and politics requires an initial focus on their roots in two distinct, but related, realms—English institutions and American colonial assemblies. American interests, such as merchants and religious groups, were ordinarily defined in local, or at most colony-by-colony, terms in the 1600s. In the twenty-five years following the Glorious Revolution (1688), English government grew in size and became more bureaucratic, and organized interests in England provided officials with a key commodity—information.[3] At the same time, trade with America was growing steadily, as were the number and diversity of American religious groups. Nonetheless, the Crown failed to increase the size of its bureaucracy in the colonies. As a result, American and English interests benefited from their ability to provide accurate information to the London-based bureaucracy, and especially to the Board of Trade. Indeed, information helped forge whatever influence American groups were likely to have in the 1690–1750s period.[4] In the absence of coercive British rule, American interests, their allied English interests, and the Crown all stood to benefit from accurate, effectively communicated information about colonial needs and governmental actions.

With increased trade, growing populations, and more commercial and governmental complexity, issues such as taxes, tariffs, land disputes, and the rules for religious practice had the potential to become highly contentious. By the early eighteenth century, interests in various colonies had begun to hire agents to address their concerns directly to Parliament and the Board of Trade. In 1712, after some years of informal representation, the

South Carolina legislature appointed a permanent agent to represent the colony's mercantile interests in London. The legislation explicitly describes the representation of mercantile interests, not persons, before the Parliament; in fact, the agent took on many of the colony's interests, with most of his efforts directed at the Board of Trade. Thus, South Carolina not only hired a lobbyist but one who shopped for the most welcoming venue to make his case.[5]

Taking this action did not mean that the colony's merchants were united in their requests of the Crown. In fact, merchants often squabbled among themselves, which made representing their interests in London a difficult task. Still, the Charleston merchants, for all their disagreements, came to appreciate the power of effective lobbying when carried out by London commercial interests. This was especially so in lengthy debates over trade restrictions on rice, when it finally became apparent in 1774 that a unified front could temper the effects of long-standing policies. Historian Rebecca Starr observes that the merchants might well have learned two lessons in their rice trade lobbying: first, that succeeding in winning mitigation of policies based on unequal power (Crown versus colonies) was just a step away from lobbying to change the balance of power itself and, second, that speaking with a unified voice was an essential precursor to convincing the Board of Trade or the Parliament of the justice of their requests.[6]

More generally, Richard Brown argues that the key figures in relations between England and the colonies were "Anglo-American politicians," who needed to satisfy constituencies in both America and England.[7] Although not all of these individuals lobbied, many did in terms of linking interests and decision makers in one venue (a colony or city) to those in another (London). Brown sees a stable system of relations developing over the mid-eighteenth century, which then began to come apart in the decade preceding the American Revolution.

Relations between American and London groups proved especially strong between 1721 and 1754, when British governments headed by three skillful prime ministers provided a stable framework for the useful exchange of information.[8] To the extent that their English agents could approach key patrons within the aristocracy and important contacts within the bureaucracy, American interests could be effectively represented as they petitioned the government on various colonial issues, such as duties, land disputes, and religious freedom.

Although some interests did become reasonably well organized during this period, American groups of the era only loosely resembled modern organized interests. Churches generally developed the most coherent organizations, both internally and in their relations with their British counterparts. Merchants, often organized around the coffeehouses that served as gathering spots, were more loosely structured, while planters and farmers were even less well organized, which is not surprising given their relative isolation.

At their best, American interests worked with their English counter-parts to gain knowledge about parliamentary and ministerial actions in order to anticipate them and provide information that might enhance or mitigate the effects of decisions. These groups became part of the regular process of governance and yet did not lobby on causes, as modern groups would.[9] Rather, American interests were most effective in petitioning for specific actions or relief from general policies, set either by the Board of Trade or the Parliament. They could thus affect policies on the ground in America by building bridges back to English groups and governmental actors, whom they could help by providing accurate information on colonial issues, desires, and concerns.

At the same time that evolving American groups became part of the London political landscape, they also interacted in significant ways with colonial governors. The most effective executives, appointed by the Crown, were those who understood that many interests had better information about London affairs than they did. Thus Virginia governor William Gooch, who served from 1727 to 1749, succeeded in working with various groups in the largest colony to maintain his tenure for more than twenty years.[10] Although many new groups were forming, especially on the frontier, Gooch acted to placate the Anglican planters, who made up a colonial elite that combined religious and economic strength. He worked with the old elite to help them understand the need to concede some power to the newer groups. Keeping the peace among the various interests allowed Gooch to become well informed about their issues and anticipate the potential consequences.

The mid-eighteenth-century American interest group system, to the extent it could be described that way, was highly oriented toward specific petitions and the exchange of useful information with London interests. American groups became central to British governance in an era of economic growth without much bureaucratic growth in the colonies. As long as strong prime ministers and a reasonably responsive Board of Trade stayed in place, this system remained stable. But after 1754, Parliament began to increase its role in Anglo-American affairs, and this meant that colonial groups' access to power decreased as British policy making became more uncertain. Groups crave access and stability, and as Parliament found its legs in the 1750s and 1760s, American interests and their London allies found themselves increasingly on the outside.

Interests and Colonial Legislatures through the 1760s: New Targets for Influence

The development of American colonial assemblies, much like the related growth of organized interests, derived directly from the British experience. Virtually all the colonies created legislatures in their early years of existence, led by Virginia, which established its House of Burgesses in 1619. The same lack of central control from London that encouraged the formation of organized interests also contributed to the development of legislative bodies. Moreover, pressure came from landowning colonial settler populations for Britain "to provide the same rights to security of property and civic participation that appertained to independent English property holders."[11] Historian Jack Greene concludes that colonial legislators were often men who sought to advantage themselves and their colleagues—in property acquisition, business dealings, or social status.[12] At the same time, the colonial legislative elites did not represent formal, organized interests. Individuals might petition the assemblies, but groups rarely approached them with the kinds of requests or demands common in contemporary legislative politics. Still, the petitioning process did lead to real changes, in that up to half the laws of some colonies originated in this way.[13]

Given the small populations of the colonies, at least in the early eighteenth century, legislators addressed the concerns of individual constituents, or small ad hoc groups, rather than those of organized groups. In many ways, "interests" were served in that landowners, merchants, churches, and local units of governments were often catered to with a host of policies, such as the provision of roads, modest social services, and protection from Native Americans or other nations' colonies.

If the forty years after 1714 witnessed the growth of American interest groups in British politics, they also saw a maturation of colonial assemblies, where increasing numbers of veteran legislators could address a changing environment in which dominant elites gave way to more pluralistic interests.[14] Effective legislatures were crucial here for reducing the potential for conflict; by the 1760s and 1770s, Green concludes, "a political system emerged [with] . . . political structures for the routinization of conflict, such as interest groups or parties [and this] was peculiarly modern in form and represented a transition from traditional to modern politics."[15]

That said, the relations between interests and colonial assemblies were scarcely "modern" in the pre-Revolutionary War era. In particular, during the early 1700s, demands upon legislative bodies were modest at best. Olson reports that just eighteen towns in Massachusetts appealed any local dispute to the assembly between 1690 and 1730.[16] The tendency was to take disputes to England, not the provincial assembly, whose decision-making authority was less definitive as it was subject to the governor's veto.

Over the course of the eighteenth century, citizen petitions to colonial assemblies became a more common tool to propose, support, modify, or oppose prospective legislation. In earlier times, petitions had been infrequent and usually had come from a single individual on a highly specific matter. By the mid-1700s, "petitions increasingly represented the appeals of informal groups for legislative action."[17] Between 1715 and 1765, the average number of yearly legislative petitions per colony almost tripled, from 26.5 at the beginning of the period to 75.7 at the end.[18] Equally important, petitions addressed bills at every stage of the legislative process; this was not modern lobbying, but such activity did represent the work of roughly organized interests that appreciated how legislation was produced.

The institutionalization of the colonial legislatures contributed to the growth of interest group actions. The speakership evolved into a more powerful office in many assemblies, but even more importantly, committees, both standing and select, became integral to legislative organization.[19] In two colonies, Virginia and Pennsylvania, the standing committees even developed subcommittees to expedite their work. Such decentralization broadly anticipated the U.S. Congress of the mid-twentieth century, and it allowed for groups to direct their attention to specialist legislators, who were often receptive and sympathetic to well-informed arguments from constituent groups. The modern parallels continued in that legislative turnover decreased substantially in many colonies, leading to a rising influence among experienced legislators serving as chairs of standing committees.[20] Linking the committees and outside groups was their mutual need for information. Legislative committees sometimes "aggressively sought information outside the assemblies, from time to time holding hearings across their respective states."[21] Interested parties did not need to go to the legislature; legislators would come to them.

In many ways these processes provide glimpses of a developing system of interest group politics. But even toward the end of this period, most interests were not well organized, often building temporary alliances through informal contacts when an important issue arose.

As Starr concludes in her assessment of the emerging South Carolina trade lobby in the first two-thirds of the eighteenth century, "An elemental familiarity with the rudiments of lobbying may be . . . said to help account for the commercial lobby's ready reception into the province's political culture. However, the integration of these elements into a systematic strategy available for repeated use, failed to develop before the 1760s."[22] In short, neither the organization of most groups nor their capacity to use recognizable lobbying tactics suggests that interests in the American colonies had developed a clear set of identifiable, organized groups or an obvious array of influence-oriented skills. But interest groups did understand that communicating effectively to the legislature, as well as to the Crown, could pay off handsomely.

American Interests in Theory and Practice, 1770s–1787

As Olson details in her authoritative *Making the Empire Work*, the eighteenth-century heyday of American-Anglo lobbying, with its cooperation between interests on both sides of the Atlantic, was coming to an end in the 1750s and 1760s. The Board of Trade and key ministers lost power to the Parliament, which proved considerably less welcoming to petitions by or on behalf of American interests, whether religious, agricultural, or mercantile.[23] But across the colonies, a host of interests had gained experience in organizing, often on an ad hoc basis, and seeking to inform and even influence decision makers, whether in London or in state capitals.

In addition, the idea of "interest" began to be defined more broadly both in rhetoric and practice. Cathy Matson and Peter Onuf state that while successful American merchants benefited from the mercantilist approach to trade, such a philosophy "could not completely disguise the subordinate, dependent status of the colonies."[24] Indeed, some colonists argued in favor of free trade, which would define the American interest very differently than being a part of the British system. Broadly inclusive American nonimportation movements of the late 1760s, which sought to attack the mercantilist imbalance, represented nongovernmental group actions to restrain trade, but they had modest success in changing British commercial policy. Nonetheless, interests had started to view themselves more expansively than simply in terms of small, local groupings of merchants or manufacturers.

Along these same lines, often-narrow American interests began to form coalitions among like-minded groups; in Massachusetts, for example, merchants and mechanics joined together to lobby but also to support particular slates of candidates in colonial elections. Such public actions illustrate a new development for American interests—the emergence of lobbies espousing causes, either narrow (ethnic societies, such as German or Irish groups, or library supporters) or broad, such as the Sons of Liberty or extensive nonimportation groups. These "public opinion" lobbies, as Olson calls them, were organized along a new, prerevolutionary dimension of opposition to the Crown.[25] This development rapidly placed established interests at risk of fragmenting as they chose sides over a new definition of what E. E. Schattschneider would call the "scope of conflict."[26] Merchants, manufacturers, and religious adherents increasingly had to choose whether to identify with the broad, radical sentiments of the prerevolutionary groups or try to maintain their traditional group identities. In the end, many longstanding American interests broke apart in this period, as the decision about whether or not to join the revolution superseded all others.

Although some groups did begin to function within a national context during and immediately after the Revolution, much of the representation of interests during this period came through the states within the highly decentralized framework of the Articles of Confederation and the Continental Congress. Relatively stable coalitions among the northern and southern colonies formed within the weak Congress, rendering it divided to the point that its stalemate led to the Constitutional Convention.[27] During the revolutionary period, economic interests actively sought to interpret free market principles within the Continental Congress, but great divisions and the weakness of the central government prevented definitive action; interests sometimes turned their attention to state governments, with better luck.[28] But until there was a stable national government, interests of all types would find it difficult, if not impossible, to defend themselves via existing national institutions. Relying on state governments gave interests some satisfaction, but it created a patchwork of policies that worked against overall coherence in either policy making or lobbying. Still, even if interests could not agree on many policies, they could come together in expressing their need for a stronger central government in which they could reliably press their demands and seek redress of their grievances on a national basis.

To a certain extent, the western-Massachusetts-based Shays's Rebellion in 1786–87 demonstrated the need for mechanisms for aggrieved interests to make their case to authoritative governmental figures. Led by Daniel Shays, an armed group of 1,000 or so farmers marched on Worcester and Springfield, provoking the fears of governmental and economic elites before being routed by local militias. In defeat, the rebellion made clear the desirability of institutions that could respond to legitimate grievances and thorny issues. The Constitutional Convention of 1787 was called in part because of the clear failure of the Articles of Confederation to provide dissatisfied interests with any adequate, predictable access to the national government.

Interests and the Constitution in Theory and Practice, 1787–1800

The members of the American political elite who framed the American Constitution also shaped its implementation over the first twenty-five years of the country's existence. Grounded in the political theory of the prior century and the practical politics of colonial legislatures, the Continental Congress, and the struggle for independence, most of the framers had participated actively within the milieu of interest groups and lobbying in the twenty years prior to the Constitutional Convention of 1787. Above all, James Madison's approach to interests—or factions—directly affected the structure of the Constitution, the politics of its ratification, and its impact on the nascent group and party systems that would develop in the first decade of the Republic.[29] No one combined a theoretical and practical approach to groups or factions better than James Madison.

Without question, Madison's most important contribution to the formation of organized interests and the ultimate encouragement of lobbying was to help raise the activities of speech, assembly, and petition to core rights in the First Amendment. American politicians, 200-plus years after the adoption of this Amendment, frequently criticize lobbying and seek to regulate it in numerous ways, but no one seriously considers banning the practice, or even seriously restricting it. The First Amendment rights are clear, and our mix of thousands of groups and tens of thousands of lobbyists continues to reflect these basic rights. Still, much as they did not foresee the development of political parties, neither did the framers understand the full implications of the First Amendment guarantees.

In *Federalist* 10 James Madison defined *factions* as

> a number of citizens, whether accounting to a majority or a minority of the whole, who are united and actuated by some common impulse of passion, or of interest, adverse to the rights of other citizens, or to the permanent and aggregate interests of the community.[30]

Although both modern political parties and organized interests fall under this broad definition, electoral parties simply did not exist in 1787, while many early versions of interest groups did. Madison had seen many factions unite "through organizations to promote, through government, interests like . . . 'a landed interest, a manufacturing interest, a mercantile interest, a moneyed interest.'"[31] In short, as he constructed a constitution that would provide for centralized national power, which most interests desired, he proposed an institutional structure that would both encourage interests to act politically and simultaneously prevent them from exercising disproportionate amounts of power.

Still, the most common Madisonian phrase drawn from *Federalist* 10 is his warning as to "the mischief of faction," and the most optimistic interpretation of his words there relies on the nature of a large republic to dilute the potentially damaging effects of faction. But Madison the practical politician proved far more accepting, even encouraging, of a positive role for organized interests. James Yoho notes Madison's active participation in a series of groups, ranging from student demonstrations at Princeton (1770), protest meetings in the 1770s, membership in a county "committee of safety" in Virginia, and a successful petition by planters to limit tobacco production in favor of more valuable revolutionary products.[32]

On an even more regular basis, Madison, as a state or national legislator, advocated on behalf of particular interests, including denominations that wished to disestablish the Anglican Church in Virginia and land speculators who were his constituents. In the latter case, "Madison found it easy enough to help his fellow Virginians by couching his position in terms of what was best for the country—which came to be his customary approach."[33] And these were just some of Madison's actions that helped particular groups, or so-called "special interests." In the end, Madison as political theorist framed factions of all sorts in negative terms, arguing for their control, not their free rein. But as a politician, whether in or out of office, he recognized the legitimacy of group actions and their claims, at least for those with whom he agreed. Overall, Madison anticipated group actions far more clearly than he did the formation of political parties, whose rapid development shaped the nation's future in profound and unforeseen ways.

Moreover, Madison helped guide one of the great public lobbying campaigns of all time in his co-authorship of the *Federalist Papers* and in his contributions to organized ratification efforts across the colonies.[34] Simultaneously, anti-Federalist forces came together as a national interest group to oppose the ratification. These opposing forces were distinctly groups, not political parties, although they would develop into partylike organizations during the course of the 1790s.

With the ratification of the Constitution and the subsequent election of the initial Congress, citizens had targets whom they could petition to address their particular concerns, redress their grievances, or clarify administrative rules. At the same time, interests, even if not well organized, could put pressure on members of Congress to lobby on their behalf, as with hotly contested tariff policies.

The first Congress witnessed a blizzard of petitions from a wide variety of sources. Although many petitions did come from individuals seeking resolution of personal grievances, a substantial number came from groups, such as tradesmen, mechanics, and shipwrights; often the group reflected the interests of a specific city or town. In addition, trade-oriented groups sometimes submitted petitions that reflected "sophisticated campaigns" based on coordination among groups in several cities.[35]

Individual members of Congress often became conduits for particular interests. Such representation was hardly surprising in that the state legislatures of the 1780s had become increasingly open to observation and interests often sought to elect their own to serve, largely so they could fulfill their given desires. Democracy was in full bloom, with frequent elections and broadened suffrage. Gordon Wood observes, "By the1780s it was obvious to many, including Madison, that a 'spirit of locality' was destroying 'the aggregate interests of the community.' Everywhere the gentry leaders complained of popular legislative practices that today are taken for granted—logrolling, horse-trading, and pork-barreling that benefited *special and local interest groups* [emphasis added]."[36]

As much as any interest, land speculators/investors sought to influence governmental outcomes for their own benefit, even if, as with Madison, they cloaked their arguments in the rhetoric of national interest. Manesseh Cutler, the clergyman-turned-lobbyist for land speculators, may have functioned as a model for other would-be lobbyists, but he was scarcely unusual in pursuing his goal of favorable treatment for an interest-based consortium. The government's role in land transactions encouraged particular corporations or groupings to seek advantage in their speculations; indeed, favorable action from the Congress could prove a necessary condition for the profitability of many ventures. In essence, as most group theories postulate, organized interests approached the government with requests for specific actions, in this case favorable land deals. But in day-to-day policy making, the central government also frequently sought out interests—and even created groups—that could contribute to the success of its policies.

The new nation's executive branch asserted itself in this way almost immediately, most notably as it incorporated the visions and carried out the preferences of Alexander Hamilton. Entering the Cabinet as arguably its most powerful and forceful member, Secretary of the Treasury Hamilton faced the formidable task of placing the fledgling nation on sound financial footing. Hamilton understood from the start how important it was to work with the largest and strongest financial interests, initially in establishing a national bank. This would come about by the government engaging "the monied interests immediately in it by making them contribute the whole or part of the stock and giving them the whole or part of the profits," thus linking "the interests of the state in an intimate connexion with those of the rich individuals belonging to it."[37] More specifically, Hamilton sought to build his overall program of a nationalistic political economy with the assistance of an organized interest of his own creation: the Society for Establishing Useful Manufactures (SEUM).

As with many early organized interests, SEUM cannot be considered a modern interest group; it was a government corporation, established in New Jersey, which was to be a model for Hamilton's broad scheme to increase trade and bolster manufacturing. In the end, Hamilton faced considerable difficulties in catering to both domestic manufacturing interests and those oriented toward free trade. Moreover, his initial choice to head SEUM was William Duer, who knew little of manufacturing, though as Hamilton's assistant at Treasury he understood the secretary's fiscal program and possessed excellent "contacts with large merchant-creditors."[38] SEUM's ventures never got off the ground with any success, in part due to too much focus on speculation. And Jeffersonian Republicans found they could build on manufacturers' distaste for this Federalist policy, especially among those smaller entities that were short of capital.[39]

More generally, the Federalists sought to construct networks of local support, often based on patronage. Hamilton built explicitly on the idea of interest in his attempt to create a strong central government "by increasing the number of ligaments between the Government and the interests of Individuals."[40] To be sure, on occasion the government might direct its attention to the highly specific interests of a given person. But addressing the shared interests of a group of individuals would prove a much more powerful initiative.

Whether in Madison's constitutional architecture, Hamilton's linkage of interests to the national government, the petitions of individuals and groups, or the political elite's comfort in working with established interests, the new nation of the 1790s was already one in which increasingly well-organized groups came to play major roles in both politics and policy making.

Setting the Stage: Interests and Groups in Eighteenth-Century America

To be clear, organized interests in American politics, to the extent they existed at all in the eighteenth century, did not look like the interest groups that formed in the late nineteenth century or proliferated in the late twentieth century. There was no significant involvement in electoral politics, nor were there scores of professional lobbyists who established strong relationships with members of Congress. Nor were there membership organizations, such as trade unions or manufacturers' associations, or interest-based groups like the National Rifle Association or the Sierra Club.

Still, looking back over the politics of the 1700s, it is remarkable how strongly the interest-based politics of that era presaged strategies and tactics that would become commonplace in group organization and lobbying as the U.S. government grew and matured. Perhaps most important, the early and continuing emphasis on providing information reflects much contemporary political science scholarship on the capacity of organized interests to affect the policy-making process.[41] Even before interests regularly hired paid lobbyists or devised extensive public relations campaign, they understood that communicating effectively with decision makers represented a powerful tool in winning favorable treatment.

In addition, eighteenth-century interests discovered that working in coalitions was useful, as was finding the proper venue for seeking action. American groups thus often ignored colonial assemblies in the early eighteenth century, as they chose to press their cases before the Board of Trade in London where they could be represented by like-minded English groups, most often merchants or religious denominations. Of special importance were the ways in which legislative development in the colonies provided useful targets for organized interests. Strong speakers and growing committee systems meant that groups could work systematically with powerful legislators, who in turn understood that they could benefit from solid ties with organized constituencies.

Finally, such crucial framers as Madison and Hamilton—regardless of their philosophical positions—became early and energetic players at interest group politics within the first few years of the ratification of the Constitution, whose design allowed, even encouraged, interests to take advantage of many access points within the national government. As the federal government took shape in the 1790s, the roots of interest group politics had already grown deep in American political soil. Moreover, with the Constitution's guarantee of rights to assemble, petition, and, above all, speak, organized interests were assured of a prominent place in the politics of the new nation.

Notes

1. Jeffrey L. Pasley, "Private Access and Public Power: Gentility and Lobbying in the Early Congresses," in *The House & Senate in the 1790s: Petitioning, Lobbying, and Institutional Development*, eds. Kenneth R. Bowling and Donald R. Kennon (Athens: Ohio University Press, 2002): 78–79. This summary draws heavily on the Pasley article, pp. 57–99.
2. Pasley, "Private Access and Public Power," 81–82.
3. Alison G. Olson, *Making the Empire Work: London and American Interest Groups, 1690–1790* (Cambridge, MA: Harvard University Press, 1991).
4. Olson, *Making the Empire Work*, 57–58.
5. Rebecca Starr, *A School for Politics: Commercial Lobbying and Political Culture in Early South Carolina* (Baltimore: Johns Hopkins University Press, 1998): 26–27.
6. Starr, *A School for Politics*, 31.
7. Richard Brown, "The Anglo-American Political System, 1675–1775: A Behavioral Analysis," in *Anglo-American Political Relations, 1675–1775*, eds. Alison G. Olson and Richard M. Brown (New Brunswick, NJ: Rutgers University Press, 1970): 14–30.
8. Olson, *Making the Empire Work*, 94ff.
9. Olson, *Making the Empire Work*, 124.
10. This section draws on Olson, *Making the Empire Work*, 126–28.
11. Jack P. Greene, "Colonial Assemblies," in *Encyclopedia of the American Legislative System*, ed. Joel H. Sibley (New York: Charles Scribner's Sons, 1994): 24. The following section draws on this article in general.
12. Greene, "Colonial Assemblies," 28.
13. Greene, "Colonial Assemblies," 30.
14. Jack P. Greene, "Legislative Turnover in British America, 1696 to 1775," *William and Mary Quarterly* 38, no. 3 (1981): 451–56.
15. Green, "Colonial Assemblies," 34.
16. Alison G. Olson, "Eighteenth-Century Colonial Legislatures and Their Constituents," *Journal of American History* 79, no. 2 (1992): 545.
17. Greene, "Legislative Turnover in British America, 1696 to 1775," 556.
18. William Sumner Jenkins's data, cited in Olson, "Eighteenth-Century Colonial Legislatures and Their Constituents," 557.
19. Olson, "Eighteenth-Century Colonial Legislatures and Their Constituents," 560.
20. Greene, "Legislative Turnover in British America, 1696 to 1775"; Jack P. Greene, "Political Power in the House of Burgesses, 1720–1776," *William and Mary Quarterly* 16, no. 4 (1959): 485–506.
21. Olson, "Eighteenth-Century Colonial Legislatures and Their Constituents," 562. Parts of this section draw generally on this article as well.
22. Starr, *A School for Politics*, 43.

23. Olson, *Making the Empire Work*, chaps. 10 and 11.
24. Cathy D. Matson and Peter S. Onuf, *A Union of Interests: Political and Economic Thought in Revolutionary America* (Lawrence: University Press of Kansas, 1990): 21.
25. Olson, *Making the Empire Work*, 164ff.
26. E. E. Schattschneider, *The Semi-Sovereign People* (New York: Holt, Rinehart and Winston, 1960): 2ff.
27. For a political science reading of this era, see Calvin Jillson and Rick K. Wilson, *Congressional Dynamics: Structure, Coordination, and Choice in the First American Congress, 1774–1789* (Stanford, CA: Stanford University Press, 1994).
28. Matson and Onuf, *A Union of Interests*, 40ff.
29. See, generally, James Madison, *Federalist* 10, in *The Federalist*, ed. Henry Cabot Lodge (New York: Putnam, 1907); James Yoho, "Madison on the Beneficial Effects of Interest Groups: What Was Left Unsaid in 'Federalist' 10," *Polity* 27, no. 4 (1995): 587–605.
30. Madison, *Federalist* 10, 55.
31. Yoho, "Madison on the Beneficial Effects of Interest Groups," 592. These paragraphs draw extensively on this article.
32. Yoho, "Madison on the Beneficial Effects of Interest Groups," 598.
33. Yoho, "Madison on the Beneficial Effects of Interest Groups," 599.
34. Yoho, "Madison on the Beneficial Effects of Interest Groups," 603.
35. William C. diGiacomantonio, "Petitioners and Their Grievances: A View from the First Federal Congress," in *The House and the Senate in the 1790s: Petitioning, Lobbying, and Institutional Development*, eds. Kenneth R. Bowling and Donald R. Kennon (Athens: Ohio University Press, 2002): 32.
36. Gordon Wood, *Empire of Liberty: A History of the Early Republic, 1789–1815* (New York: Oxford, 2009): 17.
37. Quoted in John R. Nelson Jr., "Alexander Hamilton and American Manufacturing: A Reexamination," *Journal of American History* 65, no. 4 (1979): 973.
38. Nelson, "Alexander Hamilton and American Manufacturing," 982.
39. Nelson, "Alexander Hamilton and American Manufacturing," 984.
40. Wood, *Empire of Liberty*, 107.
41. Richard L. Hall and Alan V. Deardorff, "Lobbying as Legislative Subsidy," *American Political Science Review* 100, no. 1 (2006): 69–84; Frank Baumgartner, Jeffrey M. Berry, Marie Hojnacki, David C. Kimball, and Beth L. Leech, *Lobbying and Policy Change: Who Wins, Who Loses, and Why* (Chicago: University of Chicago Press, 2009).

3

Reappraising the Survival Question

Why We Should Focus on Interest Group Organizational Form and Careers

Darren R. Halpin and Anthony J. Nownes

Since Mancur Olson's groundbreaking work on collective action, interest group scholars have paid substantial attention to the question of how interest groups form.[1] They have, however, paid relatively little attention to the question of what happens to groups *after* they form. In fact, many of them appear to assume that groups simply go on surviving. Recently this situation has begun to change, as a new cadre of interest group scholars has focused attention on the issue of group survival. These scholars, many of whom employ a population ecology (PE) approach, have questioned the extent to which groups simply "go on surviving." Some PE scholars have even made mortality an explicit focus of their attention.

Building on recent research on group survival and mortality, we push this topic further. The PE approach focuses primarily upon the question of *if* groups survive, saying very little about *how* groups survive. This is problematic. In the conclusion of their pioneering 1996 book that popularized the PE approach, Virginia Gray and David Lowery acknowledged the need for research that examines individual group histories and seeks to explain how groups survive over time.[2] Here we respond to Gray and Lowery's call, but we deviate from the approach used in most PE studies. Specifically, rather than asking, "Do groups survive?" we ask, "How do groups adapt to enhance their chances of survival?" and "In what organizational forms do groups survive?" We begin by taking stock of extant research on survival and then outline our basic plan for the study of group survival—a new approach that examines what happens to groups after they form. Our main argument is that the best way to address the topic of group survival is to utilize a historical case study method. We envision two types of studies in particular: (1) *life-history case studies* of individual organizations and (2) *small-n studies* of groups within the same population. Case studies enable us to examine change over time in the organizational form of individual groups, while small-*n* studies allow us to examine how organizational forms and therefore capacities vary across groups at a given point in time. Our goal here is to outline a basic research strategy to move forward the study of group maintenance and survival.

Background: Research on Group Survival

Early group theorists concerned themselves primarily with group formation rather than with group survival. In his classic book *The Governmental Process,* David Truman contended that social change and disturbances led to the formation of interest groups.[3] This notion, which rested upon the naïve proposition of more or less automatic group formation, stood as the conventional wisdom on group formation for the next decade. Truman said relatively little about group survival, seemingly assuming that a group would continue to survive until its social or economic base disbursed or shifted. This line of thought implied an almost infinite growth in the number of interest groups.

Rational-choice approaches thoroughly decimated Truman's argument. Mancur Olson argued that shared interests did *not* automatically lead to group formation.[4] The failure of a group to form, he argued, may reflect a lack of selective incentives rather than an absence of collective interest. In another rational-choice study, Robert Salisbury argued that group formation was a function of "entrepreneurs" who constructed incentive systems capable of attracting members.[5] Utilizing the basic Olsonian incentive theory framework, others have emphasized the role of patronage and benefactors in group formation.[6]

The Question of Maintenance

In the wake of Olson and Salisbury, scholars of group organization began to take a close look at the related process of group survival.[7] The core proposition in early studies of group maintenance is that after formation, the imperative driving group leaders' actions is *organizational survival* rather than policy influence. Inherent in this argument is the vulnerability of organizations that pursue political goals—their members may not agree on these goals, or these goals may be unachievable or lose relevance over time, and politics may not be enough to attract sufficient numbers of supporters. In the face of such vulnerabilities, the stability and survival of the group is secured by managing incentives. Terry Moe summarized this general position: "The key to maintenance, then . . . rests instead with the continuing provision of an appropriate mix of political and nonpolitical inducements— where what is appropriate varies with constituency characteristics as well as the direction and success of leader efforts to influence them."[8] This framework for understanding group survival identifies internal factors—principally the changing motivational preferences of members—as decisive. In this formulation, the role of group entrepreneurs is largely determined by member preferences for selective incentives, be they material, symbolic, or political. While maintenance clearly is about survival, much scholarly discussion of maintenance overemphasizes managing incentives at the expense of more diverse considerations.

So-called "niche theories" were also developed to account for maintenance and survival. As James Q. Wilson put it: "The easiest and most prudent maintenance strategy is to develop autonomy—that is, a distinctive area of competence, a clearly demarcated and exclusively served clientele or membership, and undisputed jurisdiction over a function, service, goal, or cause."[9] In other words, group leaders steer groups into "clear water" where they can operate in a noncompetitive environment. William Browne has identified the propensity for groups to limit policy competition by operating in ever-narrowing issue niches.[10] Groups compete for policy makers' attention, and in this competition they differentiate themselves from other groups by specializing in particular sets of issues. A group "gains a recognizable identity by defining a highly specific issue niche for itself and fixing its specified political assets (i.e., recognition and other resources) within that niche."[11]

Those familiar with group life will no doubt recognize that the scholarly work on group survival is more diverse than the term *maintenance* implies, noting that it is hard to persist as a group without engaging in both influence activities and fundraising.[12] The image of survival as transitioning from a political organization to some type of social or trading organization seems hard to reconcile with our everyday knowledge and observations about real-world interest groups.

PE and the New Focus on External Variables

For the most part, scholars of group maintenance operating in the wake of Olson and Salisbury paid little attention to the question of whether or not groups actually *would* survive over time. Their apparent assumption was that groups would survive as they tinkered with incentive packages to attract support from members and/or patrons. In the 1990s, the PE approach, which focused specifically upon the vital incidents of group birth and group death, cast doubt upon this assumption.[13] The PE approach is too complex and variegated to summarize here. Suffice it to say that the PE approach has contributed a number of important insights about both the nature of group formation and survival and the way we should study them. Among the most important insights are the following:

First, group formation is not infinite. Empirical studies show that group populations have carrying capacities, that the number of groups forming is limited, and that many groups that successfully form do not survive.

Second, the PE approach has demonstrated the value of studying group communities and populations rather than (or in addition to) individual interest groups. PE research demonstrates that we can learn a lot about interest group formation and survival by focusing on sets of groups rather than individual organizations.

Third, PE studies have shown that both population levels and the life chances of individual groups are affected by environmentally induced population pressures. Specifically, it appears that the size and heterogeneity of a given constituency, the attention of government, and population density (that is, the number of like groups) all affect group birth and death rates.

PE studies, unlike most previous work on group maintenance, emphasize environmental forces that select out poorly adapted groups and dampen birth rates. In other words, the PE approach shifts focus from internal group variables to external variables. This approach is enormously valuable. Yet by its practitioners' own acknowledgment, the PE approach offers blunt tools to examine mortality. Survival is appraised only in terms of the dual events of group birth and death. While PE acknowledges that not all groups in a given population survive (because there is some competition for finite resources among like groups), it says very little about the ways groups overcome harsh survival pressures. On the one hand, the PE approach considers the question of survival an important one, as it assumes (guided by the ecological metaphor) that to survive, groups need to find a good "fit" with prevailing conditions. On the other hand, PE scholars marginalize the importance of studying group survival, as their perspective implies that in a given group population there is a single optimal recipe for survival and thus little diversity in organizational form across groups.

But what if this implication is incorrect? What if groups can in fact follow multiple recipes to survive difficult circumstances? This question is far from trivial. Consider, for example, a hypothetical group population that contains several groups, each of which uses a different recipe for survival. One of the groups has few if any members and as such is poorly equipped to engage in grassroots lobbying. But it is well funded and staffed by well-trained professionals; as such it is well placed to conduct research that may reframe policy questions in important ways. Another group in the population has a few million members and uses these members as assets in large-scale grassroots lobbying campaigns. These brief examples show that groups bring different (and potentially complementary) capacities to the policy process. A group's capacity, we believe, is embedded within its organizational form. Thus, a variety of forms leads to a set of groups with different sets of capacities.

In short, the PE approach does a valuable service in highlighting the importance of survival but studies survival only in terms of how it manifests in overall group numbers. For the most part PE studies fail to explore what happens between formation and death. This is problematic because a growing body of evidence suggests that groups do not simply persist, waiting to be picked off by souring environmental conditions. Rather, adaptive change does indeed take place within groups. For example, the Consumers Union in the United States transformed itself from a radical organization seeking to regulate corporate behavior into a more conservative scientific organization dedicated primarily to disseminating information to consumers.[14] There is even evidence that groups in the same general field vary significantly in their form. Douglas Imig's case study of poverty action groups in the United States, for example, found nonuniform responses to the same challenging operating environment.[15] Imig wrote:

> For one group, budget reductions forced organizational retrenchment, while for another, budget reductions led to increased fundraising and new issue domains. One group with an expanding budget shifted its policy agenda to less confrontational issues in order to maintain a stream of resources, while a second, flush with resources, employed lobbying tactics new to the social welfare sector to pursue an agenda particularly confrontational to governmental institutions.[16]

In all, new research suggests that contrary to the assumptions of much PE research, the *same* challenging environmental conditions prompt *different* responses. Groups do not respond to environmental pressures by simply "matching" environmentally prescribed "ideal type" forms. As interest group scholars Anthony Nownes and Allan Cigler argued, "there is no *one* road to group success."[17]

How Groups Survive

The question of *how* interest groups survive is an important one. It speaks to a number of other important questions, including the following: (1) Why do we have the particular constellation of interest groups we have instead of some other assemblage that we might imagine? (2) Why are some interests better represented by interest *groups* than others? (3) What factors affect interest groups' life chances? (4) What can a group's leader do in the face of environmental change to improve the group's chances of survival? and (5) Are group leaders who wish to ensure group survival powerless in the face of population pressures? Although scholars have addressed these questions, they have not provided adequate answers.

In what follows, we develop an approach that places such questions at the forefront. Our primary goal is to impress upon students of interest groups that when they think of "maintenance," they should pay due attention to the "form" in which groups continue to survive. We also emphasize the fact a group may change its "form" over the course of its life—or what we call its "career."

Group Careers

The first step in outlining our basic approach is to introduce the concept of the *group career*. We define *group career* as the course or projection of a group's existence. Rather than having questions of formation and maintenance and mortality treated separately, we look at how they are linked within an overall career. To do so, it is important to recognize that contemporary groups have not necessarily always been as we find them. We ought to be curious about how they came to be as we find them, as scholars have often been in the study of political organizations generally. Many students of political parties, for example, talk of a need to focus on party "careers."[18] And there is a scholarly tradition of comparing shifts in party "forms" (for instance, from "mass" to "cartel" parties).[19] The "career" approach to studying organizations is also evident in the social movement literature.[20]

The concept of a group career suggests at least some organizational change over time. It is hard to imagine that a long-lived group will survive by simply maintaining the shape of its initial formation. Lengthy group careers will likely develop because groups adapt their initial forms to new and changing circumstances. As straightforward as this proposition sounds, the challenge is to find a way to identify what form or shape a group takes at any particular point in time—a baseline for tracking changes over time. How can we know if and how a group has changed if we do not know what it used to be and what it is now?

Organizational Form

How can we identify when a single group has changed as it moves through its "career" and describe the various ways in which groups are organized within populations? To address these questions, we utilise the term *organizational form*, a term that has a long and varied use in organizational studies.[21] Here, we define organizational form as the organizational configuration a group conforms to at any single point in time. To systematize our approach, we suggest that an organizational form at any moment manifests three broad components/layers: (1) organizational identity, (2) organizational features and strategies, and (3) technical settings. Not only is this a way to describe a group's form at a given moment, but it also provides a language to describe changes over time. We assume that these components constitute levels at which group adaptive change can occur. Thus, change can be assessed over time both in terms of alterations to individual components and in the cumulative impact of these changes on overall group organizational form.

Let us elaborate on these components of form (see summary in Table 3.1). It is helpful to think of an interest group as having a broad identity that reflects its core purpose. Like people, groups ask themselves "Why are we here?" and "What should we be doing?" One way to think about this is in terms of what the group stands for—its mission. We can discern a group's identity from its public statements to key audiences of policy makers and supporters (members and patrons). This fits with recent work arguing that groups aspire to, and proactively cultivate, their own unique identities.[22] An identity is not a statement of what a group actually does. Rather, it is a statement about what a group purports or promises to do. As will become clear, aspirations may often be somewhat disconnected from strategies and technical settings; that is, promises often lag behind practices. A group communicates its aspirations through its name, its promotional material, and its public proclamations. We restrict our definition of identity to what the *leadership* of the group wants or claims it to be rather than the views or interpretations of others, such as policy makers or members. Although an identity is often contested, we do not believe such alternative views should be incorporated into our definition of identity. Rather, at any time we see a *dominant* group identity. We further assume that we can then study efforts to change or challenge this identity. While each group will—much like people—have a unique identity, groups tend to develop some more or less

Table 3.1   Group Organizational Form and Change

Change	Description	Examples of Change
First order [Technical settings]	• Settings for organizational features • Technical approaches to implementing features • Means to achieve strategic purposes	• Develop telemarketing program to recruit members. • Develop Web site. • Develop relationship marketing program. • Change annual general meeting (AGM) format. • Recruit new staff expertise.
Second order [Organizational features and strategies]	• Policy strategy • Resource acquisition strategy • Formal organizational structures	• Change from "outsider" to "insider" lobbying strategy. • Change from small member support to large donor support. • Expand constituency coverage. • Narrow policy area of interest.
Third order [Organizational identity]	• Aim(s) • Mission	• Change from advocacy to service delivery. • Change from representative-based focus to issue focus.

common identities. Michael T. Heaney suggested that groups tend to pursue either an issue-based or a representative-based identity. In terms of aims, some groups focus primarily or solely on policy advocacy, while others lean heavily on service delivery, change "on the ground," or broad "public education" and "awareness."[23] In reality, most groups combine both foci, but Heaney found that groups tend to emphasize one over the other.

If identity is about mission or purpose, organizational features and strategies emerge in response to the question "How should we be organized to achieve our aims and mission?" Thus, organizational features and strategies refer to how a group organizes itself to serve its overall identity. Groups have an almost infinite number of features and strategies, such as recruiting staff, communicating, etc., but some are more crucial to group organization than others. Interest groups, by definition, are *formal* organizations engaged in two core tasks—mobilizing support and resources and engaging in advocacy activities. Therefore, a group's most relevant organizational features and strategies include (1) the pursuit of policy influence, such as "outside" or "inside" lobbying strategies; (2) the generation of the financial support and human resources needed to survive; and (3) basic formal organizational structures, like the level of group centralization and reliance on professional staff.

On the first count, groups need to decide what style of lobbying to engage in. Should they pursue a "system-changing" stance and be critical of government? Or should they generally try to strike a pragmatic tone? A related consideration might be how narrowly or broadly to engage on policy issues. On the second count, groups have to decide how to procure the money they need to survive. Do they seek government funding or donations from a few large benefactors? Or do they try to build a large membership base? The third element emphasizes the structures of the group. As formal organizations, groups possess attributes such as the level of professional staffing and the hierarchy among suborganizational units.

While not dwelling upon them here, we could also focus on the precise technical settings associated with implementing the organizational features. For instance, once a group has built a mass supporter base as a method of obtaining resources, the issue of implementation remains—that is, the means by which supporters are recruited. For example, are they solicited via word of mouth, through newspaper appeals, through e-mail campaigns, or by professional recruiters? These types of micro settings can change frequently. Micro settings also reflect the tactics a group uses in a specific policy battle. To wit, should the group engage in litigation or try to mobilize a grassroots consumer boycott? This level of detail is difficult to identify in population level studies and thus is best reserved for case studies (see below).

As for changes in these three components of organizational form, we hypothesize that altering identity is the most difficult. A group might seek to emphasize one or another *facet* of its identity—perhaps to emphasize, say, representativeness one day and issue expertise the next—but we do not see much evidence that a group can shift its *overall* organizational identity often or quickly. When a group shifts its reason for being—for example, from being a service provider to a mass membership advocacy group—it does so over time, not all at once. What about changes in organizational features and strategies and technical settings? Do they affect a group's identity? We hypothesize that changes in lower tiers will mostly occur without any impact on identity. For instance, a group may update member recruitment using new Web-based technologies, but doing so will not affect its basic reason for being. In short, we suggest that a hierarchy of change exists. But much empirical analysis is required to uphold this hunch.

The two concepts we introduce here—group career and organizational form—are valuable heuristic devices that we can use to study group change and adaptation. The concept of organizational form focuses our attention on the configuration in which a group survives at any single point in time. With this concept comes language we can use to start describing individual groups and how they change over time. We surmise that most changes in form are minor in nature—that is, they involve variations in strategies and/or technical settings. Changes in identity are more infrequent. In our formulation, a group career consists of strings of changes in a group's organizational form. By studying individual group careers, we can learn more about how, to what extent, and to what effect, groups change.

Implementing the Approach

In this section, we develop some illustrative vignettes to demonstrate that ours is a worthwhile approach to learning about interest group behavior. Specifically, we will present several mini–case studies of organizations that have changed over the course of their careers. These will show our basic approach in action. In addition, they will demonstrate that the approach can help us understand the general processes of group maintenance and survival.

Variation in Organizational Form among Groups in the Same Population

The thrust of this chapter would be unnecessary if groups within the same population were homogenous in their form. But we know that this is not the case. Empirical studies have shown that groups within the same population respond differently to the same circumstances. One does not have to dig far to find groups in the same population that are organized differently. Consider, for example, organizations representing blind persons in the United Kingdom.[24] By the mid-twentieth century, three major national organizations of or for the blind existed. First, the British and Foreign Blind

Association (BFBA) was formed in the late 1800s by wealthy blind persons to seek better life conditions for the blind by providing them with embossed literature. The group admitted nonblind persons as supporters and never actively sought to represent the blind so much as to work *for* them.

Second, the National League of the Blind and Disabled (NLBD) was established in 1899 as a trade union for blind and disabled workers (associate membership was allowed for partially sighted workers). Increasing numbers of blind persons gained employment within sheltered workshops, and the League organized these new workers.[25]

Finally, almost half a century later, the National Federation of the Blind of the United Kingdom (the "Federation") was established as a direct membership organization. It pursued membership among blind people who worked in white-collar and professional roles, a constituency for whom the League's industrial role was less relevant. In common with the League, it had a strong face-to-face branch structure. Both the League and the Federation were constructed from birth as representative organizations of the blind for the blind. Moreover, both organizations were strongly opposed to the preponderance of sighted persons on bodies governing their welfare, believing that such people could not be as committed to the cause as the blind themselves.[26]

Together, the basic backgrounds of these three groups indicate that the condition of blind persons during the period in question did not in and of itself seem to recommend a particular type of organizational form. The groups took three distinct forms.

Other populations of groups provide further support for the notion that different groups within the same population take different forms. For example, in their seminal work on US policy change, Baumgartner and Jones identified all citizen groups listed in the *Encyclopedia of Associations* published by Gale Research that were active on environmental issues.[27] The population of groups they described is large and amazingly diverse. To show the variety of organizational forms present in the population of environmental groups, they contrasted the American Phytopathological Society with the Sierra Club. The former is a professional association of plant scientists with a primary focus on public education, while the latter is a citizen group that emphasizes aggressive political advocacy. In short, even within the same broad group populations, individual groups can have very different identities and forms.

Formation: The Importance of Establishing a Group's Organizational Form

To understand how a group changes form over time, it is necessary to discover how the group established itself initially—that is, to understand the form it took at birth. Establishing this baseline organizational form for a group under study provides us with a reference point for examining change over time.

The early years of group life are often characterized by jousting over the basic purpose of a group. In short, group identity is not "given"; it needs to be *formed* or chosen. For example, the Soil Association, a UK organization formed by proponents of organic farming in 1946, was established with at least three stated purposes in mind: (1) public education, (2) scientific inquiry, and (3) farmer knowledge exchange. The report of the first annual meeting records the resignation of one founder over the crystallizing view that the group should be about public education and admit the broader public—not just organic farmers—into membership. The founder in question strongly preferred that the group establish an identity as a traditional amateur scientific society distributing homespun experimental results to its constituent organic farmer members. But other founders had a different vision.

In all cases, a choice has to be made about group identity at inception. But this choice is often contested and subject to internal political processes and debate. In the Soil Association case, a choice of becoming a scientific society, for example, would have implied local branch structure; scientific content in the group's published materials; and the maintenance of its research farm, which was donated to the group by its founder in 1945 and sold in 1982. But out of a lengthy formative period when various alternatives were jousting for dominance a different identity and form crystallized, secured by strong early leadership.[28] The group chose a secretariat of well-seasoned environmental campaigners and established a media staff. It organized so as to attract the attention of and engage with the broader British public, rather than primarily aggregating and representing the interests of organic farmers. Today most members are nonfarmers, and no branch system was ever developed. The recruitment of members increasingly relied on direct marketing, with appeals emphasizing incentives such as magazines, reductions on insurance, and similar packages of selective goods.

The broad point here is that students of groups will be less likely to take it for granted that groups have always existed as currently organized if they look first at group origins. The Soil Association is a modern, resource-rich, professionally staffed and led environmental citizens group. But it took this form only after several decades of battles over its "proper" identity. It is also worth noting that a group's organizational form has real and important implications for its policy behavior. In its current incarnation, the Soil Association lobbies for consumers and the soil rather than for the sectoral interests of professional organic farmers.

Radical Change: Shifts in Identity

Interest group scholars are especially interested in the most radical changes in organizational form. Aside from their intrinsic interest, such case studies also provide broad insights into group maintenance and survival, as can been seen in the following two instances of identity shifts.

The Australian Conservation Foundation.   The Australian Conservation Foundation (ACF) is a group that underwent radical identity change. The ACF commenced life as a "semi-scientific body" of prestigious scientists working in academia and government.[29] From its inception, the group had active annual general meetings and contested elections for a board, which then set the group's strategic direction. Beginning in the early 1980s, the group started pursuing a more radical "green" agenda; it engaged explicitly in political advocacy, including federal-level electioneering, and opened its membership to the mass public. In the latest period (1985–present), John Warhurst explained that the ACF appointed a lawyer as director and a rock star as its president (Peter Garret from Midnight Oil). In short, the organization for senior scientists had transformed itself into a mass affiliation group that pursued an environmental agenda through political advocacy.

The ACF started life as a group of professional ecologists concerned with the environment. Its legitimacy arose from the democratically derived view of its professional membership. Today it actively seeks a mass supporter base, which in turn will illustrate to government that a broad public views the environment as a high priority. Warhurst noted that while "the culture of the organization is participative . . . the leadership has tended to overshadow the membership."[30] Indeed, the ACF itself now talks of supporters and volunteers; its Web site does not explicitly show how a member can influence the group's decisions.

That the ACF has fundamentally changed its overall form is beyond dispute. The change is not only important in its own right, but it also has implications for how the group behaves politically. In its early years, the ACF was a good reference point for scientifically formulated positions on conservation. This nonpolitical identity provided the group with a certain credibility, but it precluded the group from engaging in overt political advocacy and mobilizing mass membership for causes. The endorsement of the current ACF of policy proposals is less about attaching a veneer of scientific respectability and more about confirming widespread societal support.

The Royal National Institute of Blind People.   The case of the ACF shows that radical shifts in purpose are not unheard of. This is an exciting finding in and of itself, and it is consistent with work in the social movement literature that shows how voluntary sector groups move among advocacy, service provision, and representation.[31] But precisely *how* does radical change come about?

To illustrate how our approach can help us understand such change, we will briefly examine the case of the Royal National Institute of Blind People (RNIB). The RNIB was founded in 1868 as the British and Foreign Society for Improving Embossed Literature for the Blind. The group was established by a group of wealthy blind men as a benevolent organization that primarily developed written materials and offered rehabilitation services for the blind, and the group championed the use of the Braille system in printed materials. Since its formation the group has undergone five name changes.[32] Appraised from a contemporary viewpoint, the group has undergone a significant change from its initial form. Specifically, the RNIB has evolved from being a provider of services to the blind in the tradition of philanthropic benevolence to an overtly political organization representing the blind before government. A brief look at the group's last ten years shows how this change took place.

The past decade has been a momentous one for the RNIB. In 2002, the group announced a series of organizational changes. Most important, the group decided to affiliate the blind into direct membership. Since 2002, the group has offered "full membership" to those who are blind and partially sighted. Essentially, the group became an organization *of* the blind and partially sighted rather than just *for* the blind and partially sighted, changing its rules to reserve a majority of spots on its governing body for the blind and partially sighted.[33] This significant alteration from the group's origins would be expected to have major effects on other organizational features. In short, the RNIB has changed from advocating for the blind to organizing the blind to advocate for themselves. The RNIB of the early twenty-first century is not the same organization that it was in the late nineteenth century. But how can we articulate this change? The group's own claim of momentous change is not disputed. But the question is whether or not the *process* of change conforms to the image conveyed by the group's own reportage of a one-off "decision" or whether it was the result of incremental adaptations over several decades.

Close inspection of the group's history suggests that there was no single moment of rapid and radical change. Changes were made by the group's governing body and formalized in the group's Royal Charter and bylaws in 2001. But the notion that this resulted from a short period of rapid and comprehensive change is erroneous. The most recent name change—from the Royal National Institute of the Blind to the Royal National Institute of Blind People (2007)—is the symbolic "cherry on the cake" in terms of demarcating change for the group. The historical record suggests that this final change was the accretion of decades of smaller modifications and, further, was made possible by precedents and decisions made half a century beforehand.

A convenient empirical indicator of the extent to which this radical change has been realized in RNIB practice is the percentage of blind persons in the main decision-making organ of the group. Fortunately, RNIB annual reports allow us to track how this number has changed over the years.[34] This statistic provides a proxy measure of the distance traveled between the two points—the extent to which the "new" representational organizational identity has been realized (see Table 3.2).

As background, it is important to know a few historical facts about the governance of the RNIB. Prior to the 1920s, for almost sixty years, the RNIB was run by a group of mostly blind men.[35] Working for the group was a purely voluntary endeavor. The roots of the contemporary reforms to the RNIB regarding blind representation can be traced back to developments in 1925–1926, 1931, and 1937. These successive and tightly bound waves of reform altered its composition and thus its internal politics. As government started to take over care for the blind in the early 1900s, the RNIB came under pressure to share its substantial fundraising wealth with local charitable organizations and local government. The British government proposed a national body be established to achieve coordination, and it suggested the RNIB assume this mantle. The group did so, but in return it had to allocate representation on its council to member organizations from local government and other organizations of and for the blind. In essence, the National Institute for the Blind (NIB), as it was then called, became a group of groups. This change in internal governing structure did *not* change the group's overall identity, as it retained its focus on delivering services to the blind.

Returning to group evolution, the share of blind persons in the RNIB's governing body provides an indicator of the distance traveled from its initial form as a benevolent group to its current form as a group representing blind persons directly. As Table 3.2 illustrates, the percentage of blind persons within the council has varied over time but has grown incrementally over the past half century. The major outcome of the 2001 reform process was a constitutional guarantee that governance structures would have a blind majority. In fact, blind persons have constituted a majority since the 1980s.

Interviews with former leaders reveal that blind persons *within* the organization sought, and won, successive reforms to the group's constitution to convert the RNIB into an unofficial representative group of the blind. In short, to take the 2001 reforms and name change as the tipping

Table 3.2   Composition of Executive Council of RNIB 1966–2001, Selected Years

	1966	1971	1975	1980	1986	1996	2001
Total	100	105	120	115	93	111	117
Percent blind	20	26	40	45	58	65	65

Source: Royal National Institute of Blind People, *Annual Report* [Various years] (London: Royal National Institute of Blind People).

point in the evolution of the RNIB would be to miss a great deal. Moreover, a great deal of first- and second-order change went on without immediately undermining or directly challenging the RNIB's philanthropic form. Slow, adaptive, yet significant change added up to transformative change.

Again, the shift in group organizational form has implications for what the group can do in public policy. The RNIB went from being a benevolent organization to one with representative legitimacy. This enabled it politically to represent the blind—to voice the interests of blind persons—not simply to show solidarity with them or to help them.

Minor Change Consistent with Established Identity: Organizational Features, Strategies, and Technical Settings

Rapid and frequent change of identity is rarely easy, and for most groups maintenance involves changing organizational features and strategies or only technical settings *within* an overarching identity. In short, organizational forms evolve most often through nonradical change that retains overall identity.

Change among Homosexual Rights Interest Groups in the United States.   In 1980, veteran gay rights advocate Steve Endean founded the Human Rights Campaign Fund (HRCF). The group, which excised "Fund" from its name in 1995, is now a gay rights advocacy behemoth. It boasts 700,000 members and annual revenues of over $20 million. According to its official history, "Ever since its founding in 1980, HRC has led the way in promoting fairness for GLBT [gay, lesbian, bisexual, and transgender] Americans."[36] This declaration is a bit of an overstatement for it obscures the fact that HRC did not add the words *transgender* and *bisexual* to its mission statement until 2001. The case of the HRC is not unusual. Over the past fifteen years, one by one, most (but not all) American gay and/or lesbian organizations have expanded their boundaries to encompass the interests of transgender individuals. Within the GLBT community this is known as "adding the *T*." For example, Parents and Friends of Lesbians and Gays (PFLAG) "added the *T*" in 1998, while both the National Gay and Lesbian Task Force (NGLTF) and the National Center for Lesbian Rights did so in 1996. No definitive and thorough study has been done on this topic. As part of a different project, however, we chose eighteen nationally active, American gay and/or lesbian rights interest groups at random and found that between 1995 and 2004, all but one (the lone holdout was the right-leaning Log Cabin Republicans) had broadened their missions to encompass the interests and issues of transgender individuals.[37]

Scholars disagree over precisely why so many gay and/or lesbian rights groups expanded their boundaries in the 1990s and 2000s. Our own research suggests that gay and lesbian rights groups chose to expand their boundaries and reach out to a new constituency to compete with newly prominent transgender interest groups such as the National Transgender Advocacy Coalition, the Transgender Law and Policy Institute, and the National Center for Transgender Equality; in other words, groups changed to enter a new market and garner new resources from members and patrons. Other scholars disagree, citing more idealistic reasons.

Scholarly debates notwithstanding, the facts concerning organizational change speak for themselves. During a ten- to fifteen-year period, the population of gay and/or lesbian rights interest groups in the United States underwent substantial change. This change, however, did not take place at the overall population level, where PE scholars focus their attention. Rather, it took place among groups *within* the population. Groups of all shapes and sizes expanded their boundaries and reached out to a new constituency. In short, the case of the population of gay and/or lesbian rights interest groups provides overwhelming empirical evidence that second-order change among interest groups is not uncommon. In fact, in this population second-order change was the rule rather than the exception. There are now close to 100 nationally active homosexual rights interest groups in the United States.[38] Over the past fifteen years, one by one, most (but not all) of them have expanded their boundaries to encompass the interests of transgender individuals

The Federation of Small Businesses.   The Federation of Small Businesses (FSB) in the United Kingdom has undergone substantial change. Its identity, however, has never changed—it is and always has been a group organizing small businesspersons and representing their interests before government. Since its establishment in 1974, the organization has intermittently revised and "upgraded" its policy strategies and recruitment strategies. In its initial formation phase, the FSB (then called the National Federation of the Self Employed, NFSE) recruited members through personal contacts, and its policy stance emphasized a belligerent pursuit of policy goals. The early success of the group faded as the founding issue of National Insurance charges for small businesses receded. Starting in 1990, while the largely activist-led and outsider-style influence strategy continued, recruitment became professionalized, and the group developed into a mass membership organization predicated on selective incentives.[39] Associated with this transformation, the FSB shifted its policy strategy. Specifically, it began pursuing a more "insider" approach and moderating its tone and tactics.[40]

To summarize, in the early 1990s, after sixteen years of "outsider" policy advocacy accompanied by a disjointed and amateurish approach to member recruitment, the FSB shifted its strategy and technical settings related to exercising insider influence and maximizing support from potential members. The group changed without altering its basic identity. The group remains a representative advocacy group for British small businesspeople.

Addressing Other Questions

Understanding group adaptive change is important in its own right. But the approach we champion here allows scholars to weigh in on other important questions. Consider, for example, the ongoing debate about the democratic properties of contemporary interest groups. Recently some influential scholars have claimed that many previously democratic groups have begun to jettison participatory democratic structures and replace them with more professionalized "top-down" group structures.[41] Other scholars argue that many groups retain democratic properties and that the "professionalization of advocacy" thesis is incorrect.[42] In our parlance, the debate is over whether or not large numbers of groups are shifting from a participative organizational form to a more elite-driven form. By recourse to our basic framework, which posits that there are levels of change in form, we can begin to unpack how such change might manifest itself.

In the United Kingdom, much has been written about the propensity of contemporary citizen groups, particularly environmental ones, to adopt a form whereby they are supported by a remote membership base consisting of individuals who are enrolled through direct marketing and who each contribute small amounts to the group. Jordan and Maloney used the term "protest business" to describe these kinds of groups.[43] Students of interest groups might ask, Is a shift in this direction a shift in organizational form? Our approach allows us to address this question. Here we will briefly examine three UK citizen groups: (1) the Royal Society for the Protection of Birds (RSPB), (2) Oxfam UK, and (3) the National Trust (NT). Each of these groups is more than sixty years old, being created in 1889, 1942, and 1895, respectively. Each group has had to adapt in some way to survive for so long. Each operates within the UK environment and conservation policy field. And all broadly share a similar organizational form; specifically, each is an issue-based advocacy group lobbying to protect the environment. They also employ "insider" lobbying tactics, utilize expertise and science to support their case, and rely financially on large and relatively remote/passive mass membership bases. In short, each of these groups is the prototypical "protest business" group.[44]

All three of these groups have come to scholarly attention because of their rapid post-1990s growth in membership. The RSPB, for instance, now has over a million members, compared to 475,000 in 1985. Research has attributed this increase in membership to the group's recent deployment of modern membership-marketing techniques and merchandizing. The adoption of innovative techniques, such as "direct-debit" payment methods, direct mail solicitation, the employment of professional performance-paid recruiters, and canvassing of "warm" leads through database mining, have led to membership increases and more income.

Each of these groups did indeed have a formative period in which it was the subject of the intense participative efforts of a small number of group entrepreneurs. For instance, the RSPB was formed by a small band of women who objected to the use of plumage from rare birds in women's hats.[45] Similarly, Oxfam started during the Second World War as the Oxford Committee for Famine Relief and, like many similar committees of its time, was run by a handful of local notables, such as church leaders and academics. The National Trust was formed by a small number of upper-class individuals, who were at first resistant to any mass membership.[46] Yet in short order each of these groups morphed into what is best described as an early "protest business." For example, by the 1920s, the NT started soliciting mass membership, and it formed a membership department in the 1940s. Similarly, only five years after its formation, Oxfam began to employ innovative business techniques to raise money. Specifically, it began selling gifts through a storefront and soliciting support through media campaigns. In the 1960s, the group adopted a "pledged gift" system whereby people were cold-canvassed at their doors to pledge support for Oxfam and provide a donation.[47] Likewise, by the end of the 1940s, the RSPB was offering its members rewards for recruiting other members and soon after produced a RSPB shopping catalog from which members could purchase merchandise.

These three cases show that the practices adopted by these groups and widely associated with "protest businesses" are consistent with each group's long-standing group identity. In other words, one lesson here is that a group that innovates by turning to direct-debit and online cold canvassing is not necessarily changing its identity or even adopting a new strategy. Rather, it is adopting a new technique in support of its long-standing strategy of fostering a passive mass supporter base, remote from leaders.

These cases illustrate the following general point: in some cases, a group changes its organizational form without changing its identity. While it is true, for instance, that in the early 1990s both Oxfam and RSPB turned to paid recruiters to increase membership (an example of strategic change) and to direct-debit instruments to maintain membership (an example of technical innovation), these changes were consistent with the long-established identity of both groups as growth-oriented mass membership organizations that used innovative business practices eschewed by many other nonprofits.[48] The changes of the 1990s were important, but they did not change each organization's identity. Instead, the changes were of a lower order and confirmed each group's commitment to its founding identity. Each of these groups was committed to a protest business identity *very early* in its history. Thus, the contemporary changes noted by some scholars[49] and normatively criticized by others[50] reflect strategic and technical variations that did not undercut a long-standing commitment to a particular group identity. Another way to put this is that each group's history suggests that it would surely have used direct debits and advanced database management linked to mail shots in its earliest days if it had the opportunity to do so. Each group has consistently utilized the equivalent member marketing technologies of its day. Thus, survival for these groups has been about low-order change—updating techniques and settings—rather than high-order identity change.

Conclusion

Interest group scholars have given a great deal of attention over the years to questions of organizational formation. This is understandable, in that new groups are the raw material that forge group populations and communities. But not all groups that successfully form are able to survive. This fact has led us to ask, What changes, if any, do groups make in order to survive? We believe that questions like this are important. Answering them will allow us to understand why we have the interest group community we do rather than some other we might imagine. Addressing such questions will also allow us better to understand group behavior.

Our overarching purpose here has been to outline a basic approach to studying interest group maintenance. First, we introduce the concepts of *group career* and *organizational form*. Neither of these concepts is novel, as each has been used previously by scholars (primarily in other fields). We argue that deploying these concepts can help us understand the postformation trajectories of interest groups.

Second, we attempt to show how these concepts can be deployed to understand group adaptive change over time. Specifically, we present several small case studies of organizational change. We believe that the case studies are valuable both substantively and demonstratively. First, they demonstrate that groups do indeed change over time. They also show *how* groups change over time. Second, the case studies are small-scale exemplars of the type of research we believe should be undertaken. Together, our case studies allow us to reach a number of conclusions about group adaptive change. While group formation continues to attract more scholarly attention than group maintenance, we believe it is time to give maintenance its scholarly due.

Notes

1. Mancur Olson, *The Logic of Collective Action: Public Goods and the Theory of Groups* (Cambridge, MA: Harvard University Press, 1965). See also Chapter 4, "Collective Action and the New Literature on Interest Groups," in Frank R. Baumgartner and

Beth L. Leech, *Basic Interests: The Importance of Groups in Politics and in Political Science* (Princeton, NJ: Princeton University Press, 1998): 64–82.

2. See Virginia Gray and David Lowery, *The Population Ecology of Interest Representation: Lobbying Communities in the American States* (Ann Arbor: The University of Michigan Press, 1996).

3. David B. Truman, *The Governmental Process: Political Interests and Public Opinion* (New York: Knopf, 1951).

4. Mancur Olson, *The Logic of Collective Action.*

5. Robert H. Salisbury, "An Exchange Theory of Interest Groups," *Midwest Journal of Political Science* 13 (1969): 1–32.

6. See, for example, Anthony J. Nownes and Grant Neeley, "Public Interest Group Entrepreneurship and Theories of Group Mobilization," *Political Research Quarterly* 49, no. 1 (1996): 119–46; Jack L. Walker, "The Origins and Maintenance of Interest Groups in America," *American Political Science Review* 77, no. 2 (1983): 390–406.

7. See, for example, Terry M. Moe, *The Organization of Interests: Incentives and the Internal Dynamics of Political Interest Groups* (Chicago: The University of Chicago Press, 1980); Walker, "The Origins and Maintenance of Interest Groups in America;" Jack L. Walker Jr., *Mobilizing Interest Groups in America: Patrons, Professions, and Social Movements* (Ann Arbor: University of Michigan Press, 1991); James Q. Wilson, *Political Organizations* (New York: Basic Books, 1995).

8. Terry M. Moe, "Toward a Broader View of Interest Groups," *Journal of Politics* 43, no. 2 (1981): 538.

9. Wilson, *Political Organizations*, 263.

10. William P. Browne, "Organized Interests and Their Issue Niche: A Search for Pluralism in a Policy Domain," *Journal of Politics* 52, no. 2 (1990): 477–509.

11. Browne, "Organized Interests and Their Issue Niche," 502.

12. Anthony J. Nownes and Allan J. Cigler, "Public Interest Groups and the Road to Survival," *Polity* 27, no. 3 (1995): 379–404.

13. See especially Virginia Gray and David Lowery, "The Demography of Interest Organization Communities: Institutions, Associations, and Membership Groups," *American Politics Quarterly* 23, no. 1 (1995): 3–32; Virginia Gray and David Lowery, "A Niche Theory of Interest Representation," *Journal of Politics* 58, no. 1 (1996): 91–111; Virginia Gray and David Lowery, "Life in a Niche: Mortality Anxiety among Organized Interests in the American States," *Political Research Quarterly* 50, no. 1 (1997): 25–47; Virginia Gray and David Lowery, "The Expression of Density Dependence in State Communities of Organized Interests," *American Politics Research* 29, no. 4 (2001): 374–91; David Lowery and Virginia Gray, "The Population Ecology of Gucci Gulch, or the Natural Regulation of Interest Group Numbers in the American States," *American Journal of Political Science* 39, no. 1 (1995): 1–29.

14. Elisabeth S. Clemens and Debra C. Minkoff, "Beyond the Iron Law: Rethinking the Place of Organizations in Social Movement Research," in *The Blackwell Companion to Social Movements*, eds. David A. Snow, Sarah A. Soule, and Hanspeter Kriesi (Malden, MA: Blackwell, 2004): 155–70.

15. Douglas Rawley Imig, "Resource Mobilization and Survival Tactics of Poverty Advocacy Groups," *Western Political Quarterly* 45, no. 2 (1992): 501–20.

16. Imig, "Resource Mobilization and Survival Tactics of Poverty Advocacy Groups," 517.

17. Nownes and Cigler, "Public Interest Groups and the Road to Survival," 397. Italics in original.

18. Richard Rose and Thomas T. Mackie, "Do Parties Persist or Fail? The Big Trade-off Facing Organizations," in *When Parties Fail: Emerging Alternative Organizations*, eds. Kay Lawson and Peter H. Merkl (Princeton, NJ: Princeton University Press, 1988): 533–58.

19. Mark Blyth and Richard S. Katz, "From Catch-All Politics to Cartelisation: The Political Economy of the Cartel Party," *West European Politics* 28, no. 1 (2005): 33–60.

20. Russell L. Curtis and Louis A. Zurcher, "Social Movements: An Analytical Exploration of Organizational Forms," *Social Problems* 21 (1974): 356–70.

21. Glenn Carroll and Michael T. Hannan, *The Demography of Corporations and Industries* (Princeton, NJ: Princeton University Press, 2000).

22. See Michael T. Heaney, "Identity Crisis: How Interest Groups Struggle to Define Themselves in Washington," in *Interest Group Politics*, 7th ed., eds. Allan J. Cigler and Burdett A. Loomis (Washington, DC: CQ Press, 2007): 279–300.

23. Heaney, "Identity Crisis."

24. We choose to examine groups within this population because one of us has studied the population extensively.

25. Gordon Phillips, *The Blind in British Society: Charity, State, and Community, c. 1780–1930* (Burlington, VT: Ashgate, 2004).

26. Benedict Nightingale, *Charities* (London: Allen Lane, 1973): 330.

27. Frank R. Baumgartner and Bryan D. Jones, *Agendas and Instability in American Politics* (Chicago: The University of Chicago Press, 1993): 185.

28. Darren Halpin and Carsten Daugbjerg, "Bringing Historical Institutionalism into Group Studies? The Evolution of the Soil Association" (unpublished manuscript, 2010), available from the authors.

29. John Warhurst, "The Australian Conservation Foundation: The Development of a Modern Environmental Interest Group," *Environmental Politics* 3, no. 1 (1994): 77.

30. Warhurst, "The Australian Conservation Foundation," 82.

31. Debra C. Minkoff, "Bending with the Wind: Strategic Change and Adaptation by Women's and Racial Minority Organizations," *American Journal of Sociology* 104, no. 6 (1999): 1666–703.

32. They are British and Foreign Blind Association (BFBA) ca. 1902, National Institute for the Blind (NIB) 1914, Royal National Institute for the Blind (RNIB) 1949, Royal National Institute of the Blind (RNIB) 2001, and Royal National Institute of Blind People (RNIB) 2007.

33. Royal National Institute of the Blind, *Annual Report 2001* (London: Royal National Institute of the Blind, 2002).

34. See Royal National Institute of Blind People, *Annual Report* [Various years] (London: Royal National Institute of Blind People).

35. Mary G. Thomas, *Royal National Institute for the Blind, 1868–1956* (Brighton, England: Brighton Herald, 1957): 44.

36. Human Rights Campaign. "Who We Are," accessed February 5, 2008, http://www.hrc.org/about_us/who_we_are.asp.

37. Anthony J. Nownes, "Sex Change: Organizational Change: Boundary Change among American Gay and Lesbian Organizations" (unpublished manuscript, November 2009), available from the author.

38. Anthony J. Nownes, "The Population Ecology of Interest Group Formation: Mobilizing for Gay and Lesbian Rights in the United States, 1950–98" *British Journal of Political Science* 34, no. 1 (2004): 49–67.

39. Grant Jordan and Darren Halpin, "Cultivating Small Business Influence in the UK: The Federation of Small Businesses' Journey from Outsider to Insider," *Journal of Public Affairs* 3, no. 4 (2003): 313–25.

40. Jordan and Halpin, "Cultivating Small Business Influence in the UK."

41. See, for example, Robert D. Putnam, *Bowling Alone: The Collapse and Revival of American Community* (New York: Simon & Schuster, 2000); Theda Skocpol, "Advocates Without Members: The Recent Transformation of American Civic Life," in *Civic Engagement in American Democracy*, eds. Theda Skocpol and Morris P. Fiorina (Washington, DC: Brookings Institution Press, 1999): 461–509.

42. John McCarthy, "Persistence and Change Among Nationally Federated Social Movements," in *Social Movements and Organization Theory*, eds. Gerald F. Davis, Doug McAdam, W. Richard Scott, and Mayer N. Zald (New York: Cambridge University Press, 2005): 193–225.

43. Grant Jordan and William A. Maloney, *The Protest Business? Mobilizing Campaign Groups* (New York: Manchester University Press, 1997). See also Christopher Bosso, *Environment, Inc.: From Grassroots to Beltway* (Lawrence: University Press of Kansas, 2005).

44. Jordan and Maloney, *The Protest Business?*

45. Philippa Bassett, *A List of the Historical Records of the Royal Society for the Protection of Birds* (Birmingham, England: The University of Birmingham, 1980).

46. Robin Fedden, *The Continuing Purpose: A History of the National Trust, Its Aims and Work* (London: Longmans, 1968).

47. Maggie Black, *A Cause for Our Times: Oxfam, The First 50 Years* (Oxford, England: Oxford University Press, 1992).

48. Black, *A Cause for Our Times.*

49. Jordan and Maloney, *The Protest Business?*

50. Putnam, *Bowling Alone.*

4

Trade Associations, the Collective Action Dilemma, and the Problem of Cohesion

Lee Drutman

A corporation seeking to influence political outcomes in Washington, D.C., has choices. It can hire its own lobbyists, either on a full-time or a part-time basis. It can join and participate in trade associations. Or, as is often the case, it can do both. Moreover, a corporation's participation in a trade association can range from making a small annual dues contribution to participating very actively in all levels of the association.

Participation in trade associations is virtually universal among companies. In one survey of 250 large companies, 100 percent reported belonging to a relevant trade association.[1] Similarly, my own survey of mixed-sized companies[2] found universal participation in trade associations. But a little less than half of the companies (43 percent) reported either being "very active" or "extremely active" in trade associations. Thus, companies are active to varying degrees.

There are more than 1,000 trade associations in Washington, D.C., a number that has increased somewhat in the last 25 years (see Table 4.1). Though many of these associations do a limited amount of lobbying, roughly 7 percent (77 associations), have lobbying budgets over $1 million (see Figure 4.1).

The most active trade associations are quite active indeed. In 2008, the top 25 most active industry trade associations (see Table 4.2) all spent at least $3.2 million in annual lobbying expenditures; this category is led by the Pharmaceutical Research and Manufacturers of America ($28.3 million), the National Cable and Telecommunications Association ($19.3 million), the National Association of Broadcasters ($13.4 million), the Biotechnology Industry Association ($10.6 million), and the Edison Electric Institute ($10 million). Interestingly, the associations vary in the degree to which they rely on political action committee (PAC) donations. Some of the largest associations, the Pharmaceutical Research and Manufacturers of America and the Biotechnology Industry Association, have relatively small PACs (both donating less than $250,000); others, most notably the Credit Union National Association ($4.3 million), the National Association of

Table 4.1   Trade Associations in the *Washington Representatives Directory*

	1981	1991	2001	2006
Trade Associations	872	937	1,099	1,067

Source: Data from *Washington Representatives Directory*, as compiled by Kay Lehman Schlozman, Sidney Verba, Henry Brady, Philip Edward Jones, and Traci Burch, "Who Sings in the Heavenly Chorus: The Shape of the Organized Interest System," paper presented at the annual meeting of the Midwest Political Science Association, Chicago, April 2008.

Figure 4.1   Industry Trade Associations, by 2001 Lobbying Expenditures

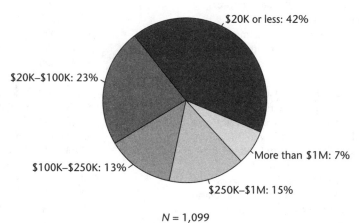

Sources: Valerie Sheridan, ed. *Washington Representatives.* Bethesda, MD: Columbia Books, 2001; Center for Responsive Politics.

Home Builders ($4 million), and the American Bankers Association ($3.9 million), all have very large PACs

Such intense participation in collective political activity poses a puzzle for classic theories of group behavior. In explaining corporate political activity, scholars commonly draw a distinction between public (or collective) and private (or selective) goods. Public goods are policy outcomes that benefit a whole industry; for example, a new federal law that promises Medicare funding for prescription drugs benefits all pharmaceutical drug manufacturers. Private goods are policy outcomes that benefit a specific company; for example, a patent extension for single drug benefits only the company that manufactures that drug.

Table 4.2 Associations by 2008 Lobbying Expenditures

Association	Lobbying expenditures	PAC size
Pharmaceutical Research and Manufacturers of America	$28,310,000	$221,974
National Cable & Telecommunications Association	$19,291,370	$2,002,483
National Association of Broadcasters	$13,402,000	$1,092,447
Biotechnology Industry Organization	$10,577,500	$257,860
Edison Electric Institute	$10,008,371	$630,059
American Bankers Association	$9,670,000	$3,987,824
United States Telecom Association	$9,330,000	$253,467
Cellular Telecommunications and Internet Association	$9,200,000	$259,655
America's Health Insurance Plans	$8,570,000	$550,410
American Council of Life Insurers	$8,127,032	$682,285
Alliance of Automobile Manufacturers	$7,900,000	none
Investment Co Institute	$7,196,817	$1,462,514
Air Transport Association of America	$7,035,000	$68,456
American Petroleum Institute	$6,449,437	none
Securities Industry & Financial Market Association Lobbying	$5,975,000	$1,279,781
National Rural Electric Cooperative Association	$5,775,000	$3,105,082
National Mining Association	$5,536,285	$222,405
Mortgage Insurance Cos. of America	$5,265,000	$77,220
National Association of Home Builders	$5,232,689	$4,003,669
Independent Community Bankers of America	$5,035,000	$1,455,088
American Chemistry Council	$4,981,895	$354,033
Associated Builders and Contractors	$4,080,000	$2,175,014
Advanced Medical Technology Association	$3,930,823	$216,774
American Forest & Paper Association	$3,650,000	$269,539
Credit Union National Association, Inc.	$3,231,734	$4,335,390

Source: Center for Responsive Politics, http://www.opensecrets.org/.

The canonical work on group activity, Mancur Olson's *Logic of Collective Action*, argues that large associations that work toward public goods should have a difficult time both forming and maintaining themselves.[3] This is because for any individual member, it makes more sense to hitch a free ride on the efforts of the association, letting others expend resources. Moreover, any individual member can see that if it expends its own resources, others will hold back and let the active member do all the work. It follows from this logic that rational corporations should underinvest in collective lobbying for public goods.

However, Olson suggests that more concentrated industries should have an advantage in overcoming this obstacle, both because it is easier for a few companies to pressure each other not to shirk and because it is more likely that one or more companies will benefit enough from lobbying on industry concerns to justify its own cost. Accordingly, Jeffrey M. Drope and

Table 4.3   Level of Participation in Trade Associations
(7-point scale)

	Mean	Median
How active are you in trade associations?	4.9	5.5

$N = 32$

Source: Compiled by author.

Wendy L. Hansen have found evidence that the more concentrated the industry, the more likely it is to have a politically active association.[4]

But the research on company-level political participation has had a much more difficult time finding a relationship between company political activity and industry concentration. Many scholars have been puzzled to find that companies in industries that are more concentrated are no more likely to be politically active than companies in less concentrated industries, a seeming repudiation of Olson's theory of collective action.[5] This has led some to speculate that individual companies must therefore lobby mostly for selective (company-level) goods.[6] Yet, in my interviews, more than half (58 percent) of the issues that company lobbyists reported working on impacted the entire industry. Further, when lobbyists were asked to rate how active they were in associations, on a scale of 1 (not active at all) to 7 (extremely active), the mean response was 4.9 (see Table 4.3).

This chapter argues that participation in trade associations is not a collective action problem because the voice that comes with participation in the trade association turns out to be its own benefit, and a valuable one at that. Companies in any given industry, after all, are competitors. And no two companies have exactly the same product lines, distribution and supply channels, or geographical footprint (among many potential differences). As a result, no two companies have exactly the same political interests, either.

Under this paradigm, the supposed puzzle of why associations thrive and prosper disappears. Companies are participating in collective lobbying efforts not because they have somehow managed to put their own self-interest aside and participate for the good of the industry. Companies are participating because they want to have a say in the industry's lobbying positions and strategies.

Are There Pure Public Goods in Corporate Lobbying?

One of the reasons that scholars of corporate political activity have had a difficult time understanding this is that they have tended, either implicitly or explicitly, to assume that the goods for which companies lobby are either purely private or purely public goods. They also assume that if companies are lobbying together, they must all share the same goal. In fact, upon showing definitively that industry concentration is not a significant predictor of corporate political activity (as Olson's theory of collective action would have predicted), Hansen and colleagues are forced to conclude that the most likely explanation is that "much business participation is aimed not only at public goods but also at private goods."[7]

But is it also possible that what Hansen and colleagues, as well as dozens of other scholars, call "the motivating assumption of the field"[8]—the claim that the collective action problem is a central obstacle to corporate political participation—is based on a faulty premise that there are such things as purely public goods? This is important, because if there are no purely public goods, there is no free rider problem, and thus there is no collective action dilemma to overcome. Hence, one finds no puzzle in why companies are so active in trade associations.

Olson's theory assumes that group members have no difficulty divining the common objective that they all seek. Olson is explicit about this: "the assumption made in this work is that there is perfect consensus."[9] Given perfect consensus, it makes sense that group members would prefer a free ride, since the group's objective is already perfectly divined and therefore cannot be affected by the participation of any member.

But Olson candidly recognizes that perfect consensus is "an unrealistic assumption" and "at best very rare."[10] He justifies building a theory based on this assumption by arguing that if even groups whose members agree completely have a hard time forming, then those groups where consensus is more elusive will have an even more difficult time forming. He spends some time discussing how painful and time-consuming it can be for large groups to reach consensus, and he suggests that if it's too hard to reach a consensus, group members will not even bother. "The contribution that each participant will make toward achieving or improving these public goods [i.e., group consensus] will become smaller as the meeting becomes larger."[11] Thus, the larger the group, the greater the likelihood the group will reach in impasse, be incapable of action, and render participation pointless.

But there is another way to think about this purported problem of agreement. Assuming that a group already exists, and is going to continue to exist, a member who doesn't participate is giving up the ability to participate in the group's internal debate. The group may be at an impasse under current conditions, but if enough members abdicate, the group may be able to come to a consensus after all. This consensus, however, will be one to which those members who left would have never agreed. Logically, then, they will continue to participate in the event they can influence an eventual decision.

A second factor to consider in thinking about groups is that neither society nor the business world is broken neatly into distinct and exclusive segments, with each individual or company having one and only one membership. Rather, as David Truman has written, "no individual is wholly absorbed in any group to which he belongs. Only a fraction of his attitudes is expressed through any one such affiliation."[12] Truman instead described a situation of "overlapping membership" and argued that "it is important never to lose sight of the group as a set of interactions."[13] Groups, after all, are made up of individuals, and both groups and their members are "constantly in the process of readjustment."[14] Truman's world of groups is a dynamic world. Group members are constantly engaged in a multidirectional game of tug-of-war, and any consensus is at best temporary. For Truman, the problem of groups is not a problem of collective action. It is a *"problem of cohesion* [emphasis added]."

Bauer, Pool, and Dexter apply this thinking more precisely to trade associations in their classic study of business lobbying, *American Business & Public Policy.* They note, "An industry is apt to have many associations covering the variety of interests represented within it."[15] Rather than consensus, they find a "pattern of multiplication and division" that "permits each association to follow the *rule of quasiunanimity* [emphasis added] within its range of issues and to permit those of its own members who have a different viewpoint to express it through another and more appropriate association."[16]

Consider Proctor and Gamble. The company reported in 2008 that it spent $9,170,408 on membership dues to 41 different trade associations, of which it estimated $1,777,609 went for lobbying. Trade associations range from the American Chemistry Council to the Food Marking Institute to the National Electrical Manufacturers' Association to the Soap and Detergent Association.[17] Most large companies belong to at least a few trade associations, each of which partially represents the interests of the company.

Associations do not fit into neat, mutually exclusive boxes. Just as companies often belong to many associations, entire industries often have many associations representing overlapping niche issues and positions. Factions arise. Members dissent. There is no clear, Platonic industry position and, hence, no clear public goods emerge. The reality is messier than Olson's elegant theorizing would suggest.

In order to understand better how this messiness impacts both companies and trade associations, let us turn to the basic mechanisms of trade association operations. Then we will explore some of the implications.

The Nuts and Bolts of the Trade Association

As we saw earlier (Figure 4.1), the lobbying activity of trade associations varies. Some have very small Washington offices, with only one person.

Others have dozens upon dozens of staff, big offices, and substantial lobbying presences. But it is important to understand that even as an association has its own logo and can appear to have an autonomous presence, it only exists and thrives to the extent that it can solicit dues from member companies. For larger companies, annual dues are typically in the range of six figures since dues are pegged to size (smaller companies pay less). Membership gives companies access to a range of benefits such as newsletters, conferences, and proprietary research. But most importantly, membership gives companies the right to participate in the governance of trade associations.

As a general rule, trade associations are structured as follows (summarized in Figure 4.2). At the top of the trade association hierarchy is a board of directors or executive committee comprised of representatives from member companies, often those companies' chief executives. This board typically meets once or at most few times a year to set and/or reaffirm the overarching priorities and positions of the association. Trade association lobbyists all describe a similar process:

> The board of directors or the executive committee within the board of directors sets the initial huge goals and major year priorities, and we work on those issues.
>
> Every year we have a CEO summit. All of our CEOs come out for a meeting and talk about the issues that are pending, what we need to focus on, what are the key issues—it's all pretty much decided there.
>
> Twice a year, we get together with all our companies and open it up to everyone and let them know our priorities for the next year. We see what we went through, what we didn't get through, and what we think we can get accomplished, and then we have a three-hour planning session.

Some associations adhere closely to the program set by the board of directors, while others tackle issues in a more ad hoc manner. Some associations are more driven by their member companies, while others, generally those in which member companies are not very politically active, are more driven by the association's staff. But all associations have a basic framework that allows representatives from member companies to decide and agree on what the baseline priorities and positions should be.

Details are hashed out at the level of specialized policy committees within the association. These committees refine policy positions on chosen association priorities. They generally comprise lobbyists, lawyers, and policy experts from individual member companies, though sometimes association employees and lobbyists participate as well, depending on how politically active the member companies are.

For example, the Information Technology Industry Council has fifteen committees, ranging from Tax to Trade to Energy and Environment. The

Figure 4.2   How Trade Associations Operate

Tax Committee "develops and recommends ITI's positions on domestic and international tax policies and regulations, including those that may affect electronic commerce." The Electronic Commerce Committee "develops and implements policy positions that promote increased access to IT products and services in domestic and global markets."[18]

In some associations, committees meet less frequently; they provide only a general framework for action and offer technical expertise and advice as needed. In these associations, staff and lobbyists do most of the work. "Committees set priorities," said one trade association lobbyist. "Our committees meet two or three times a year, augmented by conference calls. We're getting ready for the tax committee now, because there is tax legislation pending. The committee will provide us technical input and then we'll respond accordingly. But it's not cookie-cutter."

As we've already mentioned, associations have their own staff lobbyists, technical experts, researchers, and other support personnel. Many association heads are very well compensated. For example, PhRMA president and CEO Billy Tauzin earned a reported $4.5 million in 2009; American Council of Life Insurers president and CEO Frank Keating earned $2.9 million; Edison Electric Institute president Thomas R. Kuhn earned $2.5 million.[19] Association lobbyists and their support staff do a substantial amount of information gathering and monitoring and send frequent updates to member companies. Technical experts and researchers help the association to develop policy papers and supporting materials, and they try to be a resource for lawmakers and their staffs. The Investment Company Institute, for example, has a team of seventy economists with PhDs and has fashioned itself as the place to go for anybody who needs any data whatsoever about the mutual fund industry. Associations also hire Washington, D.C., lobbying firms to carry out lobbying responsibilities beyond the scope of staff time or expertise and to provide additional access.

Finally, it is important to acknowledge that despite careful planning, events have a way of developing unpredictably. Issues emerge, and associations have to respond. In such cases, association lobbyists are more likely to lead the way, and the member companies who are most actively engaged are the ones who are most likely shape positions as they emerge.

The Association's Perspective: Staying Alive

All associations only exist and thrive to the extent that they can continue to attract sizeable membership dues, and the impetus toward organizational survival plays a key role in explaining the operations of trade associations.[20] Billy Tauzin does not get to make $4.5 million in salary if PhRMA members refuse to pay their dues.

Associations first establish a presence in Washington, D.C., for many reasons. Most commonly, a group of companies realizes that it has enough shared interests in a particular set of policies that it would be cost-effective to band together and share lobbying resources. Often this understanding comes out of a new political threat to those companies.[21] For example, the Managed Fund Association, the trade association of the hedge fund industry, maintained a very small Washington presence from its founding in the early 1990s until 2005, never allocating more than $100,000 to lobbying in a year. But in 2007, with the financial sector beginning to come under political attack, the association upped its lobbying spending to $3.3 million, and in 2009, with financial reform a top priority of Congress, it spent $4.7 million.

As it turns out, trade associations have a remarkable persistence. Even as late as 2006, more than 300 associations (roughly a third of all existing organizations) had been around since before the 1950s, and roughly half of all trade associations had been in existence since the 1960s (see Figure 4.3). As one company lobbyist put it, "Trade associations are going to exist no matter what."

For trade associations, survival means keeping member companies engaged. This is done in part by providing measurable benefits; that is, showing progress and even occasional success on lobbying campaigns, keeping member companies well informed of the latest developments, and, at the very least, creating the appearance that the trade associations' representatives are key power brokers in the halls of Congress.

But keeping member companies engaged also means reminding them that membership confers the right to be part of the association's deliberations. Given that the trade association already exists and will be advocating

Figure 4.3   The Persistence of Trade Associations

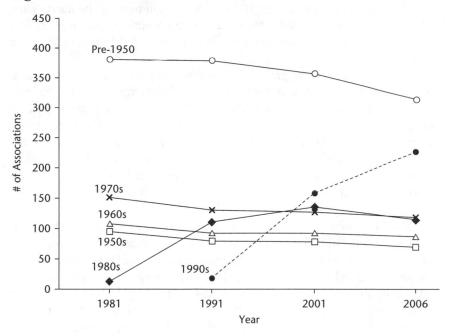

Source: National Trade And Professional Associations in the United States, ed. Valerie Sheridan (Bethesda, MD: Columbia Books, 1981, 1991, 2001, 2006).

a host of positions, companies can choose either to be inactive or to be active. As one trade association lobbyist noted, part of the sales pitch to prospective members is a reminder that "you can help drive our positions; you can help frame our materials."

Associations can also survive and thrive by dominating specific subindustry niches.[22] For example, in the wood and paper goods industry, the American Forest & Paper Association is a major trade association. With an annual budget of $38 million, it "is the national trade association of the forest, paper, and wood products industry, representing 120 companies and related associations focused on producing essential products for people from renewable and recyclable resources that sustain the environment."[23] It spends $4 million on lobbying, making it the most active association in the industry. But a brief perusal of associations in the industry finds many other lesser-known groups representing smaller industry groupings: the Alaska Forest Association, the American Paperboard Packaging Environment Council, the American Plywood Association, the Black Hills Forest Resource Association, the Association of Independent Corrugated Converters, the Envelope Manufacturers Association of America, and several others. The number of niche associations varies from industry to industry. In food and agriculture, there are more than 100 representation niches, the most of any industry. Associations include, for example, the American Butter Institute, the National Yogurt Association, and the International Jelly and Preserve Association.

Niches do not just target members based on their line of business but also based on their particular policy interests. For example, in the high-tech industry, the Business Software Alliance (BSA) has staked out a claim as being the premier association for intellectual property issues. Sometimes, associations form out of long-standing within-industry battles. For example, the Computer and Communications Industry Association (CCIA) began as the anti-IBM association back in the 1970s and (backed by "I.B.M. competitors like Microsoft and Oracle") was still pushing for antitrust actions against IBM thirty years later.[24]

Finally, associations also specialize in tactics. For example, one high-tech industry lobbyist described how a particular competitor association was known for its lobbying prowess and connections on the Hill, while his association had earned its reputation as the place to go for policy development and research firepower: "The Information Technology Industry Council is a door-opening organization, and they're very effective at that. We tend to be more of a roll-up-your sleeves, work on the details organization."

The important point is that successful associations tend to be very good at making themselves indispensable in their particular representation and issue space, which allows them to survive. "You kind of have to find your own niche and differentiate yourself," said one association lobbyist. "I think different trade associations do have different kinds of characteristics, and I think different companies see different values." Or as David Hart has noted, "Once created, high-tech associations rarely disappear, but they do adapt frequently and significantly as the environment changes and new competitors appear."[25]

In representing niches, associations do their best to make themselves seem indispensable to member companies. As with any association, this involves providing valuable intelligence, access, and support on issues that companies care about. But being indispensable also means being inevitable. To the extent that associations can show that they have a seat at the table and are a power player in key discussions, a status that usually follows from successfully carving out an exclusive niche, the fear among companies is not so much that the association will no longer have resources to play this role (the classic problem of collective action) but that the association will wield its power without adequately consulting member companies (the problem of cohesion). As one company lobbyist put it simply: "There is a lot of lobbying within the trade association to promote your point of view versus another." Let us now investigate this in more detail.

Why Do Companies Devote Resources to Trade Associations?

Companies devote significant resources to trade associations, both by paying six-figure dues and by contributing the time of company lobbyists, lawyers, and sometimes executives. As one lobbyist put it: "We really strive to have our executives beyond the Washington offices playing leadership roles in these associations, so we have senior business leaders in board-level positions in all of these trade associations and the Washington office in effect staff them."

There are two primary reasons why company lobbyists report they want to be active in associations: (1) to encourage associations to push certain issues and perspectives favored by the company and (2) to make sure associations don't push certain other issues or perspectives that run contrary to a company's preferences. The assumption that "trade associations are going to exist no matter what" is widespread among company lobbyists, so they feel they should take advantage of any opportunities that present themselves lest an industry competitor do so first.

Though on certain targeted issues, companies may find it is more effective to fly below the radar and work directly with just one or two members of Congress, on many issues, if anything is going to happen, it will require the heft of an association to break through the din of constant lobbying and to reach more decision makers.[26] "Trade associations are an important tool to amplify and leverage our voice," said a company lobbyist. "It's not as effective if we have to do it on our own."

Perhaps more significantly, associations also lend more legitimacy to a position. As a lobbyist company put it, "There is value when we say something is important, but when the whole IT industry says it, well, it's just more important to go in as the industry as a whole." Marie Hojnacki notes that this might be particularly important for corporate representatives, who especially need to "broaden the scope of support for their policy objectives, and to provide a more positive image for their policy interests."[27]

Company lobbyists (particularly for larger companies) frequently spoke of trade associations as vehicles for advancing particular issues, especially sensitive ones where going it alone might make companies look greedy and narrow. The following statements from lobbyist interviews give a flavor of this perspective:

> On difficult issues, where [our company] doesn't want to be up front, it's important to have a strong association.

> We can use them [associations] to champion issues we might not feel comfortable doing ourselves. . . . We may recommend something, or send a note to a group of people on an issue we should be involved in and say we should get this trade association to advocate more forcefully.

It's good to have trade associations to represent the industry, so if there are sensitive issues or members being problematic, it's better to go up and be the face of the industry.

If certain companies are pressing the association in one direction, other companies often find that they need to push back, lest the association advance an unwelcome position. In interviews, company lobbyists repeatedly spoke of the need to stay vigilant in trade associations in order to prevent other companies from pushing for their own narrow interests:

Some companies aren't shy about using the process to advantage something they're trying to do that would disadvantage you, so you have to be at the table. And you have to be at the table to drive things that are important to your business that other people might not think are important. You need to convince them.

[Associations] can be time-consuming, and frustrating because you're dealing with people who would otherwise be your competitors and sometimes people will utilize public policy in an anti-competitive way and you need to look to the trade association almost as a broker in that context.

We go through the issues and what they're doing, and occasionally engage more heavily if it is particularly important to our business or if there are different perspectives to different firms and I'm concerned that the way legislation is drafted it would advantage one firm and not us, or advantage everyone else. I try to keep a close check on that.

There is a lot of value in just showing up. You need to participate because others push a narrow agenda.

Some company lobbyists were quite candid about using trade associations to advance particular issues, while others claimed merely to participate defensively, trying to keep watch against *other* companies who would try to push a narrow interest. Both contribute to an arms-race dynamic. Knowing that your competitors will not disarm, it would be irrational for you to disarm. But also, once you've invested in weapons, you are more likely to want to use them.

If the above is accurate, we would expect to see some predictable differences in the ways in which different companies view associations. Specifically, we would expect that large companies, who have the resources to get the most out of association membership, would view associations more favorably than smaller companies, who generally do not have the resources to be aggressive participants in associations. Let us now turn to this distinction.

The Small versus the Large

In laying out his theory of collective action, Olson deduces that "there is a systematic tendency for 'exploitation' of the great by the small."[28] Olson asserts that in an association, small companies will free ride on the backs of large companies, taking advantage of the fact that large companies have enough incentive to engage in political activity regardless of whether the smaller companies participate. The participation of large companies thus allows smaller companies to gain the collective benefits without contributing their own resources.

Empirical evidence confirms that the larger the company, the more active it reports being within an association. Figure 4.4 plots the company lobbyists' self-reported association activity on the y-axis and the size of the company (measured as the natural log of sales) along the x-axis. A fitted linear regression line shows that a systematic relationship exists between the size of the company and how active it is in trade associations.

But while Olson's theory suggests that the main reason companies don't participate actively in associations is that it is rational for them to free ride, interviews suggest that smaller companies generally do pay their dues (usually assessed on a sliding scale, with smaller companies paying less), but

Figure 4.4   Relationship of Size and Trade Association Activity

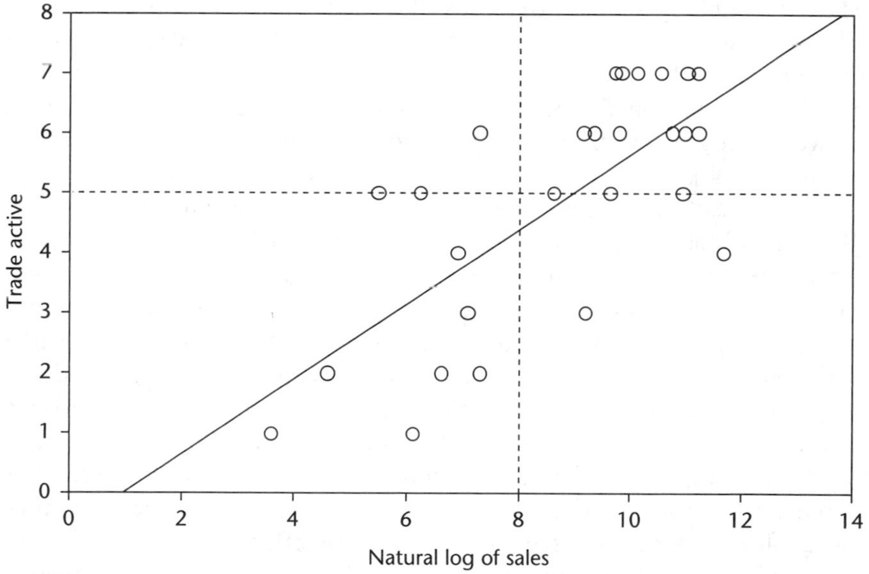

Source: Compiled by author.

they don't participate actively because they simply don't have the resources to make themselves heard. As one small retail company lobbyist put it: "The really huge large retailers who maintain a presence have a really larger share of the market, and their voices get heard a lot more. We are a very, very specific company." But this same lobbyist went on to note that the company still belongs to the association: "We can't complain if we aren't there, so at least we get to complain. We pay to complain. But our membership dues aren't that much in comparison to what we spend on other things in the business, so it's not that much to spend for us."

Another small company lobbyist put it this way: "Trade associations want membership dues, so they'll put pressure on me and encourage people to have somebody go to meetings on the Hill, but it's illogical for me to do it."

Large companies, on the other hand, see themselves as the natural leaders and want to participate. "As industry leader, our CEO would say and has said and has tried to look at his role beyond just heading [our company], really as a leadership role within the industry, to try to take a positive road on issues," said one lobbyist. "He does take seriously representation within the industry."

Some of this may simply have to do with the fact that for a lot of large companies, what is at stake is so great that the payoff is likely to be worth the investment, especially if the company already has a Washington, D.C., office and adding extra lobbying issues incurs decreasing marginal cost (since the lobbying infrastructure is already in place). Consider the case of a large technology company that took a leadership role on the patent reform lobbying issue: "We are traditionally in the top 3–4–5–6 patent recipients each year. Our R&D budget is 3.5 billion dollars. This is a top priority for our senior management," said the lobbyist. "We were told to get it done. So we're not going to free ride on the coalition; we're looking to lead the coalition."

Empirical evidence also shows that the larger the company, the more likely it will lobby for an industry good as opposed to a selective good. In interviews, I asked company lobbyists to list the top issues on which they were currently working. I then coded those issues as either being specific to the company or of general interest to the industry. Collectively, companies in the bottom third of size among the companies I interviewed devoted only 38 percent of their lobbying efforts to industry goods; the medium-sized companies (middle third) devoted 58 percent of their lobbying efforts; and the largest (top third) devoted 68 percent of their lobbying efforts (see Table 4.4). These data reinforce the claim that large companies see much more value in participating in industry lobbying efforts.

Empirical evidence suggests that issue leadership does have its privileges. A systematic relationship exists between the size of a company and how well its lobbyists think the trade associations represent the company's

Table 4.4   Company Size and Share of Lobbying Activity Devoted to Industry Issues

	Smallest Companies	Medium Companies	Largest Companies
Share of lobbying activity devoted to industry issues	38%	58%	68%

Source: Compiled by author.

Figure 4.5   Relationship of Company Size and the Value Lobbyists Place on the Trade Association

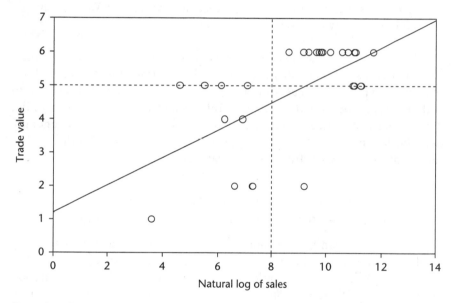

Source: Compiled by author.

interest. With only one exception, all large companies thought that trade associations represented their interests very well. Associations are most likely to work well for the companies who can devote the most resources to them. Interestingly, on a 7-point scale, not a single company lobbyist ranked association representation a perfect 7. But company lobbyists did ascribe a fair number of 6s to association representation (see Figure 4.5).

Taken together, these data suggest that associations are centers of activity primarily for those companies who have the resources to be active in them. Thus, it is not surprising that the largest and most active companies find associations to be the most valuable. As a lobbyist for a large company put it, "You get out of an association what you put into it. It's as simple as that." This lobbyist went on to elaborate on how associations are most responsive to the members who pay the most dues and devote the most activity to associations:

> If you're a small entity paying a small amount of dues, if senior executives are not on committees of real importance and don't come and participate, you're probably going to get poor to negligible service on your own unique issues. If you're a large dues-paying member but not involved, even though you might pay a large amount in dues, if you don't know the people from the head down to the bottom, your ability to influence will be minimal, so the optimal position to be in is you pay a lot of dues and you actually have executives who are very engaged and the trade association knows that you are engaged, and that empowers a good Washington office to maximize the value.

What trade associations do depends in good part on what the member companies press them to do. Large companies see trade associations as both tools in their arsenal and as something in which they need to stay active to gather intelligence on their competitors. Small companies, meanwhile, don't have the resources to participate in an effective way, so they generally don't bother. But as a result, they report being less happy with the kind of representation they get from the associations.

Limits of Associations: The Least Common Denominator and the Go-It-Alone Phenomenon

Since consensus can be a challenge, in many cases associations will only be able to take on very limited advocacy in a particular area. As one lobbyist put it: "The trade association takes everything to the least common denominator." What this means practically is that if companies in an industry can't agree on much, these companies are going to do more lobbying on their own, outside of association coalitions. While associations may be able to put issues on the table and provide general monitoring and research capability, companies will have to do additional lobbying if they want Congress to address their specific concerns. This conclusion is line with Erik Godwin, R. Kenneth Godwin, and Scott Ainsworth's conception of lobbying as a two-stage process: In the "agenda-setting" stage, companies join together in order to get an issue onto the agenda, aware that breaking the threshold of attention often takes a large coalition. But once the issue gets serious consideration by Congress, companies break off and lobby independently.[29]

Other times, the vast majority of companies in an association will agree on a position, but a few companies will dissent. "You can have an issue where nine-tenths of the companies want to do something, and then the other one can just go it alone," said one lobbyist. "Nothing stops them from going up there . . . and saying you ought to do this, too."

Consider the case of the research and development (R&D) tax credit, whose annual extension marks a perennial coalition lobbying ritual involving many associations. One lobbyist represents a company that benefited from an older version of the tax credit, no longer favored by the vast majority of the coalition: "We worked to preserve that credit for as long as possible, even though, quite honestly, as a matter of tax policy it was harder to defend. We work with a big coalition, and our voice would be the one at the table urging them, even though they came up with a new alternative credit, to allow the old one to remain in the law and have the option to stay on the old credit if you want to." That is, the company worked as part of the coalition to extend the credit generally, and then lobbied additionally in order to make sure its unique position received attention.

Associations do not want to alienate members, so they will not lobby when issues strongly divide member companies. Consensus can be elusive, and the result is often a splintering of lobbying efforts. This finding should once again reaffirm the claim that defining the industry position is never easy. In many cases, companies prefer to agree to disagree.

Real-World Challenges in Maintaining Unity

Two issues can serve as good examples of conflicts in which trade associations had difficulty maintaining unity.

Energy

One of the most controversial issues over the last few years has been energy policy. In light of increasing evidence that carbon emissions are responsible for increasing the temperature of the planet and changing the global climate, the U.S. Congress has debated ways to reduce the carbon that energy companies emit. The most prominent proposal, a cap-and-trade system, would allow companies to buy and sell permits to emit carbon over a certain amount.

Though energy producers had once presented a unified front on a number of issues, a new issue brought out many divisions within trade associations. Some companies, realizing that their mix of energy production meant that they would do relatively well under a cap-and-trade system, advocated for reform, while others, whose energy production relied more on coal and oil, either opposed reform or sought a version of reform that would heavily compensate them. Additionally, some gas producers formed the Natural Gas Alliance, because gas emits much less carbon dioxide than coal. And several large companies, most prominently the energy producer Exelon, left the U.S. Chamber of Commerce because the Chamber was opposed to climate change legislation. As a *New York Times* article noted:

> As the Senate prepares to tackle global warming, the nation's energy producers, once united, are battling one another over policy decisions worth hundreds of billions of dollars in coming decades. Producers of natural gas are battling their erstwhile allies, the oil companies. Electrical utilities are fighting among themselves over the use of coal versus wind power or other renewable energy. Coal companies are battling natural gas firms over which should be used to produce electricity. And the renewable power industry is elbowing for advantage against all of them.[30]

Many large companies who favored some regulation of carbon emissions joined the U.S. Climate Action Partnership (USCAP), a coalition of industry and environmental groups, and played a key role in helping to bring legislation to the House floor in July 2009. Yet even among the companies who had joined USCAP, some dissented with the actual details. Members Conoco Philips and BP opposed the climate change legislation, claiming it discriminates among energy producers, while Duke and Dupont registered support. USCAP member Caterpillar didn't like the provisions regarding emission standards for off-road vehicles like bulldozers, while General Motors didn't like a provision requiring automakers to produce vehicles to run on methanol.[31]

In other words, when it comes to the issue of climate policy, nothing at all like an industry position has emerged among energy companies. Individual companies, based on their energy portfolios, have fought among themselves, both within industry trade associations and by breaking off and forming their own coalitions.

Patent Reform

Starting in the 109th Congress, 2005–2007, and again in the 110th and 111th Congresses, both the Senate and the House introduced something called the "Patent Reform Act." The proposal was an attempt to raise the threshold and lower the damages for patent infringement lawsuits. Many high-tech companies argued that current US patent law made it very difficult for companies to innovate because it was too easy for patent holders to sue for patent infringement and because the damages were too high. Therefore, new companies had to be very careful that their new products did not infringe on any existing patents. However, more established companies, particularly pharmaceutical companies, argued that the current system with its strong protection for patents worked just fine, protecting their hard-earned intellectual property.

While the fight was often billed as a technology versus pharmaceutical fight (with technology companies pushing for reform and pharmaceutical companies opposing it), complicated splits appeared within both industries, depending on the individual patents that companies held and their reliance on patent licensing. As a result, industry trade associations played a less prominent role in the battles. Instead, ad hoc coalitions provided a forum for technology companies to fight other technology companies and for pharmaceutical companies to fight other pharmaceutical companies.

So, for example, when Senator Patrick Leahy (D-VT), chair of the Senate Judiciary Committee and author of the "Patent Reform Act of 2009," offered a compromise in March 2010, three coalitions took three different sides. The Coalition for Patent Fairness, which represented large technology companies like Intel, Google, Apple, Symantec, and Oracle, was disappointed that the proposal didn't go far enough and so opposed it. The Innovation Alliance, which represented many smaller technology companies, like Qualcomm and Dolby Laboratories, offered qualified support. And The Coalition for 21st Century Patent Reform, which includes technology firms such as SanDisk and Texas Instruments that hold important patents, came out in favor of the proposals. Meanwhile, IBM, a large patent holder, did not join any of the coalitions but also supported the legislation. Finally, Microsoft, Intel, and Dell, all of which were part of the Coalition for Patent Fairness, took more nuanced stances individually.[32]

In short, this was an issue that did not play out clearly along industry lines. Instead, individual companies struggled to hash out their positions, each participating to make sure that its unique voice got heard.

Conclusion

Trade associations play an important role in corporate lobbying. Associations are often conveners of industry issue campaigns. But the challenge of associations is not necessarily the Olsonian collective action problem of trying to corral companies into contributing to lobbying for goods that benefit the whole industry. The reason is simple: companies in an industry may have some common interests, but they also have many competitive interests. Thus, a particular company sees intrinsic value in participating in an association because participation means the ability to shape the association's lobbying efforts and make the association work to the company's advantage as much as possible. Participation also means making sure that competitors do not use associations to their advantage.

The reality is a messy, overlapping system of associations, far closer to the multidimensional "quasiunanimity" described by Bauer, Pool, and Dexter than the crisp pure collective goods world envisioned by Olson.

Industry associations come in many shapes and sizes. Each has its own incentive to continue to exist, and its principals are always striving to keep member companies satisfied and provide something special of value. Meanwhile, member companies seek to use associations to advance certain issues and positions, while preventing them from advancing others.

Large companies tend to dominate associations. Small companies lack the resources to shape an association's position, and as a result, they report feeling much less satisfied with the representation they are getting from associations. They do, however, pay less in dues. Rather than the small taking advantage of the large, as Olson predicted, large companies seem to do quite well.

Associations are likely to continue to thrive for the foreseeable future. Companies, particularly large ones, realize that lobbying together as an industry is usually more effective than lobbying solo, since it not only means more resources and more contacts but also a more legitimate face. When a single company lobbies for an issue, it can be seen as greedy. Companies also realize that since associations already exist, it is often better to participate in them than to ignore them.

Understanding how associations work helps to solve a puzzle that has often perplexed political scientists studying corporate political activity—that companies appear to have few problems overcoming the collective action problem when it comes to engaging in political activity and participating in associations. The puzzle dissolves when it becomes clear that there are few pure collective goods in industry lobbying. Moreover, participation in an association itself is a benefit to companies. It gives companies the ability to shape the priorities, positions, and tactics of an association.

This also means that when an association takes a position on an issue, one should not assume that the entire industry agrees on this position. The association may represent the position of large companies in an industry but not necessarily that of small companies. Or it may represent a certain faction of companies who are particularly active in the association. The world of associations is complex and dynamic, as one might expect from a forum in which competitors try to coordinate.

Notes

1. Graham K. Wilson, "Corporate Political Strategies," *British Journal of Political Science* 20, no. 2 (1990): 281–88.
2. In Fall 2007/Spring 2008, I conducted sixty hour-long interviews with company and trade association lobbyists in four industries: retail, pharmaceuticals, high-tech, and financial services. Of these, thirty were company lobbyists, fifteen were trade association lobbyists, and fifteen were for-hire lobbyists. Quoted statements from lobbyists throughout this chapter are from this research.

3. Mancur Olson, *The Logic of Collective Action: Public Goods and the Theory of Groups* (Cambridge, MA: Harvard University Press, 1965).

4. Jeffrey M. Drope and Wendy L. Hansen, "New Evidence for the Theory of Groups: Trade Association Lobbying in Washington, D.C," *Political Research Quarterly* 62, no. 2 (2009): 303–16.

5. Wendy L. Hansen, Neil J. Mitchell, and Jeffrey M. Drope, "The Logic of Private and Collective Action," *American Journal of Political Science* 49, no. 1 (2005): 150–67.

6. R. Kenneth Godwin and Barry J. Seldon, "What Corporations Really Want from Government: The Public Provision of Private Goods," in *Interest Group Politics*, eds. Allen Cigler and Burdett Loomis, 6th ed. (Washington, DC: CQ Press, 2002): 205–24.

7. Hansen, Mitchell, and Drope, "The Logic of Private and Collective Action," 163.

8. Hansen, Mitchell, and Drope, "The Logic of Private and Collective Action," 163.

9. Olson, *The Logic of Collective Action*, 60.

10. Olson, *The Logic of Collective Action*, 60.

11. Olson, *The Logic of Collective Action*, 53.

12. David Bicknell Truman, *The Governmental Process: Political Interests and Public Opinion*, (New York: Knopf, 1951): 157.

13. Truman, *The Governmental Process*, 160.

14. Truman, *The Governmental Process*, 162.

15. Raymond Augustine Bauer, Ithiel de Sola Pool, and Lewis Anthony Dexter, *American Business & Public Policy: The Politics of Foreign Trade*, 2nd ed. (Chicago: Aldine, 1972): 338.

16. Bauer, Pool, and Dexter, *American Business & Public Policy*, 339.

17. Proctor and Gamble is among a limited number of companies that voluntarily disclose their trade association contributions: http://www.pg.com/en_US/downloads/company/political_involvement/2008_NATradeAssn_matrix.pdf.

18. See http://www.itic.org/who/committees/.

19. "The Top 25 Current and Former Executives," *National Journal*, April 3, 2010.

20. As Starbuck (1965) once wrote, "The importance of survival to an organization cannot be overstated" (165). W. H. Starbuck, "Organizational Growth and Development," in *Handbook of Organizations*, ed. James G. March (Chicago: Rand McNally, 1965): 463.

21. Truman, *The Governmental Process*.

22. William P. Browne, "Organized Interests and their Issue Niches: A Search for Pluralism in a Policy Domain," *The Journal of Politics* 52, no. 2 (1990): 477–509.

23. American Forest and Paper Association. "Membership." http://www.afandpa.org/history.aspx.

24. Ashlee Vance and Steve Lohr, "U.S. Begins Antitrust Inquiry of I.B.M.," *New York Times*, October 7, 2009.

25. David M. Hart, "The Population Ecology of High-Technology Industry Associations: Assembly Rules and Resource Partitioning" (unpublished manuscript July 3, 2003).

26. Robert H. Salisbury, "The Paradox of Interest Groups in Washington D.C.: More Groups and Less Clout," in *The New American Political System*, ed. Anthony King (Washington, DC: American Enterprise Institute, 1990): 203–229.

27. Marie Hojnacki, "Interest Groups' Decisions to Join Alliances or Work Alone," *American Journal of Political Science* 41, no. 1 (1997): 61–87.

28. Olson, *The Logic of Collective Action,* 29.
29. Erik K. Godwin, R. Kenneth Godwin, and Scott Ainsworth, "Is Corporate Lobbying Rational or Just a Waste of Money?" in *Interest Group Politics,* 7th ed., eds. Allan Cigler and Burdett Loomis, (Washington, DC: CQ Press, 2007): 256–78.
30. John Broder and Jad Mouawad, "Energy Firms Find No Unity on Climate Bill," *New York Times,* October 19, 2009.
31. Stephen Power, "Climate Bill Splits Industry Coalition," *Wall Street Journal,* July 13, 2009.
32. Kim Hart, "Tech Industry Splinters over Patent Reform Proposal," *The Hill,* March 9, 2010.

5

Dissenting Doctors

The Internal Politics of the AMA during the Health Care Reform Debate

Maryann Barakso

The positions that advocacy organizations take on public policy issues often make headlines, but we rarely hear anything about the process by which groups decide what their policy standpoints should be. This is surprising because many advocacy groups are comprised of individual members and donors and have organizational structures designed to provide members with a voice in group decision making.

In this chapter I discuss the internal politics of one of the most important advocacy organizations in the recent health care reform debate, the American Medical Association (AMA). The endorsement of the AMA, whose members include about 30 percent of physicians in the United States and represent over 100 medical specialties and affiliate societies in every state, was considered critical to the success of health care reform. Although the AMA staked out a relatively moderate position on the legislation, eventually 20 percent of the AMA-affiliated medical societies (and at least one former AMA president) openly opposed the national group's stance.

Why did some state medical societies agree with the AMA's stance, while others repudiated it? One factor that might reasonably separate the fifteen state medical societies that "defected" from the AMA's position from those that decided to "defer" to its ideology would be if these fifteen groups were located in the most conservative states. In other words, their rejection of health care reform legislation would reflect the fact that their members, like other voters in their states, held more conservative political views than members and voters in other states. The puzzle is that not all AMA affiliates in conservative states rejected the AMA's position, and not all those in liberal states supported it. Arizona, Nevada, and Wyoming were among states whose vote share for Barack Obama was substantially lower than 50 percent, yet their AMA affiliates did not publicly repudiate the AMA. Conversely, a majority vote for Obama in Delaware, Florida, New Jersey, and the District of Columbia* did not prevent affiliates in those

---

*For representative purposes, the District of Columbia is considered the equivalent of a state.

states from expressing their disapproval of health care reform. Ideology alone is not an adequate predictor of which affiliates defected. Thus, we must look elsewhere to understand why state affiliates varied in their positions on the matter.

Investigating the causes and consequences of internal policy disagreements in advocacy organizations offers insight into broad questions such as these: Whose interests are being represented in the policy process, and how? How legitimate are advocacy groups' claims to represent members? What role do members play in setting policy in such organizations? Analyses of groups' internal political dynamics are also useful because they provide clues about why organizations take particular positions and why they prefer certain goals and tactics over others. Finally, understanding internal group dynamics highlights the problems organization leaders face by virtue of the fact that they must typically be responsive to multiple "audiences." To survive, groups need to satisfy their members and donors. At the same time, since advocacy organizations typically hope to advance a political agenda, their leaders need to build and preserve the groups' credibility with the public and with policy makers. Meeting the expectations of all of these constituencies is one of the most common and among the thorniest problems facing group leaders.

Advocacy groups that fail to contain internal policy disagreements face a number of negative consequences. Conflict between national levels of a group and its affiliates casts a shadow on the legitimacy of the national group's claim to represent all of its members on a particular issue, causing policy makers and the public to give less weight to that group's recommendations. At worst, internal disputes may lead to a national organization's unraveling. Affiliates also take risks when they publicly disagree with the national level of a group. Openly airing grievances could undermine their leverage among local policy makers as well as among members. Recently, when asked about a dispute within the AMA over another matter, Senator Chuck Grassley, ranking Republican on the Finance Committee, which has jurisdiction over Medicare, stated, "What I care about is what physicians in Iowa think. And what I hear from them isn't always the same as what the organization in Washington says."[1] Haberkorn and Kliff suggest that there may be a link between earlier disagreements and the current pushback the AMA is experiencing: "Months after delivering its crucial endorsement of the health care overhaul, the American Medical Association has found itself with fewer friends on Capitol Hill and more critics questioning its lobbying savvy."[2] Internal struggles between national levels of a group and its affiliates might also threaten the otherwise advantageous relationship an affiliate might have with the lead organization, as well as its level of representation in national governing bodies and the group's ability to retain old and to recruit new members.

Below I explore a few of the reasons that may have led affiliates of the AMA to decide to break with the national organization that represents them in the federal policy process. I focus on several factors that may govern the propensity to defect: ideology, the number of members an affiliate has, and the extent to which the group is politically active. As I noted above, ideology alone does not predict state affiliates' decisions to defect, but it may play a role *in concert with* membership size and lobbying expenditures. State societies with larger memberships might prove more representative of, and therefore their behavior will more closely hew to, public opinion in the state. In addition, groups with more robust lobbying operations probably also have higher levels of political interest and experience. As a result, their decisions to defer or to defect may track their state's politics more closely.

In this analysis I also consider the consequences of defection with respect to the AMA. One might expect disputes between affiliates and the national level of an association to have some measurable repercussions for the national group (since such arguments signal to interested outsiders that the national organization has failed to represent its members' interests on the issue). I examine two possible repercussions of internal dissent for the AMA: membership decline and a decline in contributions to its political action committee (PAC).

I find that when looking at state societies as a whole, decisions to support or oppose health care reform are related to the ideology of the state. However, this relationship is conditioned by the size and political activity of those state societies. There is no clear relationship between state ideology and the decision to defect from the AMA's position among small groups and those with low levels of political expenditures. However, the relationship between state ideology and defection is strong for state societies with more members and those that spend more money on lobbying.

In terms of the consequences of affiliate dissent for the AMA, I find that the AMA has not, thus far, appeared to suffer a reduction in public confidence as a result of its internal struggles. Yet, the national organization did experience a significant decline in memberships from those states that defected. As far as PAC contributions are concerned, the AMA retained a similar percentage of PAC donors in 2010 as compared to 2008 from both defecting and deferring states; however, state PACs that defected boosted their donor retention.

These findings have several implications. First, it appears that the political preferences of state medical societies with fewer members are less likely to be aligned with those of their states. This may mean that smaller affiliates are more prone to capture by ideological factions among their membership. Also, smaller groups may be less professionalized, overall, than larger organizations (and therefore be less politically savvy). Larger affiliate organizations appear to be most inclined to risk expressing public displeasure with the national group when their state's political leanings are consonant with the group's point of view. Larger groups thus may be better positioned to represent their members than those with fewer members. Furthermore, this analysis suggests that the costs and benefits of dissent are measurable. Rather than suffering for their contrariness, affiliates that defect may reap financial rewards for doing so. It may be that the media attention garnered by dissenting helps groups advertise their value to potential members and donors.

The AMA and State Medical Societies

The American Medical Association is widely cited as the peak association for medical professionals in the United States. The organization is made up of individual members who are represented in the House of Delegates, the organization's policy making body, through their membership in state and territorial associations and other constituent national medical specialty societies. In addition to setting the general policies of the organization, the House of Delegates also elects the Board of Trustees, which is the organization's 21-member governing body. In all, 180 separate medical societies (or "constituent" groups) are represented in the AMA's House of Delegates.

Although the AMA does not call these constituent groups "chapters" or "affiliates"—and to be sure, these medical societies are independent of the AMA—in practice their relationship with the national office is substantially similar to that of many other subnational groups with their parent organizations. As a condition of recognition as an affiliate, medical societies must agree to, among other things, a "Statement of Collaborative Intent" that emphasizes "collaborative partnership" and notes that

> the goals of the Federation of Medicine are to: (a) achieve a unified voice for organized medicine; (b) work for the common good of all patients and physicians; (c) promote trust and cooperation among members of the Federation; and (d) advance the image of the medical profession; and (e) increase overall efficiency of organized medicine for the benefit of our member physicians.[3]

The Statement enjoins medical societies to engage cooperatively and respectfully within the AMA's governance structure. At the same time, the Statement also emphasizes the obligations societies have with respect to expressing their views. Furthermore, the Statement highlights the steps constituent organizations should take when their views differ from those of other groups or the national organization itself.

> (e) Organizations in the Federation have a right to express their policy positions. (f) Organizations in the Federation will support, whenever possible, the policies, advocacy positions, and strategies established by

the Federation of Medicine. . . . (h) Organizations in the Federation will inform other organizations in the Federation in a timely manner whenever their major policies, positions, strategies, or public statements may be in conflict. (i) Organizations in the Federation will support the development and use of a mechanism to resolve disputes among member organizations.[4]

Thus, constituent groups play an important role in the governance of the AMA. Moreover the AMA seemed to anticipate the deleterious effects of conflict within the organization and sought to address it when admitting new medical societies to "constituent group" status.

The divisions within the AMA during the recent health care reform debate were first evidenced during the June 2009 meeting of the organization's House of Delegates. At that meeting, delegates representing the societies of the AMA debated resolutions regarding the type of plan that the AMA would endorse. However, this debate came to a standstill. On one side were liberal delegates, who favored an endorsement of a government-sponsored insurance option; on the other were conservative delegates, who opposed such a plan. In a last-ditch attempt to ensure that the House of Delegates made some statement on health care reform at the meeting, the outgoing president of the association secured support for a resolution stating that the AMA supported "health system reform alternatives that are consistent with the AMA principles of pluralism, freedom of choice, freedom of practice, and universal access for patients."[5] The resolution was vague enough to win support from a majority of delegates and, at the same time, provided sufficient leeway for the AMA's officers to endorse the variety of health care reform proposals that would be offered during the coming months.

In July 2009, just one month after this House of Delegates meeting, new AMA president James Rohack announced the organization's endorsement of H.R. 3200, "America's Affordable Health Choices Act of 2009."[6] That same month, a coalition including medical societies in Alabama, Delaware, the District of Columbia, Georgia, Kansas, New Jersey, and South Carolina announced their opposition to H.R. 3200.[7] While this initial defection was relatively moderate and the state societies were careful not to directly criticize the AMA's endorsement, the significance of the split was not lost on reporters covering the push for health care reform. Indeed, *Congress Daily* noted that the coalition of societies was "breaking from the country's largest physicians' group to mount its own push against the inclusion of a public insurance option in any overhaul bill."[8]

The next meeting of the AMA House of Delegates took place in November 2009. However, just days before that meeting took place, Rohack announced the AMA's support for H.R. 3962, "The Affordable Health Care for America Act." This endorsement sparked greater and more widespread dissatisfaction among a minority of the state societies. The Medical Association of Georgia immediately released a statement expressing the society's "disappointment" with the AMA's endorsement. It further noted that the coalition of state societies that had publicly opposed the AMA in July would advocate for the rescission of the endorsement at the House of Delegates meeting in a few days.[9] The coalition of societies did introduce a resolution to force the AMA to rescind its endorsement of the legislation at the November meeting, but the resolution garnered support from just one-third of the delegates, and the AMA endorsement remained intact.

With the AMA endorsement intact and the next House of Delegates meeting not scheduled until well into 2010, many additional state societies who disagreed with the AMA chose to publicize that dissent. By the end of 2009, several other state societies, including Missouri, North Carolina, Florida, Texas, and Tennessee, had announced their opposition to the health reform legislation that the AMA had endorsed.[10] Finally, as Congress entered the final debate on H.R. 3590 in March 2010, three more societies—Oklahoma, Arkansas, and Ohio—announced their opposition to the legislation. Thus, by the time health care reform legislation had passed Congress and was signed into law, fifteen of the fifty-one state medical societies had publicly announced a position contrary to that taken by the AMA. The following section presents the results of an analysis evaluating different explanations for these defections.

What Factors Influence State Medical Societies' Rejection of the AMA?

To understand why some state societies were more likely to defect than others, it is useful to compare the traits of those groups that did defect to those that did not. As noted above, one expectation is that state societies in conservative states were more likely to defect than those in more liberal states. To examine this hypothesis, I divided state societies into three groups—those located in states where Barack Obama won more than 55 percent of the vote in the 2008 presidential election ("blue states"), those where he won less than 45 percent of the vote ("red states"), and those where his vote share was between 45 and 55 percent ("purple states"). Figure 5.1 shows the percentage of state societies in each of these groups that opposed the health care reform legislation. The figure indicates that there is a relationship between state ideology and the propensity of groups to defect from the parent organization. Only 15.8 percent of state societies located in blue states opposed the health care reform legislation, compared with 43.8 percent of those in red states. Thus, a state society located in a red state was almost three times more likely to have defected from the AMA than one in a blue state.

Figure 5.1   Percentage of State Societies Defecting in Blue, Red, and Purple States

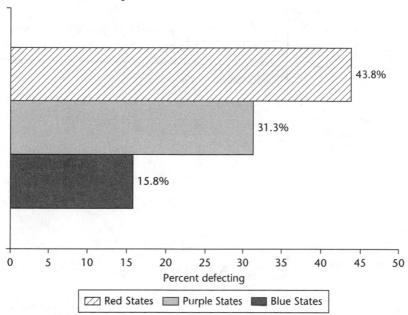

Note: "Blue states" are those where Obama received more than 55 percent of the two-party vote in 2008. "Red states" are those where he received less than 45 percent of the vote. And purple states are those where he received between 45 and 55 percent of the vote.

While the results in Figure 5.1 demonstrate that ideology is related to whether a state society defected from the AMA, this relationship may be stronger among some groups than among others. As I noted earlier in this chapter, larger groups and those with more active lobbying operations may be more sensitive to public opinion in their states. To examine whether this is the case, Figure 5.2 shows the defections rates of states along two dimensions: membership size and political activity. Data on the size of affiliates' memberships were collected from the AMA.[11] State affiliates ranged in size from 263 members in Wyoming to 17,878 in California; the average state affiliate had 4,439 members in 2009. Lobbying expenditures were collected from each state medical society's 2008 IRS Form 990, obtained via Guidestar.org.[12] The average state society reported spending $358,426 on lobbying and political activities in 2007, but that amount ranged from over $3 million spent by the California Medical Association to no reported expenditures for the medical societies in Illinois, Virginia, and North Dakota. I identified groups in Figure 5.2 depending on whether they fell above or below the median membership size and whether they fell above or below the median political expenditure.

Figure 5.2   Percentage of State Societies Defecting in Blue, Red, and Purple States by Size and Political Activity of the Societies

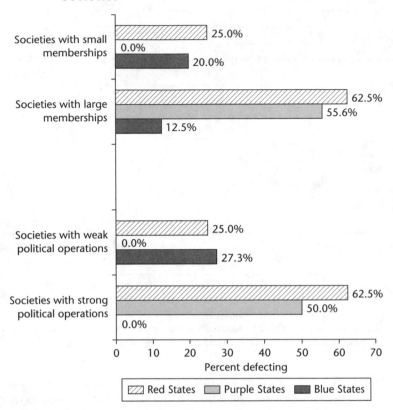

Note: "Blue states" are those where Obama received more than 55 percent of the two-party vote in 2008. "Red states" are those where he received less than 45 percent of the vote. And "purple states" are those where he received between 45 and 55 percent of the vote.

The top set of bars in Figure 5.2 report the percentage of societies in blue, purple, and red states that defected from the AMA's position on health care sorted by group membership size. The bars show that the decision to defect among large groups was closely related to public opinion, while there appeared to be no such relationship among small groups. Of small societies in red states, 25 percent publicly opposed health care reform, while 20 percent of small societies in blue states did so. The difference among state societies with large memberships was much more striking: just 12.5 percent in blue states defected from the AMA's position, while over half of those in both purple and red states did so.

The bottom set of bars in Figure 5.2 show similar results as they compare groups with stronger political operations to those with weaker political operations. The decision to defect among societies who spent below the median on political activities appeared unrelated to state ideology. Of these state societies that were located in red states, 25 percent defected from the AMA's position compared to 27.3 percent that were in blue states. On the other hand, among societies with strong political operations, state ideology was much more important. None of the state societies that had strong political operations and were located in blue states publicly opposed the health care reform legislation, while 50 percent of those in purple states and 62.5 percent in red states defected.

Thus, the results presented in Figure 5.2 demonstrate that ideology alone does not predict state defection. Instead, larger state societies and those with more active political operations are relatively sensitive to state ideology, while smaller societies and those that spend less on political activities are less so. The absence of an independent effect of state ideology on whether or not a state medical society defects may result from several factors that warrant further investigation. All affiliates depend substantially on membership dues for their revenue, and all have instituted relatively high levels of membership representation in their governance structures. As a result, particularly in smaller, more politically oriented affiliates, ideologues (members with more extreme policy views) may have extensive opportunities to advance an agenda that is different from that preferred by the population of physicians in the state as a whole. For example, affiliates rely on volunteers for many group tasks, enhancing the influence of active members. Affiliates' relatively open and accessible policy-making structures, allowing for substantial membership input, can also magnify the power of motivated members with extreme policy preferences. As a result, some smaller state societies find themselves taking stances that contrast with the view of the majority of their state's population. The next section considers the question of the costs and benefits of internal dissent for national organizations and their affiliates.

Consequences of Defection for AMA and State Medical Societies

The potential consequences of defection for the AMA and its state affiliates are several, and I explore two of these here. One place we might observe the effects of internal dissent is in changes to a group's membership rolls. Did the AMA suffer a reduction in members from states that defected?[13] One member of the AMA from Missouri, a defecting state, who was also a Republican state representative, publicized his refusal to renew his membership in the national group with the headline: "Doctors Leaving AMA in Droves."[14] But do the data support this assertion?

Table 5.1 presents the findings from a comparison of membership changes in state affiliates that defected versus those that did not. AMA

Table 5.1   Comparing AMA Membership Change in Defecting and
Nondefecting States

Group	Average Percentage Change
Defecting states	−13.1
N = 15 states	
Other states	−5.9
N = 36 states	
Difference	7.2*

*p < .05.

membership decreased by an average of 13.1 percent in the 15 state affiliates that publicly broke with the AMA, while the decrease was just 5.9 percent in the other 36 state affiliates. Thus, membership decline was more than twice as large in defecting affiliates as it was in nondefecting (or later-defecting) affiliates. This difference is statistically significant, indicating that the AMA did appear to suffer substantially more membership loss from those states that publicly broke from the organization.

Dissent between affiliates and the AMA might also affect members' willingness to contribute to either the state PAC, the AMA PAC, or both. When state affiliates publicly split from their parent organization on a policy issue, one possible result is that the parent organization's policy influence in that state will be reduced. One group of citizens for whom these policy differences may be particularly salient are those who contribute to the organizations' PACs. These citizens are highly engaged in politics and seek to invest their money in organizations that are clearly advancing their interests.[15] Thus, they might be particularly responsive to strategic decisions like those of the fifteen state societies that defected in 2009–2010. When a state society defects from the parent organization, it may signal donors in that state that they should no longer invest their funds in the national organization.

To test this possibility, I compared PAC donor retention in defecting and nondefecting states. I used individual donor data downloaded from Opensecrets.org for both the 2008 and 2010 election cycles. Opensecrets.org uses name and address algorithms to generate a unique identification number for each donor, allowing me to compare the behavior of each donor across different election cycles. Table 5.2 uses those who donated either to the AMA PAC or a state society PAC in 2008 as the baseline group to determine how successful each organization has been so far in retaining its donors in 2010. The first column of results shows that the percent of 2008 donors who gave to the AMA PAC again in 2010 was about the same (approximately 25 percent donor retention in each case) regardless of whether donors resided in dissenting states or not. On the other hand, dissenting state

Table 5.2   Comparing PAC Donor Retention in Defecting and
Nondefecting States

Group	Percent of 2008 AMA Donors Retained in 2010	Group	Percent of 2008 State Society Donors Retained in 2010
Donors in defecting states ($N = 405$)	24.2	Donors to defecting state societies ($N = 1,673$)	43.9
Donors in nondefecting states ($N = 576$)	25.2	Donors to nondefecting state societies ($N = 1,006$)	39.9
Difference	−1.0	Difference	4.0*

*$p < .05$. State society analysis includes only state societies that have an active PAC that reported individual contributions during both the 2008 and 2010 cycle.

medical societies experienced a statistically significant advantage over affiliates that deferred to the AMA's position on health care reform. State affiliate PACs that defected retained 43.9 percent of their 2008 donors in the 2010 election cycle as compared with a retention rate of 39.9 percent for those that deferred. In sum, the national group did not appear to experience difficulty retaining past donors to its PAC as a result of policy disagreement with state affiliates. Yet, it appears that the protesting state medical societies *benefited* from their rejection of the AMA's position.

Discussion

Representing the preferences of even the most homogenous group presents challenges to leaders; the case of the American Medical Association as the lead organization speaking on behalf of physicians in the recent health care reform debate proved no exception. Its pro-reform position spurred some affiliate medical societies to break publicly with the AMA, thereby casting doubt on the AMA's claim to be the legitimate representative of physicians' policy preferences on this issue.

Despite these problems, the health care reform legislation supported by the AMA passed. The data on the consequences of defection are preliminary at this point, and many of the implications may only be discerned over time. But we do have several indications of the costs of the internal debates. The influence of the dissidents at the national level may have been undermined by the successful passage of the bill they fought against. State medical societies that defected have sought to prevent the AMA from reducing their delegate allocations as a result of declining AMA memberships, thereby acknowledging that their protest may impact their level of representation in the national organization. In addition, candidates who clearly opposed reform failed to win any seats in recent elections for the AMA's Board of Trustees.[16]

The national organization will likely confront continuing fallout from the policy battle as well. For example, the AMA's president-elect (elected June 2010), noting that trust in the AMA was "damaged by the AMA's performance on health care reform," ran on a platform that called for reforms that would improve the accountability and transparency of the AMA's Board of Trustees.[17] In October 2010, the Medical Association of Georgia wrote to the board that the group had voted to "adopt a position of 'no confidence' in current AMA leadership." The letter noted that "this resolution was the subject of passionate testimony in both the reference committee and on the floor of the House of Delegates. MAG delegates expressed an overwhelming sentiment that they had serious reservations about the AMA's effectiveness and its ability to represent physicians' interests."[18] In November 2010, the AMA's CEO announced his resignation, which some suggested was linked to internal disputes over the AMA's health care reform position.[19] While the AMA's position on health care reform won the day, it is clear that this episode of internal discord continues to reverberate within the organization.

Notes

1. Jennifer Haberkorn and Sarah Kliff, "Doctors' Lobby Losing Clout on Hill," *Politico,* July 12, 2010, http://www.politico.com/news/stories/0710/39586.html.
2. Haberkorn and Kliff, "Doctors' Lobby Losing Clout on Hill."
3. K. Barton Farris and Regina Benjamin, "Guidelines for Admission of Constituent Associations to Our AMA House of Delegates," Joint Report of the Council on Constitution and Bylaws and the Council on Ethical and Judicial Affairs, presented at the annual meeting of the American Medical Association, June 13–17, 2009, Chicago: 497. Available at http://www.ama-assn.org/resources/doc/hod/a-09-other-reports.pdf.
4. Farris and Benjamin, "Guidelines for Admission of Constituent Associations to Our AMA House of Delegates," 497–98.
5. Thom Wilder, "AMA Resolution Backs Health System Reform, but Deletes Reference to Public Plan Option," *Health Care Policy Report* 17, no. 25 (2009).
6. "AMA Support for H.R. 3200: Answers to Frequently Asked Questions," July 20, 2009, http://www.amaalliance.org/site/files/625/81242/296601/410961/HR_3200_FAQs.pdf.
7. American Medical Association, "MAG Instrumental in Coalition Representing More Than 43,000 Physicians Calling for 'Patient-Centered' Health Care System," press release, July 22, 2009, http://www.mag.org/communications/press-release-archive.shtml.
8. Carrie Dann, "Physician Unrest Flares Over AMA Stand," *Congress Daily,* July 16, 2009.
9. Medical Association of Georgia, "MAG Disappointed with AMA Support for H.R. 3962, Says Bill Is Bad for Patients and Physicians," press release, http://www.mag.org/pdfs/pr_hr3962_110609.pdf.

10. Hunt, Dianna. 2009. "Texas Medical Association balks at backing Obama health-care plan, despite AMA endorsement." *Fort Worth Star-Telegram,* July 20, 2009; Medical Association of the State of Alabama et al. "Coalition Letter Opposing H.R. 3590." Letter to Nancy Pelosi and John Boehner. March 10, 2010.
11. Michael D. Daves, "2011 State Delegate Allocation," memo to executive directors—state medical associations, January 31, 2011.
12. I was unable to locate a Form 990 for Maryland's state society, so that state is excluded from the analysis.
13. Each year, the AMA compiles data on the membership in its state societies to determine how many representatives each society will be allocated in its House of Delegates. The most recent report includes information on membership as of December 31, 2008, December 31, 2009, and December 31, 2010. Using this data, I compared the average percentage change in AMA members from the group of states that defected during the health care reform debate with the average percentage change in AMA members from all other states.
14. Rob Schaff, "Doctors Leaving AMA in Droves: Represented Less Than 20% to Begin With," *AFP Missouri Blog,* December 22, 2009, http://www.americansforprosperity.org/122309-doctors-leaving-ama-droves-represented-less-20-begin.
15. Henry E. Brady, Sidney Verba, and Kay Lehman Schlozman. "Beyond SES: A Resource Model of Political Participation." *American Political Science Review* 89, no. 2 (1995): 271–94.
16. Andis Robeznieks, "At AMA Annual Meeting, Action but No Clear Consensus," *Modern Physician,* July 12, 2010, http://www.modernphysician.com/article/20100712/MODERNPHYSICIAN/307129998/1116#.
17. Peter W. Carmel, "AMA President-Elect Candidates Share Views: Peter W. Carmel, MD." *American Medical News,* May 3, 2010, http://www.ama-assn.org/amednews/2010/05/03/prsd0503.htm.
18. E. Dan deLoach. "Letter to Ardis D. Hoven, M.D., Chair, AMA Board of Trustees," Medical Association of Georgia, October 27, 2010, http://www.mag.org/pdfs/hod_action_deloach_coven_102710.pdf.
19. Dan Bowman, "AMA CEO's Resignation Linked to Group's Reform Support," *FierceHealthcare: Daily News for Healthcare Executives,* November 5, 2010 http://www.fiercehealthcare.com/story/ama-ceos-resignation-linked-groups-reform-support/2010-11-05/.

6

Learning Civic Leadership

Leader Skill Development in the Sierra Club

Matthew Baggetta, Chaeyoon Lim, Kenneth T. Andrews,
Marshall Ganz, and Hahrie C. Han[1]

In the 2009 Seattle mayoral race, political novice Michael McGinn upset renowned incumbent mayor Greg Nickles.[2] Although Nickles had become an international eco-star in 2005 by leading a campaign to make municipal carbon reduction commitments in the face of the George W. Bush administration's recalcitrance, McGinn "out-greened" America's greenest mayor in America's greenest city in this election. How did McGinn, who had never held public office, know how to design and run a successful grassroots organizing campaign that could unseat such a prominent political figure? Nickles and McGinn shared political credibility on environmental issues, a necessary feature for local political candidates in Seattle. Nickles, however, was known for "machine-style" insider campaigning and governing, while McGinn's campaign reached out, showing a particular savvy for grassroots organizing.[3] The McGinn campaign included no paid staff and engaged a broad set of volunteers, which included some people far younger than those typically involved in Seattle politics.[4] McGinn inspired local activists while also managing the media, especially on issues of "greenness." He was, for example, regularly photographed biking to campaign events. As with any election, many factors played into the final outcome, but it is hard to ignore the grassroots organizing skill demonstrated by McGinn's campaign—skills developed by McGinn during his fourteen-year tenure as the chairperson of the Cascade Chapter of the Sierra Club.[5]

The path from association leader to mayor of a major city may surprise contemporary observers. Today's political figures often make a name for themselves in business or law (McGinn is a lawyer) or may simply pursue a public political career almost from the start (as Nickles did). In past eras, however, membership in, and often leadership of, national fraternal orders, service groups, and other major federations was a common prerequisite for public leadership. For example, as sociologist and political scientist Theda Skocpol reports, in the 1950s and 1960s roughly 90 percent of Massachusetts state senators publicly listed multiple affiliations with popular cross-class membership associations. Nearly half of those senators listed membership in the American Legion alone—far outpacing the membership rates for the rest of Massachusetts' male citizenry (about 5–6 percent) in that era.[6] In similar fashion, many African-American activists who had risen to leadership positions in the NAACP and other civil rights organizations won elected office following the 1965 Voting Rights Act.[7] Women leaders also emerged from associations with varying goals and ideological perspectives; these organizations included the National Organization for Women, the League of Women Voters, and Concerned Women for America.[8]

Michael McGinn's ascendance to Seattle's mayoralty exemplifies this long-standing, if currently less common, pattern. While his affiliation with the Sierra Club likely helped bolster his overall green image with Seattle's environmentally conscious voters, his years of formal and informal training as a Sierra Club leader may well have laid the foundation for his success in the practice of political organizing. What might he have done and learned in that position that prepared him for his move to elected public office? This question motivates the research presented in this chapter.

The Sierra Club is an example of a civic association—a self-governing organization made up of individual members who joined voluntarily. These associations "depend upon voluntary efforts of their members, decentralize decision making across local units, govern themselves through elected volunteer leaders, and enable their members' collective voices to be heard."[9] Scholars from French observer Alexis de Tocqueville in the 1830s to political scientist Robert Putnam in the 1990s have investigated the connection between joining voluntary groups and the development of civic skills, values, and beliefs. Despite the long-standing scholarly interest in this relationship, however, we have surprisingly limited knowledge about it. A good deal is known about rates of associational joining[10] and the effects this can have on political participation.[11] The specific mechanisms connecting associational participation to political engagement are less well established, especially regarding leaders. In particular, we would like to know what activities local leaders do in civic associations like the National Rifle Association, the Knights of Columbus, the Veterans of Foreign Wars, or the U.S. Bowling Congress and what skills they develop through those actions. Do all leaders develop the same skills? And are some skills more likely to be honed effectively than others through these activities?

This chapter looks inside associations to reveal how volunteer leaders spend their time within their organizations and to explore the skills they do (and do not) take away from those experiences. We begin by briefly reviewing prior work on civic associations and leaders, uncovering some helpful guidance but few empirical findings, and then introduce our case study of the Sierra Club. The structural features of the Sierra Club—a federated national association with self-governing state and local units—make it relevant for understanding the development of leaders' civic skills, especially with respect to the particular relationship between leader activity and civic skill improvement. We detail the ways the Sierra Club's volunteer leaders invest time in a variety of organizational activities and identify dimensions of skills that leaders can develop. In the end, we find that some associational leadership activities, especially the work of mobilizing people, are strongly related to skill improvement, but that not all skills are equally likely to be developed.

Leadership in Civic Associations

Civic associations are self-governing organizations made up of individual members who joined voluntarily. To clarify their unique character, it is helpful to note what they are *not*. Many contemporary interest groups and service-providing nonprofits do not fit our definition of civic associations. Rather, they are centralized, professionalized, bureaucratic organizations. While many groups have "members," a typical form of membership is paying an annual subscription fee and receiving a newsletter or magazine. These organizations generate revenue by recruiting "checkbook" members, raising other donations via professional marketing efforts (door-to-door, over the phone, or via the Internet), and winning grants from government or foundations. This revenue is used to support the work of professional, paid staff.[12] Executives in these groups (e.g., the American Automobile Association, the AARP) engage with individual "members" as consumers or clients; the relationships are those of economic exchange. In that context, core "leadership" tasks are managerial. As is the focus in for-profit corporations, managers must ensure efficient production of goods and the maintenance of a satisfied consumer base—and they are financially compensated for doing so. Even when paid canvassers and grassroots lobbying firms engage in face-to-face activities, such as street solicitation, their interactions usually fail to produce meaningful civic learning, generate enduring forms of social capital, or inspire new leadership.[13]

Civic associations, on the other hand, offer substantial opportunities for civic skill learning because they engage citizens in leadership activity. Civic associations are organizational vehicles for the expression of collective identities and the assertion of public voice, in which members participate as constituents rather than consumers.[14] In this context, leaders must "mobilize and direct the commitment, accountability, and cooperation, of voluntary participants" if the organization is to be successful.[15] The organization must recruit (and often hold elections for) volunteer leaders, develop their capacity for making decisions about organizational governance, and create organizational structures for engaging additional volunteers in the work of the group. Because ordinary citizens are drawn into these core leadership activities, strong potential exists for civic skill development.

America has a long-standing tradition of this kind of civic associational-ism. Organizers throughout much of US history formed large, nationally federated associations that drew strength from millions of members in thousands of local chapters.[16] These local chapters were grouped into regional and state level units, which came together as cohesive national associations. This structure, modeled on the federated structure of the US government, provided stable sources of income for organizations (from member dues and materials purchases) and connected individuals into trans-local networks of political information and support that spanned the nation. This classic federated structure allowed organizations to maintain highly personal connections with members at the local level while simultaneously aspiring for national political clout.

In addition, America's civic associations created countless leadership positions for ordinary citizens.[17] Men and women from all walks of life had the opportunity to learn various organizational and leadership skills, long considered important for democratic citizens.[18] In 1910, for example, the Odd Fellows, a major fraternal order with 1.5 million members in 16,245 chapters, recruited members to serve in 276,813 leadership posts, 99.8 percent of which were at the local level. This means at any one time, about one out of every five members of the Odd Fellows served in a formal leadership role. Similarly, the Grange, the oldest agricultural organization in the United States, at one point had 450,000 members, 77,775 of whom held leadership positions, of which 99.3 percent were local.[19]

Despite the shift from this classic civic association form to more managerial styles of organization since the 1960s,[20] many prominent organizations like the National Rifle Association,[21] Common Cause,[22] the National Organization of Women,[23] and the Sierra Club[24] still rely on state and local units, and the members and leaders within them, to play important roles in governance and other organizational activities. Recent scholarship suggests that still today roughly a quarter of all local groups are affiliates of national associations.[25]

Many studies have examined who joins and actively participates in civic associations. We still, however, know much less about what people actually do as leaders in these organizations and what civic skills they develop as a result. The knowledge of how to be an effective association leader must be learned, and some leaders undoubtedly learn more than others. This leads us to ask, What might association leaders actually be doing within their groups, and what skills might they actually be developing through those activities?

In one notable study of anti-drunk-driving organizations, sociologists John McCarthy and Mark Wolfson provide evidence that certain leaders (chapter presidents and vice presidents) commit substantial amounts of time to their organizations, spending at least some of that time on many public appearances and attending a variety of membership and leadership meetings.[26] Their study, however, does not detail the *relative amount* of time committed by leaders to the various possible leadership activities they might undertake. In what areas do leaders invest the most (and least) time?

Beyond relative time commitment, we are also interested in how leaders' skills develop as they engage in these activities. Alexis de Tocqueville, after touring America in the 1830s, argued that "in democratic countries knowledge of how to combine is the mother of all other forms of knowledge"[27] and that for the conditions of democracy to flourish, the "art of association must develop and improve" among citizens.[28] In their recent examination of improvement in the "art of associating," political scientist Sidney Verba and his colleagues asked survey respondents whether and where they practiced four particular actions—attending a meeting, organizing a meeting, writing a letter, and making a speech.[29] They then connected the practice of these actions to subsequent political involvement. Others have followed up on this research by looking at organizational contexts that foster the opportunity for practicing similar actions, finding a variety of chances available in churches, political groups, service organizations, and even arts groups, but these studies say little about what skill sets leaders actually improve.[30] We are left, then, with two individual-level questions. What are the civic skill dimensions along which leaders might develop, and how much do leaders really develop along these dimensions through their experiences in civic associations? These are the empirical questions we pursue in this remainder of this chapter.

The Sierra Club

The Sierra Club is one of the oldest, largest, and most influential environmental associations in the United States.[31] It is regularly involved in the environmental policy-making process at national, state, and local levels and is arguably the best-known American environmental group. Despite its prominence in environmental politics, the Sierra Club maintains its commitment to outdoors activity, organizing and sponsoring everything from local day hikes to extensive high-peaks expeditions. The Sierra Club was founded in 1892 by John Muir and a set of San Francisco Bay area notables with an affinity for the mountains of northern California.[32] From the start, the Sierra Club was both an alpine club for outdoors enthusiasts and a political advocacy group that lobbied for the preservation of natural spaces.[33] That dual purpose remains, as individuals and organizational units at all levels of the Sierra Club pursue a mission to "explore, enjoy, and protect" the natural environment.[34] The Sierra Club continues to play a leading role in the environmental movement as the organization's breadth and openness allow it to engage new issues and ideas.

The Sierra Club has followed a historical trajectory common to classic American voluntary associations, beginning with a federated structure that became more complex and professionalized after the 1970s.[35] Membership in the club was modest for much of its early history, due in part to a local, California focus and to a system in which potential members needed a current member to sponsor their application for membership. By 1940 the group numbered only about 3,500 members. Following World War II, however, the Club changed strategies, rapidly expanding to develop a truly federated structure. The Club formed state chapters throughout the country and shifted to an open membership format, which dramatically increased its size. By the end of the 1960s, the club had 33 state and regional chapters and was approaching 100,000 members. In the 1970s, the Club added new city-based subunits, creating a layer of local organizations called Sierra Club groups. By the time of our study in 2003, Club membership exceeded 750,000 in 62 chapters—1 in every state plus several regional chapters in California—and more than 300 local groups.

As the organization grew older and more complex, the Sierra Club developed some of the key characteristics common to many advocacy organizations founded since the 1970s.[36] For example, paid staff (at the national and state level) handle organizational maintenance tasks like fundraising and publishing, and the organization has professional lobbyists, lawyers, and field organizers. In 2003, the Club had 163 national staff members in the San Francisco headquarters, another 52 in the Washington, D.C., office, 169 staffers working in 8 regions, and an additional 124 employees in individual chapters.[37] The Sierra Club also recruits members through direct-mail campaigns, and for a majority of members, writing checks and receiving a magazine is the only way they relate to the organization. Adopting these practices undoubtedly has contributed to the rapid growth of the organization and its success as one of the most prominent environmental groups in the United States. These changes have also expanded the organizational focus from the Club's early days as a small, almost exclusively face-to-face organization.

Nonetheless, many volunteer members play central leadership roles. Elected leaders at all levels of the Sierra Club—local (groups), regional/state (chapters), and national—commit substantial personal time to governance and activity. Beyond the elected leadership, thousands of volunteer activists contribute time and effort leading political campaigns, guiding outings and outdoors programs, coordinating public education activities, and conducting research. Political scientist Ronald Shaiko compared five national environmental organizations and found that the Sierra Club had the highest proportion of active members.[38] About 10 percent of the members considered themselves active in the organization, and almost a quarter of them were on special mailing lists and responded to issue alerts by writing to their members of Congress. In 2003, an internal Sierra Club database indicated that more than 3,000 volunteers directly participated in governance across all levels as members of "executive committees," which are senior decision-making bodies in every unit at each organizational level. These executive committee members are the leaders we focused on in our study. Our primary data come from a survey of 1,624 executive committee members (51 percent of all executive committee members in the Club) conducted in 2003.[39] We use these data to examine how elected leaders allocate their time in the Club and what skills they develop through their service.

What Do Leaders Do?

To begin, we examine the total number of hours respondents committed to Sierra Club activity. Although all the people included in our survey are elected leaders of the Sierra Club, they likely vary a great deal in the time they commit to the organization. The median executive committee member spends about fifteen hours per month on Club activity (see Figure 6.1). Separating chapter (regional/state level) leaders from group (local level) leaders, we find that the former typically devote more time (twenty hours per month) than the latter (twelve hours per month). These "typical" figures, however, disguise the substantial variation in time commitment from leader to leader. A few leaders reported spending five hours or less a month on Sierra Club activity, while on the other end of the continuum, some 20 percent of the leaders said that they spent forty hours or more per month— an average of ten hours per week.

These numbers reveal that the volunteer leaders in the Sierra Club belong to the most civically active segment of the American population. To put these numbers into perspective, about 26 percent of American adults volunteered through or for an organization at least once between September 2007 and September 2008.[40] The median volunteer spent about 52 hours during that one-year period—roughly an hour a week. A typical Sierra Club group leader would spend 144 hours per year and a chapter leader about 240 hours. Moreover, at least two-thirds of our respondents reported that they also participated in at least one other civic association, and almost half (46 percent) held at least one leadership position in another organization. For many of these leaders, activism is an important, time-consuming part of their lives.[41]

Given the time commitments of Sierra Club leaders, what do they do during the hours they devote to the organization? We asked the leaders to break down the hours they spent for the Club into several categories.[42] Figure 6.2 shows the relative distribution of leader hours across different categories of activity, sorted from most to least common. The activity that takes up the largest proportion of time is "administrative activities," which includes writing and editing newsletters, maintaining websites, keeping up with administrative e-mail, and other organizational logistics. This is

Figure 6.1 Time Invested in Sierra Club Work by Executive Committee Members

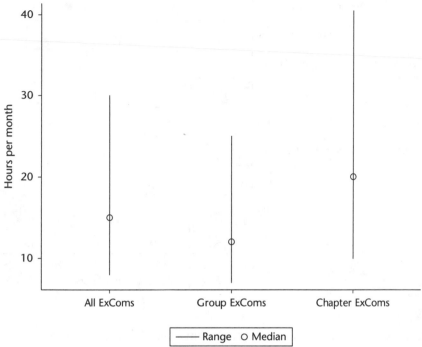

Source: Data for these and all succeeding tables and figures have been compiled by the authors.

followed closely by time invested in meetings. Together, almost half of the typical Sierra Club leader's time is spent doing administrative activities or attending meetings. The other half of leaders' time is divided among a variety of other activities, the most common of which is attending planned activities, events, or celebrations (17 percent).

How should we think about this distribution of time use? Perhaps most striking is the fact that the vast majority of time is spent doing work with other leaders or by oneself. This behind-the-scenes work may go unnoticed by those who focus only on the public side of leadership. Without prior studies for comparison, additional interpretation is speculative. Nevertheless, several theoretical traditions suggest ways we might begin thinking about the patterns we see here.

From the broadest perspective, Sierra Club groups and chapters are formal organizations. Organization scholars have suggested that creating and maintaining a formal organization for collective action requires substantial "overhead" for organizational maintenance and coordination.[43] Associations like the Sierra Club are no exception. Informally hiking with friends may not require extensive planning, coordination, or administration. A

Figure 6.2   Percentage of Leader Time Spent in Various Activities

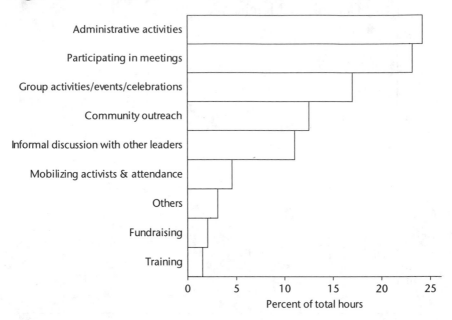

Sierra Club hike, however, needs to be announced in the newsletter, have a list of individuals signed up to participate, have a trained leader assigned to the outing, and, if it is a particularly challenging outing, perhaps have legal release forms on hand. These kinds of tasks might fall within the categories of administration or informal communication with leaders. In addition, group leaders must create a plan for making the hike happen and must see the plan through to completion. The planning and implementation processes all require coordination, which may help explain the amount of time that leaders devote to meetings. Organization scholars, then, might not be surprised to see the relatively large amount of time Sierra Club leaders devote to administration and meetings.

Students of social movement organizations might suggest similar insights. Sustained collective effort requires ongoing organization, which is typically carried out by leaders and other committed activists in formal organizations.[44] For example, a study of all public events (including cultural and sports events as well as protest events) that occurred in one year in Madison, Wisconsin, found that the large majority of events were sponsored by formal organizations that transcended the events themselves.[45] Similarly, a study of public events in Chicago concluded that the most important factor in explaining rates of public events in neighborhoods was the density of formal organizations in the area.[46] Unless organizational leaders carry out the necessary groundwork and absorb much of the costs—including meetings to decide on a course of action and administration to keep the organization afloat while actions take place—these public events are unlikely to happen and even less likely to happen in a sustained fashion.[47] Again, the relative time devoted to administrative activities and meetings makes sense from this perspective.

Scholars of civic associations similarly note the amount of attention leaders must pay to core activities that build and sustain organizations, but they draw our attention even more specifically to the unique nature of leadership activity in this context. Leaders of voluntary associations differ from managers in bureaucratic organizations with paid employees. Leaders must find potential volunteers, motivate them to participate, facilitate the development of relationships with them and among them, secure their commitments for activity, identify those with leadership potential, and develop them into the next generation of leaders. For the association to endure, leaders must build organizational capacity—useful organizational structures and skilled people to fill those structures—that outlasts any particular activity or program. Leaders must engage in strategic work, deciding on various courses of possible action and interdependently working with one another on complex tasks.[48] From this perspective, the administration and meetings taking place in civic associations may not simply be organizational maintenance activities. Rather, these may be the sites where leaders' most creative and consequential activity occur.

Social movement theories and the civic association perspective also draw our attention to related (if less commonly reported) activities in Figure 6.2, in particular community outreach and mobilization. These actions relate closely to the capacity-building leadership that associational leaders must undertake. Leaders doing community outreach are investing time in direct communication with decision makers as well as testifying at hearings, making public speeches, staffing informational tables, and engaging in other efforts to reach out to the broader community. The average Sierra Club leader devotes about 13 percent of his or her time to this kind of work. Leaders also mobilize people for activity, ranging from protests and rallies seeking political influence; to river cleanups and trail-maintenance efforts to restore the natural environment; to hikes, trips, and outings to enjoy the outdoors. Leaders reported investing less than 5 percent of their time in mobilizing people to become active participants or to attend events and activities.[49] This relatively limited time investment is surprising in light of social movement scholarship that notes the significance of organizers' efforts in getting people to participate in movement activity.[50] If we assume that higher levels of mobilization are beneficial to the Sierra Club's efforts, we might expect more leader time to be devoted to mobilizing.

In sum, Sierra Club leaders contribute a substantial number of hours to the organization, divided across a range of activities. They invest a lot of time in administrative activities and meetings; a substantial amount of time participating in activities, events, and celebrations; and relatively less time in outreach and mobilizing. Theories of formal organizations, social movements, and civic associations lead us to think the relative emphasis on administration and meetings is to be expected, although the relatively limited investment in outreach and mobilizing comes as something of a surprise.[51]

Although these patterns are intriguing on their own, what are their implications for leader skill development? A critical task for any self-governing civic association is the development of leadership.[52] More skilled leaders should produce better outcomes today, and a steady development of leadership capacity helps ensure the organization's future success. Toward these ends, in an effective association, leaders' skills should be improving. What does this particular distribution of time investment mean for developing these skills? If doing administrative tasks leads to substantial civic skill improvement, the Sierra Club will reap the benefits of many more civically skilled leaders. If, however, mobilizing activity is more of a teacher of skills, Sierra Club leaders are improving less than they might, given their modest time investment in these activities. To explore these possibilities, we turn now to leader skill development.

What Skills Do Leaders Develop?

While civic associations have long been described as "schools of democracy"[53] in which people can learn various civic and organizational skills, the kinds of skills they learn through associational experience are not widely understood. In most studies, this relationship has been studied indirectly by considering whether association members are engaged in other political or civic activities (e.g., voting, attending public meetings) more than nonmembers. If association members participate in other activities more, it is assumed they must have learned some civic lessons through their participation and become more motivated to participate in political or community events.

In our study, we measured in close detail the civic skills leaders were developing. In the survey, we offered Sierra Club leaders a list of nineteen specific skills that could be fostered by playing a leadership role in a civic association. These included, for example, "accepting responsibility," "working with the media," and "challenging others to be more effective." For each item, we asked the leaders how strongly they agreed or disagreed that their skill had improved through service as a volunteer leader in the Sierra Club. In other words, the questions do not try to measure the absolute level (or stock) of skill the leaders possess, but rather the development of the skill through experience in the organization.[54]

Our goal in utilizing these items was not to produce an exhaustive list of all possible civic skills that might be important for civic association members in general or environmental activists in particular.[55] Rather, we sought to identify sets of skill items that might indicate common dimensions of civic knowledge. Using factor analysis, a data reduction technique that searches for common dimensions underlying multiple survey questions,[56] we identified three major skill dimensions (see Table 6.1). The numbers in each column are "factor loadings," which indicate how closely each specific skill is correlated with the underlying skill dimension (a zero would mean that specific skill had no correlation with that skill dimension; a 1 would be perfect correlation; higher values mean stronger correlations). Because all the specific skill items relate to civic learning, they all have some correlation with all three underlying skill dimensions, but it becomes clear that certain skills are central to one of the three dimensions. We examined which items loaded on each factor and then named the factors according to the kinds of skills most strongly related to each.[57]

Table 6.1 Specific Skill Factor Loadings on Three Skill Dimensions

Type of skill	Managing self	Managing others	Managing public work
Accepting responsibility	**0.81**	0.18	0.22
Listening to other people	**0.77**	0.16	0.18
Accepting criticism	**0.68**	0.27	0.23
Thinking creatively	**0.67**	0.19	0.31
Managing my time	**0.48**	0.39	0.17
Challenging others to be more effective	0.18	**0.77**	0.28
Holding others accountable	0.26	**0.72**	0.20
Delegating responsibility	0.28	**0.73**	0.15
Asking people to volunteer	0.05	**0.75**	0.26
Coaching and mentoring others	0.29	**0.57**	0.49
Providing others with support	0.52	**0.53**	0.20
Asking for help	0.50	**0.54**	0.07
Working with media	0.11	0.15	**0.82**
Working effectively in coalition	0.12	0.20	**0.80**
Speaking in public	0.30	0.17	**0.70**
Planning and carrying out a campaign	0.24	0.28	**0.64**
Working effectively with public officials	0.31	0.23	**0.63**
Organizing and running a meeting	0.33	0.37	**0.54**
Managing internal conflicts	0.30	0.37	**0.53**
Percent of Total Variance Explained by Factor	21	21	19

We call the first skill dimension *managing self*. These are skills a leader needs to work effectively with other people in an organization. The most central items to this dimension (i.e., those with the highest factor loadings) emphasize taking responsibility for one's own work. Leaders with these skills take responsibility for the things for which they are accountable. They listen to other people. They fulfill their own responsibilities effectively. "Managing self" does not require changing other people's attitudes or behaviors; developing these skills is about a leader changing herself. Skills for "managing self" enhance the internal capacity of the organization through the improvement of individual capabilities.

We call the second skill dimension *managing others*. These skills involve one leader getting other people within the organization to take action or to change their behaviors. "Managing others" builds organizational capacity by getting other group members to perform more effectively, be it by volunteering more time, delegating responsibility, or holding them accountable for their actions.

The third skill dimension is called *managing public work* and involves working with institutions, organizations, and the public beyond the association. Leaders developing these skills make efforts to influence the general public and public officials, and they often work with other organizations to do so. "Managing public work" builds external organizational capacity—the ability to "change the world."

Based on our construction of these three civic skill dimensions[58]—managing self, managing others, and managing public work—we then assess how the leaders improve (or not) through their Sierra Club experience. Table 6.2 shows the percentage of Sierra Club leaders who "agree" or "strongly agree" that a specific skill has improved through their organizational activity. Sierra Club leaders report highest rates of improvement on "managing self" (41 percent) and "managing public work" (40 percent). Within these two dimensions, particular skills stand out: in "managing self," 62 percent report improving on "listening to other people" and just over half see improvement at "accepting responsibility." "Managing my time," however, is a skill that only about a quarter think has improved through their service to the Sierra Club. Within the "managing public work" dimension, nearly half (48 percent) of leaders report improving on "organizing and running a meeting" and 45 percent see enhancement of their public speaking ability. Less than a third of leaders, however, report improving on "working with media" or "managing internal conflicts."

In contrast to "managing self" and "managing public work," Sierra Club leaders report relatively less improvement in "managing others," with an average reported improvement rate of only 32 percent.[59] Still, certain specific skill enhancements are more common, like "providing others with support" (45 percent). While some leaders report improving their "managing

Table 6.2 Particular Skill Improvement by Skill Dimension

Type of knowledge	Percent of leaders who report improvement
Managing Self	
Listening to other people	62
Accepting responsibility	51
Thinking creatively	38
Accepting criticism	29
Managing my time	26
Managing Self Average	41
Managing Others	
Providing others with support	45
Asking for help	41
Asking people to volunteer	37
Delegating responsibility	30
Coaching and mentoring others	29
Challenging others to be more effective	23
Holding others accountable	18
Managing Others Average	32
Managing Public Work	
Organizing and running a meeting	48
Speaking in public	45
Working effectively with public officials	42
Working effectively in coalition	40
Planning and carrying out a campaign	39
Working with media	32
Managing internal conflicts	31
Managing Public Work Average	40

others" skills through their service to the Club, overall it appears that substantially fewer skills in "managing others" are being developed than those surrounding "managing self" or "managing public work."[60]

Overall, the experiences of volunteer leaders in the Sierra Club offer significant opportunities to improve on various skill dimensions. Some skills, however, appear to be more likely to be improved than others. "Managing self" seems to be what many leaders are most likely to improve on through their service in the Sierra Club, followed by some "managing public work" skills. "Managing others," however, which consists mostly of skills required for working collectively with other people in the organization, appears to have been improved on by only a minority of the leaders. In some ways this is surprising, as civic associations are dependent on collective action to succeed and, as we noted earlier, civic associations are one of the few (and, perhaps, best) contexts available for improving these kinds of skills. Skills for "managing others"—especially those involving challenging others to accept responsibility and be accountable—might also translate particularly well into additional civic and political success for individual leaders beyond their groups (as the Michael McGinn example we opened the chapter with suggests).

If an organization wanted to improve its leaders' rates of skill improvement, the first step would be to gain a better understanding why some leaders improve on these dimensions, while others do not. Knowing what experiences are most closely related to improvement on each skill dimension would allow an organization either to encourage more engagement with current "learning" activities or to reform other, less effective activities to produce a stronger learning context.

Leader Time and Skill Development

In our final set of analyses, we examine what factors are related to the development of skills in "managing self," "managing others," and "managing public work," focusing in particular on the relationship between how leaders invest their time in the organization and what types of skills they improve. Since many other factors could also affect skill development, it is important to control for those factors to make a meaningful assessment of the effect of time use. For example, perhaps leaders who have been active in the organization longer are more likely to have improved more skills. In order to see the real relationship of time investment to skill learning, we need to take these potential confounding factors into account. We use multiple regression analysis to control for various factors, including a variety of standard demographic characteristics (e.g., age, sex, education), leader's experience in the Club (e.g., activist tenure in the Club, the number of training programs attended), and features of particular organizations (e.g., executive committee size, membership size, whether a leader serves on a group or chapter executive committee). Regression analysis allows us to "hold constant" all of these background factors while we focus on the relationship of time spent in particular activities to particular civic skills developed.[61]

Figures 6.3 to Figure 6.6 present the patterns that show how improving on different skill dimensions relates to leaders' activities in the Sierra Club while controlling for other background factors.[62] Figure 6.3 shows how the total number of hours devoted to Sierra Club activities is related to the three different skill dimensions. Each line in Figure 6.3 represents the probability that leaders who commit a certain number of hours agree that they have improved (on average) on the skills on that dimension.

First, leaders who invest more time in the Sierra Club are significantly more likely to agree that they have improved on all three types of skills. One must keep in mind that this is the relationship after controlling for many other factors that could influence skill development. For example, the

Figure 6.3   Total Time Investment and Skill Improvement

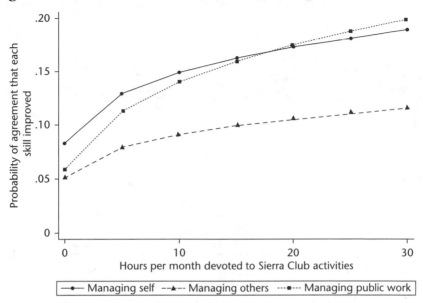

length of time a person has been active in the Sierra Club plays a major role in explaining how many skills he has improved. Similarly, as the number of leadership positions a person holds increases, the number of skills that person reports improving also increases. The relationship between time investment and skill improvement appears even after we control for these important factors.

A second pattern in Figure 6.3 is also clear. As noted earlier, skills for "managing others" seem less likely to be improved with increased time investment compared to the other two types of skills. Although leaders who put in thirty hours per month with the Sierra Club are significantly more likely to report that their "managing others" skills have improved than those who spend just one hour per month, the rate of the improvement is much smaller than for "managing self" and "managing public work." An average leader spending one hour each month with the Sierra Club has about a 5 percent chance of reporting improvement on "managing others" and just less than 6 percent chance of reporting improvement on "managing public work." If that same leader began committing thirty hours per month to the club, the chances of reporting improvement on "managing public work" would increase to nearly 20 percent, but the chances of reporting improvement on "managing others" would increase to only 11.6 percent.

Simple time commitment, however, is only the beginning of the story. What may matter more is how that time is invested (see Figures 6.4, 6.5,

Figure 6.4 Relative Time Investment and "Managing Self"

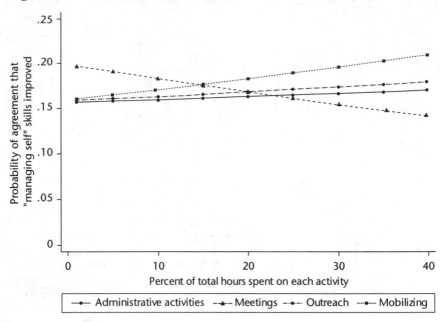

Figure 6.5 Relative Time Investment and "Managing Others"

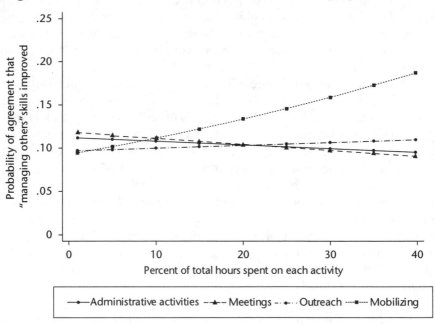

Figure 6.6   Relative Time Investment and "Managing
                  Public Work"

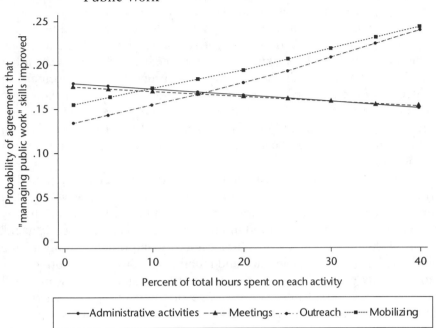

and 6.6). We again control for a large set of background factors that could
explain reported skill improvement. Most importantly, we control for how
long a leader has been active in the Sierra Club and the number of Sierra
Club training programs she has gone through, both of which have strong,
positive relationships to all three kinds of skill improvement. In addition
we, also control for the total amount of time a leader commits to the Club
(the pattern illustrated in Figure 6.3). In Figures 6.4, 6.5, and 6.6 we add to
the mix four of the types of time use we discussed earlier: administrative
activities, meetings, outreach, and mobilizing.[63] Controlling for other factors, how does spending relatively more time on any one of these activities
relate to skill improvement?

The types of skills leaders improve on seem to reflect the kinds of
activities to which they devote more of their time. Investing time in administrative activities and outreach shows a small, positive relationship to
reported improvement in "managing self" (see Figure 6.4). Investing time
in mobilizing activity shows a much stronger, positive relationship to skill
improvement, even though variability in the data makes it difficult to
establish the absolute certainty of these relationships.[64] However, a clear,
statistically significant, negative relationship does exist between meetings

and "managing self." A greater percentage of leader time spent in meetings is related to lower reported levels of improvement in skills like listening to other people, accepting responsibility, and creative thinking.

Figure 6.5 tells a similar story in that investing time in administrative activities and meetings both show negative relationships with the improvement of "managing others" skills. Investing time in mobilizing, on the other hand, shows a strong positive relationship to reports of improvement in "managing others."[65] Leaders who devote a larger proportion of their time to getting basic Sierra Club members to become active participants and recruiting people to attend events and activities are much more likely to report improvement on "managing others" skills (e.g., holding others accountable).[66]

Finally, Figure 6.6 displays the results of the same analysis applied to the relationship of time investment and "managing public work" skill improvement. Here, administrative activities and meetings show a slightly negative relationship to reported improvement on "managing public work" skills like planning and carrying out a campaign and (ironically) organizing and running a meeting. Outreach and mobilizing, however, are both clearly and strongly positively related to reports of "managing public work" skill improvement. Sierra Club leaders who devote more of their efforts to getting members to participate actively or who work to communicate to the broader public are much more likely to report being better at working with the media, engaging with coalition partners, and giving speeches.

Before we continue, we should note the causal direction of these relationships. There are two possibilities. First is a situation where participation in certain Sierra Club leadership activities facilitates learning. In this situation, devoting relatively more time to certain activities could lead to higher levels of reported improvement because each additional hour a leader spends on an activity produces more learning about the skills associated with that activity (in the same way that a student who chooses to focus more homework time on math than on English may develop more quantitative skills than verbal skills). Second is a situation where learning facilitates participation in certain kinds of Sierra Club activities. In this situation, learning particular skills encourages a leader to invest more of her time in activities where those skills are useful (as a student who has successfully completed one math course may choose to take more courses in math and fewer in English). We speculate that the former process (participation facilitating learning) is more likely in the Sierra Club, in part because our analyses have controlled for the number of formal trainings that a leader has engaged in and in part because the research literature suggests such a learning process,[67] but the possibility for both causal processes is present. While our speculations on causal direction inform some of our subsequent discussion, we must withhold final judgment until more research is done on the topic.

With that in mind, what might these patterns tell us? First, leaders are more likely to report improving all three types of skills as the proportion of time they devote to mobilizing increases. The relationship is relatively large in all three contexts (and conventionally statistically significant in two of three). If a "participation facilitates learning" process is at work here, then it would seem that activities that get leaders reaching out in acts of recruitment and engagement are more likely to teach skills ranging from thinking creatively (a component of "managing self") to delegating responsibility ("managing others") to working effectively with public officials ("managing public work"). Outreach also shows a positive relationship to improved skills, but in a more limited way. Again if "participation facilitates learning," investing time in activities like lobbying decision makers and communicating with the public appears to teach leadership lessons in "managing public work," the skills used in organizing meetings or speaking in public. Of course, as we saw in Figure 6.2, outreach and mobilizing do not appear to dominate the average Sierra Club leader's schedule. The time devoted to these activities may be producing learning, but these leaders are devoting smaller proportions of their time to these activities than to others.

What about administrative activities and meetings? The data often show no relationships, and at times even show negative relationships, between increasing meeting and administrative time investment and reported skill improvement. From the perspective of organization scholars, this is perhaps unsurprising.[68] While activities like newsletter production and regular e-mail correspondence may be critical for keeping a complex organization up and running and able to support sustained collective action, something about the nature of such activities (perhaps in general, perhaps just as they are practiced in the Sierra Club) may not be providing many opportunities for learning how to better listen to others, delegating responsibility, or managing internal conflicts. From the civic association perspective, however, these patterns—especially the negative relationship between meetings and reported skill improvement—is more surprising. For a self-governing civic association, meetings may be the primary location for learning experiences to take place. These are the occasions when leaders must work together to do things like think creatively, hold each other accountable, and plan campaigns. How is it that Sierra Club meetings do not seem to produce any of these types of learning in leaders (and may even reduce the likelihood of learning them)?

Perhaps this result is due to the nature of the meetings themselves as they are currently practiced in the Sierra Club (and likely in many other civic associations). In principle, meetings in these groups could be critical sites of learning in these voluntary "schools of democracy." While we do not have data on how meetings are run, we can speculate (given our other findings here) that the meetings in the Sierra Club currently do not offer opportunities to practice "managing others" skills such as "challenging other people to be effective" or "delegating responsibility." Instead, meetings may be sites where individual leaders offer committee reports and describe ongoing activities without evaluating those activities or deliberating about future directions for the organization. Some executive committees may even have meetings that are burdened by ongoing conflicts among leaders that undermine learning opportunities. In addition, the content of what is discussed (not only how it is discussed) could also matter. Meetings might be more civically rewarding when leaders collectively discuss organizational goals and deliberate on how to mobilize people and resources to achieve the goal. Perhaps the Sierra Club's current meetings do not regularly address such topics. If this is the case, these groups are missing a significant opportunity to improve the skills of their leaders. Speculation aside, meetings can take many different forms, and our results show that the particular type of meetings held in these Sierra Club groups and chapters are not positively related to skill improvement in leaders.[69]

Given these findings, we argue that looking deeper into what is really going on in particular meetings and administrative activities in the Sierra Club, and other groups like it, is a crucial task for researchers (and civic organizers) going forward. As we saw in Figure 6.2, a large proportion of Sierra Club leaders' time is devoted to these activities, while few civic learning returns are being realized on that time investment. Generating skill improvement in meetings and administrative contexts could be an important supplement to the skill development already taking place in mobilizing and outreach activities.

Clearly a relationship exists between time spent on Sierra Club leadership activities and skill improvement. The more time people spend working with the Club, the more they report skill improvement in multiple dimensions. But the learning is not uniform across different types of skills and activities. In general, the type of learning is consistent with the type of skills leaders need for the activities they do. Leaders who spend more time on administrative tasks are most likely to report improving on "managing self" skills, while leaders who spend more time on mobilizing others for participation are more likely to report improvement on "managing others." Meetings, as they are practiced within the Sierra Club, present a conundrum because leaders who spend more time in meetings report less skill improvement overall. Teasing out the precise causal relationships among these findings is tricky, but they do provide a foundation for thinking about the way that civic organizations like the Sierra Club can fulfill their Tocquevillean promise as "schools of democracy."

Conclusion

In the days following Michael McGinn's inauguration as mayor of Seattle, he quickly began falling under the scrutiny of a critical media and a restless public. His first year in office produced mixed results. He struggled in early interactions with the city council and the governor, facing accusations of using an overly gruff, uncompromising style. As the year progressed, however, he worked more smoothly with a variety of people and institutions around the city, moving forward several new initiatives and shifting the debate on some highly contentious issues.[70] It remains to be seen how he will fare over the remainder of his term, but there are signs that he is learning the ropes and adjusting his approaches to the tasks at hand. We might have reason to believe that he will continue to adapt and find himself successful in the long run.

Why? If his campaign efforts and his first-year adjustments are any indication, it would appear that McGinn was, during his years at the helm of the Sierra Club's Cascade Chapter, quite likely one of those leaders who learned substantive lessons about managing himself, managing others, and managing public work. We have seen so far that Sierra Club leaders often commit substantial time to their leadership activities, divided across a variety of tasks, some geared more toward the creation and sustenance of collective action, others toward organizing and influence seeking. Many leaders are developing skills, although improvement is more likely to come in some skill dimensions than in others. Devoting more time overall is related to skill improvement in general, but a closer look shows that leaders who focus a greater share of their attention on mobilizing and outreach report the best results.

Given these patterns, what *should* civic association leaders be doing? A cursory answer might be "stop meeting and start doing"—a recommendation to simply refocus leaders' time commitments away from meetings and administrative activities and toward mobilization and outreach. Such an answer would miss much of the essence of civic associations. The Sierra Club is a complex formal organization, and a substantial effort is required to direct that organization effectively in the generation and sustenance of collective action. As such, it is unlikely that a major reallocation of time from meetings and administration to other activities is possible—or even desirable. Rather than simply refocusing leaders' time, a better approach might be to reform the activities leaders are already doing to take advantage of the potential skill development opportunities. Investing in systematic, ongoing, focused training for leaders on how to run better meetings and how to challenge their colleagues could improve skills for particular leaders and help them to create more productive learning opportunities for others.

Stated more simply, perhaps the key lesson is to "be like Mike." Michael McGinn's mayoral campaign engaged lots of volunteers. Meetings happened in the course of recruiting, training, and deploying those activists—meetings undergirded with a serious imperative to mobilize effectively. Perhaps these meetings were run better than the typical Sierra Club group or chapter executive committee meeting. Importantly, activity did not stop with the meetings. Once the initial round of volunteers was in the mix, many hands reached out to the community, found interested individuals, and transformed them into active campaign participants. In so doing, the campaign could draw on civically skilled leadership and activists to deliver clever, politically savvy public events—like sending out Mike on his bike. McGinn's civic leadership training before the campaign helped prepare him to run successfully for public office. The way he then ran his campaign may well have prepared a new generation of potential Seattle politicians and community leaders to follow his example.

In an era of declining civic engagement and declining prevalence of the kinds of associations that provide opportunities for developing civic skills, organizations like the Sierra Club provide a critical civic resource for the nation. They are partially succeeding in the task of helping citizens and potential community leaders develop civic skills, but the data also show that at the moment they may not be doing enough. In addition, they may be part of a dying breed of organizations that provide any opportunity for civic learning. If organizations like the Sierra Club fail to live up to their civic-training potential, or if they end up closing their doors altogether, where will the next Michael McGinn be trained? And where does a society in need of civically skilled leaders find its next set of rising stars?

Notes

1. The first two authors contributed equally to this chapter and are listed alphabetically. The second two authors were co-principal investigators on the research project.
2. William Yardley, "Surprising Victory in Seattle Mayor's Race," *New York Times*, November 9, 2009.
3. Emily Heffter, "What the Different Styles of Seattle Mayoral Candidates Might Tell Voters," *Seattle Times*, September 24, 2009.
4. Christopher Frizzelle, "The Case for Mike McGinn: Part 4," *The Stranger*, October 27, 2009.
5. Jonathan Martin, "For McGinn, Activism Began as Law-Office Daydreaming," *Seattle Times*, October 6, 2009.
6. Theda Skocpol, *Diminished Democracy: From Membership to Management in American Civic Life*, The Julian J. Rothbaum Distinguished Lecture Series 8 (Norman: University of Oklahoma Press, 2003). See especially Figures 5.8 and 5.9.
7. Lester Salamon, "Leadership and Modernization: The Emerging Black Political Elite in the American South," *Journal of Politics* 35, no. 3 (1973): 613–46; Kenneth T. Andrews, *Freedom Is a Constant Struggle: The Mississippi Civil Rights Movement and Its Legacy* (Chicago: University of Chicago Press, 2004).
8. Elisabeth S. Clemens, *The People's Lobby: Organizational Innovation and the Rise of Interest Group Politics in the United States, 1890–1925* (Chicago: University of Chicago Press, 1997); C. M. Mueller, "Collective Consciousness, Identity Transformation, and the Rise of Women in Public Office in the United States," in *The Women's Movements of*

the United States and Western Europe, ed. Mary Fainsod Katzenstein (Philadelphia: Temple University Press, 1987).

9. Kenneth T. Andrews, Marshall Ganz, Matthew Baggetta, Hahrie Han, and Chae-yoon Lim, "Leadership, Membership, and Voice: Civic Associations That Work," *American Journal of Sociology* 115, no. 4 (2010): 1192, doi:10.1086/649060.

10. Sidney Verba, Kay Lehman Schlozman, and Henry E. Brady, *Voice and Equality: Civic Voluntarism in American Politics* (Cambridge, MA: Harvard University Press, 1995); Sidney Verba, Kay Lehman Schlotzman, Henry Brady, and Norman H. Nie, "Citizen Activity: Who Participates? What Do They Say?" *American Political Science Review* 87, no. 2 (1993): 303–18.

11. Steven J. Rosenstone and John Mark Hansen, *Mobilization, Participation, and Democracy in America,* Longman Classics in Political Science (New York: Longman, 2003); Henry E. Brady, Sidney Verba, and Kay Lehman Schlozman, "Beyond SES: A Resource Model of Political Participation," *American Political Science Review* 89, no. 2 (1995): 271–94.

12. Skocpol, *Diminished Democracy;* John McCarthy, "Persistence and Change among Nationally Federated Social Movements," in *Social Movements and Organization Theory,* ed. Gerald F. Davis, Doug McAdam, W. Richard Scott, and Mayer N. Zald (New York: Cambridge University Press, 2005).

13. Dana Fisher, *Activism, Inc.* (Stanford, CA: Stanford University Press, 2006); Edward T. Walker, "Privatizing Participation: Civic Change and the Organizational Dynamics of Grassroots Lobbying Firms," *American Sociological Review* 74, no. 1 (2009): 83–105.

14. Marshall Ganz, "Leading Change: Leadership, Organization, and Social Movements," in *Handbook of Leadership Theory and Practice,* eds. Nitin Nohria and Rakesh Khurana (Cambridge, MA: Harvard Business School Press, 2010).

15. Andrews, Ganz, Baggetta, Han, and Lim, "Leadership, Membership, and Voice," 1192.

16. McCarthy, "Persistence and Change among Nationally Federated Social Movements"; Theda Skocpol, Marshall Ganz, and Ziad Munson, "A Nation of Organizers: The Institutional Origins of Civic Voluntarism in the United States," *American Political Science Review* 94, no. 3 (2000): 527–46.

17. Theda Skocpol, Ariane Liazos, and Marshall Ganz, *What a Mighty Power We Can Be: African American Fraternal Groups and the Struggle for Racial Equality* (Princeton, NJ: Princeton University Press, 2006); Skocpol, *Diminished Democracy;* Skocpol, Ganz, and Munson, "A Nation of Organizers."

18. For a helpful review of theories regarding associations, see Archon Fung, "Associations and Democracy: Between Theories, Hopes, and Realities," *Annual Review of Sociology* 29, no. 1 (2003): 515–39.

19. Ganz, "Leading Change," 510.

20. Theda Skocpol, "Advocates without Members: The Recent Transformation of American Civic Life," in *Civic Engagement in American Democracy,* ed. Theda Skocpol and Morris P. Fiorina (Washington, DC: Brookings Institution Press, 1999); Robert D. Putnam, *Bowling Alone: The Collapse and Revival of American Community* (New York: Simon & Schuster, 2000); Steven E. Schier, *By Invitation Only: The Rise of Exclusive Politics in the United States* (Pittsburgh: University of Pittsburgh Press, 2000); Matthew A. Crenson and Benjamin Ginsburg, *Downsizing Democracy: How America Sidelined Its Citizens and Privatized Its Public* (Baltimore: The Johns Hopkins University

Press, 2002); Jeffrey M. Berry, *The New Liberalism: The Rising Power of Citizen Groups* (Washington, DC: Brookings Institution Press, 1999); Jeffrey M. Berry, *Lobbying for the People* (Princeton, NJ: Princeton University Press, 1977).

21. Kelly Patterson and Matthew Singer, "The National Rifle Association in the Face of the Clinton Challenge," in *Interest Group Politics*, 6th ed., ed. Allan J. Cigler and Burdett A. Loomis (Washington, DC: CQ Press, 2002).

22. Lawrence Rothenberg, *Linking Citizens to Government: Interest Group Politics at Common Cause* (New York: Cambridge University Press, 1992).

23. Maryann Barakso, *Governing Now: Grassroots Activism in the National Organization for Women* (Ithaca, NY: Cornell University Press, 2004).

24. Michael P. Cohen, *The History of the Sierra Club, 1892–1970* (San Francisco: Sierra Club Books, 1988); Ronald Shaiko, *Voices and Echoes for the Environment: Public Interest Representation in the 1990s and Beyond* (New York: Columbia University Press, 1999); Philip Mundo, "The Sierra Club," in *Interest Groups*, ed. Philip Mundo (Chicago: Nelson-Hall, 1992).

25. McCarthy, "Persistence and Change among Nationally Federated Social Movements"; Kenneth T. Andrews and Bob Edwards, "The Organizational Structure of Local Environmentalism," *Mobilization* 10, no. 2 (2005): 213–34. Also, while we do not address them here, a variety of other types of associations may share some of the characteristics of the national, federated associations we discuss and therefore may also offer similar civic benefits. See David Horton Smith, *Grassroots Associations* (Thousand Oaks, CA: Sage, 2000).

26. John D. McCarthy and Mark Wolfson, "Resource Mobilization by Local Social Movement Organizations: Agency, Strategy, and Organization in the Movement against Drinking and Driving," *American Sociological Review* 61, no. 6 (1996): 1070–88.

27. Alexis de Tocqueville, *Democracy in America*, ed. J. P. Mayer, trans. George Lawrence (New York: Harper Perennial, 1969): 517.

28. de Tocqueville, *Democracy in America*, 517. Previous scholarship suggests that participants learn civic values as well as skills. By working side by side with fellow citizens for a common purpose, activists form bonds of trust that may cross the boundaries of existing social cleavages; Putnam calls this process "bridging social capital," and Tocqueville referred to it as "self interest properly understood." This dimension of civic learning has stimulated a great deal of recent research and debate. While certainly interesting, these debates fall beyond the scope of this chapter. See, for example, Putnam, *Bowling Alone;* Robert D. Putnam, *Making Democracy Work: Civic Traditions in Modern Italy* (Princeton, NJ: Princeton University Press, 1993); Eric M. Uslaner and Paul Dekker, "The 'Social' in Social Capital," in *Social Capital and Participation in Everyday Life*, ed. Paul Dekker and Eric M. Uslaner (New York: Routledge, 2001); Bob Edwards and Michael W. Foley, "Civil Society and Social Capital beyond Putnam," *American Behavioral Scientist* 42, no. 1 (1998): 124–39; Elizabeth Theiss-Morse and John R. Hibbing, "Citizenship and Civic Engagement," *Annual Review of Political Science* 8, no. 1 (2005): 227–49.

29. Verba, Schlozman, and Brady, *Voice and Equality;* Brady, Verba, and Schlozman, "Beyond SES"; Nancy Burns, Kay Lehman Schlozman, and Sidney Verba, *The Private Roots of Public Action: Gender, Equality, and Political Participation* (Cambridge, MA: Harvard University Press, 2001).

30. Paul A. Djupe and Christopher P. Gilbert, "The Resourceful Believer: Generating Civic Skills in Church," *The Journal of Politics* 68, no. 1 (2006): 116–26; Matthew

Baggetta, "Civic Opportunities in Associations: Interpersonal Interaction, Governance Experience, and Institutional Relationships," *Social Forces* 88, no. 1 (2009): 175–99.

31. Christopher J. Bosso, *Environment, Inc.: From Grassroots to Beltway* (Lawrence: University of Kansas Press, 2005); Edwin Amenta, Neal Caren, Sheera Joy Olasky, and James E. Stobaugh, "All the Movements Fit to Print: Who, What, Where, When, and Why SMO Families Appeared in the New York Times in the Twentieth Century," *American Sociological Review* 74, no. 4 (2009): 636–56.

32. Stephen Fox, *The American Conservation Movement: John Muir and His Legacy* (Madison: University of Wisconsin Press, 1981).

33. Cohen, *The History of the Sierra Club, 1892–1970.*

34. http://www.SierraClub.org/.

35. Skocpol, Ganz, and Munson, "A Nation of Organizers"; Skocpol, *Diminished Democracy;* Berry, *The New Liberalism;* Jack L. Walker, *Mobilizing Interest Groups in America: Patrons, Professions, and Social Movements* (Ann Arbor: University of Michigan Press, 1991).

36. Rothenberg, *Linking Citizens to Government;* Andrew S. McFarland, *Common Cause: Lobbying in the Public Interest* (Chatham, NJ: Chatham House, 1984); Skocpol, *Diminished Democracy;* Bosso, *Environment, Inc.;* Berry, *The New Liberalism;* Walker, *Mobilizing Interest Groups in America;* Kay Lehman Schlozman and John T. Tierney, *Organized Interests and American Democracy* (New York: Harper and Row, 1986).

37. Staff numbers are tallied from Sierra Club employment records as of December 31, 2003.

38. Shaiko, *Voices and Echoes for the Environment.*

39. See Andrews, Ganz, Baggetta, Han, and Lim, "Leadership, Membership and Voice," for more details on the data collection.

40. Based on authors' analysis of September 2008 *U.S. Current Population Survey Volunteer Supplement.*

41. Explaining why these leaders commit the hours they do is another interesting issue beyond the scope of this paper. See Matthew Baggetta, Hahrie Han, and Kenneth T. Andrews, "Explaining Volunteer Time Commitment: Civic Resources, Personal Motivations, and Organizational Characteristics," in *American Sociological Association Annual Meeting* (San Francisco, CA: 2008); Rothenberg, *Linking Citizens to Government.*

42. The categories were constructed in consultation with experienced Sierra Club leaders and staff members who had substantial insight into the range of possible activities that leaders might pursue. The survey included fifteen time use categories: (1) informal discussions with other leaders, (2) responding to questions from members/community, (3) administrative/logistical work (including keeping up with communications, especially e-mail), (4) participating in group or chapter activities/events, (5) community outreach (including tabling, public speaking, etc.), (6) communicating with decision makers (including lobbying, testifying, etc.), (7) mobilizing members to become activists, (8) mobilizing attendance for events/meetings, (9) training, (10) participating in meetings, (11) participating in celebrations, (12) working on the newsletter and/or Web site, (13) fundraising, (14) staff oversight (chapters only), (15) other. We have combined several of these categories for theoretical relevance in analysis and to clarify presentation. In Figure 6.2, "Administrative activities" includes both (3) and (12); "Group activities/events/celebrations" includes (4) and (11); "Community outreach" includes (2), (5), and (6); and "Mobilizing activists & attendance" includes (7) and (8). "Staff oversight" (14) is

not displayed in the figure, as it only applies to the small subset of chapters (and no groups) that have staff and represents only a tiny fraction of those chapter leaders' time commitment. Respondents may not have considered some of these categories to be mutually exclusive. For example, one might work to mobilize members to participate in a political rally while at an outings event. Since there could be some overlap between the activity categories, the sum of the hours reported across categories might exceed an estimate of the total hours spent per month. We separately asked respondents for an overall estimate of their time commitment. The correlation between overall estimates and the sum of estimates in categories is quite high (Pearson's $r = .9$), suggesting that the detailed categorization is an accurate reflection of largely exclusive time-usage categories. The measures can give us a reasonable approximation of how the work of leaders in the Sierra Club is structured.

43. Michael T. Hannan and John Freeman, "Structural Inertia and Organizational Change," *American Sociological Review* 49, no. 2 (1984): 149–64.

44. Mayer N. Zald and John D. McCarthy, *Social Movements in an Organizational Society* (New Brunswick, NJ: Transaction, 1987).

45. Pamela Oliver and Daniel J. Myers, "How Events Enter the Public Sphere: Conflict, Location, and Sponsorship in Local Newspaper Coverage of Public Events," *American Journal of Sociology* 105, no. 1 (1999): 38–87.

46. Robert J. Sampson, Doug McAdam, Heather MacIndoe, and Simón Weffer-Elizondo, "Civil Society Reconsidered: The Durable Nature and Community Structure of Collective Civic Action," *American Journal of Sociology* 111, no. 3 (2005): 673–714, doi:10.1086/497351.

47. Pamela Oliver and Gerald Marwell, "Mobilizing Technologies for Collective Action," in *Frontiers in Social Movement Theory*, ed. Aldon D. Morris and Carol McClurg Mueller (New Haven, CT: Yale University Press, 1992).

48. Ganz, "Leading Change."

49. Of course, efforts designed to mobilize participation may also be discussed in meetings or included in newsletters, meaning some mobilizing time is captured in those other categories.

50. Bert Klandermans and Dirk Oegema, "Potentials, Networks, Motivations, and Barriers: Steps Towards Participation in Social Movements," *American Sociological Review* 52, no. 4 (1987): 519–31; Dirk Oegema and Bert Klandermans, "Why Social Movement Sympathizers Don't Participate: Erosion and Nonconversion of Support," *American Sociological Review* 59, no. 5 (1994): 703–22; Marshall Ganz, *Why David Sometimes Wins: Leadership, Organization, and Strategy in the California Farm Worker Movement* (New York: Oxford University Press, 2009).

51. Comparative data on other organizations will be especially important to gather in the future to more thoroughly assess this point. It is possible that Sierra Club leaders' limited relative investment of time in mobilizing and outreach is not typical of civic associations in general. It may, instead, be a particular challenge for the Sierra Club, at least in 2003 when we conducted our study.

52. Andrews, Ganz, Baggetta, Han, and Lim, "Leadership, Membership, and Voice."

53. Arthur M. Schlesinger, "Biography of a Nation of Joiners," *The American Historical Review* 50, no. 1 (1944): 1–25.

54. It should be noted that these measures are reports by individuals of their perceptions of self-improvement over time. As of this time, no standard measures exist for externally verifying these kinds of civic skill development perceptions—a clear area for additional research and measurement technique development. The highly

self-reflective nature of the questionnaires, the serious time and care with which Sierra Club leaders filled them out, and the degree of meaningful variation across leaders observable within each measure give us greater confidence that the indicators are capturing meaningful patterns of civic learning.

55. For a broader theoretical discussion of leadership capacities in social movements and civic associations see Ganz, "Leading Change," and Aldon D. Morris and Suzanne Staggenborg, "Leadership in Social Movements," in *The Blackwell Companion to Social Movements*, ed. David A. Snow, Sarah A. Soule, and Hanspeter Kriesi (Malden, MA: Blackwell, 2004).

56. For an introduction to factor analysis, see Jae-On Kim and Charles Mueller, *Factor Analysis: Statistical Methods and Practical Issues*, Quantitative Applications in the Social Sciences 14 (Newbury Park, CA: Sage, 1978).

57. Our interpretations of the factors, and the names we assigned to each, are most heavily influenced by those items that are most strongly related to the factor.

58. We expect that, were we to include additional specific skill items in a larger bank of questions and conduct a similar analysis in other civic associations, similar underlying factors would emerge repeatedly.

59. There are two possible explanations for this low level of reported "managing others" skill development through Sierra Club experience. First is that leaders are coming into the Sierra Club with substantial collective action skills (learned elsewhere) and therefore have little room left to improve. However, patterns of associational effectiveness in the Sierra Club (see Andrews, Ganz, Baggetta, Han, and Lim, "Leadership, Membership, and Voice") and patterns identified below regarding the kinds of leadership activities in the organization related to certain skill improvements suggest that this is not the case. Rather, the second possibility—that Sierra Club leaders start with low levels of "managing others" skills and, after participating, report relatively little improvement on this dimension, is the more likely scenario.

60. The pattern of variation within this dimension is interesting. It is possible that skills that do not involve conflict (e.g., listening, supporting others, running meetings) are more likely to be improved than skills that require challenging others (e.g., holding people accountable). While all of these skills relate to "managing others," future research should more closely investigate this potentially important distinction.

61. The following figures and related discussion address only the key outcomes of interest. Complete regression results are available from the authors upon request.

62. The regression analyses behind Figures 6.3 through 6.6 include controls for respondent age, gender, level of formal education, tenure as an active member in the Sierra Club, number of leadership positions held, number of training programs in which the leader has participated, whether the respondent is a group or chapter leader, the number of members in the group or chapter (logged), and the size of the executive committee for the entity (logged). Figures 6.4 through 6.6 also include a control for the number of hours (logged) spent on Sierra Club activity (the variable examined in Figure 6.3).

63. In this section we focus on the relationship between skill improvement and administrative activities, meetings, outreach, and mobilizing. Preliminary analyses (not shown) suggest that the other time use categories displayed in Figure 6.2 show little consistent relationship to skill improvement.

64. Uncertainty in the data leads to large standard errors for these three coefficients. They fail to reach conventional levels of statistical significance.

65. The relationship between outreach and collective action is small and positive, but it does not reach conventional levels of statistical significance.

66. To ensure that these relationships are not entirely driven by similar items included on both sides of the equation (i.e., "mobilizing members to become active" as a type of activity and "asking people to volunteer" as a part of "managing others"), we dropped those items and reran the regression models. The results were very similar to the ones reported in this chapter.

67. Verba, Schlozman, and Brady, *Voice and Equality;* Doug McAdam, *Freedom Summer* (New York: Oxford University Press, 1988); James Max Fendrich, *Ideal Citizens: The Legacy of the Civil Rights Movement* (Albany: SUNY Press, 1993); Matthew Baggetta, "Civic Development in Apolitical Associations" (doctoral dissertation, Harvard University, 2009).

68. Hannan and Freeman, "Structural Inertia and Organizational Change."

69. Meetings also have other potential outcomes for individuals. For example, while Sierra Club meetings may not currently be producing skill improvement, perhaps they are increasing leaders' sense of collective identity and commitment to the organization and the causes the organization supports. See Eric L. Hirsch, "Sacrifice for the Cause: Group Processes, Recruitment, and Commitment in a Student Social Movement," *American Sociological Review* 55, no. 2 (1990): 243–54; James M. Jasper, *The Art of Moral Protest* (Chicago: The University of Chicago Press, 1997); Francesca Polletta and James M. Jasper, "Collective Identity and Social Movements," *Annual Review of Sociology* 27, no. 1 (2001): 283–305.

70. Chris Grygiel, "Top Political Stories of 2010," *Seattle Post-Intelligencer Blogs,* December 29, 2010; Joni Balter, "Seattle Mayor Mike McGinn's First Year: A Study in the Politics of Chaos," *The Seattle Times,* December 29, 2010.

II. GROUPS AND THE ELECTORAL PROCESS

7

Interest Group Money in the
2008 Federal Election

Allan J. Cigler

The past four decades have witnessed a spectacular increase in the number and types of organized interests seeking to influence campaigns and in the breadth and intensity of their involvement.[1] This escalation of activity has been accompanied by a huge increase in the financial resources many groups devote to electoral purposes. Some of this money is directly given to candidates and parties through political action committees (PACs); these contributions are limited and open to public scrutiny—so-called "hard money." But in recent elections, an ever-growing portion of group funds is spent independently of parties and/or candidates; is unlimited in terms of amount; and is collected and spent in an often secretive, undisclosed manner—so-called "soft money." The magnitude of spending by special interests to influence elections has been and remains especially controversial, allegedly contributing to widespread political cynicism.

The concern over interest group money in federal elections is relatively recent.[2] Campaigning for office in the early years of the republic, including running for president, was largely an individual endeavor; the cost was modest, and funds typically came from family and friends. By the mid-1820s, in an era characterized by the extension of mass enfranchisement and the growth of party organizations, the cost of running for office increased, with patronage employees, party workers, and wealthy individuals bearing the brunt of campaign expenditures. After the Civil War, with the nation in the midst of an industrial revolution, groups increasingly turned to Washington, D.C., with their policy concerns and lobbying activities, but the electoral side of politics, including campaign funding, remained in the hands of parties and a number of wealthy industrialists. Groups at the time, such as those representing agriculture interests and a fledgling labor movement, found the parties too closed and entrenched for meaningful change. Thus, they largely eschewed electoral involvement, including making financial contributions to the major parties and their candidates. On a few occasions they created and financed their own short-lived, third parties to contest elections.

The early twentieth century saw more groups become involved in campaigns, but efforts were typically directed at mobilizing their own members rather than contributing funds to candidates and/or working closely with parties during campaigns. Group money strategies started to change in the 1930s and 1940s as first organized labor, followed by a number of business organizations, began to contribute funds regularly to candidates and to spend money on electioneering beyond their immediate memberships. The cost of politics continued to spiral upward in the 1950s and 1960s as campaigns increasingly relied upon radio and television to get their messages across.

By the 1970s a variety of factors were converging to make it possible for interest groups to play a significant role in campaigns, most notably at the expense of political parties. Early in the decade, for example, party reform efforts "opened up" the nomination process, particularly in the Democratic Party, enabling groups to influence the selection of candidates directly through either party primaries or caucuses, a process previously controlled by party officials.[3] The influence of the mass media, especially television, as well as the existence of increasingly educated and sophisticated voters, was creating a context hostile to partisanship. Electoral contests had grown to be largely candidate rather than party centered, and campaigning was becoming the domain of technical specialists—campaign consultants, pollsters, direct mail practitioners, and communications/advertising specialists. Using all these resources necessitated raising a lot of money. But it can be argued that an elaborate set of new campaign finance laws, designed to decrease the role wealthy individuals, so-called "fat cats," was the most important factor leading to an expanded role for group financial involvement in elections.

Group Financial Impact on Campaigns: The Framework and the Loopholes

The Federal Election Campaign Act (FECA) of 1971 and its 1974 amendments,[4] coupled with modifications found in the Bipartisan Campaign Reform Act (BCRA) of 2002,[5] provide the basic guidelines for organized interest involvement in campaigns in 2008. The early 1970s provided a context ripe for comprehensive campaign finance reform. The ballooning cost of campaigning not only drew the attention of the media and reformist elements like Common Cause and Ralph Nader–sponsored public interest groups, but it also had become a worry for many members of Congress. The latter were concerned with both the mounting burden of raising funds and the potential threat of wealthy challengers. In the aftermath of the Watergate scandal and the unseemly amounts of money spent by some of President Nixon's supporters in the 1972 election, FECA was a comprehensive law that, among other provisions, put a ceiling on how much candidates could spend in campaigns and a cap on individual and group contributions.

A substantial portion of FECA was struck down by the Supreme Court in *Buckley v. Valeo* (1976) for violating the First Amendment; primarily problematic were those provisions that capped both contributor giving and candidate spending. The Court, concerned about political expression, linked money with speech, noting that "virtually every means of communicating ideas in today's mass society requires the expenditure of money."[6] What remained of FECA, however, proved to be a boon for the expansion of group money in campaign politics. The law weakened the role of political parties in campaigns by limiting the amount they could contribute to or spend in coordination with their preferred candidates' campaigns. But more important, the law spelled out clearly how a group could legally participate financially in elections and had the effect of implicitly encouraging group formation for electoral purposes.

FECA's primary device to control the campaign excesses of organized interests became requiring such interests to create and register a PAC with the Federal Election Commission (FEC).[7] Two types of PACs are possible: (1) a separate, segregated organizational unit linked to a corporation, a union, or an association (called a connected PAC) or (2) a group of like-minded individuals who simply register with the FEC with the express purpose of influencing elections (an independent PAC). Connected PACs have some advantages. While corporations and unions cannot use their funds to fund a PAC, administrative expenses can come from the company or union treasury. Administrative costs for running an independent PAC must come from funds raised for that purpose.

PACs may raise unlimited sums of money for electioneering purposes, but they face constraints on their direct contributions to candidates and parties. PAC donors must be disclosed, and contributions to candidates must be reported to the FEC. Multicandidate PACs, those supporting at least five candidates, have their contributions limited to a maximum of $5,000 in a primary, $5,000 in a general election, and $5,000 in the case of a runoff election. No more than $5,000 may be contributed to candidates seeking party presidential nominations, and no more than another $5,000 may be contributed in the presidential general election (if the candidate does not accept public funding). Registered multicandidate PACs may contribute $15,000 per year to each national party political committee.

The Court ruled in *Buckley v. Valeo* that limitations on direct donations by PACs to candidates is not an infringement on free speech, since the donor loses control of a contribution once it is accepted by a candidate or party committee. Besides direct contributions, PACs can also increase their leverage by using their hard money to engage in unlimited "independent spending" in support of or against a candidate, as long as it is not coordinated in any way with the preferred candidate or his or her opponent. Independent spending data are disclosed to the FEC.

The independent-spending provision provided an opening for groups intent on using large amounts of money to influence elections.[8] By the late 1970s and early 1980s, several PACs became notorious for spending large sums on independent advertising against a number of senators, some of whom were defeated in close votes. In 1982 the National Conservative Political Action Committee spent more than $3 million against six liberal senators. The negative tone of such efforts prompted strident criticism from the media and even from other candidates who worried that a confused electorate might blame them for the negative ads.

Other groups learned to leverage their money beyond the $5,000 PAC contribution limits. One such group was EMILY's List, an independent PAC that solicited from its membership individual contributions made out to pro-choice women candidates for Congress who had been endorsed by the group. Using a technique known as "bundling," the group collected the individual checks made out to the endorsed candidate and presented them as a "bundle" to the candidate. In 1986, for example, the group raised more than $350,000 from its members for two women running for the U.S. Senate.[9]

Another way groups (as well as individuals) leveraged their financial influence after the adoption of FECA was through the use of "soft-money" contributions to the national parties. By the late 1970s, PACs, especially the independent, more ideological PACs, were beginning to be viewed as a serious threat to political parties. They were perceived as especially threatening to state and local parties, which had traditionally been responsible for mobilizing the electorate. Various FEC rulings and the 1979 amendments to FECA were intended to encourage national parties to solicit funds for "party-building" purposes at the state and local level in order to strengthen such volunteer activities as get-out-the-vote drives. The opening created a means for organizations such as corporations and unions, prohibited from making direct hard-money contributions in federal elections, to contribute from their treasuries unlimited amounts to party soft-money accounts. The contributions, often over $1 million, were aggressively sought by the two major parties and represented the fastest growing source of organized interest money in elections.[10]

Party soft money came to be used far differently than originally intended, including for uses typically reserved for hard money, such as campaign ads. Party soft-money contributions did not need to be disclosed until 1992. In 2002 Congress passed another reform law, the Bipartisan Campaign Reform Act, which banned soft-money contributions to the national parties.

But the most formidable barrier to controlling interest group money in elections has been the difficulty of distinguishing "issue advocacy" from "express advocacy." In a footnote in the *Buckley* decision, the Court, worried about the suppression of free expression, spelled out what has come to be known as its "express advocacy" guidelines: any legal limitations on spending to influence elections would apply only to communication expressly advocating the election or defeat of a candidate. Such communication could be identified if it used wording such as "vote for," "elect," "support," "cast your ballot for," "Smith for Congress," "vote against," and "reject."[11] In practical terms, these so-called "magic words" came to mean that any federal election communication with voters that does not use these or similar words is beyond the scope of government regulation; disclosure of donors or amounts expended is not required either. Advertisers could claim that ads without any of the magic words were speech-protected "issue ads."

Not until the 1990s did groups begin to electioneer extensively with issue ads paid for with soft money.[12] But by 2000, with so much of the money spent by groups outside of FEC jurisdiction, a leading campaign finance scholar claimed that the system "bore a greater resemblance to campaign finance prior to the passage of FECA than to the patterns that were supposed to occur after it."[13]

Congress passed BCRA in 2002, a law upheld by the Supreme Court in a close 5–4 decision, in an effort to control issue advertising (party soft money was used for it as well). An important provision in the law was that soft money paid for issue ads was now considerd to be a form of "electioneering communication" and could not be used within thirty days before a primary or sixty days prior to the general election. Outside of this window, issue ads could still be used without limitation by groups as long as they did not participate in any hard-money activities that would come under the aegis of the FEC.

The Contextual Dynamics of the 2008 Election

The role played by organized interests in campaigns is in constant flux, depending upon the competitive party balance and the issue context at the time. The 2008 election was no exception. For the first time in half a century, no incumbent vice presidential or presidential candidate was in the contest. In both parties, the nomination was genuinely open: interest group support was eagerly sought by all candidates very early in the process. While conventional wisdom suggested that Republicans had little chance to recapture control of either house of Congress, the primary target of both parties and their group allies was the U.S. Senate. Republican allies, such as the U.S. Chamber of Commerce and other business groups, believed it was crucial that Democrats be prevented from obtaining sixty seats, the number needed to invoke cloture or to stop debate on legislation and bring it to a vote. Democratic-allied groups, such as labor unions, believed that if Democrats continued to hold both houses, added a few senators to get to the magic number of sixty in that chamber, and won the presidency, policies could be adopted even in the face of united Republican opposition.

The issue context in 2008 was also distinctly different than that of the previous two decades, during which cultural/moral issues played a significant role in framing the campaign debate. Economic concerns dominated the 2008 campaign agenda, especially the cost and provision of health care and the escalation of energy costs, as gasoline prices careened to over $4 per gallon during the peak summer driving season. The Iraq War was in its sixth year with no end in sight, and the costs associated with it appeared to be escalating out of control. All signs suggested it was going to be a Democratic year; President Bush was blamed for much of the nation's economic woes and the mood of the country was "distinctly sour."[14] The climate of opinion grew even worse for Republicans after their nominating convention in mid-September, when the subprime mortgage crisis hit Wall Street. This was accompanied by a huge decline in stock prices and a near collapse of the banking system, and consumer confidence dropped to its lowest point on record.[15]

Not surprisingly, with the economy being the dominant issue, labor and business groups were the most active organized interests during the campaign. One of the most prominent divisive issues was "card check." Organized labor's highest priority was to make it easy to unionize by having workers opt for union representation by simply signing a card.[16] If a majority of workers signed the card, a business would have to recognize the union within 120 days or face binding arbitration. Business interests viewed card check as a threat. Groups like the U.S. Chamber of Commerce argued that it would not give businesses time to make their case against unionization and, absent a secret ballot requirement, would lead to worker intimidation by pro-union forces.

Social/cultural issues such as abortion, stem cell research, gay marriage, and gun rights, so important in a number of recent presidential year elections, played a minor role in 2008. The Christian right, a prominent Republican ally since the early 1980s, was in organizational disarray, and many of its adherents were unenthusiastic about eventual Republican nominee John McCain, who largely avoided commenting on social issues during the campaign. Overall, Democratic groups were more energized than their Republican counterparts, sensing that the climate of opinion was on their side.

Groups also had to operate in a campaign finance regulatory environment that had changed somewhat from the previous presidential election. Especially significant were changes that impacted the operation of Section 527 committees. Party soft money was banned by BCRA in 2002, and in

2004 much of the money that had been previously given to parties found its way into 527 committee coffers. Reformers and the media complained that the large sums spent in implicit partisan support of candidates violated the intent of campaign finance laws. Responding to the criticism, the FEC issued a series of guidelines meant to rein in 527s, saying that they had to abide by the same guidelines as PACs, including limits on individual contributions to the group.[17] After the election, the FEC collected more than $3 million in fines from 527s that had been active in 2004, including the Swift Boat Veterans and POWs for Truth on the political right and the League of Conservation Voters on the left, for acting as political committees by implicitly endorsing or opposing the election of a candidate, crossing the gray area between "issue advocacy" and "express advocacy." One prominent 527 in 2004, the Media Fund, agreed to pay a fine over $580,000 on the charge that it had "failed to register and file disclosure reports as a federal political committee and knowingly accepted contributions in violation of federal limits and source prohibitions."[18]

But the Supreme Court appeared to be going in another direction, viewing with suspicion efforts to limit free expression in any way. In *Wisconsin Right to Life v. Federal Election Commission* (2006), the Court ruled that certain organizations could become even more active as 527s in funding their operations. Its ruling appeared to permit organized interests to broadcast, without restriction, ads that any "reasonable person" would regard as having some policy issue content.[19]

The Court and the FEC seemed to be going in opposite directions, a situation that posed a dilemma for those using a 527 committee to leverage their funds for electioneering purposes in the 2008 campaign. Some observers felt that 527s could now operate unencumbered. Others believed the specter of FEC fines would have a chilling effect upon 527 activity, creating a substantial risk for groups that tried to negotiate the threshold between express and issue advocacy. Still others believed that even if the FEC prevailed, the fines were so small compared to overall budgets that many of the larger 527s would view them simply as a cost of doing business and nothing would change.

The Tools of Influence in 2008: Political Action Committees

From the late 1970s to the early 1990s, observers of American elections would have been hard pressed to name a feature of financing elections more odious than the role of PACs. By 2008, the attitude toward PACs had largely reversed, some reformers even arguing that more incentives for groups to form PACs should be put in place and contribution limits should actually be expanded. With so many organized interests, especially 527 committees and 501(c) organizations, falling outside the disclosure limits of the FEC and practicing issue advertising without meaningful reporting, PACs had become the vehicle of choice to limit the excessive influence of well-heeled groups.

Direct PAC Contributions in the 2007–2008 Election Cycle

PAC activity remains the way most groups attempt to influence elections, and making direct contributions to candidates continues to be the central purpose of most such organizations.[20] Figure 7.1 presents the growth in total PAC contributions since the 1979–1980 presidential year election cycle. The $412.8 million contributed in the latest election cycle represents a 32 percent increase over the previous presidential election cycle and sets a record.

PAC donations have typically reflected a pro-business bias, and such was again the case in the latest cycle. Overall, corporate PACs dominated giving, contributing $144 million, while trade associations contributed nearly $108 million. Together they represented roughly 64 percent of all direct contributions to candidates. Labor PACs, in contrast, contributed

Figure 7.1   PAC Candidate Contributions, 1979–1980 to 2007–2008

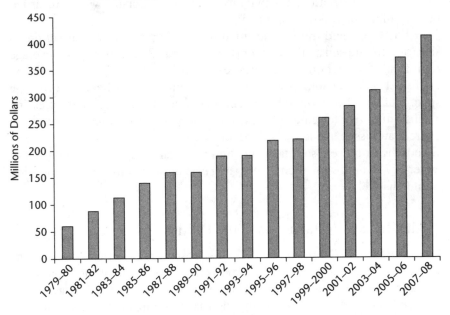

Source: Federal Election Commission, "Growth in PAC Financial Activity Slows," press release, April 24, 2009 (http://www.fec.gov/press/press2009/20090415PAC/20090424PAC.shtml).

Note: The data on which this graph is based are not adjusted for inflation.

$61 million to candidates. Nonconnected or independent PACs, typically more ideologically oriented entities, surpassed $61 million in contributions. Examples of nonconnected PACs include organizations such as EMILY's list, a liberal group founded to raise money for women Democrats running for office, and the Club for Growth, a libertarian group promoting free-enterprise, conservative candidates. Contributions from nonconnected organizations is the fastest growing category of PAC contributions, up 64 percent since the 2000 election.

The PAC system has always been known for its incumbent bias, and the generalization again held true in the most recent election cycle (see Table 7.1). But there were some different dynamics at work in 2007–08 compared to the previous presidential year cycle. In the 2008 Senate races, 72 percent of PAC money went to incumbents, while House incumbents garnered 82 percent; these percentages were similar to those of 2004. But strategic giving was evident. In 2004, majority party Republican candidates (incumbents, challengers, and open-seat candidates) held a $28 million advantage over Democrats in terms of PAC money raised; in 2008, the now-majority-party Democrats raised more than $63 million more than the Republicans. The Senate was even more revealing of group strategies. Groups, particularly Republican allies, were less enamored with protecting incumbents and more concerned with preventing Democrats from extending their majority to sixty; Republican candidates actually reversed their 2004 funding disadvantage by a small margin. Overall, Republican and Democratic Senate candidates received $387.9 million from PACs, a 34 percent increase over 2004.

Business interests were especially pragmatic in terms of partisan giving. Corporate PACs normally are access oriented and risk averse. Many altered their giving patterns in 2008 compared to the previous election, especially for House candidates in the body now controlled by Democrats. For example, while 69 percent of corporate PAC money went to Republicans in the 2003–04 cycle, only 49 percent of such money went to Republicans in the 2008 election. Labor PACs, on the other hand, behaved in a strictly partisan manner, overwhelmingly supporting Democrats at a 90 percent rate in 2004 and a 96 percent rate in 2008.

It should be pointed out, however, that direct PAC contributions to candidates have traditionally been, and were again in the 2007–08 cycle, a relatively small component of congressional fund-raising: most election funds come from individual contributions. PAC contributions were 30 percent of all the money raised by House candidates and 18 percent of all funds raised by Senate candidates. There were partisan differences. House Democrats received 33 percent of their funds from PACs, while Republicans garnered 26 percent. On the other hand, Republican Senate candidates received 26 percent of their funds from PACs, 9 percent more than Democratic Senate candidates. Although the overall percentages are not

Table 7.1 PAC Contributions to Candidates and Parties, 2000–2008 (in millions of dollars)

Item	2000			2004			2008		
	Democratic	Republican	Total	Democratic	Republican	Total	Democratic	Republican	Total
Senate candidates	18.7	33.2	51.9	28.4	35.3	63.7	33.9	45.9	79.8
Incumbents	9.5	24.0	33.5	19.1	20.2	39.3	20.3	37.5	57.7
Challengers	5.2	1.9	7.1	2.0	3.5	5.6	7.7	5.3	13.0
Open seat	4.0	7.3	11.3	7.3	11.6	18.8	5.9	3.2	9.1
House candidates	98.2	94.7	193.4	98.6	126.6	225.4	185.6	122.4	308.1
Incumbents	76.0	74.1	150.1	80.9	106.3	187.1	149.9	103.6	253.5
Challengers	12.9	7.0	19.8	8.6	7.0	15.6	24.7	11.0	35.7
Open seat	9.3	13.7	23.0	9.2	13.3	22.5	11.1	7.8	18.8
Presidential candidates	0.0	2.6	2.6	0.6	2.4	3.0	2.2	2.3	4.5
Political parties	11.7	10.3	21.9	15.8	19.3	35.0	22.8	20.5	43.3

Sources: Federal Election Commission, "Growth in PAC Financial Activity Slows," press release, April 24, 2009 (http://www.fec.gov/press/press2009/2009/2009415PAC/20090424PAC.shtml); Federal Election Commission, "Party Financial Activity Summarized for the 2008 Election Cycle," press release, May 28, 2009 (http://www.fec.gov/press/press2009/05282009Party/20090528Party.shtml).

huge, as we shall see later, much of the money was strategically targeted in competitive races, and PACs remain a central part of incumbent advantage.

The presidential campaigns are not highly dependent upon PAC funds, as Table 7.1 indicates. During the nomination season, federal matching funds are not available for PAC contributions, and candidates rely on individual contributions. And presidential candidates must forego federal funding during the general election if they accept PAC funds. In the past, this option was an unlikely choice for a candidate, but Obama did not use federal funds in 2008. Numbers do not tell the whole story, however. Many of the largest individual contributors to campaigns represent the same interests as the PACs (e.g., officers of corporations).[21] Also, PACs support presidential campaigns in ways other than direct giving, including by running independent express advocacy ads with their hard money in support of their chosen candidate and by doing grassroots canvassing or direct mailings.

The PAC universe, especially the connected PAC component, is typically stable from one election to the next and is largely composed of organized interests that have participated in electoral politics over a long period. Access to the policy process rather than ideology is the prime concern. Table 7.2 lists the top twenty PACs in terms of contributions to candidates. The groups on the list represent the usual mix of businesses and blue- and white-collar unions typically found active during each presidential election year. The National Association of Realtors has been the leading PAC contributor for many years; in the 2007–08 cycle, this group set a record by contributing over $4 million to candidates. Just under half of the groups on the list are labor unions, led by the AFL-CIO-affiliated International Brotherhood of Electrical Workers.

While union contributions overwhelmingly went to Democrats, as they always do, examination of the actions of large, individual business interests reveals somewhat more pragmatic behavior. For example, in 2007–08, with Democrats now in control of Congress and the country facing an impending housing crisis, both the National Association of Realtors PAC and the National Association of Home Builders PAC, typically Republican oriented, gave far more to Democrats than they had in 2003–04. The National Association of Realtors contributed 58 percent of its funds in 2007–08 to Democrats, compared to 42 percent in the previous presidential year cycle. The National Association of Home Builders contributed 67 percent of its funds to Democrats in 2007–08, compared to 54 percent in 2003–04. AT&T, the telecommunications giant, decreased its support for Republicans from 65 percent in 2003–04 to 53 percent in the most recent cycle. The National Beer Wholesalers Association, the fourth largest contributor on the list for 2007–08, went from contributing 76 percent of its funds in 2003–04 to Republicans to contributing a majority of its funds, 53 percent, to Democrats in 2007–08.

Table 7.2   Top 20 PAC Contributors to Candidates, 2007–2008 (in dollars)

Rank	PAC Name	Total
1	National Association of Realtors	4,013,900
2	International Brotherhood of Electrical Workers	3,333,650
3	AT&T Inc.	3,122,200
4	National Beer Wholesalers Association	2,869,000
5	National Automobile Dealers Association	2,864,000
6	American Bankers Association	2,811,550
7	International Association of Fire Fighters	2,709,900
8	American Association for Justice	2,700,500
9	Honeywell International	2,515,616
10	National Association of Home Builders	2,480,000
11	International Association of Machinists & Aerospace Workers	2,326,600
12	Credit Union National Association	2,310,049
13	Service Employees International Union—COPE	2,289,250
14	American Federation of Teachers, AFL-CIO	2,265,250
15	National Air Traffic Controllers Association	2,236,475
16	International Brotherhood of Teamsters Union	2,202,300
17	International Union of Operating Engineers	2,191,475
18	Air Line Pilots Association	2,115,500
19	AFSCME	2,112,593
20	United Parcel Service Inc.	2,082,707

Source: Federal Election Commission, "Growth in PAC Financial Activity Slows," press release, April 24, 2009 (http://www.fec.gov/press/press2009/20090415PAC/20090424PAC.shtml).

Independent Spending by PACs

As noted earlier, independent spending by PACs developed a negative reputation in the years immediately following the 1976 *Buckley v. Valeo* case, especially because funds were typically used for negative advertising. Negative ads earned the wrath and criticism of the media, the public, and elected officials alike and proved potentially embarrassing for donors. As a consequence, many of the most aggressive independent PACs went out of business by the mid-1980s because of fund-raising difficulties. By the 1990s, the rise of issue advocacy advertising, which used soft money outside of the FEC regulatory umbrella, seemed a better option for many groups. Groups could accomplish essentially the same goal of supporting or opposing a candidate without revealing the identity of their donors. By the 2000 election, only 125 PACs engaged in independent spending, with outlays of a modest $21 million.

Attempts by Congress and the FEC rulings to expand disclosure laws to include 527 committees made independent spending by PACs again fashionable. Also contributing to the popularity of PACs was the BCRA, which took effect in 2004. Paid for with hard money collected by the PAC, express advocacy ads could be broadcast up to and including election day, unlike soft money ads.

FEC data indicate that PAC independent spending experienced a resurgence in the latest presidential year cycle. Over $135 million was spent, more than double that spent in the previous cycle and five times what was spent around the 2000 election. Most of the funds (73 percent) were directed toward the presidential race, primarily in the form of radio and television ads and express advocacy canvassing in a number of competitive swing states. The FEC also collects data on whether campaign activity was positive or negative in tone. Overall, 63 percent of funds were spent in support of a candidate rather than against his or her opponent.

Table 7.3 presents a list of the leading independent expenditure PACs. Labor unions dominated this form of activity, with fully 66 percent of all reported activity being spent by one group, the Service Employees International Union (SEIU), two million members strong. The union reported spending $38.8 million independently, and SEIU Local 1999 reported another $4.8 million. The pro-Democratic group was active in both primaries and the general election, and a large portion of its expenditures was not used for direct advocacy advertising but rather for extensive canvassing, polling, and get-out-the-vote drives. Besides unions, nonconnected, more ideological PACs were active on behalf of Democrats; these included MoveOn.Org, active in the presidential general election. Some were very active in the primaries. A good example is EMILY's List, which supported Senator Hillary Clinton in key Democratic primaries, including in Pennsylvania.[22]

It is unusual for corporate or trade association interests (one notable exception being the National Association of Realtors), which dominate PAC giving to candidates, to be involved in extensive independent spending, typically a visible activity that might offend consumers or stockholders. The Republican allies that are most likely to engage in independent spending are the nonconnected PACs with a strong conservative or libertarian bent. The leading independent spender among such organizations during the 2007–08 cycle was the National Rifle Association (NRA), which reported spending $17.9 million, followed by the Club for Growth, which spent nearly $4.9 million. In the 2007–08 cycle, almost all the money spent by such groups was on radio and television advertisements.

It should also be noted that PACs also have a responsibility to report to the FEC all the communications they have with their members or employees that meet the test of express advocacy. Technically, any communication urging the defeat or endorsement of any federal candidate, providing that communication costs are greater than $2,000 per contest and that the "primary" intent is the election or defeat of a particular candidate, must be reported. No doubt this activity is underreported, given the ambiguous reporting criteria. Examples of groups that report spending on "internal

Table 7.3 Independent Expenditures by Top Groups, 2007–2008*(in dollars)

Committee	Total	Spent in Support of Democrats	Spent in Opposition to Democrats	Spent in Support of Republicans	Spent in Opposition to Republicans
Service Employees International Union	38,791,967	33,121,380	250,060	0	5,420,526
National Rifle Association	17,938,707	188,370	13,620,549	4,129,788	0
AFSCME	8,733,023	2,758,639	162,543	0	5,811,840
National Republican Trust PAC	7,646,712	0	7,373,019	273,692	0
National Association of Realtors	6,737,804	3,590,180	0	3,147,623	0
MoveOn.org	6,445,504	4,993,510	0	0	1,451,993
Club for Growth	5,227,120	0	1,363,524	1,096,836	2,766,663
United Auto Workers	4,867,469	4,444,381	0	0	423,087
Service Employees Int'l Union Local 1999	4,787,893	4,787,893	0	0	0
Republican Majority Campaign	4,742,493	0	4,685,339	57,154	0
American Federation of Teachers	4,057,323	4,057,323	0	0	0
Defenders of Wildlife	3,863,545	453,527	0	44,792	1,633,412
EMILY's List	3,731,441	2,890,416	345,097	0	495,927
National Right to Life	3,357,141	1,638	54,375	3,277,566	13,003
Let Freedom Ring Inc.	3,267,492	0	3,038,374	229,118	0
Planned Parenthood	2,925,203	809,206	0	0	2,115,996
League of Conservation Voters	2,622,871	1,502,443	0	0	1,120,427
Advancing Wisconsin Inc.	2,223,442	1,917,511	0	0	0
National Campaign Fund	1,895,104	0	511,774	1,375,573	0
Life & Liberty PAC	1,871,595	0	1,871,595	0	0
Progressive Future Incorporated	1,563,538	1,472,817	0	0	90,721

Organization					
American Medical Association	1,554,898	836,939	0	717,958	0
United Food & Commercial Workers Union	1,445,914	1,445,914	0	0	0
NARAL Pro-Choice America	1,414,648	601,886	21,734	0	791,027
International Association of Fire Fighters	1,368,949	1,026,576	1,209	0	341,163
Sierra Club	1,352,562	688,960	50	0	663,551
National Federation of Independent Business	1,233,305	0	1,233,305	0	0
Environment America Inc.	1,145,358	1,135,400	0	0	5,739
Focus on the Family Action	1,034,770	0	22,490	1,012,279	0
Legacy Committee	985,924	0	90,529	895,395	0
National Education Association	933,648	125,173	0	0	804,375
League of Conservation Voters	841,209	437,883	0	0	403,325
Our Country Deserves Better PAC	733,763	0	546,790	186,972	0
Womencount PAC	714,483	714,483	0	0	0
American Hospital Association	683,947	405,824	0	278,122	0
American Association of Orthopedic Surgeons	667,805	0	0	667,805	0
Environment California Inc.	660,604	660,364	0	0	240
PowerPAC.org	642,295	642,295	0	0	0
Humane Society of the United States	540,082	98,287	0	15,077	420,604
Credit Union National Association	530,419	336,816	0	193,603	0

Source: Center for Responsive Politics (OpenSecrets.org), "Independent Expenditures," January 15, 2009 (http://www.opensecrets.org/overview/indexp. php?filter=A&Display=M).

*Columns for some groups do not add up to 100 percent of the total spent for independent spending. Some groups may have engaged in independent spending for or against independent/third-party candidates and/or included certain communication costs in their filing.

communications" include organized labor, teachers' unions, business associations, and certain membership groups like the politically aggressive NRA. In the 2007–08 cycle, organizations reported spending $21.3 million. Of this amount, $9.5 million was spent by one union, the American Federation of State, County, and Municipal Employees (AFSCME). In almost all cases the money was spent on a positive endorsement of a candidate, most often in the presidential race.

Other PAC Activity

Direct contributions to candidates and parties and independent spending activities, such as radio and television advertising, are most associated with PAC influence in elections. But PACs may become involved in a broad range of other activities as well. Contributions to candidates and parties, for example, may not be necessarily monetary: in-kind contributions such as sharing a poll with a candidate, "lending" a staff member to a candidate, or allowing a party or candidate access to a PAC's phone-bank facilities may have an important influence on an election. PACs can also contribute to other PACs and political committees.

Some PACs neither engage in a substantial way in contributing to candidates/parties nor become active in typical independent spending activities, yet their impact may be substantial. The prime example in the 2007–08 cycle was an organization called ActBlue, which billed itself as "the nation's largest source of funds" for Democrats.[23] The registered PAC "created and deployed the next generation of online fundraising tools, enabling individuals and groups to raise money for the Democratic candidates and committee of their choice." Founded in 2004 by two computer whizzes, ActBlue set up and maintained a user-friendly platform for fund-raising by Democratic candidates and targeted small donors (the median contribution was roughly $50). Political committees for candidates set up pages that were accessed through the central ActBlue Web site and solicited contributions that were sent to ActBlue. ActBlue, in turn, collected and forwarded the contributions to the relevant party or candidate. According to the group, between 2004 and 2008 ActBlue sent nearly $140 million to 3,200 candidates and committees from 420,000 donors.[24]

In the 2007–08 cycle, ActBlue was a valuable Democratic ally, impacting a number of races.[25] Democrat John Edwards raised $4 million to keep his presidential nomination alive through ActBlue efforts. Barbara Boxer (D-CA) raised $928,000 for her leadership PAC through ActBlue, money that she later contributed to other House and Senate campaigns. In the North Carolina U.S. Senate race, ActBlue raised $450,000 for Kay Hagen in her winning campaign against incumbent Republican Elizabeth Dole. After raising $450,000 on ActBlue for a potential campaign, supporters encouraged former Virginia governor Mark Warner to run for the U.S. Senate.

The Democratic Congressional Campaign Committee collaborated with ActBlue in raising money for twenty-nine congressional races. The Obama campaign did not use ActBlue; the campaign had a model similar to ActBlue's for online fund-raising from small donors and did not need a third-party Web site.

Finally, it should be pointed out most PACs are small and a number were inactive during the 2007–08 cycle. Overall, only forty-eight PACs reported spending at least $3 million in all their activities, and just 4 percent of all registered PACs out of the 4,611 organizations registered by year-end 2008 reported spending $1 million or more. Fourteen percent of PACs had no disbursements at all. Clearly the big PAC money continues to be concentrated among a relatively few organizations.

The Soft Money Groups: 527s and 501(c) Committees

Over time the campaign finance system has evolved to include a group of organized interests that attempt to influence elections outside the hard-money guidelines of federal law. The motivations of such organizations are clear; they hope to avoid the disclosure provisions of federal law in order to protect donors from unwanted publicity about hard-hitting issue ads paid for with large sums of money. At the same time, contributions to the groups are unlimited, potentially maximizing donor influence. Over the past three decades, there has been a constant battle between regulators, who desire that all campaign monies come under FEC oversight, and forces seeking no regulation at all. The regulators have won some battles and lost others.

At the forefront of the recent debate have been Section 527 committees, organized under the provisions of the US tax code, not the FEC. A 527 committee is a political group, association, fund, or other organization operated primarily for the purpose of "influencing or attempting to the selection, nomination, election or appointment of any individual to any Federal, State, or local office or office in a political organization, or the election of Presidential or Vice-Presidential electors."[26] Such committees are purely political organizations with tax advantages over many groups (for example, donors do not pay the federal gift tax on contributions above $10,000), are easy to form (one just files a statement of formation with the Internal Revenue Service [IRS]), and are often formed by a few individuals or even one person. A 527 may not engage in any hard-money activity (such as giving a donation to or endorsing a candidate), and it may not coordinate its activities with party or other political committees. As long as such groups refrain from express advocacy of any kind, they can spend unlimited amounts on issue advocacy, earning them the title "stealth PACs."[27] The IRS now discloses the identity of donors.

Although the potential for forming 527 groups has been part of federal tax law since the early 1970s, few 527 organizations were formed until relatively recently. Concern over 527 groups came to a head during the 2004 presidential election, when they were widely created to circumvent the provisions of BCRA. Most 527 groups were clearly partisan in orientation in 2008. Some of the more prominent ones were created by former party employees who had been let go when party soft-money funds were no longer forthcoming, although they were officially forbidden from coordinating their activities with their respective parties. Data now available from the IRS indicate that 527 committee spending was $424 million in 2004, more than the combined total of direct giving and independent spending by PACs in that year.

But 527 activity, while substantial, was not nearly as widespread or important in the 2008 election. The IRS reported that 527 expenditures totaled $258 million during the 2007–08 cycle. A number of explanations may be offered for the large decrease. No doubt the more restrictive FEC rules governing 527 committees put in place after the 2004 election, including certain restrictions on fund-raising, as well as the desire of the FEC to treat such committees in the same manner as PACs (including donor identification and limitations on contributions), reduced the attractiveness of 527s. Fines for noncompliance perhaps played a role, particularly for smaller 527s. The ambiguity of the definitions of *electioneering communication* and *issue advocacy*, and uncertainty over their application, no doubt raised concerns among some groups about whether they were unknowingly violating the FEC guidelines.

Other factors, related to the dynamics of the presidential campaigns, may have played a role as well. Early in the 2007–08 cycle, 527s appeared to be on pace to set fund- raising and spending records.[28] On the Democratic side, this changed once Obama secured the nomination. His campaign implicitly discouraged 527 activity, perhaps fearful that issue advertising by allied groups might be an impediment to getting the candidate's message across. Also, such committees were perhaps viewed as competitors for the same wealthy donors.

On the Republican side, while businesses could now fund 527s out of their treasuries, in a period of declining profits it was probably difficult for corporations to justify spending money in this way. Further, the Republican nominee John McCain was himself one of the biggest critics of 527s, resenting their ability to flout the spending limits and their use of "issue advocacy" to circumvent the intent of the campaign finance laws, of which he had been a principal architect.

One also suspects that as the presidential election became less competitive during the final six weeks that both Republican and Democratic 527s had difficulty raising funds. No doubt the attention of the 527s turned to where the action was taking place, competitive Senate races.

Table 7.4 lists the top 527 committees during the 2007–08 cycle, ranked by receipts. Note that a number of the groups had federal PACs as well, and most had a partisan orientation (twenty-nine out of the forty-three on the list were Democratic allies). The universe of 527s is very diverse, ranging from unions to ideological groups to party entities. A few, such as the Alliance for North Carolina, were active in only one state.

The Service Employees International Union, which also headed the hard-money, independent-spending list, was the leading 527 in terms of receipts. Closely following was America Votes, an independent, pro-Democratic group that was instrumental in 2008 in coordinating the efforts of more than forty progressive groups, helping to avoid duplication in their activities and targeting races in swing states.

Among Republican allies, American Solutions for Winning the Future was the leading 527. Created by former Republican House Majority Leader Newt Gingrich, the group's aim was to affect the issue agenda of the presidential campaign by making energy policy the first priority, specifically reducing the nation's dependency on foreign oil. The group advocated permitting offshore oil drilling along most of the US coastline.

Big-money interests were the main funding sources for 527 committees. Table 7.5 presents IRS data dealing with the top contributors to such committees. SEIU again headed the list; it is recorded as having transferred $36.7 million from its treasury to support its own and other 527s. In some cases, individuals played a key role in 527 funding, although the amounts contributed paled in comparison to those of the 2004 election, when billionaires George Soros and Peter Lewis contributed more than $20 million each to a number of 527s dedicated to defeating President George Bush. During the 2007–08 cycle, Fred Eshelman of the Pharmaceutical Product Development corporation, who sponsored a number of anti-Obama ads in the campaign, was the fourth-ranking 527 contributor, personally contributing all the funds that his corporation reported to the IRS. Soros himself was a $5 million contributor to pro-Democrat 527s during this cycle. The Las Vegas Sands Corporation and Shangri-La Entertainment, casinos based in Nevada, were the fifth and sixth leading contributors. Sheldon and Miriam Adelson were the sole contributors representing Las Vegas Sands; Steven Bing was the only Shangri-La Entertainment contributor. Bing favors Democrats, while the Adelsons favor Republicans. For individuals seeking to spend as much as they wish on elections, 527s remain the vehicle of choice, especially if public disclosure is not an issue or, perhaps, is actually desired.

For organizations that want to keep the identity of their donors secret, there are other options. They may register as one of a number of 501(c) organizations with the IRS. Such organizations are tax-exempt, but they

Table 7.4   Top 527 Organization Receipts and Expenditures, 2007–2008 (in dollars)

Committee	Total Receipts	Expenditures	Federal PAC
Service Employees International Union	24,857,467	25,819,624	X
America Votes	23,633,214	20,749,364	
American Solutions for Winning the Future	19,676,873	19,594,558	
EMILY's List	12,592,282	10,848,170	X
The Fund for America	12,142,046	12,014,130	
GOPAC	8,192,347	8,100,840	X
RightChange.com Inc.	6,508,218	3,406,359	
College Republican National Committee	6,066,036	6,458,084	
Citizens United	5,644,344	5,238,329	X
Int'l Brotherhood of Electrical Workers	5,529,861	5,668,122	X
Club for Growth	4,986,012	5,897,982	X
Alliance for New America	4,890,621	4,890,620	X
United Brotherhood of Carpenters	4,461,701	2,099,833	
Gay & Lesbian Victory Fund	3,961,763	5,145,721	X
Patriot Majority Fund	3,930,127	3,794,584	
United Food & Commercial Workers Union	3,792,526	3,713,470	X
Friends of Fred Thompson	3,462,355	625,743	
American Leadership Project	3,459,035	3,435,564	
ActBlue	2,674,331	2,859,669	X
Young Democrats of America	2,531,108	2,676,629	
Majority Action	2,406,000	2,494,046	
Laborers Union	2,353,071	2,171,876	X
Progressive Media Action	2,124,430	2,124,430	
Citizens for Progress	1,980,000	1,561,875	
National Education Association	1,836,090	2,186,530	X
Sheet Metal Workers Union	1,805,164	1,826,825	X
Public Campaign Action Fund	1,616,620	1,688,134	
Unity 08	1,584,539	1,731,541	
Pioneer Majority	1,541,921	1,507,085	
League of Conservation Voters	1,508,572	1,167,865	X
National Public Education Action Fund	1,500,000	0	
California 2008 GOP Delegation Corporate	1,278,666	1,055,285	
National Federation of Republican Women	1,276,763	2,737,821	X
Plumbers/Pipefitters Union	1,223,636	1,249,020	X
Citizens for Strength and Security	1,207,000	1,163,352	
American Dental Association	1,150,181	1,165,225	X
Grassroots Democrats	1,129,532	1,161,615	
League of Education Voters of America	1,126,000	1,015,192	
Foundation for the Future	1,105,000	1,018,323	
Ironworkers Union	960,718	959,957	X
Democrats 2000	957,917	260,436	
Planned Parenthood	950,000	599,838	X
California Corrections Peace Officers Association	946,180	1,837,250	
Illinois Hospital & Health Systems Association	857,793	1,330,182	
Democracy for America	758,050	734,432	X

Source: Center for Responsive Politics (OpenSecrets.org), "527 Committee Activity: Top 50 Federally Focused Organizations, "December 3, 2008 (http://www.opensecrets.org/527s/527cmtes.php).

Note: These data are based on records released by the Internal Revenue Service on Wednesday, December 3, 2008.

Table 7.5   Top Twenty Contributors to 527 Committees, 2007–2008 (in dollars)

Rank	Contributor	Total
1	Service Employees International Union	36,708,275
2	American Federation of State/County/Municipal Employees	14,710,447
3	United Food and Commercial Workers Union	5,879,050
4	Pharmaceutical Product Development Inc.	5,250,000
5	Soros Fund Management	5,250,000
6	Las Vegas Sands	5,000,000
7	Shangri-La Entertainment	4,850,000
8	Fund for America	4,600,528
9	Institute for Student Achievement	3,787,000
10	Democratic Governors Association	3,765,000
11	Friends of America Votes	3,531,425
12	Oak Spring Farms	3,480,000
13	Laborers Union	2,826,179
14	Carpenters and Joiners Union	2,876,690
15	National Association of Realtors	2,651,942
16	Sheet Metal Workers Union	2,239,297
17	International Union of Operating Engineers	1,865,000
18	Plumbers and Pipefitters Union	1,777,289
19	Newsweb Corporation	1,625,000
20	America Votes 2006	1,450,000

Source: Center for Responsive Politics (OpenSecrets.org), "Top Contributors to 527 Committees 2008 Election Cycle" (http://www.opensecrets.org/527s/527$contribs.php$cycles=2008).

may engage in influential election activity. Charities, for example, register as 501(c)(3) organizations. Contributions to them are tax deductible, but the organization must not be involved in campaigns or directly impact election activities in a way that could be construed as partisan (encouraging voting and citizen participation is acceptable).

An organization may elect to register as a 501(c)(4) group under IRS guidelines; while contributions are not tax-exempt, the group may advocate ideas in the public forum, including during elections. Contributors are not identified. Electoral activities must not be the primary purpose of the group, and any advocacy must be nonpartisan. The Club for Growth is an example of such a group.

Unions and agricultural groups typically are 501(c)(5) organizations and may engage in election activities of all types. Contributions to them are not tax-exempt, but contributors can avoid public scrutiny.

Finally, 501(c)(6) organizations are typically business groups or trade associations that are not organized for profit. They may involve themselves in the whole range of electoral activities as long as such activities do not represent the primary purpose of the organization. The U.S. Chamber of Commerce and the National Association of Realtors are 501(c)(6) organizations.

The 2007–08 election cycle saw spending by 501(c)(4), (5), and (6) organizations on election-related matters more than triple, according to a study by the Campaign Finance Institute, going from an estimated $60 million in 2004 to $196 million in 2008.[29]

The Impact of Interest Group Soft Money in 2008

Compared to some of the most recent presidential and congressional elections, organized interest activity and money appeared to play a less significant role in 2008, though the totals spent for their activities was a record. A number of factors combined to let group financial activity fly under the media radar and remain relatively inconspicuous to the public. Media coverage of money in the 2008 elections focused on candidate fund-raising more than interest group spending, especially on the Democratic side, where Senators Hillary Clinton and Barack Obama raised record amounts of money from individual donors. With the election geared toward economic issues rather than wedge issues like gun control or abortion, many of the colorful, controversial organizations on the left and right seemed more restrained and less engaged. It is difficult to remember one ad from the 2008 presidential race; no contentious, memorable issue advocacy ad, like those run by Swift Boat Veterans and POWs for Truth against John Kerry in the 2004 race, captured the imagination of the electorate. But in certain states, the role of interest group money was extensive and arguably determinant, though not often highly visible.

Some groups had a broad impact on this election, with unions playing a central role. No doubt the SEIU was the most ubiquitous organization and the one that spent the most money. It was both a hard- and soft-money group. Its PAC both gave to candidates and engaged in independent spending, its active 527 committee was instrumental in funding other 527s, and the SEIU used its 501(c) status to engage in some activities. In the presidential race, SEIU was active in nineteen states.[30] Union volunteers were active during the Democratic primaries and caucuses, although state organizations variously supported Hillary Clinton, John Edwards, or Barack Obama; national endorsement of Obama did not occur until February 2008.

In the general presidential contest, SEIU concentrated its television advertising on seven swing states, running soft-money-funded commercials that featured Republican candidate McCain claiming he knew nothing about economic matters. Senator McCain said, "I'm going to be honest: I know a lot less about economics than I do about military and foreign policy issues. I still need to be educated."[31] The ads were run in mid-September just after the stock market decline.

But it was the grassroots, on-the-ground campaigning that most characterized the SEIU effort. Both separately and as part of the Change to Win coalition of unions, SEIU cooperated with the AFL-CIO voter mobilization initiative and was part of America Votes' nationwide effort to register voters and get them to the polls. Election Day efforts in the urban-industrial states were especially impressive, as the union called on its members for volunteer activity.[32] In Ohio, for example, roughly 3,000 members and staff were deployed for the last six weeks of the campaign. In Indiana, SEIU claimed to have knocked on 64,000 doors, made 85,000 phone calls, and driven 1,000 early voters to the polls. The effort was concentrated in the northeast corner of the state where it sought to increase the turnout of African-Americans and Latinos.

Health care was one of the key issues of SEIU concern.[33] The group targeted health care workers in nine presidential swing states that also had a competitive Senate race. After conducting focus groups and polling health care workers, SEIU sent 2.5 million pieces of mail to the targeted group. Also, white senior citizens were targeted in a number of swing states, like Pennsylvania; a quarter of a million DVDs were sent out explaining and criticizing the McCain health care plan (which the union deemed inadequate).

While presidential swing states and states where the group had a large membership bases garnered most of the group's attention, even states like New Hampshire, which had a competitive Senate race, received some attention ($1 million in television ads and $300,000 in direct mail costs). In states like Colorado and New Mexico, where the Obama campaign took the lead in voter registration and turnout activity, SEIU was financially helpful to the most active 527s.

Perhaps the main strategy of the Obama campaign was to increase voter turnout among minorities and young and first-time voters. Here unions like SEIU and others paralleled the efforts of the Obama campaign.[34] The United Farm Workers, for example, lent the Obama campaign some of its top field directors to organize get-out-the-vote efforts in Colorado, where turnout of the Latino vote was key. The Teamsters Union in Ohio made an impressive effort to turn out its own members on Election Day. Group volunteers and staff visited more than 1,000 teamster job sites in this state, a key Obama target, and more than 65,000 of the group's members voted on Election Day.

Republican allies, now that Christian right elements were basically sitting out the election, could not muster on-the-ground grassroots efforts equivalent to those put forth by the pro-Democratic groups. The most active, pro-business Republican ally was the U.S. Chamber of Commerce. Mostly using its status as a 501(c)(6) organization, the Chamber, like labor, concentrated its early efforts in states that had a competitive Senate race. But once the presidential race seemed to be noncompetitive (that is, after the mid-September financial crisis hit Wall Street), the Chamber and other business groups, such as the Business Industry Political Action Committee and the National Federation of Independent Business, virtually abandoned the presidential contest to concentrate on competitive Senate races. The Chamber's foremost aim, according to its magazine, was to "target key House and Senate races that could make all the difference in building a firewall in the next Congress—a firewall that stops the worst ideas and advances positive proposals for a competitive American economy."[35] In short, preventing Democrats from getting a filibuster-proof Senate was the highest priority for business interests.

Besides running the expected pro-business advertisements, which came under the rubric of issue advocacy, the Chamber engaged in computer-driven, grassroots activity. The group developed a sophisticated Web site operation where users could register to vote; learn about absentee or advance voting; sign up for a variety of free e-mail services; and get customized candidate profiles, the most current polling information, and detailed race reports. The national organization offered to create customized election Web sites for member or employee communication.[36] The Chamber claimed to have operations in 144 congressional districts.[37] In some areas, the grassroots effort went beyond technology, with Chamber members going door to door, hitting, in the words of one Minnesota businessperson, "almost every downtown business, including the thrift store and barber shops."[38]

In some of states, competition among rival interest groups was fierce, but it focused mostly on Senate races. A good example was Colorado, where the Obama campaign was flush with funds and ample volunteers and appeared to have a comfortable lead by early fall. The contest involved ideological contrast: the race pitted former U.S. Representative Bob Schaffer, a pro-business Republican, against U.S. Representative Mark Udall, a Democrat with a strong pro-environment reputation. Groups involved were careful not to violate the electioneering communications guidelines by advocating philosophical positions in their television and radio ads, but they used hard-hitting express advocacy in extensive direct mailings. Republican allies such as the U.S. Chamber of Commerce, which spent $1.91 million on the race, concentrated its television ads on the importance of electing free-enterprise-supporting legislators and used targeted direct mail to claim that Udall's election would lead to higher taxes and card check and make the county even more dependent on foreign oil. The immigration issue was also raised, albeit subtly.

Democratic allies, with a number of progressive groups such as the National Education Association and the League of Conservation Voters taking the lead rather than the unions, concentrated on painting Schaffer as hostile to a variety of liberal causes, particularly the environment. League television ads encouraged viewers to visit the group's Web site, where

Schaffer was portrayed as having earned the League's "dirty dozen" label in Congress due to his ties to big oil money. Although Republican allies were well funded in Colorado, outspending Democratic groups three to one in the Senate race, it didn't matter. Udall won the race handily. It was a Democratic year.

The Future

For most observers, organized interest money did not seem as troublesome in 2008 as in previous years, even though spending records were set in a number of categories. Groups on the political right and left appeared to act in a more restrained fashion in their electioneering activities; emphasis this time was more on ground-war, get-out-the-vote activities than polarizing air-war battles; much election activity took place below the threshold for media and public attention. Spending set records for various activities— PAC giving and independent spending in particular—that came under the rubric of FEC regulation. The FEC's efforts to constrain 527 committee activities, a problem since the 2000 election, appeared to be working, at least modestly. Regulators appeared to be making some gains.

Many believe the situation is likely to be reversed as soon as 2012. In January 2010, in the case of *Citizens United v. FEC*, a majority of the Supreme Court overturned two key provisions of BCRA, the cornerstone of modern campaign finance regulation. First, the Court ruled that the ban on the use of corporate general funds for electioneering activity was unconstitutional on free-expression grounds; this law had been on the books since 1907. Unions are now also free to use their treasury funds for electioneering activity. Second, the Court ruled as unconstitutional the BCRA ban on election-eering communication within the campaign window, thirty days before a primary and sixty days before a general election.

The initial reaction to the decision among most, including President Obama, was as one might expect, especially among those concerned about even greater corporate domination of the political system. Those wanting elections to be less negative were unnerved that we may again see an era in which the public is inundated with polarizing commercials around the clock up to and including Election Day.

At this point it is unclear what the future holds. The amount of money spent on elections will surely increase, and that would probably happen regardless of the Court's decision. But I suspect that officers in major public corporations are unlikely to subtract funds from company profits for political purposes, given likely negative reactions from their shareholders and the public. The corporations that would most likely avail themselves of the new opening might be privately held, family-owned entities, the kind that already take advantage of 527 committees for ideological reasons. Indeed, any wealthy individuals or corporations desirous of being big money players in elections could do so before the ruling through some of the means described in this chapter. They already contributed to the multitude of existing political committee and organizations, both directly and indirectly, and used soft-money options like 527 committees and 501(c) vehicles. Groups can also "bundle" their members' contributions to leverage their impact. And, of course, funds for ground-war activities such as voter registration drives have never fallen under FEC regulation.

More ominous is what the Court may do next. Will disclosure laws be the next target of antiregulatory fervor?

Notes

1. Burdett A. Loomis and Allan J. Cigler, "Introduction: The Changing Nature of Interest Group Politics," in *Interest Group Politics*, 7th ed, eds. Allan J. Cigler and Burdett A. Loomis (Washington, DC: CQ Press, 2007): 1–33.

2. Jasper B. Shannon, *Money and Politics*, Studies in Political Science 30 (New York: Random House, 1959); George Thayer, *Who Shakes the Money Tree? American Campaign Financing Practices from 1789 to the Present* (New York: Simon and Schuster, 1973).

3. Byron E. Shafer, *Bifurcated Politics: Evolution and Reform in the National Party Convention* (Boston: Harvard University Press, 1988).

4. Anthony Corrado, Thomas E. Mann, Daniel R. Ortiz, Trevor Potter, and Frank J. Sorauf, eds., *Campaign Finance Reform: A Sourcebook* (Washington, DC: Brookings Institution, 1997).

5. Allan J. Cigler ,"Enron, A Perceived Crisis in Public Confidence, and the Bipartisan Campaign Reform Act of 2002," *Review of Policy Research* 21, no. 2 (2004): 233–52.

6. 429 U.S. 1 (1976): 44.

7. Larry J. Sabato, *PAC Power: Inside the World of Political Action Committees* (New York: Norton, 1984).

8. Marian Currinder, Joanne Connor Green, and M. Margaret Conway, "Interest Group Money in Elections," in *Interest Group Politics*, 7th ed, eds. Allan J. Cigler and Burdett A. Loomis (Washington, DC: CQ Press, 2007): 182–211.

9. Currinder, Green, and Conway, "Interest Group Money in Elections," 190.

10. Diana Dwyre and Robin Kolodny, "Throwing Out the Rule Book: Party Financing of the 2000 Elections," in *Financing the 2000 Election*, ed. David B. Magleby (Washington, DC: Brookings Institution, 2002): 133–62.

11. 424 U.S. 1(1976): note 52.

12. Allan J. Cigler, "Issue Advocacy Electioneering: The Role of Money and Organized Interests," in *Law and Election Politics: The Rules of the* Game, ed. Matthew J. Streb (Boulder, CO: Lynn Rienner, 2005): 58–75.

13. Anthony Corrado, "Financing the 2000 Elections," in *The Election of 2000: Reports and Interpretations*, ed. Gerald M. Pomper (New York: Chatham House, 2001): 95.

14. Roger Davidson, "Partisan Surge and Decline in Congressional Elections: The Case of 2008," in *The American Elections of 2008*, ed. Janet M. Box-Steffensmeier and Stephen E. Schier (Lanham, MD: Rowman and Littlefield, 2009): 79–98.

15. Conference Board, "Consumer Confidence Index Plummets to All-Time Low," press release, October 28, 2008, http://www.paymentsnews.com/2008/10/consumer-confid.html.

16. Stuart Rothenberg, "Business Interests Focus on the Fight for Senate Control," *Roll Call*, September 2, 2008: 6.

17. Anthony Corrado, "The Regulatory Environment of the 2008 Elections," in *Financing the 2008 Election*, eds. David B. Magleby and Anthony Corrado (Washington, DC: Brookings Institution, 2011): 48–85.

18. Federal Election Commission, "Media Fund to Pay $580,000 Civil Penalty," press release, November 19, 2007, http://www.fec.gov/press/press2007/20071119media fund.shtml.

19. 546 U.S. 410 (2006).

20. All of the data used in this section of the chapter come from either the Federal Election Commission Web site (http://www.fec.gov/), the Web site of the Center for Responsive Politics (http://www.opensecrets.org/), or the Web site of the Internal Revenue Service (http://www.irs.gov/). See also Allan J. Cigler, "Interest Groups and the Financing of the 2008 Elections," in *Financing the 2008 Election*, eds. David B. Magleby and Anthony Corrado (Washington, DC: Brookings Institution, 2011): 249–89.

21. See, for example, Susan Clark Muntean, "BCRA's Impact on the Political Expenditures of Corporate Interests," *The Forum: A Journal of Applied Research in Contemporary Politics* 6, no.1 (2008): article 9.

22. The organization targeted 150,000 Democratic women voters in southeastern Pennsylvania in the weeks before the April 22 Pennsylvania primary. The group ran similar programs in other states. EMILY's list's press release after Clinton's win in this primary explains the organization's efforts: http://emilyslist.org/news/releases/2008_pennsylvania_primary/.

23. ActBlue: The Online Clearinghouse for Democratic Action, "About ActBlue," http://www.actblue.com/about/.

24. ActBlue, http://www.actblue.com/about/.

25. Scott Helman, "Internet-Based PAC Driving Democratic Push," *Boston Globe*, August 7, 2007, http://www.boston.com/news/local/massachusetts/articles/2007/08/07/internet_based_pac_driving_democratic_push/.

26. Diana Dwyre, "527s: The New Bad Guys of Campaign Finance," in *Interest Group Politics*, 7th ed, eds. Allan J. Cigler and Burdett A. Loomis (Washington, DC: CQ Press, 2007): 212–32.

27. Michael Trister, "The Rise and Reform of Stealth PACs," *American Prospect* 11 (September 24, 2002): 32–35, http://prospect.org/cs/articles?article=the_rise_and_reform_of_stealth_pacs#/.

28. T. W. Farnam and Brody Mullins, "Interest Group Campaign Spending Nears Record," *Wall Street Journal*, February 5, 2008, http://online.wsj.com/article/SB120217685410343083.html; Eliza Newlin Carney, "For Interest Groups, Cash Talks," *National Journal*, March 24, 2008, reprinted at http://www.democracy21.net/.

29. Campaign Finance Institute, "Soft Money Political Spending by 501(c) Nonprofits Tripled in 2008 Election," http://www.cfinst.org/Press/PReleases/09–02–25/Soft_Money_Political_Spending_by_Nonprofits_Tripled_in_2008.aspx.

30. Jon Youngdahl, political director, SEIU, interview with David Magleby, Washington, D.C., January 23, 2009.

31. Stephen Moore, "Reform, Reform, Reform: John McCain Explains his Eclectic—and Troubling—Economic Philosophy," *Wall Street Journal*, November 26, 2005.

32. Youngdahl, interview.

33. Youngdahl, interview.

34. Anna Burger, "Remarks at 2008 Post-Election News Briefing," November 6, 2008, http://www.gwu.edu/~action/2008/chrneday08/burger110608st.html.
35. Thomas J. Donohue, "Big Labor, the Elections, and You," *U.S. Chamber Magazine,* January 22, 2008, http://www.uschambermagazine.com/content/080122.htm.
36. U.S. Chamber of Commerce, "Gearing Up for the Elections: Chamber Web Site Offers Tools for Businesses," *U.S. Chamber Magazine,* April 2008: 1, http://www .uschambermagazine.com/sites/default/files/ucmagazinepdf/0804_mag.pdf.
37. Donohue, "Big Labor, the Elections, and You."
38. Tom Hamburger, "Business Groups Target Senate Races," *Los Angeles Times,* November 2, 2008, http://articles.latimes.com/2008/nov/02/nation/na-chamber2.

8

Interest Group Television Advertising in Presidential and Congressional Elections

Michael Franz

Introduction

In early 2010, the Supreme Court of the United States issued a ruling in *Citizens United v. FEC* (2010) that fundamentally changed the campaign finance system for organized interests. The Supreme Court removed one of the main features of campaign finance law, namely restrictions on political ads funded by corporate or union treasuries that mention, depict, or expressly advocate a candidate for federal office. In the 5–4 vote, the Court sided with the claim of Citizens United—a nonprofit advocacy group that in 2007 had produced a documentary critical of Hillary Clinton—that pro- or anti-candidate messages are protected speech under the First Amendment.

In one sense, the Court ended a long debate among scholars, activists, and policy makers over what types of campaign messages from interest groups could be restricted or outlawed by Congress. Interest groups had been pushing the boundaries of these limitations for over fifteen years. To that effect, the Court said that so long as the messages were not coordinated with federal candidates, and absent a compelling and clear state interest, the First Amendment trumps federal regulation. In another sense, however, the Court's decision was merely a beginning, as it called into question a host of other restrictions and regulations on the flow of money in elections. Some predict that we are on a trajectory of campaign finance deregulation—that an election cycle with no restrictions on the flow of money in elections might be in our (near) future.

These developments are of primary importance to many policy makers and campaign finance reformers, many of whom worry that an expanded role for interest groups in elections will damage the health of American democracy. As it stands, interest groups participate in electoral politics in diverse ways, with everything from candidate contributions to get-out-the-vote efforts to endorsements and voter education. Many worry that such investments have the potential to corrupt legislators, who may feel drawn to put those interests ahead of their constituents. The potential is only exacerbated, the argument goes, in an environment where the restrictions on interest groups are breaking down. President Barack Obama alluded to this in his 2010 State of the Union address, when he chastised the Supreme Court for its ruling in *Citizens United*. He said: "The Supreme Court reversed a century of law that I believe will open the floodgates for special interests—including foreign corporations—to spend without limit in our elections. I don't think American elections should be bankrolled by America's most powerful interests, or worse, by foreign entities."[1]

Such a deep-seated concern for the health of American democracy begs a few simple questions: Why are many interest groups aggressive sponsors of political advertisements, and how intense have these investments been in recent election cycles? What are the implications of *Citizens United* for future election cycles?

The chapter begins with a discussion of two powerful motivating forces for interest group advertising, the legal and political contexts surrounding elections. To that effect, the elections of 1994 through 2010 featured a range of political and legal contexts. Congress and the White House have been up for grabs in nearly every campaign since 1994, for example, and the legal dimensions over permissible electioneering altered in significant ways in 2002, 2007, and 2010. After laying out these changes, I then focus on the intensity of the "air wars" in the presidential elections of 2000, 2004, and 2008. Each cycle featured a different profile of interest groups, largely the consequence of different rules and circumstances in each year. Across all three presidential elections, interest groups sponsored about 12 percent of all pro-candidate ads, with the greatest investment coming in 2004. After that, I switch to a discussion of interest group advertising in the congressional elections of 2000–2008, for which interest groups have been responsible for nearly one in every ten campaign ads.[2] The chapter concludes with a discussion of key questions for scholars and policy makers in approaching future election cycles.

The Legal Context

Elections take place within highly particularized contexts that vary from cycle to cycle. For example, election forecasters have long noted that the state of the economy and the popularity of the incumbent president structure, to a large extent, the orientations of voters in an election year.[3] To that effect, the economic recession of 2008 helped Barack Obama convince voters to take a chance on the Democrats, and forecasting models and even online political betting (on such sites as Intrade.com) predicted a Democratic victory long before the parties had even settled on their nominees. The issue context matters, too. The unpopular war in Iraq helped Democrats in 2006 (and 2008), for example, just as the 9/11 attacks moved voters toward Republicans in 2002 and 2004. For interest groups, two other contexts are highly important in motivating particular forms of electoral investment: the campaign finance environment (that is, the nature and strength of regulations on certain forms of electioneering) and the political environment (that is, who controls Congress and the White House and whether that control is at risk).[4]

Consider first the legal context of electioneering. There have been five phases in the changing legal context for interest groups over the last thirty-five years. Box 8.1 summarizes these five phases. The first covers 1974–1994, initiated after Congress passed extensive regulations on interest group campaign efforts in the aftermath of Watergate. These included strict limits on contributions to candidates and political parties, as well as new rules on the funding of pro-candidate independent advocacy. This period was characterized in particular by a growth in political action committees (PACs).

Box 8.1   Timeline of Evolving Regulatory Context

Phase 1   1974–1994: Congress passes major reform in 1974. Political action committees (PACs) proliferate in late 1970s and early 1980s.

Phase 2   1994–2002: Courts enforce "magic word" test of issue versus express advocacy. Unregulated political advertising by interest groups skyrockets.

Phase 3   2002–2007: Congress passes major reform, the McCain-Feingold bill. The law puts new restrictions on how interest groups can purchase political ads on television and radio, essentially expanding the "magic word" test to a "candidate mention" test. The Federal Election Commission does not enforce these rules for certain Section 527s (those that only accept contributions from individuals), causing their explosion.

Phase 4   2007–2010: Supreme Court rules in *FEC v. Wisconsin Right to Life* that certain limits on interest group ads are unconstitutional. If an ad can be thought by "any reasonable person" to be about issues, it is protected First Amendment speech. This allowed any group to air pro-candidate ads so long as they had sufficient issue content.

Phase 5   2010–present: Supreme Court rules in *Citizens United v. FEC* that all limits on interest group ads are unconstitutional so long as they are uncoordinated with a candidate or party.

PACs are formalized ways for corporations (banned from directly contributing to candidates since 1907), unions (similarly banned since 1947), and other interests to form transparent committees to contribute to candidates. Congress placed limits on the size of PAC contributions to federal candidates ($5,000 per election) and parties ($25,000 per cycle), and it mandated that the committees register with the Federal Election Commission (FEC), reporting receipts and expenditures on a regular basis and conforming to strict standards in the raising of campaign cash.[5] Since the passage of campaign finance reform in the 1970s, PACs have had a consistent presence in campaigns. According to the FEC, there were 722 registered PACs in 1975. Their rate of growth was steep in the late 1970s and early 1980s and leveled off to slight increases each year thereafter. By 2007, there were over 4,200.

PACs are especially important in congressional elections. PACs directly contributed in total over $320 million to House candidates and $91 million to Senate candidates in 2010. These numbers were historic highs. In 2008, PACs contributed $300 million to House candidates and $80 million to Senate candidates (at that time a new high). In fact, since 1980 PACs have contributed larger amounts of money to House and Senate candidates in each successive election cycle.

PACs were the focus of many campaign finance reform efforts in the 1980s. To these reformers, PACs were nothing but a legalized channel for unions and corporations to curry favor with important policy makers. The focus of reform efforts changed critically in the mid-1990s, though, when a second period began that lasted through the 2002 elections. The impetus for this change was multifaceted (and intersected with the political context described below), but a number of federal court cases in the early and mid-1990s established more firmly what came to be called the "magic word" test of interest group candidate advocacy. These cases included *Faucher v. FEC* (1991), *Maine Right to Life Committee v. FEC* (1996), and *FEC v. Christian Action Network* (1996). In total, the courts clarified the boundaries between permissible and impermissible corporate and union election speech. The courts said that if parties and interest groups avoided the use of certain action words (such as "vote for" or "vote against") in their public communications, the messages would be considered issue advocacy and not candidate advocacy. The ads could therefore be purchased with unregulated funds from corporate and union treasuries (or, in the case of the parties, with large—and unregulated—donations from wealthy individuals, unions, and corporations). Specifically, these magic words were "vote for," "elect," "support," "cast your ballot for," "[Smith] for Congress," "vote against," "defeat," or "reject."[6] This meant in practice that corporations, unions, and other interests could advocate for federal candidates without having to jump through the regulatory hoops of forming and maintaining a PAC.

This simple distinction resulted in a proliferation of political ads on television and radio. The AFL-CIO, for example, spent over $36 million on issue ads that supported Democratic congressional candidates in the 1996 elections.[7] Consider an example in contrasts. The following is a transcript of an ad aired in 2000 by National Education Association:

> As the teachers of the NEA, we know what's at stake in our schools. And Elaine Bloom has fought for our children's education her whole career. In Congress, she'll stand for Head Start for every eligible child, for smaller class size, and for increased teacher training. In Congress, Clay Shaw voted no to Head Start, no to smaller class size, and no to teacher training. The difference is clear. Elaine Bloom for Congress.

This ad was sponsored by the National Association of Realtors (NAR) in the same year:

> Cal Dooley, protecting our families, protecting our values. Cal Dooley, a leader in helping Americans buy their very first home. Cal Dooley. Voting to make the dream of home ownership a reality for a record number of Americans. Cal Dooley, supporting a bill to help our teachers and police officers purchase a home. Cal Dooley, the courage to do what's right to protect our way of life. Call him, thank him for his hard work.

The first ad contained one of the critical "magic words"—[Elaine Bloom] for Congress—and was as a consequence paid for by the NEA's PAC. The second message contained no "magic word" and was paid for by the NAR's general treasury funds.[8] While the content of this second advertisement (and others like it) was generally perceived by viewers as candidate advocacy, the lack of a specific exhortation on how to vote placed it outside the scope of federal election laws.[9]

To many in Congress, the "magic word" test was too big a loophole, and the Bi-partisan Campaign Reform Act in 2002 (known also as McCain-Feingold) attempted to rein in interest groups and parties, thus beginning the third phase in the evolving legal context with the 2004 elections. The new law made the following changes:

- It expanded the "magic word" test to include a "candidate mention" test. Now, any ad that featured a candidate (like the ad for Cal Dooley) would be considered an election ad, not an issue ad. This meant such ads could not be funded by corporate or union treasury funds.
- It applied this test to a particular time period, sixty days before the general election and thirty days before a primary election. Ads aired outside the thirty- or sixty-day windows were categorized by the old "magic word" test.

These changes were straightforward and seemed to compel groups to fund most election-time ads with regulated PAC funds. But a loophole was soon discovered. Wealthy individuals formed what are called 527s, referring to the section of the tax code where these groups are classified. Swift Boat Veterans for Truth, MoveOn.org, and Progress for America were some examples of major 527s active in 2004 with political advertisements.[10] These groups argued that so long as they pooled funds (large and small) from individuals and not corporations and unions, and so long as they avoided "magic words," the new law did not cover their ads. The Federal Election Commission, with its inaction on the issue in early 2004, signaled agreement.[11]

In one sense, these 527s broadly behaved in line with the goals of regulators. McCain-Feingold prevented these groups from accepting corporate and union money for the purpose of airing pro-candidate television ads in the weeks before a federal election. On the other hand, 527s accepted huge checks from individuals and used those to air political ads. For example, in August 2004 Progress for America received a $5 million contribution from real estate developer Alex Spanos. Businessperson Jay van Andel contributed $2 million to the group in September 2004. On the Democratic side, businessperson George Soros contributed about $1.5 million to MoveOn.org in late 2003, and film producer Stephen Bing donated nearly $1 million. These contributions seemed to flout the intentions of congressional reformers, who wanted all groups airing ads that depicted federal candidates to be paid for with regulated and capped contributions.

The FEC responded in late 2006 and early 2007 by fining the Swift Boat Veterans, MoveOn.org, the League of Conservation Voters, and Progress for America for their activity in the previous presidential election, arguing that their ads and campaigning violated some sections of the 2002 McCain-Feingold reforms. The FEC's newfound focus on regulating 527s was predicted to restrain their growth in the 2008 election, but enforcement proved less relevant than expected as a Supreme Court case in 2007 signaled the fourth phase of the evolving legal context. That case, *Federal Election Commission v. Wisconsin Right to Life*, loosened the rules established in McCain-Feingold. In short, the Court exempted from campaign finance laws any broadcast advertising sponsored by outside groups that "a reasonable person" might conclude was principally about policy issues. The Court essentially gave the green light to nonprofits, corporations, labor unions, and pro-business groups to use general treasury funds to air pro-candidate ads at any point in the campaign. The only stipulation in the ruling was that the message must contain some issue discussion—a relatively low bar for classifying an ad as issue over pro-candidate advocacy. Think again about the Cal Dooley ad—it clearly refers to the congressman's policy preferences and would easily pass the "reasonable person" test.

The fifth and current phase in the regulatory context began in 2010 with the decision in *Citizens United v. FEC*, in which the Court further expanded on its ruling in *Wisconsin* and allowed corporations, unions, and all other interest groups to directly fund pro-candidate ads with no restrictions on content, such as the presence or absence of "magic words" or the presence or absence of issue discussion.[12] The Court essentially ended the debate over what public messages could be funded by interest groups and ruled that nearly all of these messages were acceptable. Coordination with candidates and parties on political ads is still impermissible, though.

A number of other cases in the pipeline have the potential to go farther. *EMILY's List v. FEC* and *Speechnow.org v. FEC* concern unlimited contributions from individuals to nonprofit groups and registered PACs making expenditures on behalf of candidates, respectively. These cases address areas of the law not directly covered by *Citizens United*, but because that case was so sweeping in its defense of the First Amendment, most observers foresee the breakdown of numerous regulations on interest group electioneering. Moreover, the Court's significant movement toward deregulation of campaign finance laws suggests little help for a reform community that has historically sought to severely limit the role of interest groups in the electoral process.

One important feature of this evolving legal context for interest group electioneering is its accelerating nature. It took nearly twenty years for interest groups to exploit the "magic word" loophole; it took just four election cycles after that for Congress to act with McCain-Feingold; there were only two elections (2004 and 2006) under the McCain-Feingold regulatory framework; only one election cycle (2008) transpired where *Wisconsin* set the rules.

The Political Context

An evolving legal context is of primary importance to understanding how interest groups participate in elections. It is not the sole—or perhaps—most important one, however. One might wonder, for example, what compelled many interest groups to pursue more aggressive electioneering and pressure the Courts for the "magic word" loophole. One answer lies in the polarized political context characteristic of the mid-1990s through today. Beginning with the Republican gains in the 1994 congressional elections, Washington, D.C., has featured an ever more polarized and partisan context.

One way to understand this is to examine the perceived stability of the majority party's control of the House and Senate in the run-up to each election. It takes 218 seats to control the House and either 50 or 51 seats to control the Senate, depending on the party of the vice president, who breaks tie votes. In the fall of each election year, a number of political experts rank House and Senate races as competitive, safe, or leaning toward one party. *Congressional Quarterly* has done this for over thirty years, which allows for a good comparison over time. Between 1978 and 1992, for example, the Democrats were expected to win anywhere between 241 and 272 seats in the House, excluding the most competitive races. Even if they had lost all of the too-close-to-call seats, they were expected to hold onto control by at least twenty-five seats. In 1994, though, their expected total, minus competitive seats, was 211, suggesting they could lose control of the chamber, which they did. After the Republicans took over in 1995, nearly every election has been characterized by tenuous control. The GOP was expected to win at least 217 House seats in 1996, 216 in 1998, 211 in 2000, 220 in 2002, 230 in 2004, and 207 in 2006. Except for 2004, where the GOP had more cushion, majority control of the chamber was essentially a jump ball.

In the Senate, majority control has been more volatile for a bit longer. Republicans won control of the Senate in 1980, for example, and lost it in 1986, but they regained it again in 1994. Between 1994 and 2006, though, the majority party in the Senate was only expected to win (minus the most competitive races) between forty-eight and fifty-two seats. This meant that every tight Senate race in those years proved critical to each party in its efforts to win or regain control of the chamber.

On their own, these tight majorities could motivate many interest groups to invest in competitive elections. Think of it this way. Just 5,000 to 10,000 votes in a handful of competitive House and Senate races had the potential in these years to determine whether a Republican or Democrat was Speaker of the House or Majority Leader in the Senate and whether Democrats or Republicans controlled all of the committees in both chambers. This helps to explain why so many interest groups took advantage of the evolving legal context for political advertising. Put simply: interest groups sought to persuade voters of the importance of voting for Democratic or Republican candidates by using political ads to paint these candidates in a negative or favorable light.

There is more to the story, though. These tightly contested races for partisan majorities were also taking place in a political environment that was increasingly polarized along ideological lines. As been long discussed in the political science literature, Democratic and Republican party elites have become more polarized in contemporary American politics than at nearly any other time in the last 100 years.[13] Two political scientists, Keith Poole and Howard Rosenthal, have collected all of the roll-call votes on the floor of the House and Senate for every congressional session.[14] They use the data to scale each Democrat and Republican on a liberal-conservative spectrum. Using these data, we can determine a score for Democrats in each congressional session that accounts for how liberal the party was and how much ideological diversity there was. We can do the same for Republicans.[15]

The pattern shows that ideological polarization between the two parties in the House has nearly doubled between 1978 and 2008. This has essentially occurred in a linear fashion, with more polarization happening every year. In the Senate, the two parties grew 67 percent more polarized in the same time frame. Anecdotal evidence backs up this conclusion. It has become harder and harder to find liberal Republicans or conservative Democrats roaming the halls of Congress, for example. And the vitriol between the parties and heated rhetoric during important policy debates, as with health care reform in 2009 and 2010, seems to grow each year.

So far, this characterization of polarization has focused only on Congress. But the presidential elections during this time were also serious business. The election of 2000 was the closest presidential election in American history, decided by fewer than 600 votes in Florida. Green Party candidate Ralph Nader made significant headway that year, arguing that the differences between Gore and Bush were negligible and amounted to a false choice. But the actions of the Bush administration after 9/11 seemed to belie the point, as the War in Iraq was a controversial foreign policy calculation that further split the two parties. To that effect, the 2004 election was also agonizingly close, decided by some 100,000 votes in Ohio.

Of course, it is important not to overstate the case. Not all interest group advertising in federal elections or on behalf of federal candidates is rooted in partisan agenda control. Putting issues *on* the agenda, more generally, is often a group's primary concern. That is, if the group can push the campaign dialogue to focus on particular issues, it may compel the elected candidate to devote more effort to those issues in the next congressional session. There is some evidence indeed that the issue debate between candidates in an election is often followed by legislative action on those issues.[16] If a group can shift the focus of the candidate dialogue, then it can raise the chance of seeing subsequent legislative action on those issues.

Additionally, interest groups may be concerned less with helping elect Nancy Pelosi as Speaker (via the elections of competitive Democrats in other districts) than with helping particular members (friends and allies on relevant committees, for example) in a difficult race. For example, in 2010 the Pharmaceutical Researchers and Manufacturers of America (PhRMA)— a decidedly conservative advocacy lobby—aired ads on behalf of Democratic Majority Leader Harry Reid, who was in a tough reelection campaign against a much more conservative Republican.[17] Reid had helped pass Obama's health care initiative in early 2010, which was supported by the drug lobby. Certain provisions in the bill seemed to favor drug companies, and the ads represented a thank-you for Reid's efforts.

Lots of reasons explain interest groups' electoral investments, then, but there is no denying that a polarized and balanced political environment—combined with a permissive legal context—has motivated the commitment of resources for political advertising in close races in the last fifteen years. A growing literature in political science may reinforce this point. Increasingly, scholars have asked whether we should expand our understandings of parties—traditionally conceptualized as the party organizing committees at the national, state, and local level—to include a network of party organizations *and* pro-party interest groups. In other words, are 527s, nonprofit advocacy groups, labor unions, and pro-business associations so increasingly aligned with one of the two parties that they effectively become a component of the party? Political scientists Matt Grossman and Casey Dominguez located evidence for this in the electoral realm when looking at clusters of candidate endorsements and campaign contributions.[18] They discovered that one set of groups tended to support and contribute to candidates of one party, while a different set of groups coalesced around the other party. Another study examined which groups shared donor lists, and here too a liberal and conservative cluster emerged.[19] The larger theme, then, is that party polarization in Congress has migrated to many interest groups, which also seem increasingly polarized.[20]

To this point, we have simply reviewed the contexts that may have been responsible for the emergence of interest group political advertising in the last fifteen years, but we have not seen how intense the "air war"—that is, the battle in advertising—was in elections during that period. The analysis now shifts to a more explicit review of this, with a focus on the number of groups advertising in presidential and congressional elections and the shift in intensity across election cycles.

Political Advertising in Presidential Elections

The data for the next two sections come from the Wisconsin Advertising Project.[21] Since 1998, the Project has tracked all political advertisements in the top media markets in the United States. The number of tracked markets has shifted, however, from 75 in 1998 and 2000 (which covered about 80 percent of the US population) to 100 in 2004 and to all 210 markets in 2008. The data are the best available evidence of interest group investments on the airwaves. Interest groups can spend to influence elections in ways beyond television ads, of course, such as through candidate contributions, get-out-the-vote drives, voter education efforts, peer-to-peer persuasion, and telephone mobilization. These are powerful means of reaching voters, but it is also much harder to track systematically many of these efforts from year to year. As such, the analysis here is limited to a discussion of political advertising. Furthermore, for ease of comparison across time, the focus is restricted to the top seventy-five markets in all covered years.

Interest groups invest considerably more resources on political ads in some years than in others and in some races over others. Consider the 2000 presidential election. In total, interest groups in the general election phase aired over 20,000 ads in the top 75 media markets advocating for either Democrat Al Gore or Republican George W. Bush. [22] From the discussion of the legal contexts earlier in the chapter, this election took place in the second phase, when any group could avoid regulation by simply avoiding "magic words" in the ad's text.

Table 8.1 lists all interest groups that aired 100 or more ads for either candidate in the general election. Al Gore benefited from the help of seven groups: Planned Parenthood, the AFL-CIO, Handgun Control, Sierra Club, NAACP, American Family Voices, and the Clean Air Project. All told, these groups totaled 14 percent of all pro-Gore ads aired in the top seventy-five markets. Bush benefited from the investment of five groups—American Seniors, National Rifle Association (NRA), Coalition to Protect Americans Now, Republican Leadership Council, and Americans for Job Security—which accounted for just over 4 percent of all pro-Bush ads in the general election, or less than a third of Gore's total.

Some groups in Table 8.1 are likely familiar to most readers (e.g., the AFL-CIO, the NRA, Planned Parenthood). Other groups, however, are not as easily recognizable (e.g., the Coalition to Protect Americans Now). One advantage for many individuals and interests seeking to help candidates is

Table 8.1   Interest Group Advertising in the 2000 Presidential Election

Interest Group	number of ads*	Candidate
Planned Parenthood	5,851	Gore
AFL-CIO	5,320	Gore
Handgun Control	2,742	Gore
Sierra Club	1,707	Gore
NAACP	468	Gore
American Family Voices	447	Gore
Clean Air Project	191	Gore
American Seniors	111	Bush
National Rifle Association	260	Bush
Coalition to Protect Americans Now	279	Bush
Republican Leadership Council	429	Bush
Americans for Job Security	4,215	Bush
Total	22,020	
Percent of all ads	8.96%	
Pro-Gore as percent of all Gore ads	14.05%	
Pro-Bush as percent of all Bush ads	4.18%	

Source: Wisconsin Advertising Project

*Totals for ad buys in top 75 media markets and for groups with 100 or more ads

the cloak of anonymity that often comes with unregulated candidate advocacy. Because Coalition to Protect Americans Now avoided the use of "magic
words" in its ads, it was not required under the laws governing the 2000
elections to report donors to any federal regulatory body. And it was free to
form and then dissolve after the election, which proved attractive to many
organized interests.

   This is precisely what motivated Congress to reform campaign finance
laws with McCain-Feingold in 2002. But these reforms hardly stemmed the
tide. In fact, the investments from groups in the 2000 presidential election
paled in comparison to those in 2004, as demonstrated in Table 8.2. In that
year, thirty-one groups aired 100 or more ads in the top seventy-five media
markets, more than double the participation rate of 2000 with nearly five
times the number of ads aired. As with 2000, the Democratic nominee
received the disproportionate benefit. In fact, 25 percent of all pro-Kerry
ads in the general election were sponsored by interest groups, the largest
two being the Media Fund and MoveOn.org. The number is worth reflecting on. One in every four spots aired in the top markets that advocated for
John Kerry (or attacked George Bush) came not from the Kerry campaign or
the Democratic Party but from interest groups unaffiliated with either.
Moreover, the 43,000 ads from the Media Fund alone constituted 30 percent of the total ad buy from the John Kerry campaign and 50 percent of the
ad buy from the Democratic Party. Nearly one in ten pro-Bush ads was sponsored by allied groups, with the Swift Boat Veterans and Progress for American being the primary actors.

   Many of these groups took cover as 527s, which were exempt from
many of the new restrictions established under McCain-Feingold. Although
groups can maintain a number of different campaign accounts (PACs, 527s,
and other nonprofit classifications), it is sometimes difficult to link a particular ad buy to a particular campaign account. But it is notable that of the
thirty-one groups in Table 8.2, all but six maintained active 527 accounts in
the 2004 elections. Two of the remaining groups (Air Traffic Controllers and
the National Rifle Association) aired their ads through their regulated
PACs, and three of the other four groups (River Smart, Citizens United,
Americans for Job Security) aired their ads outside the thirty-day and sixty-
day windows.[23]

   The expansion of 527s in 2004, and the continuing search for loopholes
in campaign finance laws, can seem dizzying at times. One clear lesson of this
chapter, though, is that the political motivation to participate in the electoral
process will often lead interest groups to locate points of entry that circumvent whatever legal barriers that Congress erects. In other words, the political context intersects with the legal context. As such, 2004 was a banner year
for interest group television advertising, motivated by the perception of an
incredibly tight presidential election. In contrast, the political motivation

Table 8.2   Interest Group Advertising in the 2004 Presidential Election

Interest Group	number of ads*	Candidate
Media Fund	43,750	Kerry
MoveOn.org	18,750	Kerry
AFL-CIO	9,764	Kerry
Communities for Quality Education	2,739	Kerry
League of Conservation Voters	2,523	Kerry
UAWVCAP	1,883	Kerry
New Democrat Network	1,751	Kerry
Stronger America Now	1,599	Kerry
Service Employees International Union	1,121	Kerry
Citizens for Quality Education	693	Kerry
Sierra Club	501	Kerry
American Fed. of State, County, and Municipal Employees	476	Kerry
Compare Decide Vote	354	Kerry
Campaign Money Watch	290	Kerry
National Education Association	290	Kerry
Real Economy Group	283	Kerry
NRDC Action Fund	254	Kerry
The National Air Traffic Controllers Association	208	Kerry
River Smart Organization	152	Kerry
Win Back Respect	150	Kerry
Greater New Orleans Republican Fund	125	Bush
Citizens United	141	Bush
Save American Medicine	196	Bush
Americans for Job Security	248	Bush
Let Freedom Ring	252	Bush
National Rifle Association	502	Bush
Softer Voice Org.	468	Bush
Americans United to Preserve Marriage	598	Bush
Club for Growth PAC	1,576	Bush
Swift Boat Veterans for Truth	5,198	Bush
Progress for America	9,283	Bush
Total	106,118	
Percent of all ads	19.33%	
Pro-Kerry as percent of all Kerry ads	25.16%	
Pro-Bush as percent of all Bush ads	9.24%	

Source: Wisconsin Advertising Project

*Totals for ad buys in top 75 media markets and for groups with 100 or more ads

was not as dominant in the 2008 presidential election. Because Barack Obama opted out of general election public financing and raised over $300 million to fund his campaign, many pro-Democratic interests did not participate in the presidential campaign.[24] And because McCain was historically opposed to interest groups' pro-candidate efforts, many conservative groups stayed out of the contest as well. Add to this the fact that the campaign was not generally competitive: Obama won with more than 360 electoral votes and 53 percent of the popular vote. In 2008, groups aired over 23,000 ads (more than in 2000 but significantly less than in 2004), but they accounted for only 5 percent of all ads aired in the general election—the lowest proportion of the three elections (see Table 8.3). Still, 19 groups did air more than 100 ads for Obama and McCain in the general election.

It is worth perusing again the list of groups in Tables 8.1–8.3. Only one group—the AFL-CIO—is featured in all three elections, though it purchased only 127 ads in 2008, significantly less than its ad buys in 2000 and 2004. Nine additional groups invested in two of the three elections: American Federation of State, County, and Municipal Employees (AFSCME); Americans for Job Security; Let Freedom Ring; MoveOn.org; the National Rifle Association; Planned Parenthood; Service Employees International

Table 8.3   Interest Group Advertising in the 2008 Presidential Election

Interest Group	number of ads*	Candidate
Service Employees International Union	4,191	Obama
United Auto Workers	1,555	Obama
MoveOn.org	1,498	Obama
American Fed. of State, County, and Municipal Employees	782	Obama
VoteVets.org	646	Obama
Health Care for America Now	556	Obama
Defenders of Wildlife Action Fund	384	Obama
Planned Parenthood	202	Obama
United Food and Commercial Workers	199	Obama
PowerPAC	193	Obama
Bring Ohio Back	178	Obama
AFL-CIO	127	Obama
BornAliveTruth.org	543	McCain
Republican Jewish Coalition	963	McCain
Let Freedom Ring	1,112	McCain
American Issues Project	1,354	McCain
National Republican Trust PAC	1,448	McCain
Committee for Truth in Politics	2,051	McCain
Vets for Freedom	5,158	McCain
Total	23,140	
Percent of all ads	5.02%	
Pro-Obama as percent of all Obama ads	4.08%	
Pro-McCain as percent of all McCain ads	6.20%	

Source: Wisconsin Advertising Project

*Totals for ad buys in top 75 media markets and for groups with 100 or more ads

Union (SEIU); the Sierra Club; and the United Auto Workers. It is telling that of the fifty-one groups organizing to air ads on behalf of presidential elections, forty-one took part in only one election. If we could look deeper at the funding of many of these one-time participants (and we can look at the funders of PACs and 527s but not other groups—an issue discussed in more detail in the conclusion), we might see that there were many consistent funders, but the organizational form takes different shapes in different years. This is largely a function of the legal rules surrounding the election (for example, is it better to be a 527 this year or not?) and the desire of large funders to remain in the shadows.

Political Advertising in Congressional Elections

Interest groups have also devoted considerable resources to congressional races in the last twelve to fifteen years. As noted earlier, the congressional context has become far more competitive and polarized since the 1980s, and the two major parties in Congress now see every competitive House and Senate seat as crucial to securing or winning majority control of the chamber. But not every election features the same level of advertising from interest groups. The specific instances in each year create greater or lesser incentives for aggressive investment in pro-candidate television ads, and some groups make calculations that other types of electoral action ("get-out-the-vote" [GOTV] drives, direct mail, radio) might provide more bang for their bucks. For example, labor in the late 1990s calculated that peer-to-peer contact among union households might be more effective than television advertising.[25] Some groups thus go off the air, not for reasons related to the political or legal contexts, but because of strategic calculations related to the perceived effectiveness of certain electioneering efforts.

Having said that, one way to assess the level of investment in television ads from interest groups is to look at aggregate group involvement in specific House and Senate races. For example, Table 8.4 lists the top twenty Senate races by interest group involvement, ranked as a percent of all ads aired in the race. The analysis only covers the elections of 2000, 2002, 2004, and 2008, because the Wisconsin Advertising Project did not track advertising in the 2006 elections. In addition, the table only shows ads aired in the top 75 media markets and covers only races where candidates aired at least 1,000 ads. This allows us to look at interest group involvement in races where candidates were active participants.

The top race was the 2008 Colorado Senate contest between Democrat Mark Udall and Republican Bob Schaffer, where interest groups sponsored nearly 40 percent of the total ad buys in the primary and general election phases of the race. The election featured fourteen separate interest groups, seven for Udall and seven for Schaffer. Pro-Schaffer groups aired

Table 8.4 Top Twenty Interest Group Investments in Senate Elections (2000, 2002, 2004, and 2008)*

State	Year	Open seat	Dem. cand. ads	GOP cand. ads	Dem. Party ads	GOP ads	Pro-Dem. interest group ads	Pro-GOP interest group ads	Group ads as % of total
Colorado	2008	Yes	6,268	2,716	2,615	2,193	3,840	4,932	38.9
Maine	2008	No	3,842	4,994	1,642	0	804	2,398	23.4
Colorado	2002	No	2,367	2,616	2,639	2,699	2,133	921	22.8
Louisiana	2008	No	2,094	1,494	633	726	566	645	19.7
Oregon	2008	No	5,655	10,084	8,646	2,984	2,898	3,733	19.5
New Mexico	2008	Yes	4,755	4,928	0	0	908	1,149	17.5
Michigan	2000	No	5,156	7,502	4,172	3,733	1,847	2,395	17.1
New Hampshire	2008	No	2,561	654	3,190	1,750	614	989	16.4
North Carolina	2008	No	6,667	8,789	11,630	4,881	1,557	3,698	14.1
New Mexico	2000	No	1,018	174	0	0	0	184	13.4
Oklahoma	2004	Yes	6,507	7,656	3,546	2,412	1,138	1,945	13.3
Minnesota	2008	No	6,644	6,210	4,223	3,450	713	2,386	13.1
Georgia	2008	No	1,917	1,733	3,422	498	692	428	12.9
Missouri	2002	No	4,383	3,327	4,670	3,993	1,250	876	11.5
Colorado	2004	Yes	3,667	4,703	1,805	1,069	911	405	10.5
Kentucky	2008	No	16,036	18,782	3,130	0	1,658	2,700	10.3
Delaware	2000	No	581	657	999	0	0	254	10.2
Iowa	2002	No	1,746	1,469	1,528	1,238	253	417	10.1
Arkansas	2002	No	4,273	2,783	2,493	3,152	849	548	9.9
Washington	2000	No	9,658	2,717	270	1,633	402	1,160	9.9

Source: Wisconsin Advertising Project

*Totals only include races where the candidates aired at least 1,000 ads. Ad totals combine primary and general election ads in the top 75 media markets. Ad totals do not include 2006 or 2010 elections.

more ads than the Republican Party and even more than the candidate himself. Pro-Udall groups aired more ads than did the Democratic Party.

The second most significant involvement—as a percent of total ads aired—was in the Maine Senate election between incumbent Republican Susan Collins and Congressman Tom Allen in 2008. In that election, interest groups sponsored nearly one in every four ads aired. Collins benefited from almost 2,400 ads in the Portland media market, with support from the U.S. Chamber of Commerce, the National Federation of Independent Business, Mainers for Employee Freedom, the Coalition for a Democratic Workplace, the American Medical Association, and America's Agenda Health Care for Kids. Allen received help from the People for the American Way, VoteVets.org, and American Rights at Work.

As Table 8.4 demonstrates, top interest group involvement can account for 10–20 percent of ads aired in tight races. Of particular note is that ten of the top twenty races were in 2008. Four of the top twenty were in 2000, four were in 2002, and two were in 2004.[26] The aggressive ad buys in 2008 likely resulted from the resistance of the presidential candidates to interest group help, as described above. As a consequence, interest groups that had mobilized after the 2007 *Wisconsin Right to Life* case had substantial sums they could more freely invest in close elections below the presidential level. Although the Senate was safely in Democratic hands in 2008, there was some concern that a strong performance could propel the Democrats to a filibuster-proof sixty-seat majority. Indeed, Democrats did eventually get to sixty votes after the election of Al Franken in Minnesota was finally certified. The supermajority was short-lived, however, after Edward Kennedy of Massachusetts died and was replaced in a special election by Republican Scott Brown. The opportunity to capture sixty seats conferred on Senate races a particular relevance. A closer look at Table 8.4 also shows that pro-Republican interest groups aired more ads than their Democratic counterparts in nine of the ten races in 2008. This lessened the Republican Party's disadvantage in many of these races stemming from the fact that the Republican Party committees sponsored fewer ads than the Democratic Party in eight of the ten races.

This analysis is repeated for House races in Table 8.5. Again, it is restricted to the top seventy-five media markets and to races where the candidates sponsored at least 1,000 ads.[27] In this context, interest group investment is even greater than for Senate races, with the ad totals ranging from 20 percent of the total ads aired to nearly 50 percent of the total ad buys in New Hampshire's 2nd congressional district in 2000.[28] In that race, the AFL-CIO backed Democrat Barney Brannon, and Citizens for Better Medicare supported incumbent Republican Charlie Bass.

Note that, unlike Table 8.4, where half of the top races were in 2008, ten of the twenty top House investments came in the year 2000, with six in

Table 8.5 Top Twenty Interest Group Investments in House Elections (2000, 2002, 2004, and 2008)*

District	Year	Open seat	Dem. cand. ads	GOP cand. ads	Dem. Party ads	GOP ads	Pro-Dem. interest group ads	Pro-GOP interest group ads	Group ads as % of total
NH-2	2000	No	805	404	61	78	556	777	49.72
CA-49	2000	No	1,343	1,008	1,386	466	1,724	2,050	47.31
WA-5	2000	No	752	1,328	777	1,306	1,859	1,816	46.89
NC-8	2000	No	472	1,043	1,599	178	902	1,865	45.67
NM-1	2000	No	1,469	1,497	546	71	1,351	1,078	40.40
KY-3	2000	No	1,860	2,538	1,763	425	2,750	1,223	37.63
FL-22	2002	No	1,379	835	0	0	0	1,290	36.82
AR-4	2000	No	1,376	1,089	1,276	1,282	1,206	1,323	33.49
PA-10	2000	No	1,916	1,621	1,304	1,100	854	2,013	32.55
MI-15	2002	No	2,275	0	0	0	997	0	30.47
WI-4	2004	Yes	1,252	0	0	0	502	0	28.62
IL-19	2002	No	469	1,316	436	0	378	493	28.17
CO-4	2008	No	1,634	1,468	859	627	1,782	0	27.97
NC-8	2002	No	816	823	323	714	143	866	27.38
KY-6	2000	No	1,542	2,811	1,939	1,822	1,342	1,693	27.22
MN-6	2000	No	1,161	924	231	456	324	646	25.92
PA-17	2002	No	2,233	1,227	1,807	2,638	746	1,856	24.76
MD-1	2008	Yes	1,545	2,722	1,585	205	0	1,668	21.59
AZ-5	2008	No	1,472	819	1,696	0	0	1,069	21.14
MI-9	2002	No	904	753	0	0	0	412	19.91

Source: Wisconsin Advertising Project

*Totals only include races where the candidates aired at least 1,000 ads. Ad totals combine primary and general election ads in the top 75 media markets. Ad totals do not include 2006 or 2010 elections.

2002, one in 2004, and three in 2008. This makes sense given the political context. In the run-up to the 2000 elections, *Congressional Quarterly* projected that the Republicans were likely to win 211 seats, not counting the outcomes of 16 too-close-to-call elections. This was seven seats shy of the total needed to control the chamber. In 2002, the Republicans had a decent grasp on 220 seats, just 2 more than needed to retain majority control. These two very tight cycles likely explain why sixteen of the top twenty interest group–funded races came in those years. In 2004, the Republicans were likely to win 230 seats, giving them a decent advantage; moreover, in that year only 6 seats ranked as too close to call, the lowest total in a generation. As a consequence, there just was not much expected change in the seat margins that year. In fact, the one election from 2004 included in Table 8.5 concerned a primary. In Wisconsin's 4th Congressional District, EMILY's List backed Gwen Moore in her primary campaign against fellow Democrats Matt Flynn and Tim Carpenter.[29] In 2008, the Democrats had close to 241 seats secured in the final weeks before the election, also dampening the motivation to invest in tight races.

The EMILY's List ad buy in the Wisconsin congressional race is a good reminder that many interest groups invest in campaigns for reasons beyond agenda control. In Gwen Moore's case, she was helped by a group committed to electing female candidates to the House and Senate. Other groups may choose to support candidates who are strong allies for the group's issue agenda, whether it is education, health care, or foreign policy. There is no denying, though, that a $1 million ad buy is a costly effort to help a single friend in need. The investment becomes more relevant if that race is crucial to a party's effort to win control of Congress.

The Future

Interest groups will continue to invest large sums of money in political advertisements in House, Senate, and presidential elections, and there are three key points of reference with respect to that future. The first is the legal context. This will continue to broaden. The current Roberts Supreme Court values First Amendment guarantees over congressional concerns about corruption or the appearance of corruption. As the flow of cases into the legal system challenges the regulated boundaries of interest group (and party and candidate) electioneering, more and more innovations will likely be permitted and with less and less regulation.

To that effect, 2010 was the first election cycle post–*Citizens United*, and the initial evidence indicates that many groups took advantage of these looser regulations. According to data from the Wesleyan Media Project, which tracked ads in 2010, interest groups sponsored 12 percent of all House ads and 15 percent of all Senate ads.[30] In terms of the count of ads aired, interest groups sponsored 168 percent more ads in House races than they did in 2008 and 44 percent more ads in Senate races. It should be noted, though, that candidates also purchased far more advertising in 2010, given that so many elections were competitive. But, overall, interest groups were more active participants in the "air war" than in any previous cycle.

Outside groups, as in previous years, were highly active in specific races. For example, interest groups sponsored 27 percent of all ads aired in the last sixty days of the highly competitive Senate race in Nevada between incumbent Democrat Harry Reid and Republican Sharon Angle. Groups were responsible for 26 percent of the ads in the Senate race in Kentucky, 28 percent in the Missouri Senate race, and 32 percent in the Senate battle in Colorado. There were also twenty-eight House races where interest groups were sponsors of at least 20 percent of the ad buys in the final sixty days.

For many, the laxer rules that allow outside groups to raise millions in large donations for ad campaigns is troubling and portends worse things to come. As a consequence, the new campaign finance battleground concerns disclosure laws, which Congress is currently seeking to expand in the wake of *Citizens United*. Disclosure of campaign activity is seen by many as a crucial weapon by which citizens, as well as journalists and political opponents, can keep tabs on political participants. All funds raised and spent by candidates, parties, and PACs, for example, are tracked and made public by the FEC. Much candidate advocacy by interest groups outside of PACs, however, is not tracked. Money raised and spent by 527s is made public by the IRS, but after *Wisconsin* and *Citizens United*, group efforts are increasingly funded through organizational forms that are not subject to disclosure, such as through 501(c)(4) organizations.

501(c)(4) groups are tax-exempt, social welfare nonprofits that are allowed to sponsor pro-candidate ads, so long as that activity does not account for more than 50 percent of their budgets. Many interests in past cycles, including 2010, used the (c)(4) classification to shield their donors. In one postelection symposium in December 2010, for example, the political director of American Crossroads—one of the dominant players in the just-completed midterms—admitted that it had formed two organizations in 2010, one that disclosed donors to the FEC and a 501(c)(4) that raised money from donors who wanted their names kept private.[31] This was such a concern that the Democrats tried to make it a campaign issue, hoping to embarrass Republican candidates, the primary beneficiaries of much of the outside spending that year.

Many worry that voters see an avalanche of ads from groups with important-sounding names but lack the means to track those groups' financial backing. And such disclosure is seen not simply as a public good.

Reformers posit that if they cannot stem interest group advertising efforts with content-based regulations, they may stymie the many groups worried about public distribution of their donor lists.[32]

On the other hand, one legal argument currently asserts that disclosure of political contributions is an unconstitutional infringement on a right to political anonymity and that forced disclosure as a tactic to reduce money in campaigns amounts to a chilling effect on free speech.[33] It is unlikely that the Court will side with the more extreme claim of anonymity as a widespread right, and so disclosure may be the last barrier to completely unregulated campaign financing of elections (at least with respect to interest groups).[34] Nonetheless, efforts in Congress to expand disclosure face stiff opposition.[35]

In the wake of a more permissive set of rules on the funding of political advertisements—increased disclosure notwithstanding—interest groups will remain aggressively involved in tight federal elections. Corporations, unions, and nonprofits will see little barrier to entry, and as issues enter the agenda, relevant groups will likely hit the airwaves to convince voters that certain candidates should be elected or defeated. The intensity of the advertising in 2010 may merely be prologue, then, as many interest groups saw the midterm elections as a testing ground for more intense mobilization in the coming presidential cycle.

This is all the more true given the second point of reference, the polarized political context. Indeed, the long-term political horizon suggests continued tight control over House and Senate majorities. For example, in the run-up to the 2010 elections, the Democrats controlled fifty-eight seats in the Senate but were projected to lose between four and eight seats. They ended up losing six seats, leaving their majority much smaller. A similar story was true for House elections. Democrats had 257 seats going into the election, but lost 63, along with majority control. In practical terms, this means that the 2012 and 2014 elections will remain hard-fought. Of the sixty-six Senate seats contested in both upcoming elections, for example, the Democrats are incumbents in forty-two of them (64 percent). Defending these races with only a three-seat majority will be motivation enough for liberal interests to wade into each competitive contest, and conservative groups will follow suit. Moreover, if President Obama's job approval continues to hover in the mid-40s, Republicans will see the White House as up for grabs. In the aftermath of the midterm elections, in fact, Senate Minority Leader Mitch McConnell indicated rather bluntly that Obama's defeat in 2012 should be the Republicans' primary objective.

Finally, a third point of reference could have a large influence on the level of interest group political advertising. This involves the changing nature of media in American elections. On the one hand, the 2008 elections featured more campaign advertising on television than in any previous election cycle. Candidates, parties, and interest groups in the top 75 media markets aired nearly 600,000 ads in congressional races, a 37 percent increase from 2004.[36] And 2010 saw a further 36 percent increase over 2008. With fewer legal restrictions on interest group electioneering, we may see no abatement on the frequency of television advertising in future cycles. On the other hand, many features of Americans' media consumption habits suggest television ads are less effective than in previous years. For one, the fragmentation of the media market means that television audiences are spread out over more stations and online sources of news and entertainment, making larger audiences harder to reach.[37] The early period in which ads were broadcast to audiences watching a relatively small number of channels has been replaced by narrow-casted media delivered to shrinking audience share. This is further complicated by DVR and TiVo, which allow viewers to record shows to watch later while easily fast-forwarding through commercials. In this context, will it continue to be worth the cost to produce and air television ads at such high levels?

This is even more relevant given the potentially cheaper forms of electoral outreach that are increasingly popular. For example, online advertising and social networking cost less and may allow political actors to speak more directly to core supporters.[38] Moreover, online campaigning is generally unregulated by existing campaign finance laws, and reformers' attempts to impose new restrictions have fallen on deaf ears at the FEC.

Additionally, many campaigns, political parties, and interest groups are turning to microtargeting efforts in which peer-to-peer contacts, direct mail, and telephone mobilization are highly tailored to specific audiences, using sophisticated matching of registration records and consumer-purchasing data.[39] With complex statistical modeling, political operatives can send one message to one household and a slightly different message to their neighbors, all with the goal of eliminating inefficiencies inherent in macrotargeting, where lots of nonvoters and apathetic citizens see the message. With all of these developments in electoral strategy, one wonders how useful old-fashioned political advertising will be in coming years.

Final Word

All told, the message of the last fifteen years is clear: interest groups are very active in American elections, and that level of investment is likely to grow as the political context remains charged and the legal context expands to allow even more forms of pro-candidate advocacy. Television advertising is one of the primary means of helping candidates, and interest groups can account for 10–50 percent of all ads aired in competitive races or media markets. These ad buys can have decisive impacts on the outcome of close elections and potentially on the fortunes of each political party in its quest for control of the policy-making agenda in Washington, D.C. The framers of the Constitution wisely anticipated the aggressive role of "factions" in the political life of America, and they knew that very little could stem the tide of group formation. They worried a great deal about the potential tyranny of a "majority faction," so one wonders what their reactions would be to a political scene with mass media, political elites, and voters increasingly polarized into two ideological camps, and a network of party and group allies working in concert to win the few seats essential to holding the reins of power over a massive central government.

Notes

1. Barack Obama, "Excerpts of the President's State of the Union Address," January 27, 2010, http://www.whitehouse.gov/the-press-office/excerpts-presidents-state-union-address/.
2. Interest group ad totals come from an analysis of data from Wisconsin Advertising Project. I am particularly grateful to the Project's Director, Ken Goldstein, for granting me access to the data for the 2000 through 2008 elections.
3. James E. Campbell, "Editor's Introduction: Forecasting the 2008 National Elections," *PS: Political Science and Politics* 41, no. 4 (2008): 679–82.
4. It should be noted that the legal context is largely constant for candidates. Rules for candidates on fundraising and expenditures have not really changed since major reform passed Congress in the 1970s. The political context does affect candidates, though. A favorable context for a candidate's party can make fundraising and recruitment much easier.
5. For instance, corporate-sponsored PACs can only solicit contributions from executive and administrative personnel, as well as from stockholders. Labor PACs can only solicit from dues-paying members and unions' executive and administrative personnel.
6. Magic words were actually first established in a footnote in the Supreme Court's 1976 decision in *Buckley v. Valeo.* The Court listed these eight phrases that it believed clearly established an election message. The ability to avoid these words and remain unregulated by the FEC was not really "discovered" until the 1990s. See Michael Franz, *Choices and Changes: Interest Groups in the Electoral Process* (Philadelphia: Temple University Press, 2008).
7. David Magleby, *Getting Inside the Outside Campaign* (Provo, UT: Brigham Young University Center for the Study of Elections and Democracy, 2001).
8. Such a distinction does not apply to candidate ads, since federal election laws consider any and all expenditures by candidates' campaigns as designed to affect election outcomes.
9. See David Magleby, "The Impact of Issue Advocacy and Party Soft Money Electioneering," in *The Medium and the Message,* eds. Kenneth Goldstein and Patricia Strach (Upper Saddle River, NJ: Pearson, 2004).
10. Ray La Raja, *Small Change: Money, Political Parties, and Campaign Finance Reform* (Chicago: University of Chicago Press, 2007); see also Steve Weissman and Ruth Hassan, "BCRA and the 527 Groups," in *The Election After Reform: Money, Politics and the Bipartisan Campaign Reform Act,* ed. Michael J. Malbin (Lanham, MD: Rowman and Littlefield, 2006).

11. Thomas Edsall, "FEC Ordered to Rethink '527' Rules," *Washington Post*, March 31, 2006; Thomas Edsall, "GOP Creating Own '527' Groups: Unregulated Funds Can Be Raised," *Washington Post*, May 25, 2004.

12. One might argue that because *Citizens United* seemed to broaden the ruling in *Wisconsin Right to Life* that the difference between Phase 4 and Phase 5 is negligible. On the other hand, *Citizens United* seems to represent a transition in the orientation of the Court toward rethinking major sections of campaign finance law.

13. Nolan M. McCarty, Keith T. Poole, and Howard Rosenthal, *Polarized America: The Dance of Ideology and Unequal Riches* (Cambridge, MA: MIT Press, 2006).

14. The data are available at http://www.voteview.com/. The manipulation of the data to demonstrate increased polarization is available on request.

15. To do this, calculate the ideology of the median member for each party in the House and Senate and divide that by the standard deviation for all other party members in each chamber.

16. Tracy Sulkin, *Issue Politics in Congress* (New York: Cambridge University Press, 2005).

17. Timothy P. Carney, "Drug Lobby Showers Money on its Hero Harry Reid," *Washington Examiner*, July 7, 2010, http://washingtonexaminer.com/news/business/drug-lobby-showers-money-its-hero-harry-reid/.

18. Matt Grossman and Casey B. K. Dominguez, "Party Coalitions and Interest Group Networks," *American Politics Research* 37, no. 5 (2009): 767–800.

19. Gregory Koger, Seth Masket, and Hans Noel, "Cooperative Party Factions in American Politics," *American Politics Research* 38, no 1 (2010): 33–53.

20. For a discussion of how the emergence of 527s corresponds to prevailing understandings of interest groups in American politics (and elections specifically), see Robert G. Boatright, "Situating the New 527 Organizations in Interest Group Theory," *The Forum* 5, no. 2 (2007): Article 5.

21. For information on the Project, visit http://wiscadproject.wisc.edu/.

22. In addition to counting the number of ads, there are two other ways that one could measure political advertising intensity. First, it might seem fruitful to talk about how many dollars were spent by interest groups to air pro-candidate ads. The estimates in the Wisconsin Advertising Project data are only estimates of advertising cost, however (see Michael G. Hagen and Robin Kolodny, "Finding the Cost of Campaign Advertising," *The Forum* 6, no. 1 (2008): Article 11.). Comparing across years would also mean adjusting these estimates for inflation. Second, it might be useful to discuss the number of gross ratings points (GRPs) purchased by interest groups. GRPs are estimates of the number of people who may have seen an ad. The Wisconsin data include the GRP value for each ad airing in some years but not in others. To best compare across time, then, the total count of ads is utilized here. It should be noted that ad counts and GRPs are highly correlated.

23. One other group, Let Freedom Ring, fell under a different loophole that this chapter has not discussed, the 501(c)(4) loophole. The justification for this comes from an important, though obscure, Supreme Court case from 1986: *Massachusetts Citizens for Life v. FEC* (*MCFL*). In that case, the Court argued that some 501(c)(4) groups (tax exempt nonprofits who register in that section of the tax code) could sponsor express advocacy communications (without having to form a PAC) if the ads were paid for by individuals and the *primary purpose* of the group was not political electioneering or lobbying. The *MCFL* exemption was rarely used prior to 2002 because non–"magic word" ads were permitted by any group, including corporations and unions. After BCRA passed in 2002, 527s (as discussed) became the organizational

vehicle used primarily for nonexpress advocacy. But with new focus on regulating 527s after 2004, the Court's twenty-year-old ruling in *MCFL* became particularly relevant for the 2006 elections. *Wisconsin Right to Life* and *Citizens United* made the *MCFL* classification less important, though registering as a 501(c)(4) helped groups shield their donors from public scrutiny. See the concluding section of the chapter for more information on this.

24. David C. Kimball, "Interest Groups in the 2008 Presidential Election: The Barking Dog That Didn't Bite," *The Forum* 6, no. 4 (2008): Article 2.

25. Peter Francia, *The Future of Organized Labor in American Politics* (New York: Columbia University Press, 2006).

26. If you look beyond the top 20 races, interest groups were active at some level in 54 of the 111 Senate races where at least one ad was aired by a candidate.

27. Because House races generally feature lower ad totals than Senate races, one might consider a lower threshold—perhaps 500 ads. Doing so does not generally change the look of Table 8.5. That is, even in these additional races, interest groups air a sizable percentage of the ads.

28. Of the 631 House elections where candidates aired at least one ad, interest groups were sponsors of ads in 142.

29. This also explains the totals for Michigan's 15th District race in 2002, when EMILY's List backed incumbent congresswoman Lynn Rivers against fellow Democrat and incumbent John Dingell in their primary fight after redistricting combined their districts.

30. See http://election-ad.research.wesleyan.edu/. The Project is a successor to the Wisconsin Advertising Project.

31. Kenneth P. Vogel, "SEIU, American Crossroads Look Back at 2010 Spending," *Politico*, December 13, 2010, http://www.politico.com/news/stories/1210/46355.html.

32. Carol Leonnig, "Political Ads are a Tough Sell for Image-Conscious Corporations," *Washington Post*, June 1, 2010.

33. Bradley Smith makes this argument in *Unfree Speech: The Folly of Campaign Finance Reform* (Princeton, NJ: Princeton University Press, 2001): 220–25.

34. In oral arguments for *Doe v. Reed* in 2010, even conservative Justices Scalia and Kennedy expressed concerns about a supposed right to anonymous political speech. This should mean that disclosure laws, even those broadened by Congress in future campaign finance legislation, should withstand judicial review.

35. Congress debated, but did not pass, one law in 2010 called (appropriately) the DISCLOSE Act. It would force any group airing ads that mention candidates to publicize their donor lists.

36. There was a more modest increase in the presidential race. Between June and Election Day, Barack Obama and John McCain aired over 780,000 ads nationwide. This was a 5 percent increase over the Kerry/Bush contest in 2004.

37. Markus Prior, *Post-Broadcast Democracy: How Media Choice Increases Inequality in Political Involvement and Polarizes Elections* (New York: Cambridge University Press, 2007).

38. Matthew Hindman, *The Myth of a Digital Democracy* (Princeton, NJ: Princeton University Press, 2008).

39. Sunshine Hillygus and Todd G. Shields. *The Persuadable Voter: Wedge Issues in Presidential Campaigns* (Princeton, NJ: Princeton University Press, 2009).

9

Bridging the Gap between
Political Parties and Interest Groups

Michael T. Heaney

On January 22, 2011, 180 people representing 70 organizations from the "tea party" movement met in Sharpsville, Indiana, to discuss the ouster of longtime US Senator Richard Lugar. Although Senator Lugar has long been considered a conservative stalwart, this group, calling itself "Hoosiers for a Conservative Senate," labeled him "too liberal" and sought to its unify its support behind an alternative candidate.[1] Lugar had won 87 percent of vote in 2006, when he was elected to his sixth term in the Senate, so one might reasonably believe that Lugar should not worry about a small group of rabble rousers. Yet, in the 2010 congressional elections, tea-party-backed candidates defeated incumbent candidates in Republican primaries in Alaska, Nevada, South Carolina, and elsewhere, leading the tea party to be credited as a major player in the election.[2] Clearly, the tea party is a force to be reckoned with.

While the tea party is busy attempting to upend the Republican Party, it may also play a role in upending the way that we think about interest group politics. While many people think of interest groups and political parties as clearly distinct entities, the activities of the tea party raise questions about how true that is. In some respects, the organizations behind the tea party movement—Freedom Works, Patriot Action Network, Tea Party Express, Tea Party Patriots, and others—look like traditional interest groups. They are autonomous organizations that express clear issue positions on topics such as taxation and health care. Yet they are attempting to reshape the nature of the Republican Party by fielding candidates in party primaries. Thus, in some ways, they look more like party organizations than like interest groups. So which are they?

Political parties and interest groups are more closely related to one another than is often supposed. Parties and groups are both types of political associations that seek to mediate the relationship between citizens and government. Interest groups usually seek to craft an identity based on the constituencies that they claim to represent, the issues that they work on, or their ideological perspectives.[3] They are formal organizations that advocate for relatively narrow interests, regardless of which party is in power. In contrast, political parties usually seek to build a broader coalition of interests so that they can sustain majorities to control the government.[4] However, even though interest groups themselves do not seek to control the government, they care about who does. Which party is in power makes a difference to which groups' interests are served.[5] Interest groups may care about not only *which* party governs but also *how* it governs. Likewise, political parties may not build the kind of narrowly focused constituencies that interest groups cultivate, but they may benefit from accessing those narrow constituencies for specialized tasks, such as raising money or getting out the vote. Thus, depending on the situation, interest groups and political parties often have strong incentives to work with each other, to fight against each other, or to try to control one another. As they cross paths with each other, parties and groups often step on each others' toes and, in the process, blur the boundaries between these two types of political associations.

To understand better how political parties and interest groups relate to one another, the chapter discusses four aspects of this relationship.

1. It explores how parties and groups compete for the loyalties and attention of the same activists. Looking at these connections with citizens illuminates how both parties and groups are alternative ways that citizens can become involved in politics.
2. It explains how formal institutional structures create opportunities for groups and parties to assist and exploit one another. Parties and groups have coevolved symbiotically, each providing the nutrients that the other needs to survive.[6]
3. It illuminates how parties and interest groups are embedded with one another through elite networks. These networks create the channels through which parties and groups use one another to send information and develop the trust that is necessary to make political processes work.
4. It considers how the relationships between parties and groups weigh in their strategic calculations.

The chapter concludes by reflecting on how party-group dynamics factor into how these actors are situated in American politics.

Competing for Hearts and Minds

Political parties and interest groups are both important avenues that citizens use to relate to the political system. Citizens learn about politics and are mobilized to action, in part, through their affiliations with parties and groups. These affiliations may reinforce one another, or they may pull at cross-purposes. These processes work differently in the Democratic and

Republican Parties. This section explores these issues first by addressing social identification, second by considering overlapping versus cross-cutting affiliations, and third by comparing affiliations across the two major parties in the United States.

Political scientists Donald Green, Bradley Palmquist, and Eric Schickler contend that "partisan identification is a genuine form of social identification."[7] Individuals begin to form impressions about political parties at a young age. They learn about parties and form partisan attitudes under the influence of their parents, in school, and from watching the world around them.[8] As events unfold and issues evolve, emerging generations see parties in a new light and adjust their evaluations accordingly.[9] Activists may switch parties over the course of their lives, but party switching is more likely to occur early in life than it is later in life, partly because partisans are gradually socialized to accept the issue portfolios of their parties.[10] The acceptance or rejection of political parties becomes a vital part of the way that citizens understand their place in society.

Membership in interest groups may also be a form of social identification. Individuals often form identifications with interest groups as they mature in their occupational and professional lives. Labor unions, for example, may prompt people to think of themselves as "workers," which may further a group-based identity in relation to the polity.[11] Professional associations, such as the American Medical Association, may encourage people to bring concerns of professional autonomy to their involvement in politics.[12] Church membership may facilitate identification with issue-oriented groups that oppose abortion, same-sex marriage, or gambling.[13] Some religiously based interest groups, such as Focus on the Family, develop media and educational materials designed to educate youth from the viewpoint of that group.[14] While individuals are exposed to interest group messages throughout their lives, they often seize opportunities to become actively involved in an interest group when they are at turning points in their lives.[15]

Loyalties to political parties and interest groups often reinforce one another. For example, membership in a pro-life interest group is likely to strengthen an individual's identification with the Republican Party because that party maintains a fairly reliable pro-life stance. Similarly, membership in a labor union is likely to strengthen an individual's identification with the Democratic Party because that party maintains a fairly reliable pro-labor stance. By participating in the activities of an interest group, individuals may meet like-minded partisans who will celebrate a particular party's victories and commiserate after its defeats.

At the same time, interest group membership and party membership have the potential to clash with each other. For example, a person who is both a member of the Republican Party and a labor union will be cross pressured by these affiliations. The Republican Party may encourage her to support right-to-work laws, while the labor union may encourage her to oppose them. The person could choose to ignore the cross pressures. Alternatively, she could choose to drop out of either the Republican Party or the labor union, thus costing one or the other of these organizations political support. Or, she could try to bring about change in the party or the labor union, either by pushing the Republican Party to be friendlier to the interests of organized labor (or at least to oppose them less actively) or by convincing the labor union to be a less vibrant supporter of the Democratic Party. Regardless of how the individual decides to act, the Republican Party and the labor union both have a member who has the potential to disrupt the agendas of their organizations.

The Republican union member is an example of someone who faces party-group cross pressures where the party and group in question have been antagonistic to one another throughout history. However, cross pressures may also exist in cases where the party and group are closely aligned with one another. For example, the Democratic Party and labor unions tend to be strongly aligned with one another. However, the Democratic Party sometimes takes issue positions that labor unions perceive to be adverse to their interests. When Democrats support free trade agreements, labor unions strongly object and attempt to convince the party to change its position.[16] If the party does not budge, Democrats who are in labor unions may complain that the party is not living up to its ideals, potentially making them less likely to support Democrats in the next election. These Democratic union members are unlikely to switch their votes to the Republican candidate, but they may neglect to engage in supportive activities that they usually undertake, such as making phone calls, knocking on doors, or raising money for Democratic candidates. In the Republican Party, conflicts between Christian interest groups and the party establishment are a common source of cross pressures. For example, members of Focus on the Family may want the Republican Party to take a stronger stand against same-sex marriage than some of the party's leaders view as politically wise.[17] Similarly, tea party interest groups are determined to make sure that the Republican Party takes conservative stands on fiscal issues. Cross pressures may not cause lifelong Republicans to become Democrats, but they may drain much of the usual enthusiasm from party members' participation. At the same time, some people do respond to cross pressures by switching parties.[18]

Interest groups and political parties compete for the loyalties of activists in both the Democratic and Republican Parties. However, the nature of this process is very different between the parties. In an earlier study that I conducted with Seth Masket, Dara Strolovitch, and Joanne Miller, we found significant differences between the Democratic and Republican Parties in terms of how their activists relate to interest groups.[19] We attended the Democratic and Republican National Conventions in 2008 and conducted surveys of the delegates in attendance. First, the results showed that while both Democrats and Republicans join interest groups, Democrats join approximately 35 percent more interest groups than do Republicans. Thus, interest groups have more points of access into the Democratic Party than they do into the Republican Party. Second, the analysis revealed that interest group membership in the Republican Party is more hierarchical than it is in the Democratic Party. In the Republican Party, activists coalesce around a smaller number of leading interest groups, while in the Democratic Party, activists disperse their loyalties more evenly among prominent groups. A list of these leading groups is provided in Table 9.1.[20] Thus, interest groups are a greater source of hierarchical control over activists in the Republican Party than they are in the Democratic Party, where interest groups coexist with one another on a more equal basis.[21] Third, different kinds of interest groups dominate the two parties. Democratic activists are more likely to be associated with labor unions and identity groups, while Republican activists are more likely to be associated with civic, religious, and professional associations. Few interests groups have leading activists from both parties in common, reflecting the partisan polarization of interest group politics in the United States.

Recognizing that parties and interest groups draw upon a common pool of activists is a critical step to bridging the gap between parties and groups. Activists do not necessarily care whether their interests are served by parties or groups, only that their interests are ultimately served. Thus, activists are likely to direct their energies, loyalties, and resources to whichever

Table 9.1   Leading Interest Groups among Democratic and Republican Party Delegates

Rank	Interest Group
Democratic Party	
1	Organized Labor (AFL-CIO, Change to Win)
2	MoveOn.org
3	National Education Association
3	Human Rights Campaign
3	NARAL Pro-Choice America
6	National Association for the Advancement of Colored People
6	Sierra Club
6	Progressive Democrats of America
Republican Party	
1	National Rifle Association
2	National Right to Life Committee
3	Campaign for Liberty

Source: Surveys of 738 delegates at the 2008 Democratic and Republican national conventions.

organizations they perceive to be acting most effectively on their behalf. These dynamics not only affect rank-and-file activists but also shape future party leaders who, more often than not, once belonged to the rank and file. As a result, today's candidates increasingly have backgrounds that connect them to interest groups and social movements.[22] Thus, competition for these activists—and potential future party leaders—stimulates a continuous interplay between parties and groups.

Institutional Opportunities for Cooperation and Exploitation

The relationship between political parties and interest groups is, in part, a product of the peculiar institutional structures of American government. Interest groups and political parties have coevolved within these structures such that mutual cooperation and exploitation are a routine part of their politics. Four institutional features promote party-group interactions. First, the existence of state and national platform committees provides an opportunity for activists and interest groups to influence public perceptions of a party. Second, primary elections restrict the ability of party leaders to select party candidates, providing an opportunity for interest groups to sway which candidates a party selects to stand in the general election. Third, campaign finance laws institute financial dependencies between parties and groups. Fourth, relatively recent changes in the structures of parties and interest groups create opportunities for each to have greater dependency on the other.

Party platforms are largely symbolic statements of party positions. Republican presidential candidate Bob Dole once famously quipped that he had not read the Republican Party Platform, and was not bound by it, when asked about what he thought about its plank on pro-life issues.[23] Nonetheless, platform committees, populated by activists at the state and national levels, provide an opportunity for interests groups to infiltrate parties formally and engrave their policy positions as party doctrines. In a study of state Republican Party platforms in 2000, Kimberly Conger demonstrates how Christian Right organizations penetrated the party at the state level.[24] Using state Republican platforms, she reveals how Christian Right penetration varied from state to state according to differences in religiosity, ideology, and competition. Although platforms do not bind candidates' rhetoric or positions in elections, they may influence public perceptions of a party, thus making them a potential starting point in groups' efforts to define a party.[25]

Unlike party platforms, primary elections are (usually) *binding* institutional structures that afford significant opportunities for party-group interaction.[26] In a parliamentary system of government, it is typical for party leaders to select the slate of candidates who will run on behalf of the party in the general election.[27] This procedure ensures that candidates who stand on behalf of the party reflect its policy positions, at least as understood by the party leaders. Given this institutional arrangement, it would be difficult for leaders of outside groups to dictate the agenda of a party. In the United States, however, candidates usually must stand for election in a primary or caucus before they stand in the general election. The existence of a primary or caucus expands the possibility that voters will select candidates that do not reflect the policy positions or priorities of party leaders. In the Democratic Party, in particular, the reforms of the McGovern-Fraser Commission (1968–1972) opened the primary process to the influence of outside groups.[28] Republican reforms also opened its party nominating process in the 1970s, but party organizations maintained greater control over the process than was the case in the Democratic Party.[29] Party organizations attempt to resist allowing outside groups to control nominations by creating rules and procedures biased toward party loyalists.[30] However, their ability to influence the nomination process varies from party to party and from state to state. Some state parties allow party leaders to endorse candidates before the primaries, though most do not.[31] The party establishment often uses contributions to incumbents through leadership PACs (Political Action Committees) to discourage challenges to incumbents.[32] Occasionally, party leaders offer inducements, such as promises of administrative appointments to prospective challengers, to avoid contested primaries.[33]

No matter how hard party leaders may work to avoid it, incumbents and other preferred party candidates always have the potential to be defeated in American primaries. This possibility creates an opportunity for interest groups to influence who stands on a party's slate. Indeed, some interest groups have made their reputations, in part, by challenging party candidates in primaries. The classic example of such a group is the Club for Growth. The Club for Growth was founded in 1999 with the goal of electing fiscally conservative candidates in Republican primaries. The Club has had several notable successes, including Sharon Angle's victory in Nevada's Republican U.S. Senate primary and Mike Lee's win in Utah's Republican U.S. Senate primary.[34] In 2010, Republican Pat Toomey was elected U.S. Senator from Pennsylvania after a longtime affiliation with the Club.[35] While there is no perfect parallel to the Club for Growth within the Democratic Party, MoveOn.org has sometimes played an analogous role. For example, in 2006, MoveOn.org was a visible supporter of Ned Lamont's primary challenge to sitting U.S. Senator Joe Lieberman of Connecticut.[36] Lamont and MoveOn.org claimed that Lieberman was too conservative for the Democratic Party, especially on issues of national security where Lieberman had been a vocal supporter of President George W. Bush. Lamont and MoveOn.org attained a Pyrrhic victory over Lieberman in the primary, as Lieberman was able to win the general election with the support of the Republican Party.

Political scientist Michael Murakami calls organizations such as the Club for Growth and MoveOn.org "party purity groups."[37] They are so called because they work to attain ideological purity within a particular political party. When party purity groups judge elected officials to have strayed from the party line, these groups let it be known that the candidates are vulnerable to a purity-group-inspired primary challenge. Officeholders know that a serious primary challenge raises the prospect that they will not be reelected, as they must prepare for battle on two fronts— against their own party's puritans in the primary and against the opposing party in the general election. In using this approach, party purity groups have the potential to influence politics far beyond the elections in which they actually field a candidate or win an election. If elected officials know that straying from the party line may make them vulnerable to a purity-group-inspired challenge, then they may be less likely to deviate from the party line. Thus, potentially vulnerable politicians may move their policy positions toward a perceived ideologically "pure" point in order to fend off the potential challenge.[38]

Party purity groups provide an example of how interest groups have the potential to use primaries as an opportunity to supplant party leadership. Party purity groups may aid party leaders by disciplining errant party members. But they may also create problems for the party. Rather than enforcing uniform party discipline, parties may benefit from flexibility across political contexts. For example, Democrats may have a better chance of winning political office in a relatively conservative state if they run a candidate that is slightly more conservative than the typical Democratic officeholder. The same is true of Republicans seeking office in relatively liberal states. If ideological purity is enforced, the party may wind up worse off than it would have been by allowing deviation from the national party standard. Such was the case in Rhode Island, where attacks by the Club for Growth weakened liberal Republican U.S. Senator Lincoln Chafee enough that he was replaced by the much more liberal Democratic U.S. Senator Sheldon Whitehouse.[39] The Republican Party is numerically weaker in the Senate with a liberal Democratic senator from Rhode Island than it would be with a liberal Republican senator from Rhode Island. But the Club for Growth hopes that Republican officeholders see what happened to Lincoln Chafee and, in turn, become more reliably conservative in their voting. Thus, while the Club for Growth helped to lose a Republican Senate seat in Rhode Island, it believes that it helped to gain a Republican Senate caucus that is more compliant with its vision of Republicanism. This example illustrates how, when primaries are involved, parties and interest groups may compete for control of the party system.

Even if interest groups do not wish to compete with parties for control of nominations, the campaign finance system is a third institutional structure that affords opportunities for party-group interaction. Many observers have speculated that PAC contributions to campaigns allow interest groups to have undue influence over politicians.[40] However, the relationship is more realistically characterized as a vehicle for information sharing and displays of loyalty than for raw vote buying. Interest groups (through their PACs) tend to support one party exclusively, unless their contributions are unlikely to affect electoral outcomes.[41] Rather than taking risks, PACs concentrate their funds on the politicians most likely to win elections.[42]

Although PAC contributions are the most well-known aspect of the campaign finance system, interest groups and political parties collaborate through numerous other campaign finance channels. PAC contributions are regulated by the Federal Election Commission (FEC) and are subject to strict dollar amount limits. Groups and parties have long found loopholes through these limitations. For many years, interest groups made unlimited contributions directly to political parties that were intended to support party-building activities and issue advertisements. These unregulated contributions were known as "soft" money because they could not be used explicitly to support or oppose a candidate for office (as is the case with "hard" money). This particular loophole closed when soft money contributions were banned by the Bipartisan Campaign Reform Action (BCRA) of 2002, which was upheld by the Supreme Court in the case of *McConnell vs. Federal Election Commission.*[43]

Parties and groups were quick to adapt to the new regulatory regime created by BCRA. They began to make use of a previously obscure provision of the Internal Revenue Code known as Section 527. This provision allows for the creation of independent political committees—referred to as "527 organizations"—that are unregulated by the FEC. These organizations cannot explicitly endorse or support a particular candidate, but they can undertake myriad activities that support the functions of a party, as long as those functions are not explicitly coordinated with the party. The new 527 organizations became a significant element of the party-group relationship when they were incorporated into the 2004 presidential election campaign. Despite the supposed absence of explicit coordination, a network of 527 organizations arose in 2004 that divided the electioneering functions of parties (e.g., fundraising, grassroots turnout, media) among a handful of unaffiliated but allied organizations.[44] These organizations hybridized the organizational forms used by the political parties and interest groups. Political scientist Richard Skinner goes so far as to argue that, collectively, this network of 527s constituted a "shadow party" in 2004.[45] This metaphor highlights the ways in which a network of 527 organizations was able to offer alternatives to party functions, at least for a short period of time.

In the 2008 presidential election, 527 organizations were much less active than they had been during the 2004 presidential election. Parties may have turned away from 527 organizations partly because of the difficulty of coordinating their functions across several organizations and partly because of the rise of the Internet as an effective tool for raising large volumes of hard-money contributions from individuals.[46] The 2004 presidential election may prove to have been the one moment in the sun for 527s. However, the emergence of this type of organization is revealing of the nature of the relationship between parties and interest groups. When the opportunity for groups to donate soft money to parties was foreclosed in 2002 by BCRA, parties and groups quickly adapted by seizing upon a somewhat obscure provision in the tax code. They used these innovative organizations to rally around or oppose the presidential candidate of their choice. In some ways, this network of 527 organizations served as a partial substitute for party organizations.

The changing organizational structure of political parties and interest groups creates a fourth opportunity for party-group interaction. For many years, mass political parties operated through deeply embedded grassroots structures with well-organized connections between parties and voters at the smallest geographic units, usually precincts, that spanned only a few blocks of a city or town. Since at least the 1960s, this machine-style of organization has been in decline such that it is no longer recognizable in most parts of the United States.[47] In its place, campaign organizations that focus on serving the needs of candidates have emerged. This shift has created a vacuum such that parties no longer have the organizing capacity to perform core functions, such as get-out-the-vote drives. Many of these functions have been outsourced to private companies and nonprofit organizations, such the Fund for Public Interest Research.[48] Additionally, this decline in party organizations opens the door for interest groups to replace the ancillary functions of parties. Interest groups may find that supplying the infrastructure for electoral mobilization and offering policy expertise play an even greater role than financial clout in steering the direction of parties.[49]

Working America is an example of an interest group that has stepped into the on-the-ground roles once played by the Democratic Party. Working America was founded in 2003 with financial support from the American Federation of Labor–Congress of Industrial Organizations (AFL-CIO), the nation's largest federation of labor unions. Formally speaking, Working America is a nonpartisan organization that does not endorse any particular party. But, in practice, it throws its support almost entirely to Democrats, making exceptions in only a handful of cases. This support is not expressed primarily through monetary donations but through grassroots canvassing efforts on behalf of pro-labor, Democratic candidates.[50] The Democratic

Party relies heavily on these kinds of efforts in a way that it might not if its local-level infrastructure were as robust as it once was.

Weaknesses in the institutional structures of interest groups concomitantly create opportunities for political parties. As Harvard Professor Theda Skocpol has shown, cross-class, membership-based interest groups have been in decline in the United States since at least the 1960s, if not earlier.[51] Skocpol reveals that where interest groups were once firmly grounded in chapters and local-level organizing, they now rely predominantly on national-level managers who sell a package of services to their supporters. Today's "supporters" have less of a stake than the "members" of a previous era, who developed a greater identification with organizations that more regularly allowed them to attend meetings, vote, and shape the direction of their organizations. Without these strong ties to interest groups, citizens are less likely to feel cross pressured to support their concerns when they clash with party loyalties.[52]

Many of the interactions between parties and interest groups are born from opportunity. The institutions of American politics open the door for parties and groups to lean on one another. Party platform committees, primaries, campaign finance laws, and organizational changes allow parties and groups to be solutions to one another's problems. The coevolution of parties and groups is, thus, a fundamental outcome of the institutionalized structures of American government.

Embeddedness in Elite Networks

Elite networks play a critical role in bridging the gap between political parties and interest groups.[53] These networks are composed of influential people who are linked to both parties and groups. Within these networks, people exchange information, share resources, build loyalty, and create coalitions. Getting access to these networks makes a difference to how political parties and interest groups operate. They may help to determine who selects political leaders and who influences public policy.

Lobbyists play an especially important role in linking political parties and interest groups. They generally move back and forth between working for these two types of organizations over the course of their careers. They play this role, in large part, because of the nature of the lobbyist's job. A lobbyist is someone who represents an interest group before Congress (or another governmental body). But, in order to represent an interest group effectively, the lobbyist has to be intimately familiar with the inner workings of Congress. The people who have the best knowledge of Congress's inner workings are those who have worked for it in the past, either as an elected member or as a hired staff member. Since any member of Congress is identified with a particular political party (as even so-called "independents" must caucus with either the Democrats or the Republicans), those people who have worked for Congress have known partisan identities. Someone who has worked for Senator Dick Durbin is known to be a Democrat, and someone who has worked for Representative Eric Cantor is known to be a Republican. Political scientist Rogan Kersh documented this point in a study showing that all the corporate lobbyists that he followed were known as either Democrats or Republicans.[54]

The partisan identities of lobbyists are a notable part of their work. Since lobbyists are known as either Democrats or Republicans, they have difficulty lobbying members of the party of which they are not a member. Members of Congress may be inherently suspicious of lobbyists who are not members of their party and may be more likely to trust lobbyists from their party. Democratic lobbyists are most effective in lobbying Democratic members of Congress, and Republican lobbyists are most effective in lobbying Republican members of Congress. Thus, an interest group's leaders must either consciously hire both Democrats and Republicans for their lobbying team or risk that their group will become known for the partisanship of its lobbyists.

The partisan demand for lobbyists helps to produce a partisan structure in elite lobbying networks. To understand this structure better, I interviewed health policy staff members in the offices of ninety-five members of Congress in 2003. I asked each staff member to look at a list of 171 interest groups that were highly active on health policy issues. Each staff member was asked to rate his or her office's lobbying contacts with each interest group according to their frequency (i.e., regular, occasional, never) and reliability (i.e., reliable, sometimes reliable, not reliable).[55] Figure 9.1 reports the network of these contacts. Each circle in the graph represents a Democratic congressional office, while each square in the graph represents a Republican congressional office. A line between two shapes indicates that the offices receive regular, reliable lobbying contacts from the same interest group. Larger shapes represent offices that receive more lobbying contacts, while smaller shapes represent offices that receive fewer lobbying contacts.

The polarized partisan structure of the lobbying network represented in Figure 9.1 is unmistakable. The upper left side of the network is composed almost entirely of Democrats, while the lower right side of the network is composed almost entirely of Republicans. There are only a few exceptions. First, two Democrats and two Republicans appear out of place on the periphery of the network. These anomalies are due to the fact that these congressional offices are not major players in health care policy, so their health lobbying contacts are driven more by district-based concerns than by ideology. The core of the network is almost perfectly polarized, with the office of Representative Ralph Hall of Texas serving as the only exception. At the time the interviews were conducted in 2003,

Figure 9.1   The Party Bias of Health Care Lobbying Networks in
the US Congress, 2003

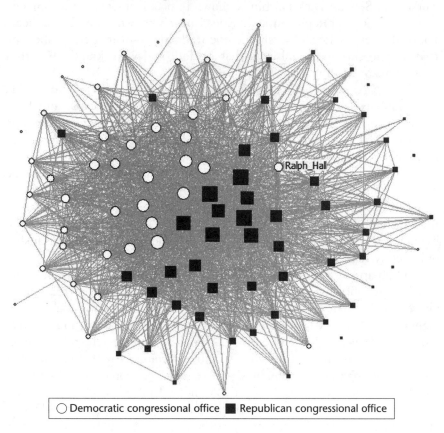

Ralph_Hall

○ Democratic congressional office   ■ Republican congressional office

Source: Interviews with ninety-five congressional staff members working on health policy in 2003.

Hall was a Democrat, so his office appears out of place since it is grouped with the Republicans rather than with the Democrats. However, in 2004, Hall switched to the Republican Party. Indeed, the network shows that in 2003, Hall's lobbying contacts were already more akin to those of Republicans than to those of other Democrats. Hall is the exception that proves the rule.

The network in Figure 9.1 reflects the strong networks that exist between political parties and interest groups. It shows that lobbying contacts are heavily influenced by party ties. Members of Congress from the same party tend to prefer to hear from the same interest groups, who tend to hire lobbyists from their party. These patterns may contribute to the polarization of interest group politics. If lobbyists have incentives to become tied to one political party, then interest groups are likely to gravitate toward only one party. Because of this polarization, interest groups that are able to reach across party lines tend to be more influential than those who are not able to do so, because of their potential to act as brokers.[56]

Networks of lobbying contacts are only one example of the ways in which parties and interest groups are connected through lobbyists. Parties and interest groups are connected through multiple kinds of networks, including networks of candidate endorsements, donations, and legislative support for pending legislation.[57] Political scientists Gregory Koger and Jennifer Nicoll Victor show that patterns of polarization are present in campaign contributions by lobbyists.[58] They observe that "the donation behavior of individual lobbyists appears to be quite partisan. About 29% of lobbyists gave almost nothing to Democrats, while another 28% gave almost nothing to Republicans."[59] Koger and Victor find that this pattern is even more pronounced among big spenders (lobbyists who gave five or more donations to members of Congress). These lobbyists tend to pick a party and stick with it. Further, two members of Congress are most likely to receive donations from the same lobbyists when they are of the same party.[60]

The networks that connect parties and interest groups can prove to be valuable resources to all involved. In an ingenious study, political scientists Gregory Koger, Seth Masket, and Hans Noel made $25 donations to an ideologically diverse set of interest groups, magazines, and party organizations using aliases.[61] They observed how organizations sold their information to other organizations by recording the new solicitations that they received. The results of the analysis showed that the information was sold within clusters that closely related to political parties. This study reveals the behind-the-scenes way in which political parties and interest groups exchange valuable information, such as the names and addresses of individuals who are likely to contribute to their causes.

Networks connecting parties and interest groups have wide implications. In their book *The Party Decides*, Marty Cohen, David Karol, Hans Noel, and John Zaller demonstrate that these networks are decisive in the selection of presidential nominees by the Democratic and Republican Parties.[62] After conducting a wide historical survey of data on party nominations, delegate selection, and candidate endorsements, they conclude that interest "groups can often get more from government by funneling their resources through a party coalition to nominate and elect officeholders friendly to their interests than by buying policies one at a time from independent officeholders after they have taken office."[63] Thus, even though members of interest groups may be numerically small in a general election contest,[64] they have disproportionate influence on the political process by helping to select presidential nominees. Interest groups are at the core of party coalitions.

The value of elite networks makes them an object of contention in the political process. If political actors gain an advantage by connecting through networks, then their opponents may try to do what they can to prevent them from benefitting from network connections. At the outset, deliberately influencing the structure of political networks seems like a difficult thing to do, since networks are highly decentralized and not always easily observable. However, two prominent Republicans—Tom DeLay, Majority Whip (1995–2003) and Majority Leader (2003–2005) of the U.S. House of Representatives, and Grover Norquist, President of Americans for Tax Reform—made changing the nature of Washington lobbying networks a cause célèbre for a decade, from the mid-1990s to the mid-2000s.[65] Prior to that time, the Democratic Party had controlled the U.S. House of Representatives continuously from 1955 to 1995. As a result, the lobbying and campaign contribution networks surrounding the House had heavily favored the Democrats. After the Republican victory in the 1994 congressional elections, DeLay and Norquist concluded that these networks should change to the advantage of Republicans. DeLay and Norquist initiated "the K Street Project" to encourage previously "Democratic" lobbyists to shift their giving to the Republicans. Further, they pressured trade associations to appoint Republican lobbyists to high positions within their organizations. By doing so, DeLay and Norquist hoped that they would be able to alter the structure of elite networks in a way that would benefit Republicans.

Attempting to influence lobbying networks, as undertaken by Republicans through the K Street Project, is ostensibly legal and ethical. For example, it is perfectly legitimate for Republicans to keep a record of campaign contributions by lobbyists and to remind them that Republicans control the majority. However, the actual implementation of the K Street Project by Tom DeLay began to raise questions. For example, DeLay was accused of insisting that the Electronics Industry Alliance name a Republican lobbyist as president if it expected favorable treatment in the provisions of the Digital Millennium Copyright Act.[66] These accusations of attempted extortion, along with other ethical irregularities, helped to force DeLay to resign his seat in the House in 2006. Through DeLay, the K Street Project also became associated with a scandal involving corrupt lobbyist Jack Abramoff.[67] As a result of this unwanted attention, Republicans began to back away from the K Street Project.

The failure of the K Street Project had numerous causes. One cause was the personal flaws and excesses of Tom DeLay, one of the project's most visible leaders. However, another cause of the K Street Project's failure was how difficult it is to bring decentralized networks under centralized control. While networking is a way in which parties and interest groups line up to support one another, this outcome is not easily dictated or coordinated by any central person or organization. Outcomes result from thousands of individual decisions made by lobbyists, members of Congress, party officials, and other political players.

Strategic Implications of Party-Group Connections

Interest groups and political parties are extensively intertwined. Both types of organizations compete for individual loyalties, draw upon institutional opportunities for cooperation and exploitation, and are mutually embedded within elite networks. What are the strategic implications of this relationship? The leaders of political parties and interest groups both are well advised to approach group-party relations cautiously. While relations may prove to be mutually beneficial, they may, alternatively, serve the interests of one side more than the other. Interest groups may be captured by parties, or groups may come to dominate the agenda of a party. Relationships once thought of as mutual may become parasitic.[68] Parties have to decide whether or not to bring interest groups into the fold. Interest groups have to decide whether to align with a party or attempt to offer an independent voice. As party-group relationships evolve over time, the leaders of parties and groups may find it wise to reevaluate these relationships.

Alliances between political parties and interest groups have the potential to be mutually beneficial, especially when the allied party wins elections. In the 2008 election, a wide range of interest groups worked to elect Barack Obama as president. His election meant that many of these groups would see the benefits of substantive policy changes along the lines that they advocated. Benefits were not distributed in an indiscriminate, spoils-system arrangement but by providing a subtle advantage to liberal groups in the policy process. Although Obama campaigned against corporate lobbyists and interest groups in 2008, these players still had a voice at the bargaining table once Obama was elected. For example, support from the U.S. Chamber of Commerce and the National Association of Manufacturers was an important factor in passing economic stimulus legislation in 2009. Yet Obama's election created disadvantages for groups representing "evangelical Christians, outdoor sportsmen, conservatives, rural residents, small business owners, financial professionals, and farmers," while providing advantages to groups representing "African-Americans, Hispanics, liberals, college students, immigrants, gays and lesbians, urban residents, government employees, lawyers, scientists, and teachers."[69] Similarly, George W. Bush's presidency benefitted conservative interest groups, such as pro-life organizations, faith-based organizations, anti-immigration groups, business associations, and energy industry associations.

While party-group alliances often pay dividends, it is also possible for alliances to be too close to benefit the group. If an interest group is so closely allied with one party that the opposing party chooses to ignore the group's interests entirely, then the group may find that its allied party also neglects it and takes advantage of its loyalty. Since such a group cannot credibly threaten to leave its allied party and support the competitor party, the allied party may chose to attend to the group's interests only when it is easy to do so. When politics get tough and important decisions are on the line, the group may find that its "allied" party is not a very useful ally. Under these conditions, the group may be said to be "captured" by its allied party.[70]

The National Association for the Advancement of Colored People (NAACP) is one group that may have been captured by the Democratic Party. In his book, *Uneasy Alliances*, Paul Frymer argues that African-American interests have suffered at the hand of the Democratic Party, which counts on loyal support from African Americans at the ballot box.[71] This capture has deep historical roots, beginning with the disenfranchisement of black voters in the south during Reconstruction, and continues to present times. For example, when he was campaigning for president in 1992, candidate Bill Clinton used an NAACP forum to attack Jesse Jackson by castigating black recording artist Sister Soulja.[72] Nonetheless, the NAACP did not seize the opportunity to counterattack Clinton. Instead, leaders of the organization, and other African-American leaders, accepted that Clinton made the attack in order to reach out to the white majority. Even if Clinton attacked a prominent member of its community, NAACP still preferred a Clinton presidency to a continuation of Republican presidential dominance. Thus, silence rather than rebuttal was the NAACP's response. This episode is symbolic of how Democratic politicians are able to take support from black interest groups for granted.

Much has changed in America since 1992, yet much has remained the same. The election of Barack Obama signals great promise for race relations—and raises the hope that black interest groups will no longer be captured within the Democratic Party. However, Obama's 2008 campaign and first-term avoidance of core black issues, such as civil rights, suggests that the Democratic Party may still have African-American interest groups captured.[73]

While captured interest groups may tend to demonstrate loyalty to their allied party, other interest groups may place greater reliance on voice and exit strategies.[74] The Log Cabin Republicans—an interest group within the Republican Party that advocates for the rights of gay and lesbians—has attempted to push the Republican Party toward more inclusive views on same-sex marriage as a reaction to the party's strong antigay stances. In 2004, the organization chose to withhold its endorsement of George W. Bush's reelection as president.[75] This move let the Republican Party know that it could not automatically count on Log Cabin's support if it was not responsive to Log Cabin's policy demands. Nonetheless, Log Cabin faced backlash within the party for its decision. Failure to endorse the party's nominee was construed as an act of disloyalty, raising questions about the legitimacy of Log Cabin as a Republican group. Opponents of gay-lesbian rights within the party expressed the opinion that they were glad to be without Log Cabin. Indeed, it is not clear whether the decision to withhold the endorsement helped or hurt Log Cabin's case for equality. In any case, Log Cabin returned to the Republican fold in 2008 by endorsing John McCain for president.

If close alignment of a group with a party risks interest group capture, then forging a bipartisan, independent stand may be an alternative way to gain political influence. In his book *Gaining Access*, John Mark Hansen recounts that the Farm Bureau rose to a position of influence in the mid-twentieth century largely due to its ability to establish recurring, reliable channels of information to elected politicians, information that was better than that provided by party organizations.[76] The Farm Bureau's independent reputation did not materialize overnight but was painstakingly cultivated for decades, from the 1920s to the 1950s. Nonetheless, political, economic, and technological changes undercut the Farm Bureau's influence in the 1960s and 1970s, as it abandoned its bipartisan posture and aligned decisively with the Republican Party.

Forging an independent role is more difficult in today's polarized political system than it once was, but attempting to do so remains a strategy available to interest groups. The greatest challenge of such strategies is to build bipartisan trust in an environment that prizes partisan loyalty. Organizations that attempt to play both sides of the partisan fence may find themselves isolated and widely distrusted.[77]

The relationships between political parties and interest groups cannot be defined once and for all. Which strategies work or fail changes over time. Interest groups representing African-Americans and gay-lesbian interests may find that the 2010s afford a more favorable environment within the parties than was true in the 1990s or 2000s. Conservative Christian interest groups and labor unions may find that their positions were more favorable in the 1990s than they are today.[78] Antiwar interest groups, such as United for Peace and Justice, worked in concert with Democratic goals from 2003 to 2006, but they found themselves abandoned by the Democratic grass roots once Democrats started to achieve electoral success in 2006.[79]

Relationships between parties and groups that once were equal partnerships may be come decidedly one-sided over time. For example, in his classic 1969 book, *Labor in American Politics*, J. David Greenstone detailed the close collaborative relationship between the American Federation of Labor–Congress of Industrial Organizations (AFL-CIO) and the Democratic Party.[80] This close collaboration was vital to passing legislation on Medicare, reapportionment, and civil rights, leading Greenstone to conclude that organized labor was not merely "a conventional interest group, but . . . an *organized constituent interest* [emphasis added] of the Democratic party."[81] In the years that followed the 1960s, however, labor received fewer dividends from its friendship with the Democrats. In an essay commemorating Greenstone's book, Peter Francia wrote in 2010 that

> American labor has done its job effectively as a campaign and electoral arm of the Democratic Party. However, for its effort, organized labor has received comparatively little in return from elected officials in the Democratic Party. This one-sided relationship raises questions about the future of the labor–Democratic Party alliance that Greenstone described some four decades ago.[82]

Labor leaders have mused about reducing support to Democrats or perhaps shifting their energies to an independent "Labor Party." They might alternatively promote their interests by seeking rapprochement with the Republican Party, perhaps in an effort to forestall the type of extreme antiunion measures pursued by Republican Governor Scott Walker of Wisconsin.[83] The difficulties that unions would face in attempting such a rapprochement is one cost that they must pay for aligning, almost exclusively, with only the Democratic Party for decades. Regardless of how labor unions reevaluate their partnership with the Democrats, a simple continuation of the 1960s status quo into the 2010s is unlikely produce significant policy victories for labor interests.

The shifting asymmetries of party-group relationships generate imperatives for these organizations to react to the inchoate factions of the American political system. As a result, strategic politicians continually craft new organizational forms out of the raw material available from parties and groups. Inventing hybrid organizational forms is one way to adapt to changing circumstances.[84] For example, in 2008, MoveOn.org merged organizing ideas from political parties, interest groups, and social movements to become a rising star in the Democratic Party network within a decade of its founding.[85] In a similar vein, 527 organizations spliced party-styled campaign tactics with the independence of interest groups.[86] If such adaptations continue to take place, then political parties and interest groups may become as unrecognizable in 2050 as MoveOn.org would have been in 1970.

Conclusion

When placed in the context of the long history of party-group interaction in the United States, the rise of the tea party in 2009 seems less anomalous than it appears on the surface. Political parties and interest groups have a long tradition of trying to seize control of one another. We might think of the tea party's attempt to upend the Republican Party in 2009 as the natural counterpoint to the Republican Party's effort to discipline business associations through the K Street Project in the late 1990s and early 2000s. The tea party's ascendance in 2009 benefitted from conservatives' anxieties over recession, a unified Democratic federal government, and a president whose unique background made him seem somewhat "other" to many Americans. With the Republican Party establishment still licking its wounds from its decisive defeat in 2008, the tea party helped to fill a void in leadership and enthusiasm within conservative ranks. Because midterm elections, more often than not, turn against the party of the president, the tea party was well positioned to claim credit for Republicans' electoral success at the ballot box in 2010. Most participants in the tea party do not want to form their own political party, per se.[87] Rather, they seek use tea party organizations as a vehicle to advance their views within the structure of the Republican Party. With the Republicans again in power in the U.S. House of Representatives, much of the anger among tea party activists had abated by 2011. Given the fragmented and decentralized nature of the tea party (and other social movements), it is unlikely to continue to dominate the Republican Party for long, though it promises to be a significant factor in the 2012 Republican presidential primaries.

In order to make sense of the tea party and see it as a typical product of the American political system, this chapter offers a framework for bridging the gap between political parties and interest groups. Parties and groups compete to mobilize the same activists, they seize upon institutional opportunities for cooperation and exploitation, and they are jointly embedded in elite networks. These interdependencies compel parties and groups to strategize over relationship formation. We can understand these strategies better by thinking about activists, institutions, and networks as key parameters of parties' and groups' competitive environments.

E. E. Schattschneider, one of the great theorists of American democracy, wrote that "it is nearly impossible to translate pressure politics [i.e., interest group politics] into party politics [emphasis removed]."[88] Schattschneider saw the principal difference between parties and interest groups as a difference of scale: parties mobilize large numbers of citizens around broad political concerns, while interest groups mobilize comparably smaller, but much more intense, groups of citizens. Schattschneider assumed that these numerical weaknesses would prevent groups from competing with parties.

The argument of this chapter demonstrates that Schattschneider's view of party-group competition is fundamentally wrong. Groups and parties *do* compete directly with one another. The political game is not simply one of counting bodies. Parties may be "larger" than groups, but groups have institutionally created advantages that allow them to navigate behind the scenes of partisan politics. Thus, instead of referring to the "two-party" system in America—which has become a hegemonic way of thinking about politics[89]—it would be more accurate to refer to the American "factional system." The factional system is the complex result of the strategies of parties and interest groups, continuously coevolving over time.

Notes

1. Associated Press, "Retire, Tea Party Tells Lugar," *Journal Gazette,* January 23, 2011, http://www.journalgazette.net/article/20110123/NEWS07/301239902/1002/ LOCAL/; Kate Zernike, "Tea Party Gets Early Start on G.O.P. Targets for 2012," *New York Times,* January 29, 2011, http://www.nytimes.com/2011/01/30/us/ politics/30teaparty.html.
2. Kate Zernike, "Shaping Tea Party Passion Into Campaign Force," *New York Times,* August 25, 2010, http://www.nytimes.com/2010/08/26/us/politics/26freedom.html.
3. Michael T. Heaney, "Outside the Issue Niche: The Multidimensionality of Interest Group Identity," *American Politics Research* 32, no. 6 (2004): 611–651; Michael T. Heaney, "Identity Crisis: How Interest Groups Struggle to Define Themselves in Washington," in *Interest Group Politics,* 7th ed., eds. Allan J. Cigler and Burdett A. Loomis (Washington, DC: CQ Press, 2007): 279–300.
4. E. E. Schattschneider, *The Semisovereign People: A Realist's View of Democracy in America* (Orlando, FL: Harcourt Brace Jovanovich, 1975).
5. Matt Grossman, "Who Gets What Now? Interest Groups under Obama," *The Forum* 7, no. 1 (2009): Article 5.
6. Christopher Witko, "The Ecology of Party-Organized Interest Relationships," *Polity* 41, no. 2 (2009): 211–34.
7. Donald Green, Bradley Palmquist, and Erick Schickler, *Partisan Hearts and Minds: Political Parties and the Social Identities of Voters* (New Haven, CT: Yale University Press): ix.
8. Philip E. Converse, "Of Time and Partisan Stability," *Comparative Political Studies* 2, no. 2 (1969): 139–71.
9. Laura Stoker and M. Kent Jennings, "Of Time and the Development of Partisan Polarization," *American Journal of Political Science* 52, no. 3 (2008): 619–35.
10. Geoffrey C. Layman, Thomas M. Carsey, John C. Green, Richard Herrera, and Rosalyn Cooperman, "Activists and Conflict Extension in American Party Politics," *American Political Science Review* 104, no. 2 (2010): 324–46.
11. Rawi Abdelal, Yoshiko M. Herrera, Alastair Iain Johnston, and Rose McDermott, "Identity as a Variable," *Perspectives on Politics* 4, no. 4 (2006): 695–711, http://papers. ssrn.com/sol3/papers.cfm?abstract_id=1100064/.
12. Paul Starr, *The Social Transformation of American Medicine* (New York: Basic Books, 1982).
13. Ziad W. Munson, *The Making of Pro-Life Activists: How Social Movement Mobilization Works* (Chicago: University of Chicago Press, 2008).
14. Nathaniel J. Klemp, "Beyond God-Talk: Understanding the Christian Right From the Ground Up," *Polity* 39 (2007): 522–44.
15. Munson, *The Making of Pro-Life Activists,* 55–61.
16. Michael Dreiling and Brian Wolf, "Environmental Movement Organizations and Political Strategy: Tactical Conflicts over NAFTA," *Organization and Environment* 14, no. 1 (2001): 34–54.

17. Klemp, "Beyond God-Talk."
18. Mary Grisez Kweit, "Ideological Congruence of Party Switchers and Nonswitchers: The Case of Party Activists," *American Journal of Political Science* 30, no. 1 (1986): 184–96.
19. Seth E. Masket, Michael T. Heaney, Joanne M. Miller, and Dara Z. Strolovitch, "Networking the Parties: A Comparative Study of Democratic and Republican National Convention Delegates in 2008" (paper presented at "The State of the Parties: 2008 and Beyond," Ray C. Bliss Institute of Applied Politics, University of Akron, Cuyahoga Falls/Akron, OH, October 15–16, 2009).
20. Interest groups are included in this table if they were among the top ten organizations listed by Democratic and Republican convention delegates. Convention delegates also mentioned non–interest group organizations (such as party organizations), which are not reported here.
21. Jo Freeman, "The Political Culture of the Democratic and Republican Parties," *Political Science Quarterly* 101, no. 3 (1986): 327–56.
22. Doug McAdam and Sidney Tarrow, "Ballots and Barricades: On the Reciprocal Relationship between Elections and Social Movements," *Perspectives on Politics* 8, no. 2 (2010): 529–42.
23. "At Conventions, It's Television, Not the Platform, That Counts," *New York Observer,* July 7, 2008.
24. Kimberly H. Conger, "Party Platforms and Party Coalitions: The Christian Right and State-Level Republicans," *Party Politics* 20 (2010): 651–68.
25. Similarly, the myriad activities of national party conventions provide opportunities for symbolic involvement by interest groups, such as sponsorships of events inside the convention hall or protests outside of it. See Mark J. Rozell, Clyde Wilcox, and David Madland, *Interest Groups in American Campaigns: The New Face of Electioneering,* 2nd ed. (Washington, DC: CQ Press, 2006): 52–54.
26. Rozell, Wilcox, and Madland, *Interest Groups in American Campaigns,* 46.
27. Pippa Norris and Joni Lovenduski, "'If Only More Candidates Came Forward': Supply-Side Explanations of Candidate Selection in Britain," *British Journal of Political Science* 23, no. 3 (1993): 373–408.
28. Byron E. Shafer, *Quiet Revolution: The Struggle for the Democratic Party and the Shaping of Post-Reform Politics* (New York: Russell Sage Foundation, 1983).
29. Rozell, Wilcox, and Madland, *Interest Groups in American Campaigns,* 48.
30. Seth E. Masket, *How Informal Party Organizations Control Nominations and Polarize Legislatures* (Ann Arbor: University of Michigan Press, 2009).
31. Peter F. Galderis and Marni Ezra, "Congressional Primaries in Historical and Theoretical Context," in *Congressional Primaries and the Politics of Representation,* ed. Peter F. Galderis, Marni Ezra, and Michael Lyons (Boston: Rowman and Littlefield, 2001): 11–26.
32. Paul S. Herrnson, "The Roles of Party Organizations, Party-Connected Committees, and Party Allies in Elections," *Journal of Politics* 71, no. 4 (2009): 1207–24.
33. Michael D. Shear and Jeff Zelany, "Bill Clinton Urged Democrat to Quit Florida Senate Race," *New York Times,* October 29, 2010.
34. Michael Connolly, "Club for Growth PAC Runs the Table Again, Undefeated in 2010," *Club for Growth BLOG,* June 23, 2010, http://www.clubforgrowth.org/perm/?postID=13577.
35. Michael T. Heaney, "Linking Political Parties and Interest Groups," in *The Oxford Handbook of American Political Parties and Interest Groups,* eds. L. Sandy Maisel and Jefffrey M. Berry (Oxford, UK: Oxford University Press, 2010): 568–87.

36. MoveOn.org, *MoveOn Members Endorse 2006*, http://pol.moveon.org/2006/endorsed .html.
37. Michael H. Murakami, "Divisive Primaries: Party Organizations, Ideological Groups, and the Battle over Party Purity," *PS: Political Science and Politics* 41, no. 4 (2008): 918–23.
38. For a similar argument related to the threat of entry into elections by third-party candidates, see Daniel J. Lee, "Anticipating Entry: Major Party Positioning and Third Party Threat," *Political Research Quarterly* (January 24, 2011): 1–13, doi:10.1177/1065912910391476.
39. Heaney, "Linking Political Parties and Interest Groups."
40. Philip M Stern, *The Best Congress Money Can Buy* (New York: Pantheon Books, 1988).
41. Thomas L. Brunell, "The Relationship Between Political Parties and Interest Groups: Explaining Patterns of PAC Contributions to Candidates for Congress," *Political Research Quarterly* 58, no. 4 (2005): 681–88.
42. Michael M. Franz, *Choices and Changes: Interest Groups in the Electoral Process* (Philadelphia: Temple University Press, 2008).
43. 540 U.S. 93 (2003).
44. Robert G. Boatright, "Situating the New 527 Organizations in Interest Group Theory," *The Forum* 5, no. 2 (2007): Article 5.
45. Richard M. Skinner, "Do 527's Add Up to a Party? Thinking About the 'Shadows' of Politics," *The Forum* 3, no. 3 (2005): Article 5.
46. Michael T. Heaney, Matthew E. Newman, and Dari E. Sylvester, "Campaigning in the Internet Age," in *The Electoral Challenge: Theory Meets Practice*, 2nd ed., eds. Stephen C. Craig and David B. Hill (Washington, DC: CQ Press, 2011).
47. John H. Aldrich, *Why Parties? The Origin and Transformation of Political Parties in America* (Chicago: University of Chicago Press, 1995): 252.
48. Dana R. Fisher, *Activism: How the Outsourcing of Grassroots Campaigns is Strangling Progressive Politics in America* (Stanford, CA: Stanford University Press, 2006).
49. Brett M. Clifton, "Romancing the GOP: Assessing the Strategies Used by the Christian Coalition to Influence the Republican Party," *Party Politics* 10, no. 5 (2004): 475–98.
50. Anya Sostek, "AFL-CIO: Knock, Knock, Knocking on Voters' Doors," *Pittsburgh Post-Gazette*, October 19, 2006.
51. Theda Skocpol, *Diminished Democracy: From Membership to Management in American Civic Life*, The Julian J. Rothbaum Distinguished Lecture Series, vol. 8 (Norman: University of Oklahoma Press, 2003): 90–91 and 194–95.
52. David Truman, *The Governmental Process: Political Interests and Public Opinion*, 2nd ed. (Berkeley: Institute of Governmental Studies, University of California, 1993): 156–87.
53. Mildred A. Schwartz, *The Party Network: The Robust Organization of Illinois Republicans* (Madison: University of Wisconsin Press, 1990).
54. Rogan Kersh, "Corporate Lobbyists as Political Actors: A View from the Field," in *Interest Group Politics*, 6th ed., eds. Allan J. Cigler and Burdett A. Loomis (Washington, DC: CQ Press, 2002): 225–238.
55. For details of the research methodology, see Michael T. Heaney, "Brokering Health Policy: Coalitions, Parties, and Interest Group Influence," *Journal of Health Politics, Policy and Law* 31, no. 5 (2006): 887–944.
56. Heaney, "Brokering Health Policy."

57. Matt Grossman and Casey B. K. Dominguez, "Party Coalitions and Interest Group Networks," *American Politics Research* 37, no. 5 (2009): 767–800.

58. Gregory Koger and Jennifer Nicoll Victor, "Polarized Agents: Campaign Contributions by Lobbyists," *PS: Political Science and Politics* 42, no. 3 (2009): 485–88.

59. Koger and Victor, "Polarized Agents," 486.

60. Gregory Koger and Jennifer Nicoll Victor, "The Beltway Network: A Network Analysis of Lobbyists' Donations to Members of Congress" (paper presented at the Annual Meeting of the American Political Science Association, Toronto, Canada, September 3–6, 2009).

61. Gregory Koger, Seth Masket, and Hans Noel, "Partisan Webs: Information Exchange and Party Networks," *British Journal of Political Science* 39 (2009): 633–53; Gregory Koger, Seth Masket, and Hans Noel, "Cooperative Party Factions in American Politics," *American Politics Research* 38, no. 1 (2010): 33–53.

62. Marty Cohen, David Karol, Hans Noel, and John Zaller, *The Party Decides: Presidential Nominations Before and After Reform* (Chicago: University of Chicago Press, 2008).

63. Cohen, Karol, Noel, and Zaller, *The Party Decides*, 34.

64. Schattschneider, *The Semisovereign People*, 46–59.

65. Burdett A. Loomis, "Does K Street Run through Capitol Hill? Lobbying Congress in the Republican Era," in *Interest Group Politics*, 7th ed., eds. Allan J. Cigler and Burdett A. Loomis (Washington, DC: CQ Press, 2007): 412–430; Nicholas Confessore, "Welcome to the Machine: How the GOP Disciplined K Street and Made Bush Supreme," *Washington Monthly*, July/August 2003, http://www.washington monthly.com/features/2003/0307.confessore.html.

66. Lou Dubose and Jan Reid, *The Hammer* (New York: Public Affairs, 2004).

67. Frank Rich, "The Rabbit Ragu Democrats," *New York Times*, October 4, 2009.

68. Christopher Witko, "The Ecology of Party-Organized Interest Relationships," 230.

69. Matt Grossman, "Who Gets What Now?" 9.

70. Paul Frymer, *Uneasy Alliances: Race and Party Competition in America* (Princeton, NJ: Princeton University Press, 2010).

71. Frymer, *Uneasy Alliances*.

72. Frymer, *Uneasy Alliances*, 119.

73. Frymer, *Uneasy Alliances*, 207–36.

74. Albert O. Hirschman, *Exit, Voice, and Loyalty: Responses to Decline in Firms, Organizations, and States* (Cambridge, MA: Harvard University Press, 1970).

75. Heaney, "Linking Political Parties and Interest Groups," 583.

76. John Mark Hansen, *Gaining Access: Congress and the Farm Lobby, 1919–1981* (Chicago: University of Chicago Press, 1991).

77. One interest group that suffered this fate was AARP (formerly the American Association of Retired Persons). In 2003, AARP tried to play both sides of the party system in the debate over the Medicare Prescription Drug, Improvement and Modernization Act. AARP failed to draw the Republican Party to its side, but it also alienated many of its longtime Democratic allies. See Heaney, "Identity Crisis."

78. Clifton, "Romancing the GOP."

79. Michael T. Heaney and Fabio Rojas, "The Partisan Dynamics of Contention: Demobilization of the Antiwar Movement in the United States, 2007–2009," *Mobilization: An International Journal* 16, no. 1 (2011): 45–64.

80. J. David Greenstone, *Labor in American Politics* (New York: Vintage Books, 1969).

81. Greenstone, *Labor in American Politics*, 352. The collaboration of the Congress of Industrial Organizations (but not the American Federation of Labor) with the New

Deal is a similar example. See V. O. Key Jr., *Politics, Parties, and Pressure Groups* (New York: Thomas Y. Crowell, 1947): 73.

82. Peter Francia, "Assessing the Labor-Democratic Party Alliance: A One-Sided Relationship," *Polity* 42 (2010): 294.

83. By A. G. Sulzberger, "Union Bill Is Law, but Debate Is Far From Over," *New York Times*, March 11, 2011, http://www.nytimes.com/2011/03/12/us/12wisconsin.html.

84. Andrew Chadwick, "Digital Network Repertoires and Organizational Hybridity," *Political Communication* 24, no. 3 (2007): 283–301; Kristin A. Goss and Michael T. Heaney, "Organizing Women *as Women:* Hybridity and Grassroots Collective Action in the 21st Century," *Perspectives on Politics* 8 (2010): 27–52; Elisabeth S. Clemens, *The People's Lobby: Organizational Innovation and the Rise of Interest Group Politics in the United States, 1890–1925* (Chicago: University of Chicago Press: 1997).

85. Masket, Heaney, Miller, and Strolovitch, "Networking the Parties."

86. Boatright, "Situating the New 527 Organizations in Interest Group Theory."

87. Vanessa Williamson, Theda Skocpol, and John Coggin, "The Tea Party and the Remaking of Republican Conservatism," *Perspectives on Politics* 9, no. 1 (2011): 25–43.

88. Schattschneider, *The Semisovereign People*, 52.

89. Lisa Jane Disch, *The Tyranny of the Two-Party System* (New York: Columbia University Press, 2002).

III. GROUPS AND POLICY MAKING

10

Issue Advertising and Legislative Advocacy in Health Politics[1]

Richard L. Hall and Richard Anderson

In the fall of 1993 President Bill Clinton announced his plan for comprehensive health care reform, and an unremarkable political commercial appeared on American television screens in a handful of states. The ad portrayed a conversation "sometime in the future." A middle-class couple named Harry and Louise sit at their kitchen table discussing how good their health insurance coverage used to be and how bad it had become. With a discordant piano refrain playing in the background, the foreboding voice of the narrator intones that "the government may force us to pick from a few health care plans designed by government bureaucrats." "If they choose," Harry begins, "we lose," Louise concludes. A simple admonition, "Get the Facts," then appears on the television screen, while the narrator tells the viewer: "For reforms that protect what we have, call toll free. . . ."

Fast-forward fifteen years. Similarly ominous music plays in the background, and we again see the characters Harry and Louise sitting at their kitchen table, this time dressed for work. Harry has been reading the newspaper and lays it open in front of Louise: "Health care costs are up again. Small companies are being forced to cut their plans." Displeased but not surprised, Louise mentions a family friend who has just been diagnosed with cancer. "He's covered, right?" Harry worriedly asks. "No," responds Louise, "He just joined a start-up and he couldn't afford a plan." "Just too many people are falling through the cracks," Harry opines; then Louise concludes that the next president needs to "make something happen."

These two examples represent a form of political advocacy typically referred to as "issue advertising." Issue advertisements are mass-media appeals intended to promote an interest group's favored policy, much as business firms use commercials to promote retail products. Indeed, many of the Madison Avenue techniques for influencing consumers are used by political consultants to influence citizens. And like conventional commercials, issue advertisements appear through a variety of media: newspapers, television, radio, the Internet, even highway billboards. Unlike commercials selling retail products, however, issue ads typically exhibit one or both of

221

two purposes: to alter or intensify viewers' beliefs about a particular public policy and/or to induce viewers to communicate those beliefs to elected officials that represent them.

Achieving these purposes, in turn, is a means to a more distant, Washington-centered end: changing the behavior of those officials in order to influence the policy being advertised. In fact, the first Harry and Louise ads were widely credited with having killed the Clinton health care plan.[2] Subsequent research has shown that claim to be greatly exaggerated,[3] but politicians are a risk-averse lot. They ignore communications from constituents—mail, e-mail, phone calls, comments or protests during "town hall" meetings—at their peril, and a good issue ad campaign can produce a flurry of messages. Such a campaign can also "prime" a legislator's constituents for subsequent appeals.[4] And spending on an ad campaign itself, independent of its effect on citizens' behavior, signals a group's willingness to reward legislators who help it and punish those who don't.

Issue advertising is not new in the practice of advocacy, of course, but its use has expanded substantially in the two decades since Harry and Louise first appeared on our television screens, and that trend shows no signs of slowing. In this chapter, we examine issue advertising, treating it as a particular form of grassroots lobbying. We describe briefly the rapid expansion of issue advertising in US national politics. We review what we know about the effectiveness of issue ads in changing citizens' beliefs and behavior: How do interest groups frame their messages? How do they evoke emotions to best effect? We then explore the relationship between issue advertising strategies and legislative strategies: Which legislators do interest groups target when making their advertising buys, and why? What effects do targeted advertising campaigns have on congressional policy making? In addressing these questions, we focus on the role of issue advertising in health policy making, one of the most contentious policy domains of our time and a site of some of the most intense issue advertising campaigns in recent memory.

Issue Advertising as Outside Lobbying

As we use the term here, *issue advertising* is a particular form of grassroots advocacy or "outside" lobbying.[5] Outside lobbying occurs when organized interests attempt to influence elected representatives indirectly by influencing the attitudes and/or behavior of citizens whose subsequent votes the reelection-minded representative will seek. Our definition thus focuses on advertising that is about specific issues and occurs between elections, not during them. In applying this definition, we hasten to emphasize, this chapter employs a distinction that is becoming increasingly blurry in American politics: namely, between legislative advocacy and campaign advocacy, or between "pure" issue ads and "sham" issue ads. The latter are campaign ads that, until very recently, had to masquerade as issue ads to escape Federal Election Commission (FEC) regulation. We come back to that distinction in the concluding section in order to speculate about the legal and practical future of issue advertising. For now, we focus on issue advertising that is distinguishable from candidate-centered advertising and draw on cases and data that encompass almost exclusively the former.

Like other forms of outside lobbying, most issue advertising aims to influence politicians by mobilizing citizens. Thus, most ads contain admonitions that the viewer contact his or her representative(s) in Washington and contain information that facilitates such contacts.[6] Alleging that special interest groups were misleading the public on health care reform, for example, one 2009 AARP ad urged viewers to "tell Congress not to let myths get in the way of fixing what's broken with health care." The ad then directed them to the group's Web site, where they would find links to congressional Web sites. On the opposing side, one ad in a $1.5 million campaign by The 60 Plus Association alleged that reformers wanted government to decide "if older patients are worth the cost." It then ended with the plea: "Tell Congress: Don't Pay for Health Care Reform On the Backs of Our Seniors."[7] The final frame displayed a phone number. The viewers who called it were patched through to their own representatives' offices.

Some issue ads are tailored to more specific audiences, sometimes identifying particular legislators for praise or scorn. For example, a 2009 ad run by Health Care for America Now (HCAN) charged that the Republicans were blocking health care reform because of $14.3 million dollars they allegedly received from the health care industry. The ad opened with photos of the Republican leadership, including the respective chambers' minority leaders, Senator Mitch McConnell and Rep. John Boehner. Similarly, a conservative ad that likened health care reform to a prescription drug with bad side effects was repeated in selected districts and identified their specific representatives: "Call Collin Peterson (202–225 . . .). Tell him to oppose a government takeover of health care." Peterson, a moderate House Democrat from Minnesota, had already announced that he would vote against his party's reform package when it came to the House floor, but he never got the chance to vote against a government takeover of health care. No such measure was proposed by either party in either chamber.

Not all issue ads are intended to incite immediate action by the audience, however. Some ads simply call attention to the larger policy problem, raising its salience in the minds of the voters. In the year-long lead-up to health care reform in 2009, AARP broadcast hundreds of spots in a multi-million-dollar "Divided We Fail" campaign, "demanding" that Congress reform the health care system. Appearing in television, radio, and print media, the ads featured average citizens highlighting the problems they faced because of rising costs and declining coverage. The ads for this campaign said nothing about what sorts of reforms AARP supported, so at first glance, they might seem strategically ill conceived; media strategies that have no actionable message are unlikely to generate much action.[8] However, such ads might prove effective in priming citizens for subsequent messages or signaling legislators about interest group resolve, mechanisms that we discuss below.[9]

The Rise of Issue Advertising

Issue advertising in the United States has a rich and varied history. As citizens of England, colonial agitators used petitions to protest excessive taxes and the quartering of British troops. The first antislavery petitions date at least to 1783, when several hundred Pennsylvania Quakers signed a resolution urging the young Congress to abolish slavery. Petition drives are still useful instruments of grassroots activism, but issue advocacy has changed more than it has stayed the same, both in scope and technology. For example, telephone campaigns conducted through "robo-calls" can reach pre-programmed quotas of citizens at a relatively low cost, encouraging them to "let Washington know" how strongly they support or oppose a piece of legislation. Almost all grassroots organizations active today develop their own Internet networks. When an organization has a priority that is ripe for action, it can quickly send out to attentive sympathizers an "action alert"—a well-timed message asking them to contact their respective representatives.

Comprehensive data on the full variety, number, and cost of issue advertisements are not available, but most agree that this category of interest group spending has been rising rapidly since the mid-1990s. The most extensive and systematic analysis to date comes from two studies by the Annenberg Public Policy Center.[10] The reports focus on the 107th (2001–02) and 108th (2003–04) Congresses, respectively, and they only examine advertising within the Washington, D.C., media markets. Nonetheless, they show that interest groups are spending remarkable sums on issue advertising. The study of the 107th Congress estimated that $41 million was spent on television issue ads. The study of the 108th Congress found that that number had increased over fivefold—to $225 million. Combining both broadcast and print totals for the Washington area, issue ad expenditures went from $105 million in the 107th Congress to $404 million in the 108th.[11]

The Annenberg reports also break down spending by topic. Over the two Congresses, health care ranked second among the twenty-eight policy areas that generated nonnegligible advertising buys. In the 108th Congress, Medicare prescription drug legislation, not comprehensive reform, was on the agenda. Yet in that two-year period advocacy groups spent $80.4 million in and around Washington,D.C., a sum greater than spending for the entire country on the 1993 Clinton reforms, which would have affected every health sector. By way of comparison, all campaign contributions by all health PACs to all federal candidates during the 108th Congress totaled just $31.6 million, less than 40 percent of issue advertising costs in the Washington media market. We should note, too, that the Annenberg categorizations exclude from the health category several health-related areas: tort reform ($5.9 million), substance abuse ($1.6 million), and abortion ($0.7 million).

Data from several sources permit a rough comparison of issue ad spending on the Clinton health care reform bill in 1993–94 with the Obama reform bill considered in 2009–10. On the 1993 Harry and Louise issue ads alone, one study found that the insurance industry spent approximately $14 million in 1993–94.[12] Summing across all groups that were contacted, in turn, the same study estimated interest group spending on television issue advertisements at $60 million, with the lion's share spent by groups against the Clinton bill.[13] Compare this to the 2009–10 debate over comprehensive health care reform. In March 2010 a *Time* article reported that in the single week leading up to the final House vote, television spending on issue ads was about $24 million, and that sum came on top of approximately $200 million that had already been spent during the yearlong debate over the bill.[14] Millions more were spent on radio and print advertising during both fights, so these estimates are undoubtedly low.[15] Nonetheless, they suggest that in the fifteen years between health care reform initiatives, issue advertising increased substantially, perhaps dramatically. "From both the left and the right," a 2009 *Time* article concludes, " . . . political campaign ads are saturating our television screens with arguments for and against President Obama's health-care-reform effort."[16] The *Washington Post* echoes this sentiment, observing that the "heated fight over health-care legislation is saturating the summer airwaves, with groups on all sides of the debate pouring tens of millions of dollars into advertising campaigns."[17]

Omitted from the above numbers is the increasingly important use of issue advertising on the Internet.[18] In the health care reform fight of 2009–10, groups from both ends of the political spectrum placed issue ads on such websites as *Politico, The Drudge Report, Talking Points Memo*, and others whose audiences included politically attentive individuals who are most easily mobilized. Internet ads were also used to mount old-style petition drives with new technology. For instance, the antireform group, the Association of American Physicians and Surgeons, used Google search ads to generate signatories to their petition to "Fight ObamaHealth Care."[19] Move.On, HCAN, and AARP likewise purchased Google search ads in

2009 to dispel a false claim propagated by Sarah Palin and Rush Limbaugh that the Obama plan would create government "death panels" to advise seniors when to end their lives. The *Los Angeles Times* reported that the Palin allegation generated far more Internet advertising than any public policy issue to date, including the Iraq War. At one point in September 2009, over ninety different organizations had purchased Google ads related to the health care reform debate.[20]

Targeting the Legislator's Audience

Interest groups do not often spend huge sums on issue advertising absent a larger strategy about how to achieve their policy objectives. As we have noted, the two-step purpose of most ads is to influence the attitudes and/ or behavior of citizens, who will then influence the behavior of their Washington, D.C., representatives. However, even the richest groups running the most expensive campaigns cannot cover the entire country. How do interest groups decide at whom they will target their advertising buys?

The receptivity of citizens to an advertising appeal counts as one important factor; in this respect, issue advertisements are like most types of outside lobbying.[21] Issue ads that advocate a major expansion of Medicaid are unlikely to play well in highly conservative areas, where most citizens want the size of the welfare state to contract, not expand. Similarly, ads about gaps in Medicare prescription drug coverage will mobilize more viewers in districts that have disproportionately high numbers of senior citizens.

Antireform groups followed this logic in 1993–94, encouraging individuals predisposed to dislike President Clinton's "Health Security for All" proposal to participate politically. The insurance companies' media consultant, Ben Goddard, would later report that they "targeted involved Americans, people who were registered to vote, wrote letters to editors or public officials, attended meetings and made political contributions."[22] But the only media venue that Goddard mentioned other than the major news networks was Rush Limbaugh,[23] whose far-right audience hated "Hillary-Care." Ken Goldstein's interviews with lobbyists active on the same bill also found an interest group tendency to target "reliable supporters."[24]

Unfortunately, no data are available on the incidence and placement of issue ads directed at the Clinton reform bill, but we do have systematic evidence about a related and more recent case. The data come from the Wisconsin Advertising Project, which catalogued the number of television issue advertisements in the top 100 media markets that dealt with the Medicare Prescription Drug and Modernization Act (hereafter, the MMA).

Enacted by Congress in 2003, the MMA created for the first time government-funded prescription drug coverage for Medicare recipients. Early polls showed that seniors had misgivings about a new government plan, but by the time the legislation was adopted, their attitudes had changed in the bill's favor. Moreover, senior citizens meet all of the criteria for good targets that Goddard had applied in 1993–94. They are disproportionately more likely to vote, write letters, and otherwise participate in politics.

Figure 10.1 reports the average number of advertisements that ran in each state according to the number of prescriptions written for individuals over age sixty-five. As the bar graph shows, the greater the prescription drug demand generated by a state's retirees, the more television ads health advocacy groups ran in that state. In fact, groups on both sides followed this pattern. Groups promoting the new coverage anticipated major political benefit once coverage began for the bill's beneficiaries. The Association of Retired Americans (ARA), which ran issue ads opposing the bill, did so not because it opposed the new coverage; rather it thought the new benefit was not generous enough.[25]

Figure 10.1   Targeting Interested Constituents: Issue Advertising on the MMA of 2003

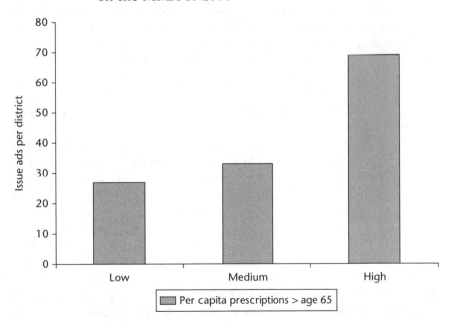

Source: Based on data provided by the Wisconsin Advertising Project, http://wiscadproject.wisc.edu/project.php.

A second factor in determining which audiences to target is the degree to which a group has an organizational presence in the member's constituency. Unions and other federated organizations may have one or more chapters or locals in a district or state, which provide a group with greater access to the press, better developed networks within the area, and a base for political mobilization around specific issues. Similarly, corporations enjoy connections to a geographic constituency to the extent that they have headquarters, offices, or manufacturing plants and therefore employees among a member's constituents. In such areas, issue ads should prove more effective in that a subset of citizens will have a predisposition—perhaps a self-interested incentive—to contact their representatives.

How much does a group's connection to a member's constituency affect the number of issue ads it will run there? In his study of advocacy on the Clinton health care bill, Goldstein asked interest group strategists about their organization's outside lobbying activities, one of which was issue advertising. He found that a group's connectedness to a district mattered a good deal. For example, a group of pharmaceutical companies hired a political consultant to fashion a message that would appeal to its stockholders and employees. Using that message in a telephone campaign, "nineteen thousand retired workers and stockholders were patched through to twenty different congressional offices."[26] Goldstein also cites a newspaper report that large corporations opposed to reform developed similar communication strategies to influence their employees in key congressional districts.[27] A spokesperson for one of the organizations behind the 2009 Harry and Louise campaign explained: "Most of [the advertising buys] will come in targeted congressional districts where our companies have a significant economic presence, or in districts where members [of Congress] can still be persuaded to support comprehensive health-care reform."[28]

Do such patterns hold for other health policies and health advocacy groups? To help answer this question, we return to the Wisconsin Advertising Project's data on the Medicare prescription drug legislation. For each of the five groups that ran television ads regarding the MMA, we counted the number of organizational sites—for example, headquarters or regional offices, state or local chapters, research sites, manufacturing plants—in each state. These groups ran advertisements in 46 states for a total of 230 group-state observations. The relationship between organizational presence (sites per congressional district) and issue advertisements is shown in Figure 10.2. The pattern is striking. On average, the five groups that advertised on the MMA ran about 25 ads per congressional district in states where they had a low number of sites (the lowest third), about 80 ads where their presence ranked in the middle, and over 180 ads per district in states where their presence was high (the top third).

Figure 10.2   Issue Advertising Close to Home: Targeted Ads on the MMA of 2003

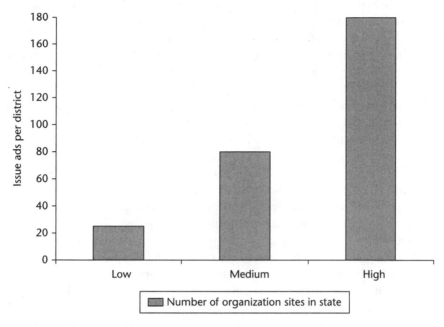

Source: Based on data provided by the Wisconsin Advertising Project, http://wiscadproject.wisc.edu/project.php.

Targeting Legislators

From the previous section, we can conclude that groups tend to advertise in areas where the public is likely to be attentive or can be made attentive and where the citizenry (or some significant subset of it) is receptive to the group's position, precisely the two factors that Ken Kollman concludes are important for all outside lobbying.[29] But influencing constituents is not an end in itself. Ad campaigns outside of Washington are ineffectual inside Washington if they neglect the districts of (potentially) influential legislators.[30]

Most accounts of outside lobbying, both academic and journalistic, characterize it as an instrument for swaying pivotal legislators to support the interest group's position. In fact, legislators take positions in several ways that can affect a bill's progress. A member might cosponsor the bill (or a competing bill), either before or after it is formally introduced; she might sign (or dissent from) a committee report; she might sign a "Dear Colleague" letter or issue a statement supporting (opposing) it. But the most visible and important position taking occurs when the roll is called—when members must vote yea or nay on a bill, any amendments to it, and any procedural choices that affect it.

In his study of the Clinton health care fight, Goldstein interviewed interest group strategists to identify the members they targeted using outside tactics, one of which was issue advertising. He found that outside lobbying campaigns mainly targeted "persuadable" legislators, that is, the members in the middle.[31] Because the Clinton reforms never came to the floor in either chamber, Goldstein found, most of these targets were in the committees of jurisdiction, and most groups—sixteen of twenty-one or 67 percent—focused on "undecided" legislators.[32] One of Goldstein's respondents commented, "We figured out who was for us and who was against us and threw the kitchen sink at everyone in the middle."[33]

The American Medical Association (AMA) applied similar tactics in the summer of 2008 when the Senate was considering legislation to increase doctor reimbursement rates under Medicare.[34] The governing statute set rates according to a long-outdated formula, but because Congress had not devised a better one, it had been adopting year-to-year adjustments. Absent such an adjustment, reimbursement rates would drop steeply in July of 2008. By a ratio of six to one, the House passed a one-year fix giving doctors a 1 percent increase rather than the formula's 10.6 percent cut, but the bill stalled in the Senate due to opposition by key Republicans. The AMA responded by launching an aggressive issue advertising campaign. One television ad warned that the government would "slash physician Medicare payments," forcing doctors to cut back on medical care for seniors. Applauding the House for "doing the right thing," the ad charged that a group of senators had committed "an outrage," conspiring with insurance company lobbyists to maintain the industry's inflated payments under Medicare Advantage plans. The AMA ran the ads in the states of ten senators who were holding up the bill.[35]

The AMA's strategy in this last case also suggests that groups tend to focus on members of Congress who are electorally vulnerable. Of senators targeted by the AMA in 2008, 70 percent were up for reelection in the 2008 cycle as opposed to the one-third up in any given cycle. More generally, the prospect of a close election concentrates the mind of ambitious politicians, making them especially hesitant to alienate single-issue voters. Interest group advocates understand that tendency and put their knowledge to strategic use whenever possible. Returning to the MMA case, the number of Medicare prescription drug issue ads in 2003 ran more than 30 percent higher in states that had a senator up for reelection. So too in the Obama health care case: the conservative group 60 Plus ran a series of ads against the reform package, announcing that it was going after eighteen electorally vulnerable Democrats.[36]

The advertising data from the 2003 MMA debate provide additional evidence of the importance that groups attach to approaching floor votes. In the 2003 time-series of group advertising buys, the number of ads spiked at three times. The first was April 2003, when the House committees held the first hearings of the 108th Congress on Medicare prescription drug coverage. But the other two spikes appeared, respectively, in the two weeks before the July floor votes and the two weeks prior to the November votes on the conference report. From February through early June, the number of Medicare issue ads averaged about 1,000 per week nationwide. In the two weeks before the first floor votes in June, the number of ads jumped to 3,000 per week. In the two weeks before the November votes on the conference report, the weekly incidence of ads dropped to about 500. But in the two weeks before adoption of the conference report, the number of ads shot up to almost 6,000 per week.

In sum, advertising buys can increase dramatically as important floor votes approach. But do those ads therefore target only the swing legislators? Not entirely. Patterns of issue advertising in the MMA case indicate that winning over undecided legislators directly was not the only or even the most important goal served by issue ad campaigns. Groups also targeted states heavily represented by members already friendly to their cause. In states where the percentage of allies in a delegation was high, for example, the number of ads was approximately twice the number as in states where the percentage of swing members was high and four times the number in states with a high percentage of opponents.

Why would groups focus on members whose positions one doesn't need to change? One possible explanation is that a group does so strategically— that is, it mounts an advertising campaign to anticipate or offset (advertising-induced) pressure on its allies from the other side, a strategy analogous to "counteractive lobbying" inside Congress.[37] But a more complete answer depends on the importance of legislative activities other than voting. Influence in Congress goes to those who work at it. It comes from labor-intensive efforts, such as drafting and introducing legislation, offering amendments, planning strategy, trading favors, and otherwise spending scarce time and political capital.[38] One of the most important of these activities, in fact, may be the legislator lobbying his or her colleagues on how to vote. Issue ads provide incentives for group-friendly members to do such lobbying and other work on an issue where the group and legislator share a common purpose. By raising the salience of an issue among a friendly member's constituents, issue ads can increase the political credit that that member can then claim for effective work in Washington.

Conversely, groups can and sometimes do use ads to lay blame at the feet of legislators who were steadfastly opposed to the advertising group's position. Running negative ads about a bill can short-circuit subsequent attempts by the member to claim credit for helping to pass it. They may even "prime" a member's constituents for subsequent issue ads that blame the legislator for promoting an unpopular bill.[39] Were they to work in this way, negative issue ads could thus "demobilize" a member by turning visibility on an issue into a political liability.

In the MMA case, blame-focused ads were relatively rare. Of the issue ads that named a particular member, in fact, the vast majority were laudatory, not accusatory. In the 2009–10 health care reform debate, no systematically collected data are available, but even during this unusually negative, strident debate, many of the leading advocacy groups ran ads expressing praise or appreciation for the actions of their legislative allies as the fight unfolded. The AFL-CIO, Americans for Health Care Reform, Americans United for Change, Catholics United, Families USA, the Pharmaceutical Research Manufacturers Association (PhRMA), Healthcare for America Now (HCAN), and the Service Employees International Union (SEIU) together spent tens of millions of dollars on ad campaigns crediting key Democrats for their actions in supporting health care reform. Conservative groups, including the 60 Plus Association and the Susan B. Anthony List, likewise ran ads praising specific antireform members. Other antireform groups spent millions of advertising dollars on ideologically right-wing Internet sites, talk radio, and television that reached conservative audiences represented by conservative members.

Journalistic reports on the issue ad campaigns suggest that positive ads targeted at legislative allies were much less frequent than ads targeting undecided legislators or legislators opposed to the group's position. Numerous organizations on both sides aggressively targeted wavering legislators and publicly announced that they were doing so. The pharmaceutical spokesperson quoted above stated they were doing so with the latter-day Harry and Louise ads. Similarly, the pro-reform groups Health Care for America Now and MoveOn.org and the antireform groups U.S. Chamber of Commerce and 60 Plus announced campaigns that would focus on undecided legislators or legislators whose electoral vulnerability might make them so.[40]

However, most stories in the press reported on television ads that attacked legislators either for their support for or their opposition to the bill. Such ads were especially common from ideological groups that opposed reform, such as the Club for Growth. Indeed, these ads continued to run after the bill's passage. Emboldened by opinion polls that showed much of the public dissatisfied with the Obama legislation, antireform groups went after Democratic incumbents who had voted for the bill by supporting their challengers who vowed to repeal it.

In general, we do not know the degree to which either side targeted allies, undecided members, or opponents during the 2009–10 health care reform fight, but issue advertising on this issue broke all records. Given the tens of millions spent on health care reform ads, it should come as no surprise that some groups could use their advertising capacity to reward friends, attack opponents, and pressure undecided members.

Issue Advertising Messages and the
Political Psychology of Citizens

To this point we have examined the nature and purpose of interest group advertising strategies. That many groups spend millions of dollars on issue ad campaigns suggests that they think their strategies bear fruit. But are they right? To what extent do issue ads induce citizens to change their views? And what features of issue advertisements make them more or less effective?

Research in political psychology provides some insight into the process by which political advertisements can influence voters. We have already referred to one mechanism, what the political psychologists refer to as "priming."[41] In this context, priming refers to the way in which previous, often repetitious, ads affect a viewer's implicit memory in such a way that some aspects of a complex issue are more easily retrieved. In the year leading up to the Obama administration's health care reforms, for example, AARP ran an expensive advertising campaign that characterized the current health care system as broken in ways that could no longer be ignored. When the legislative debate over reform got underway in 2009, aspects of the debate that reflected the "broken status quo" might then be evoked more easily.

Research also shows how features of advertisements as subtle as the background music will cue different emotional reactions from viewers.[42] Ominous music with discordant chords arouses listener fear or anxiety, but those emotions also increase individuals' willingness to consider new information and reassess their opinions. Advertisements with patriotic or inspirational music that evoke enthusiasm, on the other hand, cause experimental subjects to report higher likelihood of participation, an effect that should be important if the purpose is to mobilize citizens to contact their representatives.

We can see these tactics in action by comparing the two advertisements that opened this chapter. The first is from the original Harry and Louise ad campaign, which was aired by the Health Insurance Association of America (HIAA).[43] In 1993, when these ads were run, public support for Clinton's health care reform was high. To undercut this support, the insurance industry ad needed citizens to rethink their positions. The ad imagines a Harry and Louise conversation after reform about how bad their health insurance has become. The negative message is thus clear, but the music reinforces the effectiveness at an emotional level. A discordant piano refrain plays in the background as the foreboding voice of the narrator warns viewers that they will lose control of their own health care.

In the second commercial, Harry and Louise return to the airwaves, this time representing a pro-reform message.[44] In 2008, support for health-care reform was high, but the form it should take was being contested in the presidential campaign. The pro-reform advocates thus needed to do two things: warn the public about how bad the private health care system had become, but also deliver a positive message about what reform could do. The music in the ad reflects the two-part nature of the ad's purpose. In the first half, the actors are asking viewers to rethink their satisfaction with the current system, so the music is ominous and discordant. But near the end of the ad, the music shifts to uplifting, resonating chords as Louise looks to the future and the importance of the issue in the next election: "Whoever the next president is, health care should be at the top of his agenda, bringing everyone to the table and making it happen." The implicit emotional cue to the viewer is to get out and vote, and vote with health policy reform in mind.

Of course, issue ads are designed to work through message as well as emotion. Both scholars and practitioners emphasize the potential for issue ads to *frame* a policy message in terms that, if internalized by the public, advantages one side. In research on political communication, framing is a psychological concept that refers to one's perception about "what the debate is about."[45] Is health care reform about government bureaucrats denying choice to average Americans, as the first Harry and Louise ads suggested? Or is it about expanding insurance coverage to the "too many people" who are "slipping through the cracks," as the latter-day Harry and Louise characterized it?

Ben Goddard, the head of the media consulting firm for the insurance industry in 1993–94, described the development of the original ads that cast Harry and Louise as two average Americans whom health care reform would hurt:

> The key thing in advertising is finding the right message and messenger. In putting together the materials, we tested as spokespersons high-pro-file celebrities, doctors, and academic experts. Bill Gradison then gave a speech and said, 'this issue is going to be decided around people's kitchen tables.' My first reaction was skepticism, but we tried it with a couple around a kitchen table and it was a huge success over other formats. People respond to a familiar environment. The kitchen is a symbol for family decisions. Our research told us that people would respond to the message and that they would like the messenger.[46]

Of course, media consultants such as Goddard were not the first to discover the importance of framing in health politics. Analyzing a century of failed attempts to adopt universal health insurance in the United States, historian Colin Gordon emphasizes the skill of the American Medical Association in framing all reform proposals as "socialized medicine," a mischaracterization that in 2009–10 once again gave opponents of reform good traction.[47]

Work in psychology and political science also shows that citizens are not indiscriminate in the messages they accept. The source of the message matters. If a viewer is exposed to an advertisement sponsored by a group whose ideology they know and disagree with, that viewer will discount that information. Likewise, ads that contain messages reflecting the self-interest of the sponsor are considered less trustworthy.[48] Groups interested in running advertising campaigns recognize this, however, and often select ambiguous and nonoffensive names that mask the policy biases of the group.[49] In one study, for instance, participants were presented with advertisements sponsored either by the "United Seniors Association," a highly active group financed largely by pharmaceutical interests, or by "pharmaceutical or drug companies." Respondents held the innocuously named "United Seniors Association" in much higher esteem, reporting a 5 percent disapproval rating, compared to the 58 percent disapproval rating given to the generic "pharmaceutical or drug companies."[50]

This tactic was evident again in the health care debates of 2009–10. Working this time on the pro-reform side, for instance, the pharmaceutical industry ran issue ads using the name "Americans for Stable and Quality Care." Other groups with unrevealing monikers included the Alliance for Health, Americans United for Change, and the Alliance to Improve Medicare.

Issue Advertising and Health Policy Making

The assumption that the insurance industry won the media wars in 1993 is one reason that Clinton and his advisers listed special interest influence on public opinion as a primary cause of their defeat.[51] Other observers at the time agreed. The HIAA Harry and Louise ads were widely credited with having contributed to the administration's defeat.[52] Some academic studies later echoed the point. Goldsteen et al. attribute the precipitous drop in support for the Clinton plan in 1993 to the Harry and Louise advertising campaign, which "captured public opinion" and reversed the trend in public opinion that was undercutting the insurance industry's position.[53] Kathleen Hall Jamieson likewise reports that the health insurance industry's Harry and Louise ads attacking the Clinton bill cost $12 million and generated a remarkable 300,000 calls, the effect of which was inflated by the fact that the ads themselves attracted a great deal of free media attention.[54]

Subsequent analysis by Larry Jacobs suggests that the influence on public opinion attributed to HIAA's Harry and Louise ads has been significantly overstated, in part because the public's latent discomfort with new federal programs was already strong.[55] The poll numbers supporting health care reform were thus artificially high in 1993 and likely to come down even if HIAA had stayed off of the airwaves. The point that issue advertising is most effective when one side dominates the airwaves remains valid, however. Jacobs and Shapiro make precisely this point in their analysis of public opinion regarding Clinton's reform bill.[56] In Jacob and Shapiro's view, however, both sides used "crafted speech" in an attempt to manipulate public opinion in their favor, although the pro-reform message was promoted by the White House, for the most part, and not through not issue ads. The presence of conflicting messages, Jacobs and Shapiro argue, limited the impact of either side on the attitudes of individual citizens.

In another important case a few years later, however, Jamieson emphasizes the paucity of competing messages. In 1997, the tobacco industry mounted a multimedia ad campaign against legislation that would impose higher cigarette taxes, Food and Drug Administration (FDA) regulation of tobacco, and a $500 billion multistate settlement of cases against the industry for reimbursement of Medicaid costs.[57] Four tobacco companies joined together to spend $40 million in advertising over a five-month period. An industry spokesperson later reported that the ads generated 400,000 calls and telegrams to congressional offices. The American Cancer Society and the Campaign for Tobacco-Free Kids, in contrast, mounted a belated, bare-bones ad campaign targeted at a handful of senators. The tobacco industry's campaign, Jamieson concludes, was "a textbook example of the power of saturation advertising," which "allowed the industry to reshape the debate."[58]

Press accounts likewise point to the success of the AMA's issue ads urging Congress to correct the Medicare reimbursement rates for physicians in June of 2008, which we discuss above. The ads targeted ten senators who were blocking adoption of the reimbursement readjustment, and the AMA had the advertising airwaves to itself. Shortly after the July 4 recess, nine of the ten senators who had voted to block the bill changed their votes, more than enough to invoke cloture on the measure and move it toward passage.[59]

As in the case of tobacco regulation, evidence of advertising's influence in the doctor reimbursement matter is specific to the case, but that is not its main limitation. The problem is that any inference that the issue ads caused any senator's vote to change is more than a little tenuous. As we have seen, interest groups tend to target constituents already inclined to support their policies. And if group strategists can anticipate that reaction, so can senators. In fact, members do pay attention to constituent mail and other expressions of issue-specific opinions, such as e-mail, phone calls, and postcards. As constituent-initiated contacts increase, the probability that a sincerely undecided member will vote in the interest group's favor will probably go up. But because members of Congress *do* pay attention to constituents, and do so over long periods with good political intelligence, it is always possible that an interest group advertiser will push them where they were already likely to go.

Had the AMA not advertised, would the senators have done anything different? (Nine of ten, after all, is a good batting average in any league.) In fact, the answer is probably not. Republican support in Congress for AMA-favored policies is consistently strong; the organization's PAC gives to Republican over Democratic Senate candidates at a ratio greater than two to one. In fact, it had given generous contributions to every one of the ten senators in question in their previous election cycle (an average of $7,500 out of a maximum $10,000). The ten Republican senators did not want to cut payments to doctors, it turns out; instead they held out to protest the cuts in Medicare Advantage that the Democratic bill used to pay for the increase. Even for this simple case, the legislative effects of issue advertising are unclear.

It will be especially hard to assess whether the ubiquitous advertising about health care reform in 2009–10 had any effect on its eventual adoption. That the votes were so close in both chambers suggests that any number of factors might have made the difference. At the same time, no one voice, nor even one side of the issue, had a major advertising advantage in the print or broadcast media, much less traffic on the Internet.[60] The extraordinary frequency and diversity of ads created a political disharmony, the effects of which will require difficult research and very good data to sort out.

Conclusion: Issue Advertising and Democratic Practice

In summary, issue ads may be strategically clever instruments of political advocacy, they may command media budgets in the millions of dollars, and they may reach into the households of millions of Americans. Many of those Americans may actually watch them, and many who do watch may be influenced by them. But that does not mean that the ads have a net effect on the behavior of lawmakers, much less the shape of the laws that get made. That advertising campaigns launched by special interests can push around members of Congress is a disturbing assertion with modest empirical backing. But so would be the assertion that the millions of dollars spent on issue advertising are legislatively inconsequential. The fact is that we don't really know how much policy influence issue advertising generates.[61]

Even if one cannot show that issue advertising matters legislatively, however, it still matters democratically. In the practice of representation, we care not only who wins in the end but who participates in the process that leads to that end. Free speech and broad participation by diverse voices promote democratic deliberation and lend legitimacy to the policy process. As West and Francis point out, in fact, one of the main advantages of paid advertising is that a group can promote its perspective with the public without its views being screened and interpreted by the regular news media or political elites.[62] Other things equal, interest group participation in public policy debates is a good thing.

Issue advertising appears more democratically problematic, however, when one considers that in its most common forms it is highly expensive. Relevant here is E. E. Schattschnider's critique of American democracy, now a half century old: "The flaw in the pluralist heaven is that the heavenly chorus sings with a strong upper-class accent."[63] Social scientists since then have often found that narrow, resource-rich interests organize with relative ease, and they deploy their resources to magnify their voices in Congress. If this is also the case with issue ads, the public might hear a multitude of voices but only within a limited range. The Annenberg study for the 108th Congress found that nearly 80 percent of issue ads that ran in the Washington, D.C., media market were sponsored by corporations.[64] Within that set of groups, the vast majority of spending was done by a handful of private sector interests. The Annenberg study likewise reported an issue ad spending ratio of 5 to 1 by corporations relative to cause or citizen groups and a gigantic 100 to 1 business-to-union ratio.[65] A study of issue ads reported in the *New York Times* found a less severe bias in favor of corporations, though corporate ads were twice as common as those from nonprofit groups, some of which were themselves advocates for, and financed by, business organizations.[66] That study also found a smaller but still substantial business-to-union ratio of fourteen to one.

These patterns appear more democratically disturbing in light of the social scientific literature on framing, discussed above. Successful framing strategies structure the set of choices considered in public debate, and they are most successful when one viewpoint or one side controls the message. For the most part, antireform ads dominated the paid media during the Clinton health care debate, and almost all of those ads were financed by business interests that stood to lose from the proposed reforms. In the Medicare prescription drug case in 2003, only one organization ran any ads against the bill, and its ads were outnumbered by the insurance industry and other pro-business groups by more than ten to one. In the fight over tobacco legislation, Jamieson concludes, the tobacco industry prevailed in part because of the meager and belated public interest group effort and "a lack of counterbalancing information in the news."[67]

Of the cases we have examined here, only the debate over the Obama health care reforms in 2009–10 elicited substantial issue advertising by both sides. In this respect, the competition of ideas generated in the paid media was robust. At the same time, two important features of that competition warrant mention. First, the range of the debate was framed narrowly very early in the process. A single-payer system was never on the table, not because it lacked merit on policy grounds but because it was dead on arrival on special interest grounds. Even its diminutive cousin, a "public option" for health insurance that would compete with private plans, was gasping its last breath before the Senate Finance Committee markup had begun. Likewise omitted from the Democrats' agenda were provisions that they had championed during the MMA debate only a few years before: reimportation of pharmaceuticals and government bargaining over the pharmaceutical prices passed through to Medicare and Medicaid. Either provision would have lowered the bill's cost by billions of dollars, but neither was tolerable to the pharmaceutical industry, whose support the White House thought crucial.[68]

The second feature of the issue ad competition regarding the Obama health care reforms follows from the first. It was because the Obama administration had made major concessions to business interests at the beginning of the process that so many ads appeared on both sides of the bill. The insurance industry and U.S. Chamber of Commerce antireform advertising campaigns, for instance, were countered in part by multimillion dollar campaigns promoting the bill by the pharmaceutical industry and by health provider groups, including the American Medical Association—the nemesis of every comprehensive health care proposal for almost a century. That strong business interests weighed in on the pro-reform side may be the most important reason that comprehensive health care reform passed in 2010 after almost a century of failure. But those groups did not do it for nothing.

Notes

1. Research reported in this chapter was funded by grants from the Robert Wood Johnson Foundation Investigators Award Program and the Gerald R. Ford School of Public Policy, University of Michigan. Thanks are due to Katie Drake and Molly Reynolds for valuable research assistance. The authors are responsible for any errors that remain. Please send correspondence to Hall at rlhall@umich.edu.
2. See, e.g., Darrell M. West, Diane Heith, and Chris Goodwin, "Harry and Louise Go to Washington: Political Advertising and Health Care Reform," *Journal of Health Politics, Policy and Law* 21, no. 1 (1996): 35–68.
3. See Lawrence R. Jacobs and Robert Y. Shapiro, *Politicans Don't Pander* (Chicago: University of Chicago Press, 2000); Lawrence R. Jacobs, "Questioning the Conventional Wisdom on Public Opinion Toward Health Reform," *PS: Political Science and Politics,* 27, no. 2 (1994): 208–14.
4. Kenneth Goldstein, "Understanding Interest Group Targeting" (unpublished manuscript, University of Wisconsin, 2001).
5. See Allan Cigler and Burdett Loomis, "Contemporary Interest Group Politics: More than 'More of the Same,'" in *Interest Group Politics,* 4th ed., eds. Allan Cigler and Burdett Loomis (Washington, DC: CQ Press, 1996): 393–406; Kathleen Hall Jamieson, *Everything You Think You Know About Politics—and Why You're Wrong* (New York: Basic Books, 2000): chap. 18. The two major works on outside lobbying on which we draw in this chapter are Ken Kollman, *Outside Lobbying* (Princeton, NJ: Princeton University Press, 1998); and Kenneth Goldstein, *Interest Groups, Lobbying, and Participation in America* (Cambridge, UK: Cambridge University Press, 1999).

6. *Time* magazine ran a story in 2009 identifying the "Top 10 Fight Ads on Health Reform," providing links to the videos of each one. We refer to those ads several times in this chapter. We recommend that the reader view some of these ads as a supplement to the discussion below. See Michael Scherer, "Top 10 Health-Care-Reform Fight Ads," *Time*, August 20, 2009, http://www.time.com/time/nation/article/0,8599,1917690,00.html#ixzz12fTFXK8w/.

7. Scherer, "Top 10 Health-Care-Reform Fight Ads."

8. See especially Lawrence Wallack, Katie Woodruff, Lori Dorfman, and Iris Diaz, *News for a Change: An Advocate's Guide to Working with the Media*, Thousand Oaks, CA: Sage, 1999.

9. On priming constituents, see Goldstein, "Understanding Interest Group Targeting." On signaling by interest groups, see Kollman, *Outside Lobbying*, chap. 3.

10. Erika Falk, "Legislative Issue Advertising in the 107th Congress," a report to the Annenberg Public Policy Center of the University of Pennsylvania, Washington, DC, July 2003, http://www.annenbergpublicpolicycenter.org/Downloads/Political_Communication/LegIssueAds107Congress/2003_APPC_IssueAds107th.pdf; Erika Falk, Erin Grizard, and Gordon McDonald, "Legislative Issue Advertising in the 108th Congress: Pluralism or Peril? *The Harvard International Journal of Press/Politics* 11, no. 4 (2006): 148–64.

11. Falk, Grizard, and McDonald, "Legislative Issue Advertising in the 108th Congress."

12. West, Heith, and Goodwin, "Harry and Louise Go to Washington."

13. West, Heith, and Goodwin, "Harry and Louise Go to Washington."

14. Michael Scherer, "Heated Health-Reform Ads Give Taste of Fall Campaign." *Time*. March 15, 2010, http://www.time.com/time/politics/article/0,8599,1972364,00.html.

15. No clean comparison is possible, because the Clinton bill never came to the floor, whereas the reform package in 2009–10 saw floor action in both House and Senate and subsequent floor action on a package of amendments adopted through budget reconciliation.

16. Scherer, "Top 10 Health-Care Reform Fight Ads," para. 1.

17. Ben Pershing, "Groups Take Health-Reform Debate to Airwaves," *Washington Post*, August 5, 2009, http://www.washingtonpost.com/wp-dyn/content/article/2009/08/04/AR2009080401447.html.

18. See "Healthcare Reform Advertisers Warming Up Big Guns," *ClickZ*, November 10, 2009, http://www.clickz.com/clickz/news/1707122/healthcare-reform-advertisers-warming-up-big-guns/.

19. "Healthcare Reform Advertisers Warming Up Big Guns."

20. Peter Wallsten, "Health Care Campaigns Connect with Internet Search Terms," *Los Angeles Times*, September 4, 2009.

21. Kollman, *Outside Lobbying*, see esp. chaps. 2–3.

22. West, Heith, and Goodwin, "Harry and Louise Go to Washington," 43.

23. West, Heith, and Goodwin, "Harry and Louise Go to Washington," 43.

24. Goldstein, *Interest Groups, Lobbying, and Participation in America*, 86.

25. Besides ARA and AARP, three other groups mounted issue ad campaigns on the MMA: Alliance to Improve Medicare (AIM), Pfizer, and United States Action.

26. Goldstein, *Interest Groups, Lobbying, and Participation in America*, 86.

27. Goldstein, *Interest Groups, Lobbying, and Participation in America*, 86.

28. Pershing, "Groups Take Health-Reform Debate to Airwaves."

29. Kollman, *Outside Lobbying.*
30. Goldstein, *Interest Groups, Lobbying, and Participation in America.*
31. Goldstein, *Interest Groups, Lobbying, and Participation in America,* 42.
32. Goldstein, *Interest Groups, Lobbying, and Participation in America.* However, Goldstein's definition of "undecided" includes both "soft" supporters and "soft" opponents. See 83, n. 4.
33. Goldstein, *Interest Groups, Lobbying, and Participation in America,* 84.
34. See Robert Pear, "Doctors Press Senate to Undo Medicare Cuts, *New York Times,* July 7, 2008, http://www.nytimes.com/2008/07/07/health/policy/07medicare.html.
35. Pear, "Doctors Press Senate to Undo Medicare Cuts."
36. Jeffrey Young, "Conservative Seniors Group Launches Ads Against Healthcare Reform," *The Hill,* February 17, 2010, http://thehill.com/blogs/blog-briefing-room/news/81767-conservative-seniors-group-launches-ads-against-healthcare-reform.
37. David Austen-Smith and John R. Wright, "Counteractive Lobbying," *American Journal of Political Science* 38, no. 1 (1994): 25–44.
38. See Richard L. Hall, *Participation in Congress* (New Haven, CT: Yale University Press, 1996): chap. 1.
39. Goldstein, "Understanding Interest Group Targeting."
40. Young, "Conservative Seniors Troup Launches Ads Against Healthcare Reform"; Rachel Slajda, "HCAN Targets 11 House Dems in new TV Ads," *Talking Points Memo,* March 16, 2010, http://tpmdc.talkingpointsmemo.com/2010/03/hcan-targets-11-house-dems-in-new-tv-ads.php; Michael Scherer, "Heated Health-Reform Ads Give Taste of Fall Campaign," *Time,* March 16, 2010, http://www.time.com/time/politics/article/0,8599,1972364,00.html.
41. Priming is especially significant for the study of the news media's effects on citizen attitudes and behavior. See Shanto Iyengar and Donald R. Kinder, *News that Matters* (Chicago: Chicago University Press, 1987).
42. Brader, Ted, *Campaigning For Hearts and Minds: How Emotional Appeals in Political Ads Work* (Chicago: University of Chicago Press, 2006).
43. Video available at http://www.youtube.com/watch?v=Dt31nhleeCg.
44. Video available at http://www.youtube.com/watch?v=fOr17a4ZOIU.
45. The classic work on the subject is Amos Tversky and Daniel Kahneman, "The Framing of Decisions and the Psychology of Choice," *Science* 211, no. 4481 (1981): 453–58.
46. Quoted in West, Heith, and Goodwin, "Harry and Louise Go to Washington," 48.
47. Colin Gordon, *Dead on Arrival: The Politics of Health Care in Twentieth-Century America* (Princeton, NJ: Princeton University Press, 2003).
48. Eric W. Groenendyk and Nicholas A. Valentino. "Of Dark Clouds and Silver Linings: Effects of Exposure to Issue Versus Candidate Advertising on Persuasion, Information Retention, and Issue Salience," *Communication Research,* 29, no. 3 (2002): 295–319.
49. See, e.g., Kathleen Hall Jamieson, *Everything You Think You Know About Politics.*
50. David G. Magleby and J. Quin Monson, "The Noncandidate Campaign: Soft Money and Issue Advocacy in the 2002 Congressional Elections," *PS: Political Science & Politics* 36, no. 3. (2003): 401–03.
51. Haynes Johnson and David S. Broder, *The System: The American Way of Politics at the Breaking Point* (Boston: Little, Brown, 1996).
52. Johnson and Broder, *The System.*

53. Raymond L. Goldsteen, Karen Goldsteen, James H Swan, and Wendy Clemeña, "Harry and Louise and Health Care Reform: Romancing Public Opinion," *Journal of Health Politics, Policy, and Law* 26, no. 6 (2001): 1325–52.

54. Jamieson, *Everything You Think You Know About Politics.*

55. Jacobs, "Questioning the Conventional Wisdom on Public Opinion Toward Health Reform."

56. Jacobs and Shapiro, *Politicians Don't Pander.*

57. Jamieson, *Everything You Think You Know About Politics*, 136.

58. Jamieson, *Everything You Think You Know About Politics*, 136.

59. "Senate Passes Doctor Reimbursement Bill," *USA Today*, July 9, 2008.

60. As we discuss below, however, one reason for the diversity of the ads was that major business interests received concessions very early in the process and thus ran issue ads on the bill's behalf.

61. On this general point, see Frank Baumgarter, M. Berry, Marie Hojnacki, David C. Kimball, and Beth L. Leech, *Lobbying and Policy Change* (Chicago: University of Chicago Press, 2009). Baumgartner et al. conclude that resource-rich groups seldom win new policies when they want them. Instead their power comes in protecting a status quo that already favors their interests.

62. Darrell M. West and Richard Francis, "Electronic Advocacy: Interest Groups and Public Policymaking." *PS: Political Science and Politics* 29, no 1 (1996): 25–29. See also Jamieson, *Everything You Think You Know About Politics*, 125–131.

63. E. E. Schattschneider, *The Semisovereign People: A Realist's View of Democracy in America* (Chicago: Holt, Rinehart and Winston, 1960): 37.

64. Falk, Grizard, and McDonald, "Legislative Issue Advertising in the 108th Congress," 157.

65. Falk, Grizard, and McDonald, "Legislative Issue Advertising in the 108th Congress," 155–157.

66. Clyde Brown, Herbert Waltzer, and Miriam B. Waltzer, "Daring to Be Heard: Advertorials by Organized Interests on the Op-Ed Page of *The New York Times*, 1985–1998," *Political Communication* 18, no. 1 (2001): 23–50.

67. Jamieson, *Everything You Think You Know*, 136.

68. See Andrea Seabrook and Peter Overby, "Drug Firms Pour $40 Million Into Health Care Debate," National Public Radio, *All Things Considered*, July 23, 2009, http://www.npr.org/templates/story/story.php?storyId=106899074.

11

Gridlock Lobbying

Breaking, Creating, and Maintaining Legislative Stalemate

Jennifer Nicoll Victor

Interest groups are permanent players in the policy-making process. They seek legislative outcomes and provide a means of representation for subsets of citizens. According to The Center for Responsive Politics, a watchdog organization that monitors lobbying and archives public data on lobbying disclosures, interest groups spent $3.27 billion lobbying the US Congress in 2008. This is up from $1.45 billion in 1998, when the data were first recorded.[1] The amount of money that firms, groups, and individuals spent on lobbying in 2008 was roughly equivalent to the $3.2 billion that all congressional and presidential candidates raised in the 2008 election. Lobbying is therefore a massive presence in the US Congress, but what exactly do organized interests hope to achieve through their lobbying expenditures?

In this essay, I show how we can understand interest groups' lobbying strategies through the basic legislative spatial model. Because groups and lobbyists are ultimately interested in policy outcomes, they, like members of Congress, are strategic actors in a policy-making game. Congressional scholars have used the legislative spatial model to describe many of the strategic actions of members of Congress. I argue that interest groups act in this policy space and that we can use the legislative spatial model as a framework to understand the behavior of groups. To do so, I first describe legislative spatial models; then I add interest groups as nondecisive players in the spatial model, which provides a platform to describe interest groups' persuasion-oriented lobbying tactics.

The Basic Legislative Spatial Model

It is commonplace to use spatial terms to describe politics (e.g., Obama is *left* of McCain). Legislative scholars have applied the spatial model of politics to a variety of aspects of legislative decision making, such as elections, committee decision making, legislators' ideological preferences, and congressional parties.[2] In particular, models of legislative gridlock have recently been used to describe policy change in Congress. For example, Brady and

Volden argue that Congress only successfully changes policy when the median members of the House and Senate prefer some policy alternative to the status quo.[3] Their argument is not based on interest group lobbying, election politics, or party manipulations; rather, they argue that one can explain policy change by examining the unidimensional preferences of members of Congress, particularly those near the median.[4]

In the basic legislative spatial model, legislators exist in a one-dimensional linear space (a line) that is assumed to be a liberal-to-conservative scale that represents players' preferences over a particular policy. Each legislator has an ideal point in the policy space, and individual legislators prefer points closer to their ideal points over points farther away.[5] Using the theorem developed by Black known as the median voter theorem, the model produces a single equilibrium outcome.[6] On any one-dimensional scale (with an odd number of players) a median voter will exist, and the policy that corresponds with her preference will always be an equilibrium.[7]

We can use a hypothetical committee, such as that displayed in Figure 11.1, to describe three important consequences of the median voter theorem as applied to group decision making: (1) to determine whether a motion will pass or fail, (2) to identify the median voter, and (3) to identify the set of policies that can defeat the status quo. The hypothetical committee in Figure 11.1 has seven voters who are voting between a proposal called "Motion" and the status quo (Q). Each voter has an ideal point—or the point at which each individual receives the most utility. Each voter evaluates whether this ideal point is closer to Motion or to Q and casts a vote for the alternative closest to her ideal point. Contests are decided by simple majority rule.

1. To determine whether any given motion will pass or fail, we simply look at the model and ascertain for each voter whether he is closer to Q or to Motion. In this example, the motion would pass because David, Elaine, Faith, and Gerald prefer Motion to Q because it is closer to their ideal points than is Q.

Figure 11.1   Voters Prefer Proposals Closer to Their Ideal Points

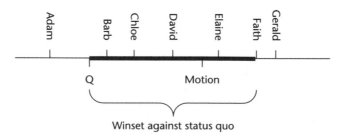

2. We can identify the median voter by simply finding the voter whose preference is in the middle of the spectrum when each voter is aligned along the one-dimensional scale. In this case, David has exactly three voters to his left and three voters to his right; David is the median voter. As the median voter, David's preference for Motion over Q will prevail.

3. Finally, we can find the set of policies that could defeat the status quo by identifying the set of policies that the median voter, David, prefers to the status quo. David will prefer all policies that are closer to him than the status quo. We call this set of policies the "winset" against the status quo, or the set of policies that could defeat the status quo. In Figure 11.1 this winset is highlighted in black. The winset against the status quo in this case extends from David's ideal point to the status quo and a distance on the other side of David's ideal point (away from the status quo) that is equal to the distance from David to Q.

One could use the median voter theorem to describe the passage and failure of bills in the chambers of the US Congress, but the US Congress does not operate by simple majority rule. Two supermajority rules are particularly relevant for understanding legislative gridlock—the filibuster and the veto. Each of these rules involves a key lawmaker (called a pivot player) who is different from the chamber median voter.

In the U.S. Senate, 60 of 100 members are needed to break a filibuster and allow a vote to proceed on a policy. A minority of at least forty-one senators can therefore prevent a bill from coming to a vote. Figure 11.2 illustrates this point. Here, M represents the median member of the Senate, and Q represents the status quo. The senators at F_L and F_R represent filibuster pivots. There are twenty senators between F_L and F_R, with forty senators to the left of F_L and forty to the right of F_R. Either of these groups of forty, plus the pivot senator, could successfully filibuster a bill. When the status quo is between F_L and F_R, gridlock occurs. That is, if a senator proposed to enact a policy just to the right of Q, the forty senators to the left of and including F_L would object and prevent a vote on such a change. The same is true for those to the right of F_R if a proposal was put forth left

Figure 11.2   Gridlock with Filibuster Pivots

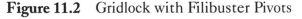
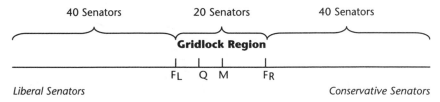

of Q. Therefore, Brady and Volden call the range between F_L and F_R the "gridlock region."[8]

The gridlock region is made larger by the institutional veto. A two-thirds vote is required in each chamber to override a presidential veto. The member in each chamber whose vote is pivotal to meet the two-thirds threshold is called the veto pivot. When the president is liberal, the veto pivot is the member who has one-third of the chamber to his left and two-thirds of the chamber to his right. When the president is conservative, the veto pivot has one-third of the chamber to his right and two-thirds to his left. Figure 11.3 provides an example of the former. The veto pivot can effectively determine whether or not a bill will pass in much the same way the median voter does. If a bill falls outside the president's winset, it will be vetoed. If a vetoed bill falls within the winset of the veto pivot, the veto will be overridden. For example, given a liberal president (as in Figure 11.3), if a bill is proposed to the right of Q, say at M, the president (P) will veto such a bill, and the chamber will not be able to muster the two-thirds super-majority to override a presidential veto.[9] The veto will be sustained by V_L and the thirty-three senators to her left (notice that all policies right of Q are outside of P and V_L's winset against the status quo). Notice that in Figure 11.3, the Motion falls outside of the winsets of P and V_L, indicating that the Motion will be vetoed and sustained.[10]

The complete gridlock region is bounded by the filibuster pivot and the veto pivot. Figure 11.4 illustrates this point using a hypothetical senate

Figure 11.3   Gridlock with Veto Pivot, Liberal President

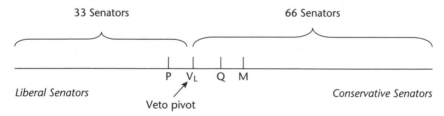

Figure 11.4   Complete Gridlock Region with Filibuster and Veto Pivots

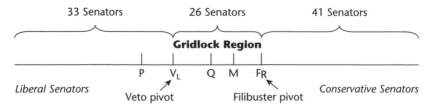

chamber (because 100 is an easy number of players to work with). If the president is liberal, a gridlock region will exist from the thirty-third senator (from the left) to the fifty-ninth senator (from the left). If the status quo is in this region of twenty-six senators, between the veto pivot and the filibuster pivot, the chamber will not be able to agree to make a policy change, even when a majority of senators seek change. The supermajority veto and filibuster rules cause this legislative gridlock. Note that the president himself could be the edge of the gridlock region if the president were more conservative (centrist) than the veto pivot. Because players who form the boundary of the gridlock region change, it is important to talk about the "pivotal players," rather than refer specifically to F, V, or M. Below, when I refer to pivotal players, I am referring to the pivots that form the boundary of the gridlock region; these are the filibuster pivot, veto pivot, median voter, or president.

To summarize, *legislative gridlock occurs when the status quo is already near the ideal policy preference of the median legislator.* The gridlock theory predicts that gridlock will persist when the status quo is within the gridlock region. If the status quo is outside of the gridlock region, policy will be amended to move it inside the region, thus achieving a stable equilibrium. This theory presumes that every legislator has equal power to filibuster, propose legislation, or override a veto—there is no agenda setter. Moreover, legislators are presumed to act as individual utility maximizers, not party loyalists. Under this theory, gridlock occurs often and under many different government circumstances (liberal/conservative president, unified/divided government). When gridlock does not occur, policies tend to pass by supermajorities because of the existence of supermajority rules like vetoes and filibusters. For example, the health care reform bill (H.R. 3590, Patient Protection and Affordable Care Act), which was signed into law in March 2010, passed the Senate with a supermajority of 60 votes. It passed the House with a bare majority of 219 votes, because there was no presidential veto threat.

Next, it is important to understand the roles that interest groups play in the creation, maintenance, and disruption of gridlock.

Interest Groups in the Spatial Model

The legislative process is characterized by many uncertainties. Members of Congress are uncertain about how a policy might work in the "real world," how constituents and voters will respond to policy changes, and about the policy preferences of their colleagues. All of this uncertainty creates a ripe breeding ground for interest groups. We know that interest groups are seen as purveyors of information in Washington, D.C., and one of their main goals is to reduce the uncertainties of members of Congress.[11] John Wright argues that interest groups "achieve influence through the acquisition and *strategic* [emphasis added] transmission of information that legislators need to make good public policy and to get reelected."[12] I argue that groups attempt to reduce uncertainty for members of Congress by strategically providing information that may alter their preferences over policy or change their beliefs about the dimensionality of the policy space. Ultimately, groups want to move policy closer to the group's ideal point—to do so, they may need to move legislators' ideal points. Lobbyists and groups attempt to do this, at least in part, by changing legislators' preferences over policy.

Based on the gridlock model, or pivotal politics model, two observations are immediately clear. First, if gridlock exists (the status quo lies between the filibuster pivot and veto pivot), a policy proposal is likely to fail because of the institutional supermajority requirements of the filibuster and veto override, as demonstrated above. Second, an interest group will prefer those policy proposals that are closer to its ideal point than the status quo, and it will oppose those proposals that are farther from its ideal point than the status quo. The set of policies an actor prefers to the status quo is the actor's winset. An interest group will support any bill in the interest group's winset and oppose any bill outside of the group's winset. These two features—the existence of gridlock and a group's preferences for policy proposals—provide the basis for understanding group behavior.

To determine how interest groups affect the spatial model of legislative policy making, we must consider the relative positions of the interest group, a proposed policy, and the status quo. The systematic consideration of these positions leads to four general scenarios in which interest groups will act and four expectations about the behavior of interest groups in legislative politics. I refer to this as the spatial model of interest group lobbying. The model shows that interest groups will engage in three general strategies when they seek to affect the outcome of a proposed policy: to break legislative gridlock, maintain gridlock, or create gridlock.[13] The model presented in Table 11.1 explains these strategies in the context of each scenario.

The upper-left cell of Table 11.1 describes what an interest group should do when legislative gridlock exists and the proposed bill falls within the interest group's winset. In such a situation, the group (IG) wants the bill (b) to pass, but it is likely to fail. The example provided in Table 11.1 highlights the interest group's winset—the interest group prefers the bill to the status quo; however, the proposal is likely to fail because the president (P) will veto the bill and it will not be overridden by the veto pivot (V) (the bill is outside the veto pivot's winset). The interest group can anticipate this outcome and attempt to change legislators' policy preferences in an attempt to *break* the gridlock that exists. To do so, the interest group would have to target the *far pivot*, or in this case V, to move to the other side

Table 11.1

	Bill (b) is IN Interest Group's Winset	Bill (b) is OUT of Interest Group's Winset
Legislative Gridlock Exists	• Interest group supports a bill that is likely to fail. • Interest group will try to BREAK gridlock by targeting the FAR PIVOT. • Example:	• Interest group opposes a bill that is likely to fail. • Interest group seeks to MAINTAIN gridlock to kill the bill by targeting BOTH PIVOTS. • Example:
Legislative Gridlock Does NOT Exist	• Interest group supports a bill that is likely to pass. • Interest group will target the MEDIAN of the chamber in an attempt to pass a bill as close to the group's ideal point as possible. • Example:	• Interest group opposes a bill that will likely pass. • Interest group will try to CREATE gridlock to kill the bill by targeting the NEAR PIVOT. • Example:

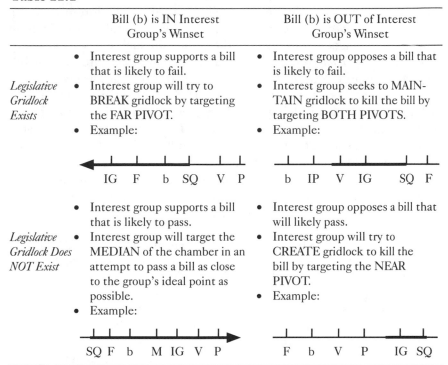

In each example, gridlock is created when the status quo (*SQ*) is between the filibuster pivot (*F*) and the veto pivot (*V*). The winset of policies that the interest group (*IG*) prefers to the status quo is highlighted in bold. When the proposed bill (*b*) falls inside the interest group's winset, the group favors the bill; when the proposed bill (*b*) falls outside of the interest group's winset, the group opposes the bill.

of the status quo. The only way to break gridlock in one-dimension is to move one of the pivots to the other side of the status quo. It would be illogical for the interest group to target the near pivot because the group would have to try to move the pivot away from the group. Rather, the group can target the pivot that is on the opposite side of the status quo relative to the group and attempt to change enough legislators' preferences such that the pivot moves to the other side of the status quo.[14] In the example in Table 11.1, this would amount to the president vetoing the bill but then a successful veto override vote if the bill were in the veto pivot's winset. Thus, it can be proposed as follows:

> Proposition 1: When legislative gridlock exists and a policy proposal is within an interest group's winset, the group will seek to *break* gridlock by targeting the policy preferences of the pivot on the opposite side of the status quo, relative to the interest group.

The upper-right cell of Table 11.1 describes a scenario in which legislative gridlock exists but the proposed bill is outside of the interest group's winset. In such a case, the interest group opposes a bill that is likely to fail—an advantageous position for the group. In such a case, the group would seek to *maintain* the existing gridlock in order to ensure that the bill dies. The group could do this by targeting both pivotal players, and the legislators near them, to encourage them to hold their positions. This would be akin to counteractive lobbying, where groups lobby allies in an attempt to counteract lobbying by their adversaries.[15] In the example shown in Table 11.1, the group's winset is highlighted. The bill (b) clearly falls outside the group's winset; however, it is also clear that the bill will be opposed by the filibuster pivot (F). Any proposal to the left of the status quo in such a case would be filibustered in the Senate because it is too far from the policy ideal points of the forty senators to the right of F.

> Proposition 2: When legislative gridlock exists and a policy proposal is *not* within an interest group's winset, the group will seek to *maintain* gridlock by targeting the policy preferences of both pivots.

The lower-left cell of Table 11.1 describes a case in which legislative gridlock does not exist and a proposed bill falls within an interest group's winset. In this case, the interest group supports a bill that is likely to pass—an advantageous position for the group.[16] The example shown in this cell of Table 11.1 indicates that the interest group has a large winset, because its ideal point is far from the status quo. However, the status quo is far from most players' ideal points and is to the left of the filibuster pivot (F), veto pivot (V), and median voter of the chamber (M). The policy proposal at b is likely to pass, and it effectively would move the status quo closer to the interest group's ideal point. While the group is pleased with such an outcome, we should expect the interest group to lobby the median voter of the chamber in this case. The bill is likely to pass at the median voter's ideal point, and the closer that point is to the interest group's ideal point, the better off the interest group is.

> Proposition 3: When legislative gridlock does *not* exist and a policy proposal is within an interest group's winset, the group will target the median voter of the chamber.

The lower-right cell of Table 11.1 depicts a scenario in which legislative gridlock does not exist and a proposed bill falls outside of an interest group's winset. In such a case, the interest group is opposed to a bill that is likely to pass.[17] The interest group would attempt to change legislators' preferences in an attempt to *create* gridlock to kill the bill. As the example in Table 11.1 shows, the bill is well outside the interest group's winset, but the bill is likely to pass because the legislative incentives are to move the status quo into the gridlock region. In its attempt to prevent that from happening, the group would target the *near pivot*, in this case *V*. If the interest group could persuade enough legislators to change their policy positions to the right such that the veto pivot moved to the opposite side of the status quo, gridlock would be created, and the proposed bill would fail.

> Proposition 4: When legislative gridlock does *not* exist and a policy proposal is *not* within an interest group's winset, the group will seek to *create* gridlock by targeting the policy preferences of the pivot on the same side of the status quo, relative to the interest group.

One might ask whether it is reasonable to assume that legislators' policy preferences can change. Might Senator Orrin Hatch (R-UT) be convinced that abortion is acceptable? Not likely. Legislators' policy goals are assumed to be fixed, but groups may be able to change legislators' beliefs about how to achieve those goals.[18] For example, suppose a legislator has a preference for low crime rates and a derived preference for capital punishment because she believes it will deter crime. The derived preference is based on a belief linking capital punishment to lower crime rates. It is this belief that interest groups attempt to affect. An anti–capital punishment group might attempt to change the derived preference of the legislator by presenting evidence that capital punishment does not deter crime. In this instance, the interest group tries to affect the member's beliefs about the connection between her stable preference and her policy preference.

We should not expect each of the four spatial scenarios outlined in Table 11.1 to occur with equal frequency. The gridlock theory of legislative politics recognizes that gridlock is a common occurrence. We are therefore more likely to observe scenarios described in the top row of Table 11.1 than in the bottom row. When groups are supportive of policy proposals in the case of legislative gridlock (upper-left cell), groups seek to break gridlock (Proposition 1). However, shifting enough legislators' preferences to break gridlock is likely to be an expensive undertaking with an often unlikely outcome.

Case Studies

Empirically, no metric exists that allows us to examine the relative positions of legislators, interest groups, and bills in the same policy space on the same scale. While testing the propositions stated above poses significant challenges, empirical evidence does exist to support them. Two recent case studies exemplify the scenarios described above. The first is an example of lobbying on a policy in gridlock. The case involves a bill in the 110th Congress (2007–08) that would move regulation of tobacco products from jurisdiction of the Department of Agriculture to that of the Food and Drug Administration. The second is an example of lobbying on a policy not in gridlock. The case involves a bill in the 109th Congress (2005–06) that would make it a federal crime to transport a minor across state lines to obtain an abortion in order to circumvent state parental notification and consent laws.

Tobacco Case—Gridlock

In 2007 and 2008 the House of Representatives and Senate separately considered legislation that would change how tobacco and tobacco products are regulated in the United States. The proposed legislation would have given jurisdiction over tobacco to the Food and Drug Administration (FDA) instead of the Department of Agriculture, which has long regulated tobacco in the United States.[19] Democrats won a majority of seats in both chambers after the 2006 elections for the first time in twelve years and promised to make a strong push to grant the FDA broad new powers to regulate tobacco, including packaging, sales, marketing, and nicotine levels.[20]

In the House, several committees fought for jurisdiction over the bill (H.R. 1108), including the House Ways and Means Committee (which has jurisdiction over tax and revenue-raising bills) and the Natural Resources Committee (which has jurisdiction over Indian Affairs issues included in the bill). The bill was sponsored in the House by Henry Waxman (D-CA), who chaired the Oversight and Government Reform Committee. In July, Chairman Waxman and Chairman John Dingell (D-MI), of the Energy and Commerce Committee, reached a compromise that allowed the bill to move forward in a form that did not require the consent of the Natural Resources Committee.[21] The House passed the bill in July by a veto-proof vote of 326–102.[22]

The Senate bill (S. 625) was sponsored by a liberal stalwart, Senator Edward Kennedy (D-MA) and a conservative pillar, Senator John Cornyn (R-TX). This team of odd bedfellows gave supporters hope that a bill would pass, but President George W. Bush had promised to veto any bill that won approval. Kennedy's position as chair of the Health, Education, Labor, and Pensions Committee (HELP Committee), which had jurisdiction of the bill in the Senate, helped to push the bill forward. However, several tobacco-state senators strongly opposed the bill, notably Senator Richard M. Burr (R-NC), and the bill became permanently stalled.[23]

Organized groups that opposed the proposed change in regulatory scheme included medium and small tobacco producers, such as Lorillard Tobacco, R. J. Reynolds Tobacco, the Cigar Association of America, and U.S. Smokeless Tobacco. These groups coordinated their efforts to oppose this bill and lobbied on few other issues during this Congress.[24]

Supporters of this bill included a surprising mix. Major tobacco producer Philip-Morris supported the bill because the marketing restrictions would give it a strong advantage over its competitors. The American College of Cardiology supported the bill because of the health ramifications of having tobacco regulated as a drug rather than purely an agricultural product.[25]

To test the predicted behavior described in the model above, I require a spatial representation of the pivotal players, the status quo, the bill, and the lobbying interest groups who seek to influence the outcome of the bill. I can determine the positions of pivotal players using Poole and Rosenthal's DW-NOMINATE scores.[26] These scores provide a one-dimensional measure of each legislator's ideology based on all votes taken over the course of a Congress. A limitation of this test is that I am assuming that the ideological scores for legislators over the course of a Congress is equivalent to legislators' preferences on tobacco legislation. In addition, it is impossible to pinpoint the location of the bill, status quo, and interest groups on the same scale as the NOMINATE scores. I use journalistic accounts of the lobbying and legislative procedure on this bill to help me infer the locations of these features of the model. Figure 11.5 depicts the spatial setup of this bill.

Here, with the benefit of hindsight I infer that the bill is in the gridlock region between the filibuster pivot and the veto pivot in the Senate. We know that the bill was ultimately filibustered, or at least blocked by the efforts of Senator Burr. Democrats had been trying to pass a bill of this type since 1995 and had been thwarted by Republicans in each attempt during previous Congresses. This is strong evidence to suggest that the bill was in gridlock. We also know that the smaller tobacco producers opposed the bill, while hundreds of health organizations supported it.[27] Given this setup, we should expect that the opposing interest groups, or smaller tobacco producers, should understand that the bill was in gridlock and lobby both the veto and filibuster pivots in order to preserve the gridlock on the bill, thereby killing the legislation (as represented in the upper-right corner of Table 11.1). Meanwhile, we should observe the supporting interest groups, such as the health organizations, targeting the far pivot or, in this case, the veto pivot in an attempt to break gridlock (upper-left cell of Table 11.1).

Figure 11.5   Tobacco Regulation in the 110th Senate

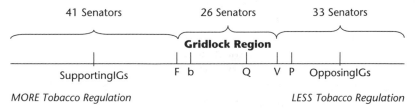

It is difficult to observe the actual lobbying behavior of interest groups, especially the exact targets of their campaigns. To overcome this challenge, I analyze the contribution behavior of the political action committees (PACs) associated with the major groups that lobbied on these bills. Using publicly available data from the Federal Election Commission and compiled by the Center for Responsive Politics, I can identify the targets of groups' PAC donations.[28] A PAC is an organization designed solely to raise money to contribute to candidates. This is a limited test because PAC contributions are not the same as lobbying. I expect the interests of a group's PAC to be broader and more diverse than the associated interest group's position on a single piece of legislation. In this way, using PAC contribution behavior should provide a *conservative* test of these propositions.

Another limitation of these data is that evidence exists that suggests campaign donations do not buy votes.[29] Rather, campaign donations are thought to buy access and serve as a legislative subsidy.[30] It might therefore be questionable to use campaign donations as evidence of groups targeting particular legislators for the purpose of persuading them to change their policy preferences on a particular bill. While I agree with the shortcomings of this method, I argue that given the absence of measures of interest group's lobbying targets for the purpose of persuasion, campaign contribution behavior provides a telling window that may reveal groups' favored legislators. While campaign contributions cannot be a perfect substitute for lobbying targets, to the extent to which PAC contributions provide a signal of legislators with whom groups would like to maintain avenues of contact, relationships, and access, these data can help reveal groups' lobbying targets without establishing a causal link between donations and legislators' votes.[31]

Also, because I do not expect groups to attempt to identify and target a single pivotal player, I examine the data for pivotal ranges of players. First, I arrange senators on a left-right scale according to their NOMINATE scores. To identify players in the veto pivot range, for example, I identify the thirty-third senator from the right (in this case it is Senator Mel Martinez [R-FL]) and include the senators whose NOMINATE scores fall within one standard deviation of the single pivotal player I identified. For the 110th Senate, the range of NOMINATE scores for 102 senators is −1.093 on the left (Senator Russ Feingold [D-WI]) to 0.89 on the right (Senator Tom Coburn [R-OK]).[32] The standard deviation of senators' NOMINATE scores is 0.476. The range of veto pivot players, in this case then, extends from Senator Jim DeMint (R-SC, score = 0.75) to Senator Ben Nelson (D-NE, score = −0.068).

In Table 11.2 I summarize the mean contributions of four organizations opposed to the tobacco bill and two organizations in favor of it. The opponents include Lorillard Tobacco, R. J. Reynolds Tobacco, Cigar Association of America, and U.S. Smokeless Tobacco. The proponents include Altria,

Table 11.2

| | Pro Regulation of Tobacco Groups | | | | Anti Regulation of Tobacco Groups | | | |
| | Contribution | | | | Contribution | | | |
	Mean	N	T	$\Pr(T)<0$	Mean	N	T	$\Pr(T)<0$
Donations *within* veto pivot range	$2,657 (567)	51	−1.95	0.027	$3,441 (918)	51	−2.97	0.0018
Donations *outside* veto pivot range	$1,353 (357)	51			$569 (300)	51		
			T	$\Pr(T)\sim=0$			T	$\Pr(T)>0$
Donations *within* filibuster pivot range	$1,509 (362)	54	1.56	0.122	$611 (291)	54	3.06	0.0014
Donations *outside* filibuster pivot range	$2,563 (590)	48			$3,573 (971)	48		

Standard errors in parentheses.

Here the expectation is that pro-regulation groups will target the veto pivot but not the filibuster pivot, while antiregulation groups will target both the veto and filibuster pivots. The results show evidence for the former, while the antiregulation groups target the veto pivot but not the filibuster pivot.

which is the parent company of Philip-Morris, and the American College of Cardiology.[33]

The results provided in Table 11.2 generally correspond to my expectations, despite the limitations of this analytic approach. I expected that supporters of the bill, including Philip-Morris and the health organizations, would anticipate the gridlock problem and target the veto pivot in an attempt to break gridlock by changing the preferences of the veto pivot players. The contribution data show that the PACs of the pro-regulatory groups gave significantly more donations to senators in the veto pivot range than senators outside of the veto pivot range ($2,657 versus $1,353, respectively). The difference is statistically significant using a Student's T distribution difference of means one-tailed test. Moreover, the pro-regulation interests did *not* significantly target senators around the filibuster pivot over those outside the filibuster pivot range ($1,509 versus $2,563, respectively). Senators around the veto pivot appear to have been the primary target of the groups who supported the legislation. This behavior is particularly telling since it suggests that groups with a liberal-leaning preference over this bill targeted conservative-leaning senators with their PAC donations. This provides strong support for the most counterintuitive theoretical claim laid out above—that groups will target a pivot far from their ideal point in an attempt to break gridlock.

I also find support for the behavior of the groups that opposed the tobacco regulation. Here, I expected groups to target both the veto and filibuster pivots in order to try to maintain the existing legislative gridlock. The results show that these groups targeted senators in the veto pivot range but not in the filibuster pivot range. Table 11.2 shows that antiregulation interest groups gave significantly more campaign donations to senators within the veto pivot range ($3,441 versus $569, respectively). However, the antiregulation groups also gave significantly to groups *not* in the filibuster pivot range ($611 to senators in the filibuster pivot range versus $3,573 to senators outside the filibuster pivot range). This finding goes against my expectation. According to the spatial model, these groups should seek to maintain gridlock by targeting both the filibuster and veto pivots to stay the course and ultimately kill the bill. However, these conservative groups concentrated their campaign donations on senators on the right side of the spectrum.

Overall, I find strong, but not unequivocal, support for the spatial model of lobbying in this single gridlock case. I make reasonable estimations of the spatial representation of the case of tobacco regulation in the 110th Senate and find that liberal groups that sought to break gridlock indeed targeted the far pivot. I also find the conservative groups that sought to maintain gridlock targeted one, but not both, of the pivots that made up the bounds of the gridlock region. Next, I examine a test case of the lower two cells of Table 11.1—a case without gridlock.

Abortion Case—No Gridlock

To test the behavior of groups lobbying when gridlock does not exist, I look at Republicans' attempt to tighten rules relating to abortion in the 109th Congress (2005–06). The political context of the 109th Congress was quite a bit different from that of the 110th. In the 109th Republicans held majorities in both chambers of Congress and had control of the White House. President Bush had just won his second term as president, and Republicans generally felt buoyant about the possibility of making good progress on passing a conservative agenda. During the 109th both the House and Senate passed different versions of a bill known as the Child Interstate Abortion Notification Act, which would have criminalized the act of an adult helping to transport a minor across state lines to seek an abortion in avoidance of parental notification laws in the minor's home state. The bill enjoyed widespread support from conservatives. Republicans held a majority of seats in both the House and Senate in the 109th

Congress, and then-president George W. Bush favored the proposal. Pro-life organizations supported the bill, and pro-choice organizations opposed it.

Ultimately, this bill failed to make it to President Bush's desk, despite the fact that both chambers passed some version of the bill. The House approved a broad version of the bill (H.R. 748) in April of 2005. More than a year later, the Senate passed a version of this bill (S. 403), but Democrats thwarted efforts to form a conference to settle the differences between the chambers. Republicans in the House then decided to take up S. 403, but the House added a last-minute amendment to penalize doctors who perform abortions on out-of-state minors who live in states with parental notification laws. The House passed this bill, but the Senate was unable to muster the sixty votes for cloture on the amended bill.[34] Evidence suggests that conservatives were confident the bill would pass: "Social conservatives appeared poised during the summer to score another win in a campaign to incrementally restrict abortions. In late July a filibuster-proof majority of 65 senators voted to pass a parental consent bill (S. 403), introduced by Nevada Republican John Ensign."[35] A lobbyist for the National Right-to-Life Committee, the premier antiabortion organization, was quoted as being "cautiously optimistic"[36] and believing that "the measure probably will pass."[37] This optimism was likely based on the Republican majority in the Senate and the fact that the Senate leadership had made passage of this bill a high priority. These descriptive accounts suggests that lobbyists at least believed gridlock did not exist.[38]

Assuming that the bill was *not* in gridlock—or at least that the key players did not believe the bill to be in gridlock—I use the same procedure as outlined above to test the propositions about groups lobbying on bills out of gridlock outlined in Table 11.1. In this case, I expect the pro-life organizations to support the bill and target the chamber median in an attempt to move the final bill as close to the group's ideal point as possible (the lower-left cell of Table 11.1). In addition, I expect pro-choice groups to seek to create gridlock by targeting the near pivot, or in this case the filibuster pivot (the lower-right cell of Table 11.1). To assess the behavior of interest groups on the left, I collect the PAC contribution behavior of Planned Parenthood, National Abortion Rights Action League (NARAL), and People for the American Way. On the right, I collect the PAC contributions and individual lobbying donations of the PAC and lobbyists associated with the National Right-to-Life Committee. Each of these groups filed disclosure reports that indicate they lobbied on this bill.[39] Figure 11.6 lays out the spatial setup of this case.

Figure 11.6 shows the status quo (Q) to be outside the gridlock region. This is the scenario that provided conservative groups with their "cautious" confidence that the bill would like pass and that policy would probably move to the right.[40]

Figure 11.6   Abortion Regulation in the 109th Senate

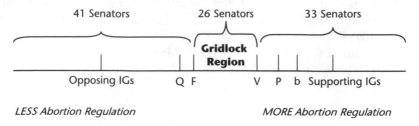

Table 11.3

	Pro-choice Groups				Pro-life Groups			
	Contribution				Contribution			
	Mean	N	T	Pr(T)<0	Mean	N	T	Pr(T)<0
Donations *within* median voter range	$345 (239)	58	1.36	0.177	$16,773 (7901)	58	−1.75	0.042
Donations *outside* median voter range	$1,041 (501)	43			$707 (707)	43		
			T	Pr(T)~=0			T	Pr(T)>0
Donations *within* filibuster pivot range	$1,245 (482)	52	−2.51	0.007	$5,249 (5249)	52	1.05	0.297
Donations *outside* filibuster pivot range	$0 0	49			$14,903 (7667)	49		

Standard errors in parentheses.

Here, the expectation is that pro-choice groups will target the filibuster pivot (which they do) and that pro-life groups will target the median voter (which they do).

Table 11.3 summarizes the contribution behavior of the pro-life and pro-choice PACs and lobbyists. I find evidence to support the spatial account of this case and the theoretical expectations noted above. Pro-life organizations are expected to target the Senate median voter. Indeed, the National Right-to-Life Committee gave significantly more to senators around the median than to those on the ends ($16,773 versus $707, respectively). Likewise, there is no evidence that this organization was concerned about the filibuster or targeted those in the filibuster range during its campaign. The National Right-to-Life Committee gave an amount to senators in the filibuster pivot range ($5,249) that is considerably less than monies given to those outside of it ($14,903), but the difference is *not* statistically significant. This evidence suggests that this organization perceived a lack of legislative gridlock and sought to take advantage of that scenario in its favorable disposition for the bill.

Likewise, pro-choice organizations should seek to create gridlock by targeting the near pivot, or in this case the filibuster pivot. Evidence suggests they did this. Pro-choice groups in fact, *only* gave money to senators in the filibuster range ($1,245 versus $0). Also, it appears that these groups were not targeting the median voter. Pro-choice groups gave a statistically similar amount of money to senators within the median voter range ($345) as to those outside of it ($1,041).

The campaign contribution behavior by interest groups that lobbied for and against the so-called "transporting minors" bill demonstrates the utility of the spatial model of interest group lobbying. Pro-life and pro-choice groups exerted interest group "influence" in the manner predicted by the theoretical model laid out above: pro-life groups sought to influence the median voter because they believed the bill they favored was likely to pass, while pro-choice groups sought to create gridlock where none seemed to exist by targeting the near (in this case, filibuster) pivot.

Conclusion

There is no shortage of evidence that interest groups are strategic actors in the legislative policy-making game. Groups have preferences for particular outcomes and possess limited resources to spend in affecting those outcomes. The challenge for scholars is to be precise about *how* interest groups exert their lobbying influence. Under what conditions do interest groups act? How do they decide which type of action to take? The legislative spatial model provides a foundation from which to understand interest group activity, because legislation is the primary target of lobbying activity. While interest groups are not decision makers in the legislative game, and "persuasion lobbying" is not the only activity in which groups engage, they are interested actors who attempt to influence policy outcomes in predictable ways.

The spatial model outlined above shows that two features of the legislative environment explain the lobbying behavior of interested groups: the spatial context of a particular bill and groups' preferences over proposed legislation. The presence or absence of legislative gridlock (which occurs when the status quo lies between pivotal players' ideal points) is a key feature of the model. When gridlock exists, interest groups that favor a bill seek to break gridlock by attempting to change the policy preferences of the pivotal player farthest from the group's ideal point. If a group can change enough legislators' minds to move the far pivot to the opposite side of the status quo, gridlock will be broken, and the group may see a preferred bill passed. When a group opposes legislation that is in gridlock, the group seeks to maintain gridlock and does so by targeting both pivots to encourage them to stay where they are. If gridlock can be maintained on a bill that a group opposes, the bill will die, and the group will have achieved its preferred outcome.

When legislative gridlock does *not* exist, a group that favors a bill will target the legislative median voter. The group is in an advantageous position under this scenario because it supports a bill that is likely to pass. At this point, the group can only add icing to its proverbial cake by moving the bill even closer to its ideal point. If a group opposes a bill out of gridlock, the group will try to create gridlock by targeting the pivot closest to its ideal point and attempting to move it to the other side of the status quo.

The relative positions of groups to the status quo, and the status quo to pivotal players in the legislative game, help us to glean insights into the lobbying behavior of organized interests. I examined a case of legislative gridlock in the 110th Congress where a tobacco regulation bill was ultimately filibustered (or at least killed in the Senate due to inaction). The groups that supported the bill behaved as anticipated and targeted the veto pivot, but not the filibuster pivot, in an attempt to break gridlock. The groups that opposed the bill behaved partially as expected and targeted one, but not both, of the pivotal players in an attempt to maintain gridlock. In the abortion case in the 109th Congress, I analyzed a case without legislative gridlock and found that groups that supported an abortion-restrictions bill targeted the median voter, as expected, in an attempt to help move a bill that was expected to pass even closer to the group. I also found that groups that opposed the bill targeted the near pivot (filibuster pivot) in an attempt to create gridlock where none existed.

The cases of tobacco regulation in the 110th and abortion restrictions in the 109th Congresses are not particularly special cases. There is no reason to believe that the findings that support the spatial model of lobbying in these cases would not generalize to other Congresses and other bills. I selected these cases because of the ease of developing measures from these high-profile cases. The empirical approach used here has limitations, and it provides a limited test of the theoretical model. It is problematic to identify the exact locations of key players and items in the spatial model, to identify the population of groups that lobby for and against bills, and to identify the targets of lobbying that is aimed at persuasion. However, the drawbacks of the analytical approach generally should make it *less* likely to find support for my claims and should result in a conservative test of the propositions.

Notes

1. The Center for Responsive Politics, "Lobbying Database," *Opensecrets.org*, April–June 2009, http://www.opensecrets.org/lobby/index.php.

2. On elections, see Anthony Downs, *An Economic Theory of Democracy* (New York: Harper, 1957); David R. Mayhew, *Congress: The Electoral Connection* (New Haven, CT: Yale University Press, 1974); Richard F. Fenno, *Home Style: House Members in Their Districts* (Boston: Little-Brown, 1978). On committee decision making, see Duncan Black, *The Theory of Committees and Elections* (Cambridge, UK: Cambridge University Press, 1958); Richard F. Fenno, *Congressmen in Committees* (Boston: Little-Brown, 1973); Keith Krehbiel, *Information and Legislative Organization* (Ann Arbor: University of Michigan Press, 1991). On legislators' ideological preferences, see Keith T. Poole and Howard Rosenthal, *Congress: A Political-Economic History of Roll Call Voting* (Oxford, UK: Oxford University Press, 1997); Keith T. Poole and Howard Rosenthal, *Ideology and Congress* (New Brunswick, NJ: Transaction, 2007). On congressional parties, see John Herbert Aldrich, *Why Parties? The Origin and Transformation of Party Politics in America* (Chicago: University of Chicago Press, 1995); David W. Rohde, *Parties and Leaders in the Postreform House* (Chicago: University of Chicago Press, 1991); Gary Cox and Mathew D. McCubbins, *Legislative Leviathan: Party Government in the House*, California Series on Social Choice and Political Economy No. 23 (Berkeley: University of California Press, 1993).

3. David W. Brady and Craig Volden, *Revolving Gridlock: Politics and Policy from Jimmy Carter to George W. Bush*, 2nd ed. (Boulder, CO: Westview Press, 2006).

4. Keith Krehbiel, *Pivotal Politics: A Theory of U.S. Lawmaking* (Chicago: University of Chicago Press, 1998).

5. In the parlance of formal theory, we would say that legislators' utility functions are symmetrical and single peaked.

6. See Black, *The Theory of Committees and Elections*. Also, for a detailed and accessible description of one- and two-dimensional spatial models of legislative voting, see Krehbiel, *Pivotal Politics;* Charles Haines Stewart III, *Analyzing Congress* (New York: Norton, 2001).

7. An equilibrium is the stable outcome that occurs when each player plays the strategy that maximizes her outcome, given that she believes all other players are also playing the strategies that maximize their outcomes. In equilibrium, no individual player can benefit by unilaterally changing her strategy, given that other players' strategies are unchanged.

8. Brady and Volden, *Revolving Gridlock*, 16.

9. One can prove this by drawing a winset for P. A winset is the set of policies a player prefers to the status quo. P's winset is therefore any policy between P and Q and policies to the left of P that extend a distance equivalent to the distance P–Q. The policy M is clearly outside this winset because it lies on the opposite side of Q from P.

10. If the Motion had been outside of the president's winset but within the veto pivot's winset, then the bill would be vetoed and that veto overridden.

11. Lester W. Milbrath, *The Washington Lobbyist* (Chicago: Rand McNally, 1963); John W. Kingdon, *Congressmen's Voting Decisions*, 3rd ed. (Ann Arbor: University of Michigan Press, 1989); Richard L. Hall and Frank W. Wayman, "Buying Time: Moneyed Interests and the Mobilization of Bias in Congressional Committees," *American Political Science Review* 84, no. 3 (1990): 797–820; John Mark Hansen, *Gaining Access: Congress*

and the Farm Lobby, 1919–1981 (Chicago: University of Chicago Press, 1991); Gregory A. Caldeira and John R. Wright, "Lobbying for Justice: Organized Interests, Supreme Court Nominations, and the United States Senate," *American Journal of Political Science* 42, no. 2 (1998): 499–523.

12. John R Wright, *Interest Groups and Congress: Lobbying, Contributions, and Influence* (Boston: Allyn & Bacon, 1996): 2.

13. Of course, interest groups engage in many activities that are not aimed at affecting policy outcomes. Much of what some groups do has nothing to do with lobbying for or against proposed legislation. Groups expend considerable resources trying to get specific policies proposed in Congress—or trying to keep policies from being proposed. Such lobbying efforts are outside the scope of this model. The model is intended to explain interest group *reactions* to proposed bills, not their *proactive* attempts to affect legislation.

14. Notice that changing the preferences of a single senator makes no difference even if that senator happens to be the pivot. To effectively change the location of the pivot and move it to the other side of the status quo, enough senators would have to change their policy preferences to shift the location of the veto pivot. The status quo does not move, but senators can. To change the location of a pivot, it is likely that many senators' preferences would have to change.

15. David Austen-Smith and John R.Wright, "Counteractive Lobbying," *American Journal of Political Science* 38, no. 1 (1994): 25–44; Frank R. Baumgartner and Beth L. Leech, "The Multiple Ambiguities of Counteractive Lobbying," *American Journal of Political Science* 40, no. 2 (1996): 521–42; David Austen-Smith and John R. Wright, "Theory and Evidence for Counteractive Lobbying," *American Journal of Political Science* 40, no. 2 (1996): 543–64.

16. It is theoretically possible, although realistically unlikely, for a policy to be proposed outside the gridlock region. In such a case, the interest group would support the proposal, but the bill would be likely to fail because of its location outside the gridlock region. Such a bill would likely be killed or amended to something inside the gridlock region. The group would lobby for an amended bill that falls inside its winset.

17. Again, it is theoretically possible, although realistically unlikely, for a policy to be proposed outside the gridlock region. In such a case, the interest group would oppose a bill that would be either likely to fail or likely to be amended to something within the gridlock region. The group would then lobby for an amended bill that falls within its winset. However, when gridlock does not exist, policy proposals are more likely to be within the gridlock region, as described in the lower-right cell of Table 11.1.

18. In his book, Keith Krehbiel argues that decision makers' utilities are based on their preferences over outcomes (basic preferences) but that they make decisions over policies. It is preferences over policies that are potentially moveable (derived preferences). See Krehbiel, *Information and Legislative Organization*, 66–77.

19. A. Lee Fritschler and James M. Hoefler, *Smoking and Politics: Policy Making and the Federal Bureaucracy* (Englewood Cliffs, NJ: Prentice Hall, 1996).

20. Drew Armstrong, "2008 Legislative Summary: Tobacco Regulations," *CQ Weekly*, December 2008, 3284.

21. Armstrong, "2008 Legislative Summary: Tobacco Regulations."

22. Drew Armstrong, "Tobacco Regulation Bill Passes House," *CQ Weekly*, August 2008, 2132.

23. Armstrong, "2008 Legislative Summary: Tobacco Regulations.."
24. The Center for Responsive Politics, "Lobbying Database.."
25. The Center for Responsive Politics, "Lobbying Database.."
26. Poole and Rosenthal, *Congress: A Political-Economic History of Roll Call Voting.*
27. Shawn Zeller, "Public Health Doctors Take on Tobacco Control Bill," *CQ Weekly*, July 2008, 1952.
28. The Center for Responsive Politics, "Lobbying Database."
29. Richard L. Hall and Alan V. Deardorff, "Lobbying as Legislative Subsidy," *American Political Science Review* 100, no. 1 (2006): 69–84; Gregory Wawro, "A Panel Probit Analysis of Campaign Contributions and Roll-Call Votes," *American Journal of Political Science* 45, no. 3 (2001): 563–79; Gregory Wawro, *Legislative Entrepreneurship in the U.S. House of Representatives* (Ann Arbor: University of Michigan Press, 2000). Also see James B. Kau and Paul H. Rubin, *Congressmen, Constituents, and Contributors: Determinants of Roll Call Voting in the House of Representatives* (Boston: Martinus Nijhoff, 1992); Sam Peltzman, "Constituent Interest and Congressional Voting," *Journal of Law and Economics* 27, no. 1 (1984): 181–210; Lawrence S. Rothenberg, *Linking Citizens to Government: Interest Group Politics at Common Cause* (New York: Cambridge University Press, 1992); John R. Wright, "PACs, Contributions, and Roll Calls: An Organizational Perspective," *American Political Science Review* 79, no. 2 (1985): 400–14; John R. Wright, "Contributions, Lobbying, and Committee Voting in the U.S. House of Representatives," *American Political Science Review* 84, no. 2 (1990): 417–38; Wright, *Interest Groups and Congress;* Janet M. Grenzke, "PACs and the Congressional Supermarket: The Currency Is Complex," *American Journal of Political Science* 33, no. 1 (1989): 1–24.
30. Regarding campaign donations as access, see Hall and Wayman, "Buying Time," 797–820; Hansen, *Gaining Access.* Regarding campaign donations as legislative subsidy, see Hall and Deardorff, "Lobbying as Legislative Subsidy," 69–84; Richard L. Hall and Kristina C. Miler, "What Happens After the Alarm? Interest Group Subsidies to Legislative Overseers," *Journal of Politics* 70 (2008): 990–1005.
31. Jennifer Victor and Gregory Kroger, "The Beltway Network: A Network Analysis of Lobbyists' Decisions to Donate to Members of Congress" (paper presented at the annual meeting of the Midwest Political Science Association, Chicago, April 2–5, 2009).
32. There are 102 senators because of two departures in 2007—the resignation of Senator Trent Lott (R-MS) and the death of Senator Craig Thomas (R-WY).
33. Altria acquired U.S. Smokeless Tobacco in 2009.
34. Keith Perine, "2006 Legislative Summary: Transporting Minors," *CQ Weekly*, December 2006: 3336
35. Perine, "2006 Legislative Summary: Transporting Minors."
36. Sheryl Gay Stolberg, "House Passes Bill Tightening Parental Rule for Abortions," *New York Times*, April 28, 2005, http://www.nytimes.com/2005/04/28/politics/28abort.html.
37. Amy Fagan, "House Approves Abortion Limits," *Washington Times*, April 28, 2005.
38. Even if gridlock did exist, lobbyists' beliefs about the spatial context of a bill are more important than the latent true state of the world since these beliefs will inform lobbying strategies.
39. The Center for Responsive Politics, "Lobbying Database."
40. This model also explains why the bill ultimately failed, as the bill (*b*) is clearly outside of the winset of the filibuster pivot.

12

Not Just Another Special Interest
The Intergovernmental Lobby Revisited[1]
Beverly A. Cigler

Governments that lobby other governments are often overlooked in the study of interest groups. However, states and local governments lobby a great deal in the American political system. The best-known organizations are membership-based organizations that represent generalists in state and local government—governors, mayors, county commissioners and executives, legislators, and other state and local elected officials. Traditionally called the "Big Seven," the intergovernmental groups include associations representing generalist officials and their jurisdictions: the National Governors Association (NGA), National Conference of State Legislatures (NCSL), National League of Cities (NLC), U.S. Conference of Mayors (USCM), and the National Association of Counties (NACo). Collectively known as SLIGs—state and local interest groups—they are supplemented by the International City/County Management Association (ICMA), which represents nonelected officials such as city and county managers but does not lobby. The Council of State Governments (CSG) also does not lobby and is unique among these organizations in representing officials from all three branches of government—the executive, legislative, and judicial. The other five organizations lobby and are sometimes helped by the nonlobbying of ICMA and CSG in weakening any perceptions that the generalist officials are "just another special interest." Most academic research on state and local government representation focuses narrowly on the Big Seven. Table 12.1 provides essential information about these organizations.

The intergovernmental lobby is an "interest group sector" or set of organized groups that share broadly similar policy concerns, much as labor, business, or ideologically oriented groups form interest group sectors. The intergovernmental associations often label themselves as public interest groups (PIGs) because they pursue benefits not limited to their members. On the other hand, others, including some national government officials, sometimes use the acronym *PIGs* in a pejorative way to argue that the intergovernmental groups operate in a closed, cozy subsystem or as part of an "iron triangle" in which they work with congressional committees and subcommittees and executive branch agencies to develop policies of mutual

Table 12.1   The "Big Seven" Intergovernmental Associations

Association	Founded	Membership	URL
National Governors Association (NGA)	1908	Incumbent governors	www.nga.org
Council of State Governments (CSG)	1933	Direct membership by states and territories; serves all branches of government; has dozens of affiliate organizations of specialists	www.csg.org
National Conference of State Legislatures (NCSL)	1948	State legislators and staff	www.ncsl.org
National League of Cities (NLC)	1924	Direct membership by cities and state leagues of cities	www.nlc.org
National Association of Counties (NACo)	1935	Direct membership by counties; loosely linked state associations; affiliate membership for county professional specialists	www.naco.org
United States Conference of Mayors (USCM)	1933	Direct membership by cities with populations over 30,000	www.usmayors.org
International City/ County Management Association (ICMA)	1914	Direct membership by appointed city and county managers and other professionals	www.icma.org

benefit.[2] Local governments also have lobby organizations at the state level; for example, the NLC has affiliate organizations in the states called municipal leagues. Counties have state-based county associations, though not affiliates of NACo. Both types of organizations lobby their state legislatures. ICMA also has affiliate organizations in the states, which, like ICMA, do not lobby.

The intergovernmental lobby at both the national and state levels does much more than lobby. Its constituent groups monitor and report on governmental actions in the legislative and executive branches, develop and analyze policies, communicate with policy makers, and mobilize political support. Robert Salisbury would describe them as "service organizations" engaged in "interest representation."[3] ICMA, its affiliates in the states, and the CSG are information generators, collectors, and disseminators; morale boosters for public service; providers of member services; and facilitators of collaborative linkages among governments and other organizations.

Are state and local governments and officials special interests? They are not united in terms of goals or ideology, and they compete with each other and other organized interests for programs and money. They employ lobbying tactics that mirror those of other organized interests, and their actions affect the other groups. The agenda of urban intergovernmental groups often dovetails with the positions set forth by members of the traditional Democratic coalition. All this creates the image of special interest, and the intergovernmental groups often complain that they are treated as "just another special interest," wishing instead to be seen as "intergovernmental partners" with the national government.[4] Public officials join the organizations not only to advance policy positions but also to promote core political-system values: responsiveness, representativeness, accountability, equity, efficiency, and effectiveness. Their organizations work toward improved intergovernmental partnerships, such as the provision of a sound, balanced, and coordinated national transportation system or manageable environmental and natural resources policies.

The generalist officials' associations pioneered the bipartisan advocacy and reformist ideas essential for collaborative national-state-local activities that contribute to national objectives. On the other hand, those same officials must face the voters and media in their respective jurisdictions. Thus, they seek political flexibility to manage the intergovernmental system for the benefit of their constituents. Much of the work of making and implementing public policy is intergovernmental. The state and local officials elected to do the business of government enhance their work through their participation in associations of generalists in state and local government. Although such associations strive to effect policy change, they are strongly oriented toward providing membership services and professionalizing government. Thus they are neither purely special-interest organizations nor purely public-interest organizations.

Empirical Research on State and Local Interest Representation

Although there is a substantial literature on interest groups and lobbying, the empirical research or theory development focused on governments lobbying governments is sparse. Allan Cigler and Burdett Loomis highlighted the importance of intergovernmental lobbying decades ago.[5] Mancur Olson's collective action work provided an early explanation for why subnational governments participate in membership organizations like the NGA, NCSL, and NLC, organizations that offer attractive collective benefits, such as a unified voice speaking on intergovernmental issues, that are denied to nonmembers.[6] These intergovernmental organizations also offer a mix of selective benefits to their members, such as publications and research. Olson's work also helped explain why the mix of collective and selective benefits offered to members may not be sufficient. What each individual member wants most for itself, such as funding or special treatment on a mandate, are selective benefits that these organizations cannot readily provide. As a result, states and cities sometimes create their own, single-representation Washington, D.C., offices. Olson helped us understand that subnational governments may seek both collective and selective benefits, sometimes from different sources.

This chapter (1) presents a typology that outlines the broad array of types of state and local interest representation within the American political system; (2) focuses on the emergence and development of Washington-based state and local government interest representation (i.e., the Big Seven); (3) examines group and sector resources; (4) highlights tactics used to achieve policy and service goals; and (5) summarizes trends affecting the sector.

Emergence and Development of State and Local Interest Representation

The state and local interest representation sector is not limited to the handful of organized groups of state and local generalists. Table 12.2 revises a typology originally developed by Beverly Cigler in 1995. Seven types of interest representation that comprise the intergovernmental sector are depicted on the table and discussed here: the Big Seven, new and resurgent generalist organizations, single jurisdictional representation, state and local interest representation in the international arena, specialist associations, public interest organizations, and the intergovernmental information infrastructure.[7]

The Big Seven: Products of the Times

The growth of government and the proliferation of intergovernmental groups are linked. Organized groups of government generalists are a twentieth-century phenomenon. New organizations formed with increasing

Table 12.2

Types of State and Local Interest Representation
The Big Seven and state level associations
New and resurgent generalist associations
Single jurisdictional representation
State and local interest representation in the international arena
Specialist associations
Public interest organizations
The intergovernmental information infrastructure

frequency during the New Deal era in the 1930s and again in the 1960s and early 1970s as programs requiring cooperation among the national, state, and local governments were created to combat an array of public problems. The NGA formed in 1908, the NCSL was founded in 1948 for state legislators and staff, the NLC in 1924, and the NACo in 1935.

Beginning with the New Deal, state and local governments grew in their responsibilities, personnel, and budgets, sparking a demand for Washington, D.C., representation. A special window of opportunity for growth occurred after the mid-1960s when new federal programs established direct links with cities. Urban programs grew rapidly in number and costs, fueled by growing national affluence, heightened concern with social issues, and a Democratic president with an ambitious domestic agenda. By the 1970s, the Washington presence of associations of state and local officials was well established.

U.S. Conference of Mayors and Relationships with Other Big Seven Organizations.   Richard Flanagan argued that the USCM, founded in 1933 to give big-city mayors an effective organizational base for lobbying Congress and for coordinating with executive branch agencies, was a major force during the New Deal and has been largely overlooked by theorists of federalism and intergovernmental relations.[8] His account of the New Deal revealed both cooperation and conflict, with cities turning to Washington for help with myriad policy needs after being rebuffed by the states. In turn, the national government often bypassed states to deal directly with cities because states so often resisted New Deal initiatives. Even in the twenty-first century, the three local government generalist organizations within the Big Seven are sometimes called the "urban lobby."

Flanagan explained that the USCM lobbying built support for stronger urban programs and national-city linkages during the New Deal. In effect, the USCM served as an informal extension of the national bureaucracy that offered program information to local jurisdictions and feedback about implementation and policy impact to the national bureaucracies that dealt with urban issues. President Franklin D. Roosevelt had close ties to the USCM, which established a pattern of politics in national urban policy that Flanagan claimed persisted until the early 1980s.[9]

This depiction of intergovernmental lobbying does not dovetail with other assessments. Samuel Beer argued that the intergovernmental lobby was a response to the Great Society, which greatly expanded the national grant-in-aid system and led to the rise of specialists—civil servants—who attempted to undercut the power of generalist elected officials.[10] Beer saw government lobbying of the federal government in the 1960s as a major change in the system of national representation. It is accurate that the mayors, governors, and county executives were a 1960s phenomenon, but the

USCM was active and influential in the 1930s, 1940s, and 1950s as well. Therefore, the expansion of the intergovernmental lobby was not as radical a departure from the past as Beer suggested. Rather, it reflected this lobby's growth and extension.

Flanagan's historical analysis challenged the notion that significant intergovernmental lobbying was a response to the programs of the Great Society, when an infusion of national funds began to flow to subnational governments.[11] More accurate may be the conclusion that the intergovernmental lobby arose simultaneously with, and helped create, the development of New Deal urban programs—in municipal financing, public housing, and work relief. The USCM in the 1930s had resources such as votes, financing, and information, but it also possessed stature in Washington politics because of its access to the Roosevelt administration. While the USCM helped cities and the administration, Roosevelt used it as a tool to support his programs for cities and worked with New York mayor Fiorello LaGuardia, who was president of the USCM from 1935 to 1945.

Several scholars have provided valuable descriptions of the intergovernmental lobby in the 1960s and performed case study research that focused on specific legislation or programs. Suzanne Farkas examined the urban lobby and the emergence of an urban issues network in national policy making in the 1960s.[12] Donald Haider examined the intergovernmental lobby from the New Deal to the early 1970s and sorted out three phases.[13] The first period, from the New Deal to 1964, was characterized by the presence of big-city mayors who wanted to bypass the states and deal directly with the national government. At the time, governors were not interested in a national presence in state affairs. This account dovetails with Flanagan's depiction of the USCM. Haider's second period extended from 1964 to 1968 and coincided with President Lyndon Johnson's administration and the growth of national programs. Governors were actively involved in competing for national initiatives and funding, as were mayors and other local government officials. The third phase came with President Richard Nixon's New Federalism initiatives, highlighted by general revenue sharing.

Anne Marie Cammisa described this last phase as one in which state and local governments received more money with fewer strings attached.[14] Cammisa's research consisted of interviews and case study analysis of three major pieces of legislation and the roles of the NGA, NCSL, NLC, USCM, and NACo. She added a fourth phase to Haider's work, from President Jimmy Carter's later years in office to 1995. She argues that President Carter's anti-Washington candidacy was linked to the eventual decline in national funding for states and cities at the end of his presidency, a trend that continued with President Ronald Reagan's policies.

The strong relationship among the principal intergovernmental lobby organizations continued throughout the 1960s and 1970s and included substantial funds from national government contracts.[15] Because cities came to be associated with racial unrest following the urban riots of the late 1960s, however, public attitudes toward redistributive programs changed quickly, as did congressional and media interest. The state and local associations that had grown up with federal urban programs were unable to mount a serious defense of these programs, and the cities and their associations experienced budget problems during the Reagan years. The steady transfer to state and local governments of administrative and fiscal responsibility for what had begun as federal programs provoked discord within the intergovernmental sector. President Reagan reduced the bureaucracy's capacity to deal with urban issues and curtailed the significant federal financial commitments to cities. The USCM's role as an extension of the national government ended, as did its national contracts. Charles Levine and James Thurber reported a 50 percent budget cut for USCM from national government contracts in a five-year period, and staff reductions ensued.[16] Overall, the Reagan administration slashed national funding to cities and states and broke the direct relationship of the federal government with cities. Today, the USCM represents 1,139 cities with populations of 30,000 or more. Cities are represented by their chief elected officials, usually the mayor.

National Governors Association.   Originally called the National Governors Conference, the National Governors Association was formed during Theodore Roosevelt's presidency; it is the oldest and arguably the most prestigious of the Big Seven. The NGA meets twice each year and otherwise operates primarily through standing committees and staff activities. Policy positions require the support of three-quarters of the governors present and voting, so strong initiatives are infrequently adopted. Governors of large states generally do not play active roles in the NGA, but there are exceptions: for example, Governor Ed Rendell of Pennsylvania served as NGA president in recent years. NGA is not only the collective voice of the nation's governors, but it also represents their senior staff members, such as policy advisers, on Capitol Hill and before the administration.

In 1967, the NGA split from the Council of State Governments (CSG) to become a separate organization. It moved to Washington, D.C., to focus on building efforts to boost the states' image in American policy making, to showcase the fifty governors, and to promote national policy debates on critical issues. In 1976, NGA moved to the Hall of the States, a Capitol Hill building that attracted other intergovernmental sector members as tenants.

Council of State Governments.   CSG is an umbrella association that generates information for all three branches of state government but provides assistance primarily to state legislatures, including their many service agencies such as legislative research organizations. CSG also serves as the secretariat for many affiliate organizations of state specialists, such as the National Association of State Personnel Executives and the National Association of State Treasurers. The association is headquartered in Lexington, Kentucky, and has a Washington, D.C., office. As noted previously, the CSG, along with the International City/County Management Association (ICMA), is not a lobbying group; this sets it, and the ICMA, apart from the rest of the Big Seven. In recent years, CSG has sought to be the forecaster of policy trends for states and territories on a national and regional basis.

National Conference of State Legislatures.   The National Council of State Legislatures (NCSL) provides legislative services to all fifty state legislatures and their staffs and to commonwealths such as Puerto Rico. Policy positions are taken by a State/Federal Assembly. The Assembly meets several times a year and consists of members appointed for two-year terms by the presiding officers of each state's two houses. Policy positions require a three-quarters majority vote of the states, not individual members. From its main headquarters in Denver, Colorado, the NCSL staffs the association's committees and conferences. It also provides direct services to member state legislatures and publishes a monthly magazine, *State Legislatures.* Much of the work of its smaller Washington, D.C., office involves monitoring and publishing information about federal legislation and mandates.

In 1976, NCSL and CSG moved their Washington offices into the Hall of the States, joining the NGA. The move helped facilitate working relationships among the associations. By the late 1980s, approximately fifty state-oriented organizations, including specialist affiliates of CSG and various single-state offices, had also relocated to the building.

The three local government generalist organizations within the Big Seven are sometimes called the "urban lobby." The U.S. Conference of Mayors represents the larger cities, the National League of Cities represents medium and small cities, and the National Association of Counties represents rural, suburban, and urban counties.

International County/Management Association.   ICMA, the remaining generalist group, was founded as the International City Managers Association. It represents a large segment of the nation's appointed local chief executives—city and county managers—as well as other local professionals such as department heads and assistant managers. The word *County* was added to the ICMA title in the 1990s, making it the International City/County Management Association. The name reflected the growing influence of counties in the American political system, but a second *C* was not added to the acronym. ICMA was traditionally less active nationally than the other Big Seven groups, tending to focus on technical issues and services. The Center for State and Local Government Excellence was created in 2007 with financial support from ICMA's Retirement Corporation to respond to the challenges facing state and local governments as they seek to attract and nurture the best workforce for the twenty-first century. The Center has conducted numerous major research projects, conducted opinion polling, and launched a campaign to bring attention to workforce challenges in the public sector. Its research, especially studies of pension systems, has been cited in congressional testimony, in professional conferences, and in the national media. The larger ICMA publishes books considered "must" reading by local professionals.

CSG and ICMA contribute to the overall functioning of the intergovernmental sector in very important ways. They link other organizations by providing information and other services. They also help to weaken perceptions that the generalist officials are "just another special interest."

The Big Seven groups often compete with each other for resources, including members, government and foundation funding, and policy access. The proliferation of federal grants in the Great Society period of the 1960s fueled that competition. Conflict occurred at many junctures: disagreements flared between state and local organizations, generalist and specialist officials, urban and rural officials, large and small governmental jurisdictions, and counties and cities.

Cooperation among the Big Seven splintered further during the Reagan years. The *National Journal, Congressional Quarterly,* and political scientists documented these organizations' troubled times during President Reagan's first term, although the groups had squabbled with each other even before the Reagan presidency. The states accused the local associations of supporting the successful elimination of general revenue-sharing funds for states. Federal aid cutbacks and program terminations, such as the elimination of all general revenue sharing and Urban Development Action Grants, were other significant setbacks. The federal government severed direct ties with local governments as federal funds came to be passed through the states.[17] The government groups complained of being treated as "just another special interest." In the Reagan White House, cuts in domestic programs were seen as a way to "defund the Left" and reduce subsidies for selfish "special interest groups." The Big Seven and other sector members felt their sense of having shared goals weaken.[18]

The external political environment posed major resource problems for the operations of the Big Seven in the Reagan years. Between 1980 and 1990, USCM lost 48.7 percent of its federal funding, NACo lost 67.5 percent, and NLC lost 97.9 percent. ICMA, the nonlobby, lost 74.7 percent of its federal funding.[19] Journalist Jonathan Walters reported that, in the early 1980s, NACo's Washington, D.C., staff was reduced from 140 to 60, NLC cut back from about 120 to 65, and USCM was reduced from 120 to 75. The funding losses caused changes in Washington office operations. Staff resources were shifted from traditional service activities toward raising dues and fees, conducting membership drives, initiating business ventures, and hiring fund-raisers. Lobbying operations were relatively insulated from the cutbacks.[20]

Diminished technical service capabilities (for example, tracking state mandates and legislation, computer networking) came to haunt local government organizations in the early 1990s, as program and fiscal responsibilities continued to shift downward in the federal system. Members of some local associations criticized their groups as being ill-equipped to deal with the increased importance of the states and of state-local relations.[21]

The state and local government members of the Big Seven have come together in agreement on a number of significant issues in recent decades. In the mid-1990s, they worked together to pass the Unfunded Mandates Act. They voiced enough agreement to stall the Voter ID Act for many years and finally significantly change it. While not in agreement on specifics, they worked together to play a major role in prompting the national government to act in several key areas, such as health care reform and immigration reform.

State-Level Generalist Associations.   The state-level associations provide a wide array of state services to their members. Because local governments are "creatures of the states," the states and their associations have advantages in dealing with emerging state-local issues. The Great Recession that began in December 2007 and continues at the time of this writing in mid-2011 has strained local funds, and a number of state-level local government associations are losing member jurisdictions that can no longer pay their membership dues. NCSL has become very active in informing state legislatures about state-local issues. State and local generalists (governors, mayors, county commissioners, legislators) continue to be important to congressional policy making.

At the state and local levels, the government lobby groups include municipalities of all types, counties, school districts, regional authorities (including transportation, waste management, water, and recreation), state and regional commissions, and a host of other organizations. All told, the amount of government lobbying in a state by governments is often the single largest category of state-level lobbying. This is the case in California, for example, based on its lobbying-disclosure Web site that allows the categorization of lobbying data by employer (http://cal-access.ss.ca.gov/Lobbying/). Many states exempt government agencies from the same lobby disclosure requirements used for private sector lobbyists, making it difficult to find data. Only six states' lobbying laws contain a definition of a public entity.[22]

Overall, the Big Seven continue to dominate intergovernmental interest representation nationally, and municipal and county associations are key lobby groups in the American states. A generalist perspective adds a spatial or "areal" dimension to the national decision-making process. The importance of this dimension has been demonstrated in the shaping of welfare reform legislation in 1988 and in strides toward Medicaid reform since. The spatial perspective also shows that "cookie-cutter" approaches pose problems, and the associations have been successful in getting the federal government to be more responsive to waiver requests when policies are implemented. Much of the current health care legislative reform debate centers on the role of states versus the national government in designing and implementing policies.

New and Resurgent Generalist Associations

Several new generalist organizations were formed in the 1980s and 1990s as some of the established groups experienced a resurgence. Some of the generalist groups think the Big Seven terminology is outdated and urge that the club be expanded to the "Big Eight" or "Big Nine." The National Association of Towns and Townships (NATaT) is a case in point. This Washington, D.C., voice represents the views of the tens of thousands of small local jurisdictions in the political system. The impetus for its creation was the perception by many small governments that the NLC and other organizations did not represent their interests well. Created in the 1960s, NATaT achieved some favor during the Reagan administration as a relatively conservative group. Since then, strong membership services and ties to township associations within several states have helped NATaT achieve a number of policy successes. NATaT plays an important role in explaining the special financial and managerial problems confronting small and rural governments in the political system.

Another emergent organization is the National Association of Regional Councils (NARC). The geographical organization of metropolitan areas does not necessarily match the nature of policy problems, which often spill over jurisdictional boundaries. Regional organizations, it can be argued, are better equipped to deal with functional policy concerns than are the generalist associations that represent officials from political jurisdictions. NARC previously published a journal and held an annual conference on regionalism. Most recently, it has not been as active as it once was. Both NARC and NATaT have experienced problems with leadership.

The National Civic League, founded in 1894 as part of the "good government" reform movement (then called the National Municipal League), is an example of a resurgent organization. This nonprofit organization promotes the active involvement of citizens in the governance of their communities. Through conferences, networking, and the National Civic Review, the National Civic League is a leading generalist organization. It provides its dues-paying individual members much of the help in focusing on the state and local levels that elected public official generalists are asking of their national associations. The National Civic League focuses primarily on making state and local governments more responsive and effective and plays a major leadership role in shaping public dialogue about the future of the federal system. Its directors and activists are a workable blend of public officials from all levels of government and the public, private, and nonprofit sectors, including academics.

An interesting splinter from the Big Seven has an explicit ideological focus. In 1973 a group of conservative state legislators, arguing that NCSL had a liberal agenda, worked with several conservative foundations to create the American Legislative Exchange Council (ALEC). ALEC's principal founder was Paul Weyrich, a leading "movement conservative" and head of the Free Congress Foundation. Weyrich also cofounded the leading national conservative think tank, the Heritage Foundation, also in 1973. ALEC is currently the largest network of individual state legislators, with more than 2,000 members from among the roughly 7,400 state legislators in the United States. It works as a well-coordinated network on a broad set of issues and writes model laws to promote conservative positions, such as antitax legislation and taxpayer bill of rights (TABOR) laws, and to oppose civil rights laws and consumer, labor, and environmental initiatives. ALEC links state legislators with right-wing thank tanks, many of which are located in state capitals.

Unlike the NCSL and the other intergovernmental lobby organizations within the Big Seven, ALEC seeks corporate members, who pay dues up to $50,000 per year and more to sit on task forces that draft ALEC's legislative initiatives. ALEC is a major success within the conservative movement, but it generally works out of public view. The organization has taken credit for passing hundreds of laws. Its lobbying is both within state legislatures and with the national government. Although ALEC is a conservative interest group that works through an intergovernmental and state lobbying effort, it has most recently looked to the local level for its organizing on policy issues.

As a response to ALEC, the American Legislative Issues Campaign Exchange (ALICE) was created, with its origins in the Center on Wisconsin Strategy, the Economic Analysis and Research Network, and other progressive groups. ALICE is very much a fledgling organization that serves as a clearinghouse of information and legislation for local governments as they lobby state government. Its goal is to support and assist 10,000 progressive local elected officials.

Still another organization, the Progressive Legislative Action Network (PLAN), was created in 2005. Similar to ALEC, PLAN develops model legislation and uses grassroots activists. The emergence of ideological groups to advance causes in state legislatures is a new development and one that may lessen the overall effectiveness of NCSL, which provides nonpartisan advice and research to state legislators. It is not yet known whether the individual-based memberships in these groups achieve more allegiance from legislators than does NCSL.

The ties between ALEC and the Heritage Foundation highlight a trend in state and local interest representation: the emergence of dozens of new think tanks at both the national and state levels. Most of these have explicit ideological concerns and receive funding from like-minded individuals and foundations. Most are conservative.

Single Jurisdictional Representation

Single states, cities, counties, and other governmental units such as special districts that seek Washington, D.C., representation are also important players in the intergovernmental sector. They can open Washington offices; work with trade or professional associations to pursue interests; establish an intergovernmental liaison office at home; or hire consultants, public relations specialists, lawyers, or lobbyists to pursue specific policies or programs.[23] By 1981, more than a hundred cities had Washington offices. At the state level, there may also be single-jurisdiction lobbyists—for a large city, county, or authority, for example. The most typical of the single-jurisdiction groups are single states lobbying in Washington. "Going it alone" is often successful.

In 1941 Governor Herbert Lehman of New York created the first federal-state relations office in Washington, D.C., to seek national funding for projects and to lobby against strong regulations. Other states created federal state offices, mostly in the mid- to late 1960s, in conjunction with the rise of the Great Society programs of President Johnson and the New Federalism programs of President Nixon. By 1985, thirty states had offices in Washington. By 1987, two-thirds of US governors had Washington offices, another third of the states had offices connected to other state entities, and only a third had no state lobbying presence. A few state legislatures also created D.C. offices, but most relied on the NCSL.

State activism continued to increase in Washington in the 1980s, but a recession led to a dwindling of national funds that went to subnational governments. Between the late 1980s and late 1990s, the number of state offices in Washington peaked at thirty-six, but it dropped to thirty-one by 1998 and has not grown since. On the other hand, state and local governments have increased their utilization of a variety of other ways to lobby the national government. Specifically, they hire lobby firms, trade associations, law firms, and other groups to do specialized work in issue monitoring, tracking legislation, and anything else that might help these governments influence national activities. In 2009 the Center for Public Integrity found that states, territories, and local governments spent $83.5 million in lobbying the national government, but the spending dropped to around $60 million in 2010 as governments at every level responded to a major recession. Nearly 1,000 government entities hire approximately 1,000 lobbyists per year to lobby the national government. In addition, individual state agencies, including state universities, hire lobbyists to work for them in Washington and in the states.[24]

Individual states' lobbying has a checkered history of success, with some state offices being better funded, more effective, and generally more successful than others, as several scholars have found. David Cingranelli interviewed Washington office directors in 1981–82 and focused on describing communication patterns.[25] John Pelissero and Robert England examined the roles, services, and strategies that the Washington offices of state and local governments employed during Reagan's first term, a time of major changes in intergovernmental relations.[26] Darby Morrisroe updated Cingranelli's early assessment and examined offices in Washington and in state capitals.[27] She asked why some states do not establish D.C. offices and found the reasons to be political. Entrepreneurial, aggressive governors tend to establish offices in Washington. Of major importance is that a governor makes the decision to establish an office, but there is no systematic explanation for governors' decisions in the aggregate. John Nugent attempted to understand states' Washington offices as a means of countering perceived encroachment of the national government on the original safeguards of federalism.[28] He viewed the state offices as a successful attempt to protect state interests and their constitutional roles. Troy Smith used case studies of Medicaid reform, crime policy, and welfare reform to assess the ability of governors and state legislators to represent and defend their interests before Congress.[29] Washington offices, of course, are just one of several means used by governors to lobby the national government. The recent research did not judge states' offices in Washington, D.C., to be effective.

The most substantial research on states' Washington offices was conducted by Jennifer Jensen, who adapted Robert Salisbury's exchange theory of interest groups to explain why some US states mobilize and create Washington, D.C., lobbying offices while others do not.[30] She expanded Salisbury's theory by considering environmental factors that could affect mobilization, and she interviewed approximately seventy directors and former directors of federal-state liaison offices in Washington and state capitals. Jensen found substantial differences between states with Washington offices and those with only state-federal relations offices in their state capitals. Relying on Salisbury, Jensen expected to find that benefits of Washington offices would be the prevailing explanation for their establishment; she found, instead, that office costs were more important. Governors' preferences led to the creation of Washington offices, and, sometimes, the political costs were a disincentive. Media and officials from other political parties complained about spending for the offices, and some state legislators, who recognized the visibility advantages for a governor, as well as an increased ability to secure national funds, were likewise critical.

The Center for Responsive Politics gathers information from lobbying disclosure reports filed in Washington, D.C. In recent years, the highest-spending states have been Pennsylvania, New Jersey, Indiana, Mississippi, Nevada, Kentucky, and Georgia. With the exception of Pennsylvania, most of those states spent between $200,000 and $400,000 a year.[31]

International State and Local Interest Representation

State governments typically have foreign trade offices to represent and promote their economic interests abroad. In 1977, 22 states had overseas offices, but by 1990 a total of 163 foreign offices were operated by 42 American states. Most of these offices are in Japan, with the second most popular location being Taiwan. The economic slowdown of the mid-1970s led business leaders and state officials to seek new foreign markets as a way to supplement waning domestic markets in an interdependent world economy. Another precipitator of state initiatives was the disengagement of federal agencies from foreign trade activities beginning in the 1970s, largely because of the fragmentation of trade responsibilities among agencies.[32]

State and local governments engage in international issues in ways previously not envisioned, building relationships far beyond the areas of economic trade promotion, cultural exchanges, and tourism. The narrowing distinction between domestic and international issues led Bayless Manning, in 1977, to coin the word *intermestic* to describe these activities.[33] The international activism of subnational governments encompasses a wide range of activities, including the climate change agenda, human rights issues, economic sanctions and related divestment policies, global finance issues, drug policy and other criminal justice issues, food safety, and more. Dovetailing with the activism is an expanded mission for state and local associations, which play key coordinative roles. Individual cities and states are active in representation in the international arena also.

Forty-four US cities, eighteen counties, and sixteen states passed or considered legislation related to the Convention on the Elimination of All Forms of Discrimination against Women (CEDAW), signed by President Carter in 1980 but not ratified by the Senate. In spring 2005, nine US mayors agreed to their own climate protection program, approved by the U.S. Conference of Mayors (USCM), and by fall 2008, 884 mayors who represented more than 81 million people had endorsed the program. The Large Cities Climate Leadership Group, now called C40, includes more than thirty-five of the world's largest cities, including some in the United States. By 2000, for example, twenty-six municipalities and four states had enacted economic sanction laws aimed at Burma, Nigeria, and other nations.[34]

Specialist Organizations

Congress is specialized in terms of functional policy areas, with program and functional specialists providing highly detailed information on Capitol Hill and in executive branch agencies. The specialist associations of state and local officials have relatively easier access than generalist associations to policy-making arenas.

Specialist associations represent nearly every identifiable administrative specialty. These were created in response to expanding political opportunities within the intergovernmental sector, such as changes in the US policy-making and service-delivery systems. These specialist organizations share much with the generalist groups, primarily a broad sense of the public interest. Their members are the professionals who staff government bureaucracies at all levels—for example, finance officers; planners; and human resource, transportation, and housing specialists. During the heyday of state and local lobbying in the 1960s, the loosely linked specialist associations were dubbed the "Dirty Dozen," and they often clashed with the PIGs.

As early as 1974, Donald Haider observed that the state and local generalist officials faced the rising influence of "functional specialists" across all levels of government.[35] Later writers, however, underrated the importance of the specialist associations, especially in explaining the "decline" of the Big Seven generalist associations during the Reagan years.[36]

Specialists face fewer obstacles to organizing than do generalists. Agency funds, along with individual memberships, help support their associations, which provide a wide variety of professional functions for members besides lobbying. The specialist associations fit well within the functional policy networks at the national level, sharing knowledge and interest with similar professionals at all governmental levels, as well as with nonprofit public interest groups that specialize in particular policy areas. The specialist associations work through vertical and horizontal ties within the political system, including those with private professional organizations. Because so much of their work is concentrated in large and medium-sized cities, they come in frequent contact with the generalist organizations. Some specialist associations are affiliates under the Big Seven umbrella.

A classic example of the clash of generalist and specialist perspectives was provided by the debate over general revenue sharing in the early 1970s. Generalist elected officials strongly supported unfettered funds that would be directly under their control. Specialists feared the use of funds by governors, mayors, and county commissioners; they desired, instead, that federal dollars be channeled through the intergovernmental bureaucracies they staffed.

Public Interest Organizations

State and local interest representation in Washington, D.C., also consists of some of the thousands of US public interest groups, especially those associated with urban and environmental issues. They compete or cooperate with the major intergovernmental groups, depending on the policy area. Competition is due to ideological and goal differences, as well as the continual quest for federal and foundation support. Unlike the Washington-based generalist officials' associations, many of these groups focus their advocacy on state governments and even some local governments.

Whenever the issues promoted by the poverty, child welfare, civil rights, environmental, and other sectors are threatened, rates of group formation increase in reaction to perceived hostility to such interests. For example, specialist group formation expanded rapidly beginning in the 1960s, and then, fueled by antagonism toward President Reagan's policies, in the 1980s. This illustrates the importance of political context and helps explain patterns of conflict and cooperation among sectors.

The public interest organizations are under increasing assault by conservative authors and right-wing think tanks who criticize what they call "taxpayer-funded lobbying." In fact, the same charge is leveled against many of the generalist and specialist organizations because taxpayers' funds are used to pay association dues. Economists James Bennett of George Mason University and Thomas DiLorenzo of Loyola University described this lobbying as an inappropriate and deleterious loophole within the government sector in which government supports groups and associations that support government's own initiatives and goals. That is, taxpayer funds are used to advance the interests of bureaucrats and politicians, a circular system of support that advances and expands government. These researchers focus on such groups as ACORN and the National Council of Churches to illustrate what they argue are perverse incentives and negative consequences of taxpayer-funded lobbying. Public interest advocates organized across such issues as consumer watch groups, energy, the environment, welfare, poverty programs, civil rights associations, seniors, legal services, and unions have been cited as the cause of an explosion of lobbying and an expansion of government.[37]

By 2011, some ramifications of the "public choice" arguments have been congressional defunding of some organizations and, at the state level, hundreds of bills introduced to curb the power of public employee unions. The research and actions taken to curb public interest group lobbying has resulted in closer scrutiny of lobbying disclosure laws at the state level for government and what are considered quasi-government organizations.[38]

The Intergovernmental Information Infrastructure

Another category of interest representation within the intergovernmental sector consists of the array of national- and state-level legislative and executive units that facilitate the overall understanding of intergovernmental issues. The national government's institutional capacity for analyzing intergovernmental issues rose in the early 1950s but began to decline in the 1980s. Beginning in 1953, several institutions were established to analyze and, in some cases, coordinate and manage intergovernmental issues. Key among these were the U.S. Advisory Commission on Intergovernmental Relations (ACIR); intergovernmental divisions in the General Accounting Office (GAO), which is now the Government Accountability Office, and in the Office of Management and Budget (OMB); and several congressional subcommittees. Many states also created units similar to the ACIR to do research on state-local issues and the effects of federal policies on state and local governments. A key example is the study of unfunded mandates from one government to another.

These organizations flourished from the mid-1960s to the mid-1980s. Their analytic capabilities dovetailed with the objectives and tasks of the intergovernmental groups, helping the Big Seven and other organizations to develop and mature. ACIR provided a forum in which officials at all levels could consider common problems and recommend improvements in grant administration and coordination, among other issues. ACIR provided technical advice to Congress and the president on proposed legislation, studied emerging intergovernmental problems, and recommended ways to make the overall policy system function more smoothly.

Through exposure to high-quality information, policy makers at all governmental levels became better informed about intergovernmental issues. The fact that the analytical organizations are governmental units themselves can help defuse the notion of state and local government groups as "just another special interest."

Since 1985, all of the national analytic organizations (ACIR, GAO, OMB, and the intergovernmental congressional committees) experienced reductions in capacity, and, in some cases, their mission was reoriented or they were terminated. This has had a major impact on the understanding of intergovernmental issues throughout the American political system. OMB's intergovernmental unit was disbanded by President Reagan. ACIR was abolished and GAO's capabilities were diminished through major budget cuts in the 1990s. In the same time frame, the House and Senate both demoted the status of intergovernmental concerns, most visibly by reorganizing subcommittees, failing to hire staffers with intergovernmental expertise, and devoting less time to coordinating activities with intergovernmental units. The information infrastructure's decline lessened the analytical abilities and access of the Big Seven and other organizations to executive branch agencies.[39]

The most significant example of the loss of intergovernmental expertise is the demise of the Advisory Commission on Intergovernmental Relations (ACIR), which was abolished in 1996. ACIR was a major source of data and analysis on intergovernmental issues. The death of ACIR and the decline of adequate assessment capacity at the top for policy making have major implications for the fate of state and local governments in a federal system. In many ways, the intergovernmental lobby fills some of the gaps in the continuing loss of analytic capacity in the intergovernmental system.[40]

Looking at analytical capacity issues from the subnational perspective provides a somewhat more optimistic view. The National League of Cities not only represents and lobbies for its members but also has affiliate state organizations, usually called state municipal leagues. NACo membership is by individual county, and it does not have affiliate organizations in the same sense as the NLC. But the forty-eight states that have counties also have state-level county associations that generally include all their counties as members. The county association executive directors from the states meet with each other and work cooperatively with NACo, as do each state's county associations. Many state legislatures have local government commissions that study state-local issues, and special commissions are created on topics such as mandate reform and local government restructuring.

Resources Used for State and Local Interest Representation

The major state and local generalist lobbying groups have less clout than many well-financed private groups. The intergovernmental associations lack resources such as political action committees (PACs) and the opportunity to participate in election campaigns. In varying degrees, however, the intergovernmental associations possess the same types of resources as do other organized interests. These include size, status and prestige, access, organizational structure, leadership skill, organizational cohesion, and intensity.

Size, Prestige, and Access Advantages

The size and prestige of the groups within the sector are impressive. The United States consists of more than 87,000 governments. Only one of those is the national government; the others are state and local governments. Not all governments can afford to be members of the associations that make up the intergovernmental sector, and not all are interested in either the membership services or advocacy provided by generalist organizations. NLC has a large and diverse membership base because cities of any size can join if they are members of their state league of cities or municipalities. USCM has expanded its membership from 600 members in the mid-1990s to over 1,300 members as more medium-sized cities experience large-city problems. The specialist associations represent professionals working at every level and in every type of government. And, as mentioned earlier, the more than 2,500 public interest groups in the United States engage in activities that represent state and local interests across dozens of issues.

Intergovernmental groups enjoy recognition and a measure of legitimacy with the media and others, which enhance their ability to influence policy. National lawmakers view elected generalists in the political system as having a legitimate right to speak on behalf of their constituents.[41] However, "where you stand is where you sit." Members of the Senate and House are not inclined to accept the policy preferences of state and local officials from their home state when those views conflict with their own. Subnational elected officials assume office on partisan ballots, which gives them additional access through their party connections.

Groups within the sector vary significantly in their status and prestige. The National Governors Association has a great deal of prestige largely because of the importance of the fifty individual governors. Historically, NACo lacked the prestige and access generally afforded to the USCM and the NLC, in part because counties were slow to modernize and did not emerge as major human-service providers in the political system until the 1990s. As local problems are increasingly regional in nature, NACo has become more important.

Cohesion and Intensity

The intergovernmental associations face drawbacks in terms of cohesion and intensity. There are many of them, and some are internally fragmented. Their perceptions are shaped by the level of government or policy area in which they operate. Sector associations possess uneven resource bases in terms of their membership size and organizational finances. A few examples are in order.

NACo, a generalist organization, is the most visible example of a group that lacks internal cohesion. The diversity of American counties in terms of political party control, size, population density, degree of shared responsibility with other local governments, degree of autonomy from state governments, economic bases, and cultural attitudes makes the national representation of counties very difficult.

Two-thirds of US counties are rural, and many rural counties are declining in population and revenues. Because NACo membership is by individual county, rural counties have tended to dominate NACo's policy and member services agendas. This has meant an emphasis on public works, especially highways, and agricultural issues. As counties have evolved into major providers of human services in our governmental system, NACo's membership has diversified. Its agenda now includes such concerns as public health, social welfare, mass transit, solid waste disposal, and county modernization. The expansion of the agenda has increased conflict among diverse counties. As counties take on more of the responsibilities held by municipalities in the political system and receive additional responsibilities and unfunded mandates, sector conflicts over revenues, responsibilities, and powers increase.

Traditional "urban policy" issues such as poverty, racism, redistribution, and spatial targeting are a tough sell in either the national or the state capitals. Urban problems have rarely generated much sustained and focused interest (intensity) among the state and local associations. Short-term surges of narrow interest have been followed by longer-term indifference. From the national government's perspective, however, the decline of large cities over decades was important for its impact on the national economy. More recently, the national government has focused attention on large cities and metropolitan areas as economic engines for growth and prosperity. The state groups, in general, were traditionally less active in seeking federal funds for their members, as were the local groups. The states were less critical, also, of national funding priorities. Twenty-five percent of total federal grants went to local governments in 1980 and 75 percent to the states; by 1988, the percentages were 15 and 85 percent, respectively. Local groups were more concerned with federal aid disbursement; the state organizations tended to focus on federal deficit reduction. Federal stimulus monies during the Great Recession that started in 2008 went directly to states, angering many local groups who sought direct funding from the stimulus monies. Differences in ideology and goals explain variations in cohesion between the state and local groups and, thus, within the overall sector.

Some state legislative officials argue that NCSL is ineffective in influencing Congress and too liberal in its views. Policy positions, however, must be approved by three-quarters of the states, voting as states and not as individual members. As is the case with so many other groups, NCSL is hampered in achieving policy consensus because of the size and diversity of its membership. NCSL's primary role is thus informational, not political. ALEC is less active in congressional lobbying than NCSL but can bring formidable resources to bear on particular issues, such as the balanced-budget amendment, largely because of its financial resources and the relative ideological unity of its membership.

Since ALEC's creation, no single organization in Washington, D.C., has represented all state legislators. ALEC is not housed in the Hall of the States; instead, its offices are with the influential conservative think tank, the Heritage Foundation. Such splintering of the Big Seven highlights, once again, the cohesion problems for the sector.

Organizational Structure and Leadership

The structure created by an organization and its group leadership capabilities are additional elements that affect group effectiveness. NACo is a case in point. NACo's diversity mirrors that of its affiliate associations, which are national organizations that represent specialist officials such as county attorneys, administrators, fiscal officers, and parks and recreation personnel. The mix of both generalist and specialist officials under the same umbrella can cause internal policy conflict; it can also lead to success in meshing spatial (rural versus urban, for example) and functional interests. On the other hand, associations that include only generalists or specialists may be hampered because of a failure to blend differing perspectives.

The local associations possess varying abilities to help their members respond to new political realities, often as a result of their organizational structure. The NLC, for example, with its dues-paying state affiliate organizations, has a relatively strong network in place to forge better linkages with state capitals. Cities of any size can join NLC. There are also statewide associations of counties and county officials, which are the primary legislative lobbyists for counties at that level. Unlike the strong relationship between the state leagues of municipalities and the NLC, the statewide associations of counties traditionally have had weak ties to NACo.

Both NLC and NACo were founded in Chicago and moved to Washington, D.C., as federal linkages to local governments grew. The USCM's only home, on the other hand, has been Washington. The large-city interests that dominate the group have led to a focus on "big-city problems," such as crime and drugs, hunger and homelessness, transportation, housing, education, environment, and AIDS. "Big-city problems" no longer affect only large jurisdictions, however. Such developments open a window of opportunity for coalition building for the association, and USCM has recently had relatively small-city mayors among its leaders. USCM leadership, however, is perceived as less willing than that of other local associations to respond to the changing domestic policy system by turning its interests toward the states.

Financial Resources

The financial resources of the various state and local organizations also affect their successes. As explained earlier, the local associations, like local governments, were hit hard during the Reagan years. As a result, their financial problems were greater than those of the state organizations in the 1980s and 1990s.

In mid-1993, several states revolted against an NGA plan to increase state membership dues. As in the 1980s, staff structure suffered in the 1990s. Dues were frozen for three years, and employees did not receive pay increases in 1993, some staff lobbyists were laid off, and revenues dropped both because of the dues freeze and partial payments by some states.

Some states argue that they do not get enough for their NCSL membership dues. State legislatures are billed according to population, with the larger states paying a couple hundred thousand dollars or more. On the other hand, because ALEC members are individuals, not legislatures, that organization can more easily assess member satisfaction.

In the mid-1990s, at least a half dozen of CSG's several dozen member groups of state specialist officials (for example, National Association of State Purchasing Officials, National Association of State Information Resources Executives, and National Conference of State Fleet Administrators) left the organization. Their departure was the culmination of a two-year internal rift over mission, administration, and money. The disgruntled groups felt that CSG was overcharging them for secretariat services. The CSG has now changed its rules for affiliate status. Prospective members must now apply for membership; membership decisions are made by CSG's administrative and elected leadership.

As is the case with other intergovernmental associations, NACo pursues corporate involvement through participation and contributions. Relationships with the private sector provide association members with knowledge and experience and contribute to providing the highest-quality services to county residents.

Sponsorship opportunities through national conferences, regional meetings, technology summits, and caucuses are available to corporate sponsors. For 2012, a corporate sponsor of NACo has provided funds to pay the NACO dues of all US counties. This is an obvious financial boost to NACo and may prove important in terms of coalition building among counties.

Tactics and Issues

Congressional and Executive Branch Liaison

Tactics used by the intergovernmental sector to influence congressional policy making often resemble the tactics used by private organized interests. The lobbying groups develop information to support their positions,

testify at formal hearings, contact legislators and administrators, and cultivate relations with the media. Prominent members often present their organizations' position. Washington staff maintain contact with appropriate
policy makers and their staffs.

The relative advantage of the intergovernmental lobbying groups in
gaining access to policy makers is not matched by significant ability to actually influence policy decisions. This is due, in large part, to enormous variations in group resources within the sector. It is also due, especially, to the
lack of cohesion and to a relatively low intensity of issue stands.

The intergovernmental issues on which generalist officials have concentrated are the cost of unfunded federal mandates to states and communities and the preemption by Congress of state laws and regulations for
product liability, credit reporting, interstate branch banking, and telecommunications, among others. Other concerns are federal intrusions on the
states' tax base, such as increases in fuel taxes and a possible tobacco tax or
other "sin" taxes to fund health care reform; an inflexible grant system; and
restrictive regulations and grant conditions designed to coerce state or local
action. Tables 12.3 and 12.4 depict the issues of interest to the Big Seven,
separating state-oriented from local-oriented organizations. The wide array
of policy concerns further makes the case that these organizations are not
typical special interest groups but, instead, are working for the broader
public interest.

State and local interest representation involves far more than dealing
with Congress on program adoption and funding issues. Washington, D.C.,

Table 12.3

Issues of Interest to State Government Lobbying Organizations
Agriculture and Rural Development
Banking, Insurance, and Financial Services
Budget and Taxation
Criminal Justice
Economic Development, Job Creation, Trade, and Cultural Affairs
Education, Preschool, K–12, Higher Education, and Vocational Education
Energy
Environment and Natural Resources
Health
Homeland Security, Emergency Management, and Public Safety
Human Services and Workforce Development
Immigration
Labor and Employment
Telecommunications and Information Technology
Transportation and Infrastructure

Table 12.4

Issues of Interest to Local Government Lobbying Associations
Agriculture and Rural Affairs
Children, Youth, and Family
Community and Economic Development
Criminal and Social Justice
Economic Development, Jobs, and Workforce Development
Education
Emergency Management
Energy, Environment, and Land Use
Finance and Intergovernmental Affairs
Health
Housing
Human Services
International Affairs
Labor and Collective Bargaining
Metropolitan Policy
Natural Resources
Public Lands
Rural Policy
Telecommunications and Technology
Tourism, Arts, Parks, Entertainment, and Sports
Transportation and Infrastructure

lobbyists also have close ties to the appropriate executive branch agencies and private sector groups who unite around particular causes. When programs cannot be changed, the task is to try to alter the way they are carried out by influencing the development of bureaucratic rules and regulations.

Because federal funding is so important to states and local governments, the Big Seven remain very active as Washington lobbyists. New mandates continue to be imposed. Tighter budgets at all levels mean more difficult policy choices and priority setting. Major policy victories by the groups, however, have been few in recent years. In many respects, the state and local groups are operating at the margins of policy—attempting, independently and in concert, to avoid the elimination of entire programs. The USCM, in 2011, was united in fighting for the retention of the federal Community Development Block Grant program, which has been a mainstay for cities since 1974.

Significant strides have been made in working with the national government to reduce the imposition of unfunded mandates, streamline the process of applying for and obtaining waivers from regulations, and establish consultative processes on intergovernmental issues. States have had more flexibility in handling Medicaid, for example, as the federal government has become more flexible in granting waivers.

Coalition Building

Each of the city organizations has its own base of support in Congress. By combining efforts, a broader base of support can sometimes be developed. For many years, NACo received strong support among suburban and Republican legislators, who were joined by many rural legislators. NACo's alliance with the USCM, with its strong ties to Democratic urban legislators from the northeast and midwest, has led to broad congressional support for particular policy objectives such as housing policy and welfare reform.

Through the years, the shared political concerns among the Big Seven encouraged the formation of alliances to enhance policy influence. The executive directors of the various organizations met regularly, and their staffs worked together on common strategies to affect national policy. The organizations jointly sponsored many service activities, and in 1970 the staffs of USCM and NLC were merged; the merger was dissolved in 1977, however.

Within-sector collaboration involves working together for the enactment or defeat of specific legislative policies, the writing of favorable regulations, the adjustment of deadlines for meeting mandates, and other, less subtle policy influences. Relations within the sector today range from "ships passing in the night" to "turf wars" to truly collaborative efforts.

The state and local government groups are using a broader range of tactics on a wider range of issues than in the recent past. Collaborative tactics have changed their form. Generalists and specialists, for example, collaborate to provide civic education to the general public, based on their shared professionalism and commitment to public service. In the Hall of the States, Big Seven association representatives and states meet with congressional staffers, state officials, federal agency officials, and even the media to receive briefings on agency and legislative developments. Such information networks continue to serve a valuable purpose in bringing organizations together to work in an intergovernmental environment.

Perhaps the largest role played by these groups is that of providing member services. Information is developed and distributed in a wide variety of formats: publications such as magazines, bulletins, directories, issue briefs, reports, and books; membership surveys; audio and video recordings; electronic networks; conferences, meetings, orientations, and training sessions; and codes of ethics. Recent examples are CSG tracking the federal stimulus funds during the Great Recession and its trends forecasts; NGAs's Best Practices Center, which assembles best management and policy ideas from across the states; NACos sustainability initiatives; and ICMA's Center for State and Local Government Excellence.

Intergovernmental issues are not sexy or exciting; they have low visibility in the daily experiences of the majority of the population. Citizens do not care which level of government delivers services; they just want efficient delivery. But crises can act as focusing events to promote change in a political system. The single issue around which the state and local groups have rallied in recent years is that of the unfunded mandate, which they collectively believed had deteriorated to crisis proportions. In October 1993, the generalist organizations cosponsored National Unfunded Mandates Day, a major effort to educate the public and media, and the Unfunded Mandate Reform Act became law soon after. Most recently, these associations have been dealing with the Great Recession. However, their efforts are more directed toward providing services to their members than toward forming a coalition around the myriad aspects of intergovernmental issues associated with the recession.

Groups within the sector also forge coalitions with private-sector institutions and interests. One recent example is the public-private partnership developed by the states named as finalists for the location of the supercollider. Other such coalitions are focused on a variety of sustainability initiatives.

Courts

The federal courts condition the problems and policies of the states and local governments. A series of cases eroded state and local protections against the expansion of congressional authority. In effect, subnational governments have been redefined by the courts as interest groups. Their associations contend, in rebuttal, that the Tenth Amendment to the Constitution places a limit on national power. Seemingly endless challenges to subnational authority and capabilities—preemption of their rights and responsibilities, unfunded mandates, unrealistic regulatory deadlines, increased service-delivery and policy-making responsibilities but decreased resources—led to the creation of a State and Local Legal Center, which the intergovernmental lobby increasingly uses to deal with policy issues of greatest concern. The Big Seven created the Academy for State and Local Government (ASLG) in 1971, a small nonprofit policy group, which houses the State and Local Legal Center.[42]

The national state and local government associations file *amicus curiae* briefs before the US Supreme Court to promote their policy initiatives regarding federalism. Until the early 1980s, state and local governments rarely filed briefs and were generally not successful when they did. The legal center aids states in filing briefs and coordinates the advocacy of state and local governmental associations in litigation before the Supreme Court.

Edward Laverty and Kenneth Palmer reviewed thirty-seven cases between 1995 and 1998 in which the associations were active and six high-profile federalism cases during the period in which the center was generally less involved. They found that the associations were more unified in raising technical issues, such as intergovernmental policy and program implementation, and prevailed in 68 percent of the cases during the period of study. In addition, the national government and state and local government interest groups usually supported similar positions before the Court on the highly technical issues. The associations succeeded less frequently when dealing with major federalism disputes, but in cases in which both the states and national government filed briefs, the states fared better than the national government.[43]

Another intergovernmental organization, the National Association of Attorneys General, which deals primarily with state issues, moved its headquarters to Washington, D.C., in the early 1980s and began engaging in national issues more often than in the past. This group has become a powerful force in American litigation, with a large number of states joining together for important lawsuits. Attorneys general from twenty-six states together plus two states independently have filed lawsuits against the national health care law that was passed in 2010. The concern is that the requirement in the legislation for individuals to purchase insurance or receive a penalty oversteps the power of Congress regarding the Commerce Clause. Originally, the Commerce Clause was intended only to regulate trade among and between the states, but it was expanded to include action within a state that has a substantial effect on interstate commerce, such as manufacturing or agriculture. States filing lawsuits opposing the health care law argue that congressional power cannot require individuals to purchase health insurance.

A 1992 Supreme Court ruling, *Quill Corp. v. North Dakota*, held that a state cannot force a company to collect that state's sales taxes from consumers unless the company has either property or employees there. In addition, the ruling said that state sales taxes cannot extend beyond state lines because they are too complex. States have worked together through the Streamlined Sales Tax Project to make their sales tax systems simpler, and they are using that effort to win congressional authorization for states to extend their sales tax to online and catalog sales. Congress has shown little interest, so it is likely that *Quill* will be challenged in the courts again. Colorado, New York, North Carolina, and Texas have been aggressive in pursuing Amazon.com and other online retailers to force them to voluntarily report and collect sales taxes on online purchases. The companies argue that revealing their sales through itemized lists is a First Amendment issue, not only for customers but also for the retailers, because the names of some online companies and interest groups can suggest overt religious, political, or expressive affiliations.

Trends in Intergovernmental Representation

Whether the generalist organizations of public officials are effective in lobbying at the national level for their members is debatable. Because the Big Seven and other organizations often compete with each other on major issues, lobbying success varies widely and may depend on the issue. It is in the realms of information production, sharing, and dissemination and the provision of other membership services that the organizations have solid performance records. The groups, however, are "not just another special interest group," as they deal with issues of broad public interest and consequence. They are major generators of information and disseminators of that information to their memberships, with conferences, publications, and consultations that provide opportunities for exchanging information and building potentially significant interstate and intermunicipal interactions. Their information, moreover, is shared widely across the political system with the general public and decision makers. Similarly, the affiliate, parallel organizations in the states that lobby state legislatures provide state-specific programs, conferences, research, and other information exchanges. In the states, these organizations shape much of state-local and intermunicipal relations, supplementing the work of state and local employees who belong to and network through subject-matter organizations.

The American policy-making system can be described as consisting of "multi-centered policy dominance."[44] State and local interests must compete with an increasing number of other groups to place items on the public and/or official agenda. Existing in a "shared power world"—and nurturing the skills to do so—presents major challenges to a sector that lacks a cohesive policy network, whose service network has been diminished by the loss of direct funding, and whose information infrastructure has eroded. Fragmentation within the intergovernmental policy community from one issue to another is difficult to overcome. Greater interdependence in collecting and sharing information is already evident, however, as is some movement toward rethinking organizational roles in a decentralized intergovernmental system.

Except for federations of local community organizations, which are dispersed among Washington, D.C., New York, Chicago, and Philadelphia, the major state and local government presence is in Washington and state capitals. To be proactive, not simply reactive, sector members must find new ways to work with each other. They must blend policy and management concerns and generalist and specialist perspectives. Common ground must be found within the context of differing ideologies and goals, whether within individual organizations or among and between them. Levels of governments, especially, must collaborate more frequently, and policy deliberations and solutions must transcend jurisdictional boundaries.

The intergovernmental associations must also deal with the seemingly endless stream of reform efforts within the political system: government reinvention, privatization, regionalization, and collaborative governance. Privatization, in particular, has posed a challenge since many issues are no longer a monopoly of government, a fact that somewhat undermines parts of these organizations' agendas. On the other hand, some current concerns within the political system create new opportunities for the sector. Societal and governmental attempts to balance citizen and group rights with responsibilities and to focus attention on the need for sector involvement in civic education. In a society that has in many ways redefined individual and group wants as needs and then redefined those needs as rights, a dialogue that helps citizens understand their rights and obligations suggests new roles for the sector. The Great Recession has led to sweeping realignments of agencies at all levels and massive budget cuts, affecting a wide range of citizens' rights and responsibilities.

Based on the notion that organizations must solicit and maintain members by offering the proper supply of incentives, recent demands by generalist officials signal the need for some internal restructuring of their associations to shape more coherent relationships between national and local affiliates. In addition, it may be important for the national organizations representing state and local governments to be concerned with state-level activities and for increased positive interaction to take place between the entire panoply of the state and the local groups.

The jurisdictional nature of representation by the generalist state and local organizations may be their greatest problem. Federal policies follow the pattern of funding people, not places. Real-world problems seldom occur neatly within jurisdictional boundaries. The interests of units of local government are not necessarily the same as the interests of their larger metropolitan or regional areas. In addition, the American public, with the aid of the media, has lost much of its sense of place.

The types of issues that the local groups deal with are unlike many other policy areas in the American political system. They involve both a governmental function (for example, community development) and a geographic area (such as a city, county, or township). Public policies are usually envisioned and handled in the political system in terms of the clusters of values, objectives, and programs related to basic government functions—for example, education, law enforcement, or transportation. Dealing with the geographic or jurisdictional dimension promoted by the local government groups continues to be problematic. The executive branch and Congress fragment decision making along functional, not spatial, lines. It is, therefore, difficult for intergovernmental generalists to penetrate the policy process. The specialists (in housing, employment, crime, education) do not consistently deal with these issues in ways that take into account their spatial implications. The sector's most significant role appears to be that of providing information services to members.

Social scientists often focus on issue networks to examine the array of actors operating within a policy domain. Such analyses may neglect the broader political context in which networks exist, including how various groups work in harmony or in conflict. This examination of the intergovernmental sector, especially the generalist associations, has included reviewing structural and strategic factors that facilitate or hamper groups' emergence and development, and sometimes lead to their decline.

Notes

1. This chapter is a revised and updated version of Beverly A. Cigler, "Not Just Another Special Interest: Intergovernmental Representation," in *Interest Group Politics*, 4th ed., eds. Allan J. Cigler and Burdett A. Loomis (Washington, DC: CQ Press, 1995): 131–53.
2. Charles H. Levine and James A. Thurber, "Reagan and the Intergovernmental Lobby: Iron Triangles, Cozy Subsystems, and Political Conflict," in *Interest Group Politics*, 2nd ed., eds. Allan J. Cigler and Burdett A. Loomis (Washington, DC: CQ Press, 1986): 202–20.
3. Robert H. Salisbury, "Interest Representation: The Dominance of Institutions," *American Political Science Review* 78, no. 1 (1984): 64–76.
4. Beverly A. Cigler, "The County-State Connection: A National Study of Associations of Counties," *Public Administration Review* 54, no. 1 (1994): 3–11.
5. See Allan J. Cigler and Burdett A Loomis, eds., *Interest Group Politics*, 2nd ed. (Washington, DC: CQ Press, 1986).
6. Mancur Olson, *The Logic of Collective Action: Public Goods and the Theory of Groups* (Cambridge, MA: Harvard University Press, 1971).
7. Cigler, "Not Just Another Special Interest."
8. Richard M. Flanagan, "Roosevelt, Mayors and the New Deal Regime: The Origins of Intergovernmental Lobbying and Administration," *Polity* 31, no. 3 (1999): 415–50.
9. Flanagan, "Roosevelt, Mayors and the New Deal Regime."
10. Samuel H. Beer, "Federalism, Nationalism, and Democracy in America," *American Political Science Review* 72, no. 1 (1978): 9–21.
11. Flanagan, "Roosevelt, Mayors and the New Deal Regime."
12. Suzanne Farkas, *Urban Lobbying: Mayors in the Federal Arena* (New York: New York University Press, 1971).
13. Donald H. Haider, *When Governments Come to Washington: Governors, Mayors and Intergovernmental Lobbying* (New York: Free Press, 1974).
14. Anne Marie Cammisa, *Governments as Interest Groups: Intergovernmental Lobbying and the Federal System* (Westport, CT: Praeger, 1995).
15. Levine and Thurber, "Reagan and the Intergovernmental Lobby."
16. Levine and Thurber, "Reagan and the Intergovernmental Lobby."
17. Beer, "Federalism, Nationalism, and Democracy in America."
18. Farkas, *Urban Lobbying.*
19. Haider, *When Governments Come to Washington.*

20. Flanagan, "Roosevelt, Mayors and the New Deal Regime."
21. Cammisa, *Governments as Interest Groups.*
22. See Jason Clemens, Julie Kaszton, Karrie Rufer, and Laura Sucheski, *State-Level Lobbying and Taxpayers: How Much Do We Really Know?* (San Francisco, CA: Pacific Research Institute, 2010), http://www.pacificresearch.org/docLib/20100309_TPFL_F.pdf.
23. David L. Cingranelli, "State Government Lobbies in the National Political Process," Rockefeller Institute Reprint Series No. 12 (Albany: Nelson A. Rockefeller Institute of Government, State University of New York, 1984): 122–27.
24. The study of this activity is continuously updated and found in multiple sections at the Center for Public Integrity's Web site at http://projects.publicintegrity.org/hiredguns/.
25. Cingranelli, "State Government Lobbies in the National Political Process."
26. John P. Pelissero and Robert E. England, "State and Local Governments' Washington 'Reps'—Lobbying Strategies and President Reagan's New Federalism," *State and Local Government Review* 19, no. 2 (1987): 68–72.
27. Darby Morrisroe, "The State of 'State Offices' in Washington: A Critical Assessment," paper presented at the annual meeting of the American Political Science Association, Boston, September 1998.
28. John D. Nugent, "Federalism Attained: Gubernatorial Lobbying in Washington as a Constitutional Function" (PhD diss., University of Texas, Austin, 1998).
29. Troy Smith, "When States Lobby" (PhD diss., State University of New York, Albany, 2008).
30. Jennifer M. Jensen and Jennifer G. Kelkres, "The First State Lobbyists: State Lobbying Offices in Washington during World War II," paper presented at the 40th annual meeting of the Northeastern Political Science Association, Boston, November 13–15, 2008.
31. OpenSecrets.org, "Lobbying: Civil Servants/Public Officials," 2010, http://www.opensecrets.org/lobby/indusclient.php?id=W03&year=2010.
32. See Beverly A. Cigler, " International Intergovernmental Relations and Impacts on American Federalism," in *Intergovernmental Relations in 2020: Theory and Practice*, eds. Kurt Thurmaier and Jack Meek (Washington, DC: CQ Press, forthcoming).
33. See Bayless Manning, "The Congress, the Executive, and Intermestic Affairs: Three Proposals," *Foreign Affairs* 55, no. 2 (1977): 306–324.
34. Cigler, " International Intergovernmental Relations and Impacts on American Federalism."
35. Haider, *When Governments Come to Washington.*
36. See Cigler, "Not Just Another Special Interest."
37. A representative publication is James T. Bennett and Thomas J. DiLorenzo, *Destroying Democracy: How Government Funds Partisan Politics* (Washington, DC: Cato Institute, 1985).
38. Clemens, Kaszton, Rufer, and Sucheski, *State-Level Lobbying and Taxpayers*
39. These points were made in John Kincaid and James A. Stever. "Rise and Decline of the Federal Government's Institutional Capacity for Intergovernmental Analysis: ACIR, OMB, GAO and the Congress," paper presented at the Annual Meeting of the American Political Science Association, Chicago, September 3–6, 1992.
40. See Kincaid and Stever, "Rise and Decline of the Federal Government's Institutional Capacity for Intergovernmental Analysis;" Cigler, "Not Just Another Special Interest;" Timothy J. Conlan and Paul L. Posner, eds., *Intergovernmental Management for the 21st Century* (Washington, DC: Brookings Institution, 2008).

41. On this point, see Parris N. Glendening and Mavis Mann Reeves, *Pragmatic Federalism* (Pacific Palisades, CA: Palisades, 1977).

42. See David E. Nething, "State Viewpoint: States Must Regain Their Powers," *Journal of State Government* (January–March 1990): 6–7.

43. Edward B. Laverty and Kenneth T. Palmer, "State and Local Government Interest Groups before the Supreme Court: Implications for Intergovernmental Policy," *Public Administration Quarterly* 24, no. 4 (2001): 522–536.

44. Farkas, in *Urban Lobbying*, makes this point.

13

The Rise and Fall and Rise of the China Lobby in the United States

Ronald J. Hrebenar and Clive S. Thomas

"When China awakes, the world will tremble."

Quote attributed to Napoleon[1]

By the dawn of the twenty-first century, it was clear even to the Americans that China had awakened and the United States had to deal with a new power in many different issue areas. The old China of centuries of military and economic weakness had disappeared, and a new powerful China was building up its military and aggressively seeking new economic opportunities around the world.

It was only a matter of time until China would once again appear on the Washington, D.C., political stage and make its policy demands known. A nation initiates or upgrades its lobbying team in Washington when its interests are being challenged or threatened. China in the latter part of the opening decade of the twenty-first century found itself in just that predicament. Stories in the *New York Times* had headlines such as "For Our China Trade Emergency . . . ," and the cover of *The Economist* depicted China as a giant, smoking dragon staring down at a seated President Obama with the headline "Facing Up to China."[2] Television ads in the 2010 congressional campaigns featured a giant dragon and a voice-over discussing free trade policies that sent American jobs to China, and they thanked the incumbent member of Congress: "As they say in China, 'Xie, xie.'"[3] Robert A. Kapp, the former president of the US-China Business Council, noted that "even though tensions had flared in the past, he had never seen China used as such an obvious punching bag for American politicians."[4] By the 2010 elections, China had become an economic villain similar to Japan in the 1980s and Mexico in the 1990s after the North American Free Trade Agreement (NAFTA). In October 2010, the House of Representatives passed a bill that would give President Obama expanded authority to impose tariffs on virtually all Chinese imports to the United States. The bill passed 348–79. It was part of a larger US government campaign against alleged Chinese currency manipulation, which has fueled increases in Chinese exports to the United States while limiting US exports to China. The Chinese, on the other hand, saw American efforts to raise the value of the Chinese *renminbi* as an attack on Chinese economic growth and China's economic role in the world. Paul Krugman, a Nobel prize–winning economist who writes for the *New York Times* op-ed page, had been penning columns with titles such as "Taking On China," supporting the bill as a "step in the right direction."[5] And then the *Economist* noted "China Buys Up the World," using very similar words as were written in the 1980s regarding Japanese buyers of property in Manhattan, Pebble Beach Golf Course, and beachfront property in Hawaii.[6]

In mid-2010, economists and statisticians declared that China had become the world's second largest economy after the United States. It had nudged Japan, the longtime number two, aside, and now the world was clearly aware of the economic miracle that had occurred after Deng Xiaoping began a new economic policy of encouraging free markets while keeping much of the Chinese economy state owned. The huge Chinese population (1.3 billion in 2010) was free to engage in business, and capitalism roared into China; a pattern of over 10 percent annual growth in China's GDP sustained itself over decades. Likewise, a record amount of wealth was generated in China from 1980 to 2010, and that wealth fueled a greater Chinese involvement in the world's economic and political arenas.

Sooner or later, China had to come to Washington, D.C., and play the game of political influence and lobbying. Actually, China had established lobbies in the US capital several times in the twentieth century under several different regimes and with various degrees of success. China as a nation, not necessarily a government, was a seasoned veteran of the Washington lobbying game, but a lack of continuity and lack of experienced players meant the reinvention of the China Lobby several times during the twentieth century. In many ways, the most recent government of China has had a more difficult time learning how to effectively lobby. One of the political handicaps of authoritarian states such as the People's Republic of China (PRC) is a lack of practical experience in how to lobby in modern democratic states. In other words, politics is very different in Beijing than in Washington, D.C. How does such a country establish a lobbying presence in America to protect its interests?

What foreign nations have the greatest influence on American public policy? Besides the powerful domestic lobbies with which many American are familiar, such as the AARP, National Rifle Association, and Goldman Sachs, some nations have quite successfully lobbied the US Congress and the executive branch. Back in the 1850s, the lobbyist for imperial Russia managed to persuade the United States to buy a seemingly worthless plot of frozen land for a few dollars—the purchase of Alaska (also known as

"Seward's Folly") during the Lincoln administration. More recently, in the 1980s, there was a great deal of discussion (and concern) about the power of the Japan Lobby. And in the last decade, there has been a lively debate over the extent of power of the so-called Israel Lobby.[7]

The Old China Lobby

A China Lobby was a major actor in American politics for most of the twentieth century. In the mid-1800s, Boston and New England shipping and whaling interests knew that China was a very profitable market, and many American fortunes were made investing in China. But, if US-China trade was to be successful over the long run, the shipping routes had to be protected across a vast Pacific Ocean with famously bad weather. US efforts to force open Japan in the 1850s were supported by the early American China Lobby, which demanded that Japanese ports be opened to American whaling ships needing repairs and supplies in the Northern Pacific and that Japan be a port of call on long voyages to and from China. China was viewed as a huge potential market for American finished products and as fertile soil for American religious missionaries seeking to bring Jesus to the Confucian Chinese masses. For years, the sons of former American Christian missionaries who lived in China taught at elite American universities, and these people composed the core of Americans who helped explain China to the United States. They were the original China Lobby.

Prior to the 1920s, other than the very vague combinations of Christian missionaries and some businessmen, there really was no China Lobby that operated on a regular basis in Washington, D.C. The term *China Lobby* became popular in the 1930s, as American media realized the significant influence of Chiang Kai-shek and the Nationalists in the US Congress. Following the Chinese Nationalist revolution in 1911, which overthrew the Manchu Dynasty, the new Republic of China was declared on April 5, 1912, and the United States became the first foreign nation to recognize it. A period of political chaos ensued as the various provinces and warlords maneuvered to see who got to control the new China. Eventually, Chiang Kai-shek, a Westernized general, emerged as the leader of a Nationalist China. During the late 1930s and early 1940s, China continued to have widespread military conflicts, and the China Lobby operated to maximize US support for Chiang's Nationalist regime in its battles against Mao's Communist Red Army and Japanese invaders. This version of the China Lobby had, like all versions, a Chinese and an American component. While Chiang and his beautiful wife and their family represented the Chinese part, the American part was also very powerful and influential.

A major part, perhaps the single most important part, of the anti-Communist, pro-Nationalist American China Lobby was famous publisher

Henry R. Luce, the publisher of *Time, Life,* and *Fortune* magazines as well as the producer of radio and newsreels for movie theaters.[8] Luce was the world's first and most successful multimedia owner, and he was the American leader of those who supported the Chiang Kai-shek and Nationalist China. Luce was an "old China hand"—the son of missionary parents, he was born and raised in China. So strong and consistent was Luce's support of Chiang Kai-shek and his wife Soong Mei-ling that they appeared on the cover of *Time* magazine eleven times between 1927 and 1955. Among the other important members of the American Nationalist China Lobby were Senator William Knowland (D-CA), Senator Joseph McCarthy (R-WI), Representative Walter H. Judd (R-MN), and Alfred Kohlberg, a New York businessman with investments in China.

While the Nationalist China Lobby spent money on lobbyists and had the media support of Luce's publishing empire, it was successful for such a long time because it also had the support of millions of Americans. The public came to support China in its war against the Japanese and in its civil war against Mao's armies. China also had the support of important American Christian missionary organizations such as the International Missionary Council. After Japan's attacks on China in 1937, the Nationalist China Lobby organized to seek strong American support for the Nationalist regime. The American Committee for Nonparticipation in Japanese Aggression and the Price Committee became the coordinating committee for the Nationalist Chinese lobbying effort. It opposed American economic ties to Japan and supported an embargo of military supplies to Japan. Among its effective political supporters was Henry Stintson, who went on to become Roosevelt's secretary of war in 1940. The Price Committee deployed a wide range of lobbying tactics to encourage support for China. Using churches, civic organizations, and universities, as well as mass mailings, press releases, and petitions, Madame Chiang came repeatedly to the United States to lobby for her government along with her brother. Madame Chiang, a very attractive, young Christian Chinese woman, was a magnet to the American press corps and thus a powerful advocate for her husband and his cause.

After the defeat of Japan in 1945, the civil war between the Nationalists and Mao's Communists resumed, and the American China Lobby portrayed Chiang and the Nationalists as one of the essential bulwarks against the spread of communism in Asia. The message it managed was a combination of democracy, Christianity, anticommunism, and pro-Americanism. The greatest Chinese stars for the China Lobby were the president of China, Chiang Kai-shek, and his wife. They became the face of China and that nation's most effective lobbyists throughout the 1930s and 1940s.

When Mao finally triumphed in October 1949 and Chiang had escaped to Taiwan, the United States delayed its decision on whether to recognize the new Communist government. Conservatives and Republicans attacked the Truman administration and charged the Democrats with "losing China." The decision to continue to recognize the Chiang Kai-shek government on Taiwan as the legitimate government of China was largely a result of the Chinese intervention into the Korean War against US forces defending South Korea. After the end of the Korean War in 1953, the United States concluded a mutual defense treaty with the Republic of China (Taiwan), and growing American involvement in Vietnam reinforced anti-PRC attitudes in the United States. The Taiwan China Lobby was successful in persuading the US government not to recognize the PRC government, and that decision was the central part of America's China policy from 1949 to 1979—an incredible three decades when the United States ignored the Communist government of mainland China and recognized Chiang Kai-Shek's Nationalist government on the island of Taiwan as the only legitimate government of China.

Gradually, the growing reality of the People's Republic of China and the fading of memories of China's war with the United States in Korea forced the United States to shift from total support for Taiwan to a recognition of the People's Republic of China. Thus, President Richard M. Nixon and Secretary of State Henry Kissinger "opened China." In July 1971, Kissinger unexpectedly visited Beijing, and several months later Nixon and Mao Zedong met and dined together in Beijing. In 1972, the United States facilitated the admission of the People's Republic to the United Nations and agreed to the expulsion of Chiang's Taiwanese government. Finally, the United States completed the American recognition of the People's Republic of China in 1979.

During the administration of Jimmy Carter (1977–1981), the PRC agreed to allow the United States to continue its "unofficial" relations with Taiwan and arms sales to Taipei. The power of the Taiwan Lobby was still sufficient to prevent the complete abandonment of Taiwan by the United States. In 1979, Congress passed the Taiwan Relations Act, and it restated American intentions to protect Taiwan from any attack by the PRC. The United States will "consider any effort to determine the future of Taiwan by other than peaceful means, including by boycotts or embargoes, a threat to the peace and security of the Western Pacific area and of grave concern to the United States." Furthermore, the Act requires the United States "to provide Taiwan with arms of a defensive character; and to maintain the capacity of the United States to resist any resort to force or other forms of coercion that would jeopardize the security, or the social or economic system, of the people on Taiwan."[9]

The "provision of arms" clause of the Act has generated a continuing lobbying effort by powerful American military arms manufacturers, such as Boeing, Lockheed-Martin, and Raytheon, to continue supplying Taiwan with planes, ships, and technology to prevent any possible future Chinese attacks. This military-industrial sector has remained an important part of the Taiwan China Lobby, with the major exception of Boeing. Boeing defected to Beijing when it became clear that the Chinese aviation market required thousands of new commercial jets and it could become for Boeing what China has become for Ford Motor Company—its largest market. Additionally, the powerful lobbying firm Cassidy & Associates has long been a key part of the Taiwan Lobby, receiving almost $4.5 million in fees from Taiwan in the 2000–2003 period.[10]

John Newhouse calls the Taiwan Lobby the "old superpower of foreign lobbies" in Washington: "From the 1940s to the 1970s, no U.S. president challenged the so-called China lobby."[11] The PRC refused to seriously lobby and left the field open to Taiwan interests. Those days have clearly changed, as the PRC has now become a permanent actor in the Washington influence game.

The New China Lobby

When the United States officially recognized the People's Republic of China in 1979, the Communist regime had no official lobbying presence in Washington, D.C. In the ensuing decades, up to the late 1990s, the PRC lobbying effort in Washington remained weak but did gradually strengthen. When China became a world power in the early 2000s, its growing wealth, trade with the United States, and search for raw materials around the world forced it to significantly upgrade its lobbying corps in America. The PRC also developed a corps of super diplomats who could operate as lobbyists with Congress.

Newhouse notes that three crises in recent decades caused the PRC to reconsider its reluctance to build a stronger lobbying presence in Washington: the American reaction to Tiananmen Square in 1989, the 1995 Clinton decision to grant a visa to Taiwan president Lee Teng-hui, and the ongoing trade imbalance with the United States. China responded to these conflicts by increasing its investments in US Treasury securities.[12] It also hired Hogan & Hartson, one of Washington's major law firms, and McDermont Will & Emery to lobby on textile issues and, in 2005, added Patton Boggs.[13] When the China National Offshore Oil Corporation tried to buy Unocal, an American oil company, the Chinese hired Akin Gump, another powerful Washington legal and lobbying firm. China eventually withdrew the offer after encountering tremendous American opposition.

The New China Lobbying Corps

When Richard Solomon and Charles Freeman Jr. researched Chinese negotiating behavior in 1999, they concluded that the Chinese "pursued interests through old friends."[14] That is why one of the oldest friends of the New

China Lobby has been the former national security adviser and secretary of state in the Nixon administration, Henry Kissinger. Kissinger "opened up China" in 1971 and orchestrated the famous 1972 Nixon trip to Beijing that catalyzed the eventual normalization of diplomatic relations. Kissinger does not appear on the lists of lobbyists employed by China, but many reports over the decades have indicated that Kissinger and Kissinger Associates, his political consulting and risk assessment firm located in New York City, have been important in advising China on how to deal with the United States. For example, in the days after the Obama administration took office in January 2009, Kissinger in a newspaper column called on the US-Chinese relationship to be "taken to a new level."[15]

Kissinger Associates was founded in 1982 by Kissinger, former Republican presidential national security advisor Brent Scowcroft, and former secretary of state and White House chief of staff Lawrence Eagleburger to advise clients on government relations throughout the world. Kissinger was able to start the firm with loans from Goldman Sachs and three other banks. The firm has had close ties with the APCO Worldwide public relations firm, the Blackstone Group, and the influential Washington, D.C., law firm Covington & Burling. Kissinger Associates has had some of Washington's power elite as associates, including Tim Geithner, Obama's secretary of the treasury, and Bill Richardson, former Democratic governor of New Mexico.[16]

Kissinger Associates has never disclosed its client list. This became an issue when Kissinger was named by President George W. Bush to chair the 9/11 Investigation Commission. When told he would have to disclose his client list, Kissinger decided he would rather not chair the committee. In 1999, Mack McLarty joined with Henry Kissinger to open Kissinger McLarty Associates in Washington, D.C. McLarty added his background as White House chief of staff under President Clinton to the Republican power brokers already at Kissinger Associates. The two firms eventually separated in 2008, with McLarty Associates operating in Washington and Kissinger Associates out of New York City. Henry Kissinger and his key associates are frequently in the news commenting on China and its relationship with the United States. In September 2010, Kissinger was profiled in a long article in the *International Herald Tribune* warning of the dangers of US confrontation with China and urging both countries to develop mutual trust.[17] Sometimes, the New China Lobby looks like an association of former American secretaries of state. In addition to the Kissinger luminaries, a list of former secretaries of state and other high-level Americans have been associated with Chinese lobbying, including George Shultz, Cyrus Vance, and Alexander Haig.

When one considers only the official lobbying of the Chinese PRC government in Washington, the China Lobby does not look very impressive. In 1997, American Ambassador to China James Sasser ranked the China

Lobby in Washington as the least effective foreign lobby in the city.[18] The PRC embassy in Washington increased its congressional relations staff in the late 1990s, but it continued to rely on hiring major lobbying and law firms for its important interactions with the American government.

The New China Lobby has operated with two primary political objectives: strengthening American political ties with the PRC while weakening US ties with Taiwan, and promoting economic ties with the United States that favor the continued economic development of the PRC. This second goal of economic development has made building a bridge to America's corporate elites a logical strategy for the PRC. China has been able to harness the American business community to effectively lobby for it. Foremost among the American business sector of the China Lobby have been the U.S.-China Business Council and the Emergency Committee for American Trade, as well as major corporations seeking greater access to the Chinese markets such as Boeing, General Motors, and AT&T. This powerful American China Lobby helped secure China "most favored nation" designation and the Permanent Normal Trade Relations Act in the 1990s.

China, as we mentioned earlier, used its strategic weight to cultivate special relationships with powerful political figures such as Brzezinski, Kissinger, and James Schlesinger. It also has developed long-standing relationships with powerful corporate leaders. Maurice R. Greenberg, the chair of AIG, has been called China's unofficial ambassador to the United States. AIG, one of the world's largest insurance companies, started in Shanghai in 1919 and returned to China in the 1970s. The ever-present Henry Kissinger is on the AIG board of advisers, and Greenberg has served as chair of the U.S.-China Business Council and as a member of the Emergency Committee for American Trade. Henry Kissinger also served as chair of the America-China Society with cochair Cyrus Vance, former secretary of state under President Jimmy Carter.[19]

The 1996 case study of the renewal of China's most favored nation status gives one a sense of the American business community's role in support of the New China Lobby. Supporters of China include prestigious US Fortune 500 companies such as Boeing, Motorola, Caterpillar, AT&T, and AIG. The leading organization is the ad hoc Business Coalition for U.S.-China Trade. It is coordinated by the Emergency Committee on American Trade, a $1 trillion coalition of fifty-five major American companies with interests in China, including General Electric, Mobil, Exxon, United Technology, Phillip Morris, Proctor and Gamble, TWR, Westinghouse, and IBM. Boeing and other major businesses spent over $20 million hiring major lobbying firms, along with Henry Kissinger and Alexander Haig, as advisers for their pro-China lobbying campaign in 1996–97.[20] It has also used many former US government officials to help mold public opinion in op-ed articles, in public forums, and on television programs. The American China Lobby has manufactured numerous opinion pieces, briefing pieces, and reports and has saturated the press with these public relations products.[21] The American China Lobby also launched a massive grassroots effort to drum up support among thousands of small businesses whose fortunes were as tied to China as those of large US corporations. For instance, Boeing alone has 40,000 suppliers located in virtually every state.[22]

Also included in the Chinese grassroots lobbying were major peak umbrella organizations such as the National Association of Manufacturers, the U.S. Chamber of Commerce, and Business Roundtable and various trade associations, including the American Petroleum Institute, the Pharmaceutical Research and Manufacturing Association, and the Business Software Alliance. Finally, there is the U.S.-China Business Council consisting of 300 members including firms in the financial, defense, pharmaceutical, automobile, financial services, retail, high-tech, and many other sectors. In total, an estimated 700 American businesses participated in the lobbying efforts, and their PACs contributed $20 million to members of Congress. The various parts of the China Lobby targeted 103 members of Congress and claimed that 101 of these voted in favor of China.[23]

Clearly, in future trade and other economic conflicts in the coming years, the Chinese will be using a mix of professional lobbying firms and powerful American businesses that have or desire to have profitable relationships with China.

The New China Lobby has had more trouble mobilizing the Chinese-American community than the India Lobby has had in mobilizing the Indian-American community.[24] Chinese-Americans have been quiet on foreign policy, lacking a policy around which they can mobilize. "China is not threatened, and unlike Cuban Americans, most Chinese Americans do not see themselves as political exiles and do not push for the overthrow of the communist government. Moreover, Chinese Americans are divided over whether to promote trade with China or to pressure Beijing to improve its human rights record."[25] Paul and Paul do not even rank the PRC ethnic lobby in the United States, but they rank highly the Indian-American and Taiwan-American ethnic lobbies.[26]

When Chinese leaders see their country portrayed on covers of Newsweek as a dragon attacking the symbol of America and books such as Martin Jacques's *When China Rules the World*,[27] which discusses the dangers of the rise of modern China, China's response has been to upgrade the various parts of its lobbying operation in the United States to counter such images and possible American legislative responses. In the fall of 2010, the Obama administration made clear that it was leading a new coalition domestically and internationally that believed China to be a threat to their various interests. "Administration officials speak of an alarming loss of trust and confidence between China and the United States over the past two years."[28]

The rise of China's economy has provided the New China Lobby with enough financial resources to hire the top lobbyists in Washington and provide campaign contributions to gain access to members of Congress and the executive branch. In the most-favored-nation lobbying battle, not only did China have Kissinger and Associates on its side but three of the best lobbyist firms in Washington: Hogan & Hartson; Patton Boggs, Hill & Knowlton; and Manatt, Phelps & Phillips. Nancy Pelosi (D-CA), who would become Speaker of the House, estimated that the China Lobby was spending over $20 million in PAC contributions to members of Congress.[29]

The lobbying blitz was described by one lawmaker, Rep. Frank Wolf (R-VA), as bordering on a "feeding frenzy of lawyers."[30] Beginning in the winter of 1994, lobbyists swarmed over Washington. They conducted briefing sessions at the capitol and brought corporate executives to Capitol Hill to personally lobby lawmakers. They mobilized letter-writing campaigns. And they distributed studies that purported to show the high cost to the American economy of revoking most favored nation status for China.[31]

The type of pressure brought to bear was illustrated at a House Ways and Means subcommittee hearing in February 1994, when one corporate speaker after another warned of the "devastating consequences" if most favored nation status were revoked. Typical of the alarms sounded was one issued by Mattel Vice President Fermin Cuza: higher import duties would have a "severe impact" on American importers, some of whom "would be quickly forced out of business." Higher tariffs, he added, would "raise retail prices by approximately 25 percent, at a minimum, [and] also put at risk many of the 32,000 U.S. jobs in the U.S. toy industry."[32] As noted above, Chinese lobbying often used small business suppliers for the big US corporations to generate grassroots support for China. These small business efforts were organized state by state by the major companies (e.g., Boeing in Washington State, Motorola in Illinois and Texas, etc.).[33] The New China Lobby was also able to count on the White House for support in the lobbying battles of the 1990s. The Clinton White House established a China Trade Relations Working Group Command Center with 150 staffers to support the China trade-lobbying effort.[34] In addition to help from the US multinationals, China fielded its own impressive professional lobbying team. The Washington office of Cleveland's Jones, Day, Reavis & Pogue, the nation's third-largest law firm, represented the Chinese embassy. The Washington office of Mudge Rose Guthrie Alexander & Ferdon, the New York law firm of former President Nixon, represented the China National Import/Export Corporation. Rollins International, the consulting company of Edward Rollins, former aide to Ronald Reagan and GOP political consultant, was the registered foreign agent for the China Chamber of International Commerce and the municipality of Nanjing, China.[35]

One set of numbers shows how far China has come in the lobbying game. In 1970, China did not have a single lobbyist in Washington, D.C. Today, no fewer than nineteen law firms and consultants, many of them representing multiple Chinese clients, have registered as foreign agents for China. And that number does not include the US multinationals who can be called on when needed. [36]

China's "soft power" lobby in the United States and around the world has been lodged in the Confucian Institutes program it created in 2004. China had established 316 Confucian Institutes by 2010 and planned to establish 1,000 by 2020. The Confucian Institutes are located in universities in over 75 nations and had taught the Chinese language and Chinese history to over 100 million students. In the United States, Confucian Institutes are located at a growing number of prestigious universities, including the University of Michigan, Michigan State University, Texas A & M University, University of California–Los Angeles, University of Chicago, University of Washington, University of Oregon, University of Utah, and University of Massachusetts. The Chinese government approaches a prospective university with a financial offer to create a Confucian Institute to assist the university in its Chinese Studies program. The University of Utah, for example, receives $100,000 for its Confucian Institute and indirect promises for additional funds if programs warrant it.

To get a sense of the "heavyweights" of the American business world who have signed on to support the American China Lobby, take a look at recent members of the U.S.-China Business Council (USCBC). The board of directors of the organization in June 2008 announced that its new chair would be Andrew Liveris, CEO of Dow Chemical. Dow has a long-term and increasing presence in China, with ten manufacturing plants in China and plans to build more. Other officers elected to the USCBC board included the CEO of Coca-Cola, the CEO of 3M, a senior vice president of Exxon Mobil, a vice chair of General Electric, and the president of global operations at Dell. As one lobbying expert noted, "Corporate America has done a good job unofficially representing the Chinese government in Washington."[37] Chinese political leaders decided that Beijing's interests would be better served by allowing US business groups to speak for them: "The New China Lobby is indeed, the U.S.-China Lobby."[38] This Chinese-paid public relations operation is willingly carried out by corporate America. The potential profits can be so huge for American businesses in China that they are willing to act as players on the Chinese lobbying team in Washington when needed.[39]

The New China Lobby has also effectively used the Chinese branches of American companies operating in China such as the American Chamber of Commerce (AmCham) of Hong Kong, which sends a sizable group of businesspeople each year to Washington, D.C., to "door knock" at congressional offices.[40] Daniel Drezer, writing in *Foreign Policy* in 2010, noted that "were it not for the power of big business, the relationship between the US and China might have gone sour years ago. . . . US multinationals . . . have made the argument that a stronger and more prosperous China is good for America."[41]

In the 2000s, individual Chinese corporations finally realized that they too had to hire professional lobbying firms to protect their interests in Washington, D.C. The Bank of China, for example, hired Public Strategies for $85,000 a month to help its initial public offering (IPO) sales in the United States. The city government of Beijing contracted with the famous Republican public relations firm Hill & Knowlton to promote the 2008 Beijing Olympics. Other Chinese companies have also hired in-house lobbyists and outside firms to represent them.[42]

The Chinese have also learned the hard way that hiring big-name lobbying firms does not always guarantee success. The failed attempt to buy Unocal by China National Offshore Oil Corporation followed a $3 million expenditure for a ninety-six-member team from Akin Gump Strauss Hauer & Feld. Most lobbying experts concluded the failure was the result of starting far too late and allowing the opposition to organize itself before lobbying began.[43]

Evaluating the Influence of the New China Lobby

Clearly, the PRC's lobby in Washington, D.C., has come a long way from its starting days in the early 1970s. But has it reached the heights of lobbying influence long reserved for the Israel and Cuba lobbies? Not yet, because according to the Congressional Research Service, China is not one of the top ten countries lobbying in Washington.[44] Eric Uslaner has written a chapter on foreign lobbies for several editions of this book and has never listed the PRC lobby as one of the most influential.[45] In one respect, the New China Lobby has been lucky in its opponents. The general anti-Chinese lobby on the business and trade issue battles has been composed of anti-communist groups, religious groups who engage in foreign policy issues, the AFL-CIO, and human rights groups. With corporate America largely on the Chinese side, the lobbying battles, while interesting, have been somewhat one-sided, with China winning all the recent fights.[46]

While China has had great support from the American business community, mobilizing the American business lobby after 2010 may be more difficult after the challenges American companies Google, Goldman Sachs, and General Electric have encountered in China. Recently, more and more American businesses are becoming aware that the roles played by the Chinese government in the PRC business environment are not the same roles that the US government and other Western governments play in their respective countries.[47] Additionally, it has been quite a while since the

American China Lobby has had to be fully mobilized. The last big China lobbying battle was over China's accession to the World Trade Organization in 2001.

Another recent change that may reduce the effectiveness of the New China Lobby has been a greater congressional assertion of its role in the trade policy-making process. Rather than dealing with Congress, China would prefer to cut deals behind closed doors with the executive branch. It opened to the Americans in 1972 based on secret meetings with Henry Kissinger long before a public announcement of the move toward normalization of relations with the United States, and China is still much more comfortable working behind the scenes than in an open lobbying-type campaign.

Asian Challengers to the New China Lobby

A battle is emerging among the rising powers of Asia for influence in Washington, D.C. India and China are the world's two most populous countries, both with well over one billion people each. They are also two of the great economic success stories of recent decades. In addition, one-time lobbying heavyweight, Japan, still has clout, and rising power South Korea is now one of the top ten economies in the world and is very comfortable establishing a powerful diplomatic, economic, and cultural lobby in the United States.

India was basically a nonactor in the Washington, D.C., lobbying game until recently. For decades, India was viewed by American politicians as leaning toward the Soviet Union and against America's ally Pakistan, India's longtime enemy with whom it fought three wars as well as seemingly constant border skirmishes. The relationship began to change after 9/11, as the United States gradually became aware of Pakistan's growing instability, India's tremendous economic growth, and the possibility of India becoming an Asian counterweight to China.

The India Lobby has largely consisted of Indian expatriots and some friendly members of Congress. India had run its lobbying in Washington on a very low budget. The India Caucus in Congress has about 180 members, but only a small number are active. Many joined the caucus to get access to financial contributions from the growing Indian business community in the United States. Others joined for pro-Israel, anti-China, or anti-Pakistan reasons and not necessarily to support India or India's political issues in America.[48]

In 2005, the Embassy of India fired its longtime lobbying firm and Washington powerhouse, Akin, Gump, Strauss, Hauer & Feld, and replaced it with the Republican firm of Barbour, Griffith & Rogers. The decision to fire Akins was because of its failure to stop an arms sale to Pakistan.

The India Lobby really emerged during the 2005 congressional debates over American sales of nuclear technology and reactor-quality enriched uranium to India.[49] The George W. Bush administration fought hard for this agreement with India, and with the help of strong American business lobbies, which also rallied to support the Indian agreement, the agreement finally won approval. What emerged from the "nuclear technology transfer" lobbying campaign was a much more professionalized and well-funded "India lobby" on Capitol Hill that clearly demonstrated its lobbying clout. Many expect this restructuring of the India Lobby to signal its emergence as one of the most important ethnic communities seeking influence over US foreign policy in the twenty-first century.

The India Lobby's recent successes have been the result of both the lobbying done by the Indian government and especially its embassy in Washington, D.C., as well as the professional lobbying firms it has retained and the mobilization of the American Indian community to politically support Indian political objectives. In this respect, the Indian community has proven to be somewhat similar to the American Jewish community. Existing scholarly literature on ethnic lobbies and American foreign policy typically focuses on communities such as Jewish Americans and Cuban Americans and argues that wealth, geographic concentration, and group cohesion are important factors explaining ethnic lobby influence in the US foreign policy process. Indian Americans as a community broadly fit the first two criteria, but until very recently they were highly segmented into particular professional and Indian language/regional associations and were largely ignored in the ethnic lobby literature. Recently, though, the community has become more unified and politically mobilized, with potentially important implications for US policy in South Asia, the broader Asian region, and the world.[50]

Another way to evaluate nations' lobbies is to look at "soft-power" lobbying resources (i.e., students studying in a nation and a wide variety of cultural institutions and exchanges). The number of 2009–10 foreign students studying in the United States indicates that the soft-power resources of both China and India have grown in recent years while Japan's have continued to erode. The number of Chinese students studying in post–high school institutions in the United States rose to 127,600—an increase of 36 percent over 2009. There were 104,900 Indian students and only 24,800 Japanese students. The Japanese total represented a drop of 15.1 percent from 2009—the largest drop among the twenty-five nations surveyed. As recently as 1994–98, Japanese students were the largest number of students studying in the United States, but their numbers peaked in 1997–98 at 47,000.[51]

As much as the India Lobby would like to see its recent victories as concrete evidence of its own power, one must see the successes more as a reflection of growing anti-Chinese feelings in the United States. Without doubt, India and Indian concerns are now much better represented in the hallways of American politics, but the India Lobby is still a relatively new lobby and not yet one of the established foreign powerhouses on the American lobbying scene.

In terms of PAC contributions and reported lobbying expenditures, only the Indian Americans and Taiwan Americans have much of a presence.[52] Of the two, only the Indian American lobby is considered to be effective in Washington. The PRC has never been able to organize a non-corporate American lobbying branch, and the Japanese-American community has simply dropped out of the lobbying game on foreign policy issues.

When one surveys the major Asian lobbies that operate in Washington, clearly the Chinese and Indian lobbies are on the rise, and the old lobbying power that was Japan has greatly declined. No longer can American scholars and media focus on the Israel Lobby as the only major foreign operation in town. The New China and India Lobbies are well organized, well funded, and serious about playing a major role in future policy discussions in the United States.

The Decline of the Japan Lobby—the Previous "Big Asian Lobby"

In the 1980s, the big Asian lobby operating in Washington, D.C., was the Japan Lobby. We have written about the Japan Lobby in previous editions of this book, and its power was considerable.[53] When trade wars loomed in the 1980s, Japan purchased the services of some of the biggest, most influential, and most costly law firms, lobbying firms, public relations firms, and think tanks in the city. To be on the Japan payroll at that time was a very lucrative place to be. But when Japan went into a two-decades-long economic tailspin following the crash of the Japanese stock market and real estate bubbles in 1990, it drastically cut back on its lobbying in Washington. Not only was the Japanese lobbying corps sharply reduced, but Japan's soft-power diplomacy lost its leading-edge presence among Asian countries, especially as compared to the emerging Chinese Confucian Institutes and the Korean Foundations. Suddenly, the once unchallenged Japan Foundation and other Japanese cultural organizations found themselves as also-rans in the game of soft-power diplomatic efforts. Japan was being outspent and out-organized in the intellectual and public opinion molding battles by its major Asian rivals.

The decline of Japan in relative economic terms and the rise of China have changed the political game in Washington, D.C., to such a degree that it is now very difficult to find much of a Japanese presence there, but Chinese money and programs are everywhere. The decline of Japanese influence is also a function of the relative decline of Japanese-Americans in the United States due to changes in immigration patterns and a large increase in the Chinese-American population. In San Francisco, for example, the ratio of Chinese-Americans to Japanese-Americans used to be 3.6 to 1; now it is 12 to 1.[54] Kent Calder, director of the Reischauer Institute at Johns Hopkins University, warns that Japan must adequately fund the academic study of Japan in the United States; otherwise, Japan will continue to be over-shadowed by its Asian competitors.[55]

Conflicts between the United States and Japan on trade, currency issues, investment, and military issues all have been solved or downgraded to the point that they can be managed without the help of massive represen-tation in the D.C. lobbying world. Significant conflicts now involve China and its economic and military rise in East Asia as well as its growing world-wide search for raw materials and markets. In the twenty-first century, the major law firms, lobbying firms, public relations firms, and think tanks are receiving contracts to represent the Chinese government and corporations. There has been a fundamental change in the rankings of Asian lobbies oper-ating in the United States, and this is now the era of the New China Lobby.

Foreign Lobbying Power in Washington

One of the keys to success for a foreign nation's lobbying efforts in the United States has been the ability to organize and implement a domestic lobbying campaign that uses Americans with identities associated with the lobbying nation. Paul and Paul, in their 2009 book on ethnic foreign lobbies in the United States, argue that such lobbies are based on four domestic characteristics: size and geographical distribution of the ethnic population, a certain level of ethnic integration into the American society, continued identification with the country of origin, and the existence of an issue of such magnitude that it focuses the attention and energy of the ethnic population. Paul and Paul's research produced a long list of lobbies but found that very few are able to combine the characteristics needed to pro-duce an effective American-based ethnic lobby. Those that do are also on the list of the most powerful foreign lobbies in the United States: Israel, Cuba, Ireland, and Armenia. The PRC does not make the list of most influ-ential ethnic lobbies in foreign policy making. The China lobby that is on this list represents Taiwan. In fact, only three Asian ethnic US lobbies seem to be particularly active in foreign policy issues: Indian Americans, Korean Americans, and Taiwanese Americans.[56]

The Rise and Fall and Rise of the China Lobby

The China Lobby has been part of the American lobbying scene for the past 150 years in one manifestation or another. It has had four distinct forms: (1) an early nineteenth-century American business lobby that was interested in the China trade; (2) a Chinese and American Old China Lobby that formed after the Nationalist Revolution in 1911 and lasted until the 1949 triumph of Mao and the Red Army; (3) the Nationalist Chinese Lobby representing the government that moved to Taiwan in 1949, which became the Taiwan China Lobby representing the anti-Communist Chinese; and (4) the lobby that represents the People's Republic of China's Communist regime. The first lobby was very successful in getting the American government to protect its goal of maximizing the opening of China to international business and opening Japan to support the China trade. The Nationalist China Lobby in its two forms (1911–1949 and 1949 to the present) effectively rallied American support for Chiang Kai-shek and the Nationalist regime against the Japanese and the Communists. Finally, the New China Lobby is effectively representing the People's Republic of China.

The rise and fall and then rise again of the China Lobby is the story of a rising power in Asia and its need to deal with the world's superpower. The PRC's and, to a much lesser degree, Taiwan's lobbying efforts represent the recent rise of China as a world economic superpower. The China Lobbies of the nineteenth and twentieth centuries represented hundreds of millions of Chinese, a huge potential market to be exploited, but today's China not only represents over a billion Chinese but its recent accumulation of wealth and growth of military power. The big difference today is that Asia has multiple formidable lobbies in Washington; not only the Japanese, as in past decades, but now the Japanese, Chinese, and Indians with other rising nations such as South Korea and Pakistan attempt to exercise influence. The Asian Lobby in the United States is newly powerful and diverse.

Notes

1. Quoted by Piers Brendon, *International Herald Tribune*, August 23, 2010.
2. Sherrod Brown, "For Our China Trade Emergency, Dial Section 301," *New York Times*, October 17, 2010, http://www.nytimes.com/2010/10/18/opinion/18brown.html; *The Economist*, February 6, 2010, front cover.
3. David W. Chen, "China Emerges as Scapegoat in Campaign Ads," *New York Times*, October 9, 2010, http://www.nytimes.com/2010/10/10/us/politics/10outsource.html.
4. Robert Kapp, quoted in Chen, "China Emerges as a Scapegoat in Campaign Ads."
5. Paul Krugman, "Taking On China," *New York Times*, March 14, 2010, http://www.nytimes.com/2010/03/15/opinion/15krugman.html.
6. *Economist*, "China Buys Up the World," November 11, 2010, http://www.economist.com/node/17463473/.
7. John Miershiemer and Stephen Walt, "The Israel Lobby," *London Review of Books* 28, no. 6, (2006): 3–12, http://www.lrb.co.uk/v28/n06/john-mearsheimer/the-israel-lobby/.
8. Robert E. Herzstein, *Henry R. Luce,* Time, *and the American Crusade in Asia* (Cambridge, UK: Cambridge University Press, 2006).

9. Taiwan Relations Act, Pub. L 98–8, 93 (1979), sec. 2(b)(4–6). Available at http://usinfo.org/docs/basic/tra_e.htm.
10. Judy Sarasohn, "Lobby Shop Forges Ties with Taiwan," *Washington Post*, June 26, 2003.
11. John Newhouse, "Diplomacy, Inc.: The Influence of Lobbies on U.S. Foreign Policy," *Foreign Affairs* (May/June 2009): 90.
12. Newhouse, "Diplomacy, Inc.," 91.
13. Newhouse, "Diplomacy, Inc.," 91.
14. Richard H. Solomon, *Chinese Negotiating Behavior: Pursuing Interests Through "Old Friends,"* with an interpretative essay by Charles W. Freeman Jr. (Washington, DC: United States Institute of Peace Press, 1999).
15. Elizabeth C. Economy and Adam Segal, "The G-2 Mirage: Why the United States and China are Not Ready to Upgrade Ties," *Foreign Affairs* (May–June, 2009): 14.
16. Sourcewatch, "Kissinger McLarty Associates," http://www.sourcewatch.org/index.php?title=Kissinger_McLarty_Associates/.
17. *International Herald Tribune*, "Kissinger Warns of Future U.S.-Chinese Confrontations," September 14, 2010, http://www.nytimes.com/2010/09/13/world/europe/13geneva.html.
18. *Harper's Magazine*, "Harper's Index," May 1997, http://www.harpers.org/harpers-index/.
19. William F. Jasper, "China's Man in America," *The New American*, October 8, 2001; Robert Dreyfuss, "The New China Lobby: Who Bought American Indulgence of China? Surprise—Multinational Corporations that Fly the U.S. Flag," *The American Prospect*, January 1, 1997, http://prospect.org/cs/articles?article=the_new_china_lobby_1197/.
20. Les Blumenthal, "Boeing Lobbies for China: Plane Maker Has Billions at Stake in Trade Status Issue," *Rocky Mountain News* (Denver), May 11, 1997.
21. Ian Urbina, "The Corporate PNTR Lobby: How Big Business is Paying Millions to Gain Billions in China," *Multinational Monitor* 21, no. 5 (2000): 7–11, http://www.multinationalmonitor.org/mm2000/052000/urbina.html. See also Xiaowei Chen, "Engineering the Continuation of a Non-Judgmental United States–China Relationship in the Tumultuous Post–Cold War World: An Overview of the 1990s Chinese Public Relations Campaign in the United States," *Journal of Promotion Management* 14, nos. 3 and 4 (2008): 327–53, doi:10.1080/10496490802632334.
22. Blumenthal, "Boeing Lobbies for China."
23. Ken Silverstein, "The New China Hands," *The Nation*, February 17, 1997.
24. John Newhouse, "Diplomacy, Inc."
25. James M. Lindsay, "Getting Uncle Sam's Ear: Will Ethnic Lobbies Cramp America's Foreign Policy Style," *Brookings* (Winter 2002), http://www.brookings.edu/articles/2002/winter_diplomacy_lindsay.aspx.
26. David M. Paul and Rachel Anderson Paul, *Ethnic Lobbies and U.S. Foreign Policy*, (Boulder, CO: Lynne Rienner, 2008).
27. Martin Jacques, *When China Rules the World: The End of the Western World and the Birth of a New Global Order* (New York: Penguin Press, 2009). See also *Economist*, "Facing Up to China," February 4, 2010, http://www.economist.com/node/15452821 /.
28. Mark Landler and Sewell Chan, "Taking Harder Stance toward China, Obama Lines Up Allies," *International Herald Tribune*, October 27, 2010, http://www.nytimes.com/2010/10/26/world/asia/26china.html.
29. *The Nation*, February 17, 1997.

30. Center for Responsive Politics, cited in Dreyfuss, "The New China Lobby"; also see Donald L. Barlett and James B. Steele, "Most Favored Lobby: China Gets What It Wants the Old-Fashioned Way," *Washington Monthly*, December 1, 1996.
31. Barlett and Steele, "Most Favored Lobby."
32. Dreyfuss, "The New China Lobby."
33. Chen, "Engineering the Continuation of a Non-Judgmental United States–China Relationship."
34. David Ho, "White House Lobbies for the China Trade," APOnline, May 10, 2000, http://www.highbeam.com/doc/1P1–26537611.html.
35. Dreyfuss, "The New China Lobby."
36. Barlett and Steele, "Most Favored Lobby."
37. Dreyfuss, "The New China Lobby."
38. Dreyfuss, "The New China Lobby."
39. Chen, "Engineering the Continuation of a Non-Judgmental United States–China Relationship."
40. Jing Zhong, "New China Lobby and Sino-US Relations in the 1990s," Institutional Reposit, Hong Kong University of Science (1999), http://hdl.handle.net/1783.1/5523/.
41. Daniel W. Drezer, "The Death of the China Lobby?" *Foreign Policy*, July 20, 2010, http://drezner.foreignpolicy.com/posts/2010/07/20/the_death_of_the_china_lobby/.
42. Li Xin and Wang Feng, "China Lobby Curries Favor with U.S. Government," *Caijing Magazine*, August 7, 2006, http://english.caijing.com.cn/2006–08–07/100014037.html.
43. Xin and Feng, "China Lobby Curries Favor with U.S. Government."
44. J. Zhang and G. T. Cameron, "China's Agenda Building and Image Polishing in the U.S.: Assessing an International Public Relations Campaign. *Public Relations Review*. 29, no. 1 (2003): 13–28, doi:10.1016/S0363–8111(02)00198–4.
45. Eric Uslaner, "American Interests in the Balance? Do Ethnic Groups Dominate Foreign Policy Making?," in *Interest Group Politics*, 7th ed., eds. Allan Cigler and Burdett Loomis (Washington, DC: CQ Press, 2007): 302–21. Also see Ronald Hrebenar, Valerie Ploumpis, and Clive Thomas, "What Happened to the Japanese Lobby in Washington? The Decline of the Japan Lobby and the Rise of the New China Lobby" in *Interest Group Politics*, 7th ed., eds. Allan Cigler and Burdett Loomis (Washington, DC: CQ Press, 2007): 322–39.
46. Chen, "Engineering the Continuation of a Non-Judgmental United States–China Relationship."
47. Drezer, "The Death of the China Lobby?"
48. Ramtanu Maitra, "China's Shadow Over India's U.S. Lobby," *Asian Times*, September 13, 2005, http://www.atimes.com/atimes/South_Asia/GI13Df01.html.
49. Mira Kamdar, "Forget the Israel Lobby: The Hill's Next Big Player is Made in India," *Washington Post*, September 30, 2007. See also Maitra, "China's Shadow Over India's U.S. Lobby."
50. Paul and Paul, *Ethnic Lobbies and U.S. Foreign Policy*, 137.
51. *Asahi Shimbun*, December 6, 2010.
52. *Asahi Shimbun*, December 6, 2010, 72 and 96.
53. Ronald J. Hrebenar, Valerie Ploumpis, and Clive S. Thomas, "What Happened to the Japanese Lobby in Washington? The Decline of the Japanese Lobby and the Rise of the New China Lobby," in *Interest Group Politics*, 7th ed., eds. Allan J. Cigler

and Burdett A. Loomis (Washington, DC: CQ Press, 2006): 322–39; Ronald J. Hrebenar and Clive S. Thomas, "The Japanese Lobby in Washington: How Different Is It?" in *Interest Group Politics*, 4th ed., ed. Allan J. Cigler and Burdett A. Loomis (Washington, DC: CQ Press, 1995): 349–67.

54. *Asahi Shimbun*, December 6, 2010.
55. Kent E. Calder, *Pacific Alliance: Reviving U.S.-Japan Relations* (New Haven, CT: Yale University Press, 2009).
56. Paul and Paul, *Ethnic Lobbies and U.S. Foreign Policy*, 38.

14

Ethnic Interest Groups and American Foreign Policy

A Growing Influence?

James M. McCormick

In March 2010, the House Committee on Foreign Affairs narrowly passed H.R. 252 by a vote of 23–22 and sent the resolution to the full House for its consideration.[1] The nonbinding resolution called upon the president to acknowledge the Armenian genocide of 1915 by Turkey. Three years earlier, the same resolution had passed the Committee by a larger margin, 27–21, but failed to reach a vote on the House floor.[2] The Armenian Assembly and the Armenian National Committee of America, the key interest groups of the Armenian community in the United States, supported and lobbied for the 2007 and 2010 resolutions. Both resolutions elicited a large number of cosponsors from members of the House of Representatives, 143 for the 2010 resolution and 212 for the 2007 one. These two resolutions also sparked intense lobbying by Turkish interests, both within the United States and from abroad. The 2007 resolution "pitted Turkey's money and high-placed connections against a persistent and emotional campaign by Armenian-American citizens' groups,"[3] and the 2010 resolution stimulated "a full-page ad in *The Washington Post*" by Turkish groups and a visit of eight Turkish parliamentarians to Capitol Hill over the impending Committee vote.[4]

Yet these resolutions caused more than just a clash between domestic interest groups and foreign lobbies on both sides of the issue; they also caused foreign policy difficulties between United States and Turkey. Just prior to the 2010 committee vote, for instance, Turkish president Abdullah Gul called President Obama, apparently to seek his help in stopping this resolution, and Turkey subsequently recalled its ambassador to the United States in protest when the resolution passed in the Foreign Affairs Committee. Turkish interests also made veiled threats about further disruption in US-Turkish relations as a result of the passage of this resolution.[5] In all, these nonbinding resolutions, advocated and opposed by competing ethnic interest groups, had the potential to disrupt foreign relations between the United States and Turkey.

To be sure, the Armenian and Turkish lobbies are relatively small in comparison to the size of other ethnic lobbies, and the nonbinding resolution may have had more symbolic than substantive effect on foreign policy. Yet this episode exemplifies how organized and mobilized ethnic interest groups can affect foreign policy debate at home and may disrupt relations abroad. Is this the case for other ethnic groups as well, or is this an isolated instance of ethnic and foreign lobbies involved in US foreign policy making? Indeed, are other ethnic and foreign lobbies more consequential for the foreign policy process?

In this chapter, we address these and related questions in an effort to assess the role of ethnic interest groups in affecting the American foreign policy process. To put this discussion in a larger context, our point of departure is to identify the number and type of foreign policy interest groups at the present time. Next, we evaluate several ethnic interest groups that have operated for some time and have had an impact on American foreign policy over the years. Then we turn to identifying and assessing the potential role of several new and emerging ethnic groups that have become active more recently. With all of these groups, we utilize several criteria to evaluate their effectiveness and judge their relative impact on US foreign policy. We conclude by considering the overall influence of these kinds of interest groups on the conduct of American foreign policy.

Number and Types of Foreign Policy Interest Groups

The types of interest groups active in foreign policy today are indeed numerous, but identifying the precise number is difficult to do for several interrelated reasons. As the foreign policy agenda of the United States has expanded from its traditional emphasis on security concerns to encompass economic, environmental, and social issues, foreign policy interest groups have grown exponentially. As this agenda has expanded, the decision-making arena of foreign policy has as well. Now more policy making involves Congress and the executive branch—and more foreign policy interest groups as well. Because such groups often form, lobby, and then disband, it is difficult to track their exact number at any particular time. Finally, and importantly, we have no single accounting mechanism or reporting requirement to identify the number or types of these foreign policy interest groups; instead, we necessarily must rely upon estimates from a variety of sources.

When we do that, the estimates of interest groups vary widely. One estimate, now a decade old, judged that there were about 11,000 firms or groups lobbying in Washington, D.C., and these firms employed about 17,000 individuals to seek to influence the policy process. Another estimate, based upon the growth of nongovernmental organizations (NGOs) worldwide, placed the number anywhere from 5,600 to 25,000 and even to 100,000 such groups.[6] These interest groups or NGOs are surely not all concerned with foreign policy (although the line is blurring between domestic and foreign policy concerns for many lobbying groups). In all, whatever the exact number, these estimates illustrate how numerous and pervasive such groups have become today and thus their potential to affect foreign policy.

As the number of foreign policy interest groups has increased in recent decades, the types of such groups have as well. Foreign policy interest groups include some traditional lobbying groups, such as business groups, labor unions, and agricultural interests, with their principal focus being on international trade issues (although increasingly these groups take stances on a broad array of other foreign policy concerns as well), and they now also include several newer groups that are active on foreign policy. These groups include religious communities, veterans' organizations, academic think tanks, ideological organizations (such as Americans for Democratic Action [ADA]), and single-issue interest groups (e.g., United Nations Association of the United States, Union of Concerned Scientists, and Americans against Escalation in Iraq).

Yet this listing does not include arguably the oldest foreign policy lobby, ethnic interest groups. Ethnic groups, or those groups of Americans who hold a particular concern for US policy toward the particular country or region of their own or their ancestors' origin, are not only the oldest foreign policy lobby but, in many ways, often turn out to be the most influential. In important ways, too, these ethnic groups are often tied to foreign country lobbies or to those groups that directly lobby the American government on behalf of another nation. (As a result of these international linkages, the US government may sometimes subject American ethnic groups to extra scrutiny to make certain that they are in compliance with the strictures in the Foreign Agents Registration Act[7] and are not acting as foreign agents of another government.) These foreign lobbies, moreover, are increasingly numerous and consequential, and they often complement the work of ethnic groups. Foreign country lobbies can appeal to American ethnic groups that share their views on a particular issue to broaden their level of support, and ethnic groups can gain support from foreign lobbies (and particularly their domestic representatives) for aid in making their case to Congress or the executive branch on a particular issue. Note, for example, in the case of the Armenian genocide resolution that both Turkish domestic groups and Turkish parliamentarians simultaneously worked to affect the outcome. In this sense, although we now turn to focus on several key ethnic groups, we will also consider the foreign lobbies that may assist them.

Principal Ethnic Lobbies

Although ethnic lobbies are increasingly numerous today, the level of activism and effectiveness by individual lobbies varies. Traditionally, Americans of Jewish, Irish, and Eastern European heritage have been the most active ethnic lobbies on foreign policy.[8] Over the past several decades, however, Americans of African, Arab, Armenian, Cuban, Greek, Hispanic, Mexican, and Turkish descent have been increasingly active on foreign policy issues as well. Recently, yet another group, Indian-Americans, has become more involved in the foreign policy process. For these interest groups, their principal foreign policy concern is American policy toward the country or region of their origin. Hence, Jewish-Americans are most often concerned with US policy toward Israel, Irish-Americans toward Ireland, Cuban-Americans toward Cuba, and so on. Because of their singular focus on policy toward a particular country or region, these individual ethnic groups tend to be highly motivated in their lobbying efforts, and that level of motivation often proves crucial in their success in obtaining their preferred policy from the American government. To be sure, some ethnic groups are more successful than others, and we discuss those first. With all of the ethnic groups that we discuss, we will identify several factors that account for their relative success as compared to others.

The Jewish Lobby

By virtually all assessments, the Jewish lobby or the Israel lobby is perhaps the most influential ethnic lobby today, with the preponderance of its attention on issues related to the state of Israel and to the Middle East more generally. The Jewish lobby has been described as a "loose coalition of individuals and organizations that actively work to shape U.S. policy in a pro-Israel direction."[9] This lobby has two umbrella organizations that coordinate its activities, the Conference of Presidents of Major American Jewish Organizations and the American-Israel Public Affairs Committee (AIPAC), but AIPAC is usually the organization most often identified with Jewish lobbying efforts. AIPAC has a relatively large membership at about 100,000 activists,[10] has "a network of 10 regional offices and nine satellite offices,"[11] and has a large and effective staff in its Washington, D.C., office. AIPAC also provides a variety of services to its members in an effort to stimulate grassroots support for key issues. The organization's Web site, for example, provides a wealth of information that would allow its members to participate in the foreign policy process: a summary of key issues under consideration by Congress, a congressional directory to facilitate those who want to contact their representatives, numerous policy statements on issues important to the organization, and a list of its policy achievements.[12] Furthermore, the Web site contains direct links, or buttons, for Capitol Hill staffers and for the press as additional ways to get its message out. Finally, and interestingly, AIPAC proudly exclaims its policy effectiveness: "The most important organization affecting America's relationship with Israel"—a descriptor provided by the *New York Times* some years ago.

The Jewish lobby, and AIPAC in particular, has indeed been successful in affecting the direction of American foreign policy toward Israel and the Middle East more generally over the years. AIPAC has largely been able to garner widespread support for legislation that it favors or stop legislation that it opposes. In the 1970s, for example, it was able to obtain seventy-six Senate cosponsors for the Jackson-Vanik Amendment to the Trade Act of 1974 that prohibited most-favored-nation (MFN) status to any state without a free emigration policy—a bill focused on the Soviet Union's restriction on Jewish emigration at the time. In the same decade, it also obtained seventy-six senators to sign a letter urging President Ford to support Israel in any peace effort in the Middle East. In the 1980s, AIPAC was instrumental in forcing the Reagan administration to alter the composition of an arms sale to Saudi Arabia, and, in 1988, Saudi Arabia purchased $30 billion in arms from Britain rather than deal with congressional opposition from supporters of Israel.[13] Currently, AIPAC points to several specific legislative actions to demonstrate the effectiveness of its lobbying: "passing more than a dozen bills and resolutions condemning and imposing tough sanctions on Iran," supporting numerous resolutions passed in Congress that "affirm[ed] congressional support for Israel's right to self-defense," and promoting legislation "requiring the administration to evaluate all future military sales to Arab states in the context of the need to maintain Israel's qualitative military edge over potential adversaries."[14] Through the past several decades, the level of congressional support for Israel has rarely wavered and has been at extraordinarily high levels across party lines in Congress.[15] Undoubtedly the best single indicator of congressional support and AIPAC's policy success with that body has been that fact that Israel has continuously received the highest amount of US foreign assistance of any country over the past three decades—at about $3 billion annually.

What accounts for the success of this ethnic lobby—or indeed any ethnic lobby? After all, the number of Jewish-Americans, 6.2 million, constitutes less than 3 percent of America's population. How can this interest group seemingly be so influential? Political scientist Tony Smith in his *Foreign Attachments* begins to provide an answer for this group and others. Smith points to two general factors: the structure of the American political system and the characteristics of ethnic groups themselves.[16] The former factor refers to the pluralist nature of the American political system, which allows interest groups access to the governmental process, while the latter refer to specific resources that ethnic groups can use to affect the process. The access that these groups have, Smith argues, are "at the local, grassroots level of party selection of officeholders during primaries," "in the divisions that naturally open between the executive and the legislature" and in "the divisions within the legislature itself in Washington."[17] Although these points of access are obviously important, the ability of ethnic groups to take advantage of them is arguably even more crucial. Smith argues that to take advantage and thus gain influence, ethnic groups potentially possess three important resources: their ability to provide votes in key areas, their ability to make campaign contributions to office seekers, and their ability to organize and lobby on key issues.[18]

Applying these three criteria to the Jewish lobby, we begin to see how that lobby can be so effective. First, America's Jewish population tends to be concentrated in several key states. States along the East Coast (New York, New Jersey, Florida, and to a lesser extent Maryland and Massachusetts) tend to have large concentrations of Jewish voters, as do the states of California, Illinois, and Ohio. Further, and importantly, Jews tend to participate in the political process at a much higher rate than other groups in American society. As a result, presidential candidates will likely be sensitive to the interests of Jewish voters in these states, especially since these states have a large number of electoral votes and especially in years with closely contested national elections. Second, the Jewish community and pro-Israel lobbying groups provide a large amount of campaign funding for congressional and presidential elections. According to the Center for Responsive Politics, pro-Israel groups provided $13.8 million in campaign contributions in 2008, with 63 percent of those funds supporting Democratic candidates and 37 percent for Republican candidates.[19] (AIPAC does not directly make campaign contributions, but it has close ties with political action committees [PACs] that can be used to make such contributions.) Moreover, the support or opposition of pro-Israel groups can be—and has been—crucial in the electoral fortunes of political candidates. Two classic illustrations of the power of these groups were the reelection defeats of Senator Roger Jepsen (R-IA) and Senator Charles Percy (R-IL) in the 1980s. As a result, rarely would congressional candidates challenge American policy toward Israel, and it is rarer still that any major presidential party candidate would not commit to supporting Israel or current policy toward that country.

Third, and as we have already noted, AIPAC has an effective and efficient organizational structure operating within Washington, D.C. With its large contingent of activists nationwide, AIPAC is well positioned to elicit a grassroots response to the Congress and the executive branch at any time. Furthermore, AIPAC has effectively tied itself into the political decision-making network in Washington. One tangible, and important, indicator of its close linkage to the political leadership is the list of regular attendees and speakers at the annual AIPAC policy conferences. At the 2008 conference, for example, three presidential candidates—Hillary Clinton, Barack Obama, and John McCain—spoke, as did outgoing Secretary of State Condoleezza Rice. Furthermore, the principal leaders of the Congress—Speaker of the House Nancy Pelosi, House minority leader John Boehner, Senate majority leader Harry Reid, and Senate minority leader Mitch McConnell—made presentations. At the 2010 conference,

Secretary of State Hillary Clinton gave a plenary address summarizing the Obama administration's continued support for Israel, but the delegates also heard presentations by public officials from across the political spectrum: Senators Charles Schumer (D-NY), Lindsey Graham (R-SC), and Evan Bayh (D-IN); Governors Martin O'Malley (D-MD) and Tim Pawlenty (R-MN); and House Majority Leader Steny Hoyer (D-MD) and House Republican Whip Eric Cantor (R-VA).[20]

Another crucial factor contributes to the effectiveness of any ethnic group. The late Senator Charles McC. Mathias Jr. of Maryland identified that factor about three decades ago, albeit in an inverse way. "Foreign lobbies," he wrote, "that lack significant domestic support exert only limited influence on American foreign policy."[21] A lack of domestic support is hardly the case for the Jewish lobby. Among the American public, the level of support for Israel remains very high. In February 2010, 63 percent of the American public expressed more sympathy with the Israelis than with the Palestinians, and such high levels of support have generally been the case for the past twenty years of Gallup polling data.[22] Moral, ethical, and political considerations are the important reasons for this substantial support among the American public for Israel. The Jewish people are viewed as deserving a homeland in light of the suffering and persecution that they have endured over time, and the state of Israel is viewed as a democratic state in a region with very few. Furthermore, Israel has been and continues to be a strategic asset for the United States, both during the Cold War and afterward.

A final important factor that impacts the effectiveness of any ethnic group is the extent to which a countervailing ethnic group is active on similar foreign policy issues. (Recall the competition for influence between the Armenian lobby and the Turkish lobby in our earlier example and how that undoubtedly contributed to a very narrow division among members of Congress.) Three pro-Arab lobbies, the National Association of Arab Americans (NAAA) founded in 1972, the American-Arab Anti-Discrimination Committee (ADC) founded in 1980, and the Arab American Institute (AAI) founded in 1985, have tended to be much less effective than the Jewish lobby over the years and thus have not served as effective counterweights. Indeed, the NAAA and ADC merged in 2001, undoubtedly in an effort to increase their effectiveness.[23] The ADC now has an organizational structure that is similar to that of AIPAC with chapters throughout the nation, governmental and legal divisions, and a range of educational activities. AAI is a Washington-based organization that "strives to serve as a central resource to government officials, the media and community groups and a variety of public policy issues that concern Arab Americans and U.S.-Arab relations."[24] Nonetheless, these groups cannot be judged as being as effective as the pro-Israel lobby. Part of the difficulty for these groups, based upon our earlier criteria for an interest group's success in gaining influence, is the lack of an effective voting bloc among the American public to which they can directly appeal for support, the limited campaign contributions that these groups (or their PACs) provide in election campaigns, and the relatively low support for Arab states and the Palestinian Authority among the American people. In a February 2010 survey of American perceptions of favorability of twenty nations worldwide, several Middle East states were near the bottom of those rankings. Iraq, Yemen, the Palestinian Authority, and Iran received favorability rankings ranging from 23 percent (Iraq) down to 10 percent (Iran). In another survey at about the same time, only 15 percent of the American public expressed sympathy with the Palestinian Authority.[25] Perhaps the founder of ADC, former US Senator James Abourezk, best summarized the challenge facing his group and the Arab lobbies more generally: "To have influence in Congress you have to have money for candidates or control lots of votes. We're trying to build a grass-roots network; it's difficult for us to raise money."[26]

Despite the Jewish lobby's success, its influence is not without controversy. In a recent controversial article, and later book, two political scientists John Mearsheimer and Stephen Walt raised questions about this lobby's undue influence on American foreign policy.[27] In particular, they contend that the strength of the Israel lobby more fully accounts for American policy toward Israel than moral or strategic explanations by the public or its leaders, and they call for a more open discussion of the power of this particular ethnic lobby on American foreign policy. They do not argue that the lobby is "a cabal or a conspiracy or anything of the sort"; rather, they argue that "it is engaged in good old-fashioned interest group politics, which is as American as apple pie."[28] In this sense, however, they contend that the lobby is a legitimate subject for debate and examination within American politics. Their critique of the power of this lobby, however, set off a firestorm of reaction and criticism of their analyses.[29] More recently, another book, *Transforming America's Israel Lobby*, assessed an array of Jewish lobbies, including AIPAC, and argued that AIPAC did not wholly reflect the views of the American Jewish community.[30]

Indeed, AIPAC policy positions—which are often seen has too hardline and often wholly supportive of the Israeli government in power—has created a division within the Jewish community, and that division has now stimulated the emergence of an opposition group. In 2008, J Street was established. (The name is symbolic, not representative of an actual location. There is no "J Street" in Washington, and this group was formed to fill a void by providing a new voice on the Middle East.)[31] Its goals are to give a "political voice to mainstream American Jews and other supporters of Israel who . . . believe that a two-state solution to the Israeli-Palestinian conflict is essential to Israel's survival." The organization not only hopes to promote this policy position but also seeks "to ensure a broad debate on Israel and the Middle East in national politics and the American Jewish community."[32] Moreover, J Street sought to broaden its base by joining with the Jewish Alliance for Justice and Peace in January 2010, and it now claims to have 150,000 supporters on whom it can call to contact members of Congress. In March 2010, for example, J Street was able to generate 18,000 signatures on a petition supporting the Obama administration's opposition to the Israeli government's expansion of settlements in East Jerusalem.[33] Furthermore, J Street has received endorsements from a considerable list of individuals across the political spectrum and was actively engaged in the 2008 election. Still, one recent analysis raises questions about its staying power and its ability to maintain support among the Jewish community. With the organizational skills of AIPAC, the intensity of AIPAC supporters for a more hardline position within the Middle East (as opposed to the two-state solution advocated by J Street), and the "deep fear of Arab intentions" toward Israel, this analyst contends, AIPAC appears to enjoy the lobbying advantage.[34]

The Cuban Lobby

A second influential ethnic group in recent years has been a Hispanic group, the Cuban Lobby. The Cuban American National Foundation (CANF), founded in 1981 by Jorge Mas Canosa, is the principal Cuban lobby. It originated with those Cuban émigrés who fled the Fidel Castro regime in Cuba after the 1959 Revolution and included some who had participated in the Bay of Pigs invasion of Cuba in April 1961. From the outset, its principal foreign policy aim was to affect US policy toward Cuba.[35] Over the years, this general aim has largely meant the maintenance of the American embargo against Cuba and the promotion of the return of democracy to that island nation as soon as possible. At present, CANF identifies its mission as directed toward producing "non-violent and meaningful" change in Cuba, providing support to those seeking to effect change within Cuba, and "working to counteract the Castro regime's propaganda machine."[36]

For a relatively small lobby, CANF has seemingly been remarkably successful in influencing the conduct of American foreign policy toward Cuba. The trade embargo against Cuba, originally imposed in the early 1960s by executive order, has remained in effect to this day. Indeed, the embargo was actually strengthened in the 1990s by two legislative actions. With the passage of the Cuban Democracy Act of 1992, the embargo was codified into law, rather than being dependent upon an executive order. Then with the passage of the Helms-Burton Act (or more formally the Cuban Liberty and Democratic Solidarity Act) of 1996, the embargo was again codified into law, and two important additional restrictions were placed upon interactions with Cuba. Title III of the Helms-Burton Act allowed Americans to sue foreign companies "trafficking in stolen property" in Cuba. That is, if a foreign company was operating on or doing business with property in Cuba that was previously owned by Americans before Castro's seizure of such property, that company could be sued. Title IV of the Act would deny American visas to officials from such companies that were "trafficking" in stolen Cuban properties.[37] CANF was involved in the development of the Cuban Democracy Act within Congress, but it was less directly involved with the Helms-Burton Act, although CANF undoubtedly applauded its passage.[38]

The continuance of the embargo and the passage of these pieces of legislation are important policy successes for CANF. Yet they are not the only evidence of its influence. CANF was instrumental in promoting the establishment of Radio Marti, a US government–sponsored station, to broadcast to Cuba during the Reagan administration. During the Clinton years, this lobby was important in stopping some administrative appointments to the State Department that it did not approve and in prodding the administration to respond to Cuba's shooting down two unarmed planes of the "Brothers to the Rescue" organization in international waters off Cuba. In 2003, in fact, CANF called for the indictment of Fidel Castro over this episode.[39] The George W. Bush administration did not change American policy during his tenure, and the Obama administration has not either. In all, there remains largely a status-quo approach to Cuba by the United States—and CANF seems one important reason why.

If we apply our earlier criteria for ethnic group effectiveness, we begin to see why this is the case. Although the Cuban-American population (estimated at about 1.2 million)[40] is relatively small within the United States, it is concentrated in some key electoral states (e.g., Florida and New Jersey), and CANF has been able to utilize that political influence to maintain influence. Furthermore, over the years, CANF was operating in a political environment in which there was public and leadership support to pressure the Cuban regime. During the Cold War years, relatively few political leaders were willing to propose the easing of the embargo against Cuba. Indeed, few leaders were willing to promote any policy that would be viewed as in any way accommodating Castro's communist regime. In this sense, CANF's position was reinforced by Cold War politics. In addition, its leadership, especially under Jorge Mas Canosa, was well connected in official Washington and was able to provide some support to favored political candidates. Moreover, CANF was also regarded as an effective lobby in Congress when it needed to be. One member of Congress put it this way: CANF "uses difficult, difficult tactics whenever you disagree with them."[41] Finally, perhaps the most compelling factor for the Cuban lobby's success is the high degree of policy motivation and intensity among its members. Their antipathy toward the Castro regime and their determination to elicit change in Cuba have been critically important to the lobby's success.

In the last decade or so, CANF has in fact experienced some difficulty in maintaining this same level of intensity and unity—and influence. Several reasons account for this change—the death of CANF founder, Jorge Mas Canosa, in 1997; the generational divide between older Cuban-Americans who experienced the Castro regime and younger Cuban-Americans born in the United States without that direct experience; and the rise of other lobbying groups—some more inclined toward improving Cuban-American relations and others more inclined toward no accommodation with Castro's regime under any circumstance.[42] Furthermore, several CANF board members resigned in 2001 over policy disagreements concerning the Castro government and formed a new organization, seemingly dismissing CANF's influence.[43]

One indicator of this changing environment for the Cuban lobby was the 2008 congressional elections in south Florida. Three Cuban-American members of Congress who had long espoused a hard-line policy toward Cuba faced challengers who favored a different strategy toward Castro.[44] Although all three incumbents ultimately won reelection, such challenges reflect the changing political culture that may be developing in the Cuban-American community. Overall, though, like the Jewish lobby, the Cuban lobby remains a formidable example of an ethnic group with an impact on foreign policy.

Greek, Turkish, and Armenian Lobbies

The Greek, Turkish, and Armenian lobbies are three other ethnic lobbies that have operated for some time. Each has sought to affect American policy toward southeastern Europe and the Middle East. The issues of concern to these three groups are often similar, but each lobby's positions (especially those of the Greek and Turkish lobbies) are often at odds with one another. Hence, the actions of these differing ethnic groups have often complicated American foreign policy making on several key issues.

The first of these three groups is the Greek lobby or the American Hellenic Institute (AHI). This organization was established in 1974, immediately after the Turkish invasion of Cyprus. A year later, the American Hellenic Institute Public Affairs Committee (AHIPAC) was created with the expressed goal to focus on lobbying on behalf of Greek-Americans.[45] The current foreign policy goals of this lobby focus primarily on American policy toward Greece, Cyprus, and the region surrounding these countries. Specifically, AHI seeks to strengthen American ties with Greece, remove the Turkish occupation from Cyprus, support sovereignty for Greece in the Aegean Sea, and oppose the use of "Macedonia" by the former Yugoslav Republic of Macedonia in its name.[46]

This lobby points to several important successes in affecting American foreign policy over the past four decades. Undoubtedly the AHI's principal success was persuading Congress to impose an arms embargo against Turkey in 1975 over that country's invasion of Cyprus a year earlier and to sustain that embargo for three years. This American action was seen as punishment for Turkey's use of US arms during its intervention and occupation of Cyprus, an action that directly violated the Foreign Military Sales Act.[47] AHI also claims as important achievements the maintenance of American military assistance to Greece at 70 percent of the level of such assistance to Turkey, Congress's elimination of economic grant aid to Turkey in 1995, and the halting of direct trade by the United States with the Turkish-controlled northern sector of Cyprus. In addition, AHI pays close attention to legislation and congressional resolutions in the House and Senate that promote Greek interests, and this lobby continuously seeks to advance them.[48]

The strength of this lobby is partially tied to the number of Greek-Americans (estimates of the Greek-American population range from 1.38 million to 3 million).[49] Despite their modest size among the American population, Greek-Americans tend to be concentrated in some urban areas, active in politics, and well connected within their communities. Hence, they have the potential to exercise some electoral influence.[50] Importantly, too, the American Hellenic Institute is well organized and effective in its lobby activities, particularly on Capitol Hill. AHI has its headquarters in Washington, only a short distance from the White House, and it has chapters throughout the country. It also has an "Action Alert" system to activate its membership on issues of current interest. Its relative success as a lobbying organization has also been tied to a number of prominent Greek-Americans who have held influential and leadership positions within Congress over the years. Former and current members of Congress with Greek ancestry include Rep. John Brademas (D-IN), Senator Paul Sarbanes (D-MD), Senator Olympia Snowe (R-ME), Rep. Michael Bilirakis (R-FL), and his son, Rep. Gus Bilirakis (R-FL). In addition, the House Congressional Caucus on Hellenic Issues with 149 members in the 111th Congress, cochaired by Rep. Gus Bilirakis (R-FL) and Rep. Carolyn B. Mahoney (D-NY), provides yet another means for the Greek-American community to influence the congressional process.[51]

A countervailing group that seeks to reduce the Greek lobby's impact is the Turkish lobby. The principal organization for promoting Turkish interests in the United States is the Turkish Coalition of America (TCA), although there is a broad array of other Turkish American groups as well. The TCA is a relatively new organization, only established in 2007, and it conducts a number of social, cultural, and educational activities. Still, it engages in numerous political activities to advance issues important to Turkey and the Middle East region. Although Turkish interests have been heavily involved in seeking to stop the passage of the Armenian genocide resolution in the US Congress, they have also been engaged over issues related to America's relationship with Greece, the issue of Cyprus, and sovereignty concerns in the Aegean Sea.

The impact of the Turkish lobby appears to come less from the size of the Turkish-American population or its campaign contributions and more from its successful efforts to engage in lobbying on Capitol Hill. The Turkish-American population is about a tenth of the size of the Greek-American population; hence, it is a substantially less significant voting bloc and source of campaign contributions than is the Greek-American community. Instead, Turkish lobbyists must stress Turkey's strategic importance for the United States when seeking to advance that country's interests with the Congress or the executive branch. In this connection, the Turkish community can routinely work with the House Congressional Caucus on US-Turkey Relations and Turkish Americans, a caucus that reached 100 members in 2009,[52] but it also relies upon support from the Turkish government to lobby the Congress and the executive branch more directly.

In this connection, the Turkish government itself has often been involved in defending its interests by employing prominent Americans as lobbyists on its behalf. At the time of the debate over the 2007 Armenian genocide resolution, for example, two prominent former members of Congress—Robert Livingston (R-LA), former speaker of the House-designate, and Richard Gephardt (D-MO), former majority leader of the House—were deeply involved in seeking to stop this resolution.[53] A crucial part of their argument against condemning the Turkish government over this incident undoubtedly was the strategic importance of Turkey for the United States. Close ties with Turkey, a NATO ally and a pivotal Muslim state in the Middle East, remain crucial for American foreign policy. Support for Turkey at the time came from other key former American officials as well: eight former American secretaries of state who served in seven different administrations—Alexander Haig, George Shultz, Lawrence Eagleburger, Madeleine Albright, Henry Kissinger, James Baker, Warren Christopher, and Colin Powell—and three former secretaries of defense—Frank Carlucci, William Cohen, and William Perry. Each group sent letters to the Speaker of the House, Nancy Pelosi, and highlighted the "critical role" that Turkey plays "in supporting U.S. national security interests in the Balkans, greater Middle East, the Black Sea region and Afghanistan."[54] While these efforts did not stop the passage of the Armenian genocide resolution in the House Foreign Affairs Committee, the resolution did not reach a vote on the House floor.

The third ethnic lobby seeking to affect American policy toward this region is the Armenian lobby. Its principal organizations are the Armenian Assembly and the Armenian National Committee of America (ANCA). As we indicated earlier, it has been extremely active in seeking passage of the Armenian genocide resolution that targets Turkey. Yet it also works to advance a number of other aims regarding American foreign policy and

Armenia. For instance, this lobby seeks to increase American assistance for Armenia and to obtain direct aid for Nagorno Karabakh. (Nagorno Karabakh is a territory wholly within Azerbaijan that is largely populated by Armenians. Since the breakup of the Soviet Union in particular, this territory has been contested between Azerbaijan and Armenia, including in a war between the two countries that ended in 1994.[55]) At the same time, it seeks to deny American aid to Azerbaijan, its regional rival, especially in light of the trade blockade by that nation toward Armenia. Finally, and importantly, this lobby promotes independence for Nagorno Karabakh.[56]

The Armenian lobby has had some success in obtaining these goals— or at least making progress on them. American assistance to Armenia since its independence from the former Soviet Union has totaled nearly $2 billion, and Armenia has also received funding through the Millennium Challenge Account, a program initiated by the George W. Bush administration to aid selected countries that met several key performance indicators.[57] The United States has also provided some direct assistance to Nagorno Karabakh, as the lobby desired. In addition, in the Freedom Support Act of 1992, Congress included a provision restricting aid to Azerbaijan, just as this lobby sought, until the Azerbaijani government takes "demonstrable steps to cease all blockades and other offensive uses of force against Armenia and Nargorno-Karabakh." Congress also passed appropriation bills in 1996 that directed the cutting of all American assistance "to any country which restricts the transport or delivery of U.S. humanitarian aid to a third country."[58] Turkey was the target of the latter action over its border closure with Armenia, and such a measure was wholly consistent with the interests of the Armenian lobby. Yet both of these measures allowed for presidential waivers in their enforcement, thus weakening the two prohibitions in the bills and reducing the lobby's overall success in achieving its aims.

The success of this lobby is somewhat surprising in that a relatively small population within the United States (446,000) claims Armenian ancestry. However, that population is politically active and involved. Much of the Armenian-American population is concentrated in the American west and, importantly, in some congressional districts in California, and that fact aids the lobby's impact. The main sponsor of the Armenian genocide resolutions in Congress in 2007 and 2010 was Rep. Adam Schiff from the 29th district in California. That congressional district has an Armenian-American population of 67,000, more than 10 percent of its total.[59] Such a concentration of Armenian-Americans in this district undoubtedly contributed to Rep. Schiff's interest in promoting this resolution (as it had done for his predecessor in that seat, former Rep. James Rogan).

The Armenian National Committee of America, however, remains politically active beyond this single district. It conducts national voter registration drives, endorses candidates for office, and issues "report cards" on members of Congress. In addition to its electoral efforts, the Armenian community has proved to be an effective lobbying organization in Washington with good connections on Capitol Hill. Like other effective groups, ANCA uses "Action Alerts" to keep its members engaged in the political process, and it even includes sample letters that its activists can forward to members of Congress.[60] Further, the Congressional Caucus on Armenian Issues, established in 1995, now has 150 members in the House of Representatives.[61] This caucus provides yet another mechanism for keeping Armenian-related issues before political leaders and the public. In all, then, this active and committed ethnic group, albeit relatively small in overall size, can affect the congressional process and has affected American foreign policy.

New and Emerging Ethnic Lobbies

Over the last several decades, a number of other ethnic lobbies have also sought to engage in America's foreign policy process. These groups have not been as continuously active, organized, or influential as those we have just discussed, but they may become increasingly consequential in the future. We focus on four of these emerging ethnic lobbies.

Mexican-American Lobby

The Mexican-American lobby is the first. The Mexican-American community is a significantly larger Hispanic group than the Cuban-American community, but it has generally been described as much less successful as an ethnic lobby. With at least 21 million and perhaps as many as 30 million Mexican-Americans in the United States,[62] this group potentially provides an enormous voting bloc, a significant source of campaign contributions, and a potent lobbying force. Part of the explanation for this lobby's lack of success is that this community is not as well organized to lobby or as committed on foreign policy issues as other ethnic groups—two important requirements for lobbying success, as we pointed out earlier. Yet its lack of success is also tied to the fact that its issue positions do not differ substantially from those of the rest of the American public and do not appear tied to those of particular foreign governments. One analyst makes the point in this way: "Mexican American policy preferences on major issues such as immigration and border control . . . differ from those of the Mexican government."[63] And another analyst is even more decisive about the effect of this ethnic lobby: "The Hispanic community exerts almost no systematic influence on U.S.-Latin American relations, or, for that matter, on U.S. foreign policy in general."[64]

Such a conclusion, however, may need to be altered somewhat, especially in light of recent Mexican-American activism on state and national legislation related to immigration. Indeed, one analyst argues that the Mexican-American community has "two effective national organizations in the National Council of La Raza and the Mexican American Legal Defense and Education Fund" and contends that this community was active in affecting the Immigration Reform and Control Act of 1986 and the Immigration Act of 1990. These measures "effectively blocked meaningful changes" over prevailing "migration patterns" and included "amnesty provisions" that "surely substantially accelerated" these patterns.[65] More recently, as Congress was taking up immigration legislation in 2006 and beyond, several Mexican-American organizations conducted nationwide demonstrations to protest this legislation. In 2010, this community also became active over an immigration law passed by the state of Arizona. On the immigration issue, the growing Mexican-American population may well play a role in shaping US policy in the future. On other foreign policy issues—the promotion of NAFTA and Mexican democracy, for example—this community has been judged as having a decidedly limited impact.[66] Yet, given the overall size of this community (particularly in some western states), the potential for foreign policy influence in the years ahead remains a distinct possibility.

The Rebirth of the Eastern European Lobby

Shortly after the implosion of the Soviet Union in 1991 and the gaining of independence of numerous states in the old Soviet empire, a new ethnic organization, the Central and East European Coalition (CEEC), emerged in the United States to promote the interests of these new nations. This organization, established in 1994, was indeed a coalition—a collection of eighteen national organizations representing Americans who traced their ancestry to Hungary, Latvia, Armenia, Belarus, Bulgaria, Czechoslovakia, Estonia, Georgia, Lithuania, Poland, and Ukraine. In a sense, this lobby might be thought of as the successor to the "captive nations" lobby of the 1950s, which had sought freedom and independence for those nations behind the Iron Curtain,[67] albeit now with goals to seek greater stability and security for this region of the world. Supporters of the CEEC argue that the economic and security interests of the United States "demand an unwavering commitment to and sustained engagement with the Central and East European countries."[68] In this sense, the well-being of these Coalition nations and the United States should be wholly tied together.

To enhance this linkage, the Coalition promotes and supports a number of ongoing American policies. CEEC, for example, has been a major proponent of NATO expansion and the incorporation of these new states in that organization to maintain their security and independence. It currently supports moving Georgia and Ukraine toward full NATO membership in accordance with NATO's Membership Action Plan (MAP). CEEC also strongly supports the principal aid and reform initiatives taken by the United States over the past three administrations—the Support for East European Democracy (SEED) dating back to 1989, the Freedom Support Act (FSA) of 1992, and the more recent Millennium Challenge Account (MCA) program of 2004—and views them as important mechanisms to advance democratic and market reforms in the countries of Central and Eastern Europe. Furthermore, the Coalition promotes more vigorous action on the part of the United States "to counter Russia's neo-imperialism," both within Russia itself and within this region of the world.[69]

American foreign policy generally comports with the principal goals of the Coalition. In this sense, it is unclear how much effect the CEEC has had in shaping these policies as compared to the general political environment of the post–Cold War years. Still, CEEC has sought to keep its principal issues before America's political leaders through a variety of informational and educational activities. With its headquarters in Washington, D.C., the CEEC and its affiliate organizations regularly hold events and discussion forums in Washington, on Capitol Hill, or even at the White House as important mechanisms for shaping the foreign policy debate about this region of the world. Furthermore, CEEC has developed a series of position papers that are routinely shared with members of the current US administration. Recent position papers, whether on Ukraine or Georgia or making a policy statement on the region at large, generally call upon the United States to provide greater commitment to the member states, whether by increasing aid to them or promoting energy diversification for the region. These policy statements also tend to be a bit more skeptical of the actions of Russia than current American policy.[70] Finally, supportive members of Congress have formed the Congressional Caucus on Central and Eastern Europe as yet another way to discuss these issues, although the impact of this caucus appears to be modest.

Through its member organizations, CEEC has the potential to reach the 22 million Americans who share an ancestry from this part of the world and serve as an important voting bloc.[71] Since most Americans with Central and Eastern European heritage are concentrated in the Midwest, this region would seem especially ripe for electoral impact if these foreign policy issues were to dominate the campaign agenda. At the present time, however, the Coalition does not appear to have a ready mechanism to mobilize this population in the way that more successful ethnic lobbies mobilize their populations. In addition, because the CEEC is truly a coalitional organization, it necessarily has to seek consensus among its member groups, a task that may be difficult from time to time. Overall, then, the CEEC cannot be judged as having as influential an effect on foreign policy as the Jewish, Cuban, Greek, or Armenian lobbies. If issues in this region were to reemerge as central to American foreign policy and if the CEEC were to experience greater organizational development, this lobby might be able to exert increased influence.

African-American Lobby

A third ethnic lobby that has emerged over the past several decades is the African-American lobby. TransAfrica (or the TransAfrica Forum) is the principal organization that promotes the interests of those with African heritage in the United States, the Caribbean, and parts of Latin America. It was founded in 1977 and pursues a number of goals related to creating greater economic justice globally, reducing American militarism, and promoting democracy in Africa and among the African Diaspora.[72] To achieve such goals, TransAfrica has taken a number of actions to try to affect American foreign policy over the past four decades.

TransAfrica's lobbying efforts began in the late 1970s, and it has continued to try to influence American foreign policy in this way during each succeeding decade. One of its initial actions focused on seeking to maintain US economic sanctions on white-ruled Rhodesia in southern Africa. By 1980, this activity, and a series of actions by a number of others, resulted in the creation of the state of Zimbabwe from this former British colony. A few years later, TransAfrica lobbied the Reagan administration to impose economic sanctions on South Africa over its apartheid policy. In 1986, the organization supported efforts by Congress to override a presidential veto and pass the Anti-Apartheid Act of 1986, a measure that strengthened the administration's executive order of 1985. By the early 1990s, TransAfrica was influential in prodding the Clinton administration to take stronger measures against those who had overthrown the democratic government in Haiti. In 1994, moreover, the Clinton administration did order an American intervention into Haiti, and the military rulers fled the country.[73]

In the twenty-first century, TransAfrica continued its lobbying effort, albeit with decidedly more mixed results. For instance, the organization opposed the African Growth and Opportunity Act that was enacted into law over concern that it might provide little actual aid to Africa, and it opposed the creation of the "Africa Command" within the American military structure because the organization viewed it as leading to a greater militarization within Africa. TransAfrica also worked to oppose the increasingly repressive Mugabe government in Zimbabwe, also with limited success.[74] At the present time, TransAfrica is focused on seeking relief for the substantial debt owed by Africa and the Caribbean countries, opposing the militarization of Africa, and seeking to promote "human rights, fair trade, and self-determination of African peoples" as "the cornerstone of U.S. policy towards Africa."[75]

Unlike many of the other ethnic lobbies that we have discussed, the African-American lobby appears to do a great deal of its work with civil society groups abroad (in various countries in Africa and elsewhere) and with Americans of African ancestry at home. In this sense, there is potentially a substantial grassroots component to TransAfrica, but the extent of its following in the United States is not clear. Furthermore, it has a limited domestic electoral base and has not been a major campaign contributor to candidates for elective office. In this sense, TransAfrica does not possess some of the characteristics that we identified as important for a successful ethnic lobby. At the same time, in the nation's capital, the organization has been involved in taking direct actions to affect American policy, both with protests and demonstrations and with its lobbying of the Congress. Trans-Africa has a natural ally in the Congressional Black Caucus (since its founding was linked to this caucus), and that tie helps it to gain access and influence in official Washington. Overall this organization appears less well organized and influential than some of the other ethnic lobbies that we have discussed. Nevertheless, TransAfrica has the potential to appeal to the African-American community within the United States, especially on issues related to Africa, a continent long neglected in American foreign policy, and on issues related to global social justice, such as the genocide in Darfur.

The Indian Lobby

The newest ethnic lobby, and the most influential of the emerging ethnic lobbies, is the Indian lobby. This lobby consists of those Americans whose ancestry is tied to the country of India. The number of Americans with Asian Indian ancestry totaled between 1.7 and 1.9 million in the 2000 US Census and was estimated at "over 2.5 million" in 2007.[76] The total is probably somewhat larger today, but even with a modest increase, the percentage of Indian Americans represents less than 1 percent of the total US population. Yet in one recent assessment, this lobby has been described as "the only lobby in Washington likely to acquire the strength of the Israel lobby."[77]

How can this descriptor be possible for such a relatively small group? As was the case with other groups of relatively small size (e.g., the Cuban lobby, the Armenian lobby), an important part of the explanation rests with the substantial motivation of members of this community, the electoral clout—both through voting blocs and campaign contributions—that the lobby possesses in particular states and districts around the country, and the improved organizational structure that it has put into place in recent years. Finally—and hardly inconsequentially—the changed international political environment over the past two decades has also aided the emergence of the Indian lobby.

Over the years, numerous disparate Indian-American organizations have existed, but these organizations were often organized "along professional-occupational lines" (e.g., the American Association of Physicians of Indian Origin and the Asian American Hotel Owners Association).[78] In

2002, however, the US India Political Action Committee (USINPAC) was formed. It established itself in the K Street neighborhood in Washington, D.C., hired a staff of professionals committed to advancing a series of important foreign and domestic policy goals, and put into place a comprehensive organizational structure for lobbying. Thus, this organization today is the principal lobbying organization for the Indian-American community, although it continues to work effectively with other organizations (primarily business organizations) in advancing its goals.

USINPAC has a number of goals, both in foreign and domestic policy. In the foreign policy arena, USINPAC is primarily interested in strengthening US-India bilateral relations across the spectrum—defense, trade, and business. It is also interested in promoting "a fair and balanced policy on immigration" and addressing the issues of international terrorism. In the domestic arena, its concerns focus on protecting the civil rights of Indian-Americans, promoting equal opportunity for members of this community, and advocating for small businesses. To achieve these goals, USINPAC conducts a broad array of activities, including holding fund-raisers for political candidates that its supports, hosting receptions and briefings on Capitol Hill, sponsoring trips to India for its supporters, and providing a listing of its key issues and events on its Web site.[79] Furthermore, this organization and its associated groups work with two congressional caucuses dealing with India: the Congressional Caucus on India and Indian-Americans in the House and the Friends of India Caucus in the Senate.[80] Finally, USINPAC also has a "National Outreach Program" that seeks to coordinate issue positions among affiliated groups, and it has been active in promoting Indian-Americans who are competing for elective offices nationwide.[81] In all, USINPAC in a relatively short period of time has established itself as a comprehensive and effective organization.

Other important characteristics of the Indian-American community also facilitate its activism and impact. Indian-Americans tend to be highly educated (with 64 percent over age twenty-five having a college degree), economically successful (with a median income almost twice that of most Americans), and well connected.[82] By one estimate, Indian-Americans own "20 percent of all the companies in Silicon Valley" in California and "the U.S.-India Business Council, which has a core committee of 200 companies that make up part of the United States' corporate elite, is closely allied with the India lobby."[83] In this sense, the Indian lobby can reach out to a number of supporters beyond its core constituents to enhance its influence in the political process. Furthermore, the Indian-American community tends to be concentrated in particularly important electoral states (e.g., California, Washington, New York, Illinois, Texas, and Pennsylvania), and it has been an increasingly generous campaign contributor to its supporters in government. Finally, as one analysis put it, the Indian-American community has gone through a generational change in which the younger generation of

Indian-Americans has become more politically active, especially with regard to lobbying the US Congress.[84]

Although these organizational and individual characteristics account for a great deal of the rise of the Indian lobby, the political and economic environment surrounding US-India relations over the past two decades also provided the occasion for this lobby to promote its foreign policy goals. First of all, with the end of the Cold War and the implosion of the Soviet Union, an opportunity developed for restarting American-Indian relations, a relationship that had been decidedly cool due to India's ties with the Soviet Union. Second, India is the world's largest democracy, and it is also one of the world's most dynamic economies. In this sense, India may well be America's new "ally," as Fareed Zakaria described the relationship in *The Post-American World*.[85] Third, in the post-9/11 era, India is located in an important, but volatile, part of the world for the United States. Strong and productive relations with India are increasingly crucial for American foreign policy. For all of these reasons, then, the India lobby has had an opportunity to affect American foreign policy.

And the Indian lobby has done so. Perhaps the most important foreign policy achievement of this lobby was the passage of legislation in 2006 that lifted restrictions on nuclear fuels trade by the United States with India. Such restrictions had been in place for several decades as part of US obligations under the Nuclear Nonproliferation Treaty (NPT) and domestic laws; they dated back to India's "peaceful" nuclear explosion in 1974 and were reinforced by India's nuclear test in the late 1990s. Despite a skeptical Congress heading into an election in the fall of 2006 and a weakened Bush presidency from the Iraq War, both houses of Congress approved this legislation. One recent analysis argues that "Indian-American mobilization was *the* critical factor behind overwhelming congressional support" for passage of this legislation. Without the "energetic efforts of a newly professionalized 'India lobby' on Capitol Hill, personal contacts with legislators and staffers by Indian-Americans, and grassroots informational and petitioning campaigns," this analyst contends, the legislation would have failed.[86] Importantly, the India lobby's success with this legislation has energized its work on a host of other trade, defense, and immigration initiatives involving US-India relations. In all, the India lobby is increasingly a potent force seeking to influence American foreign policy.

Ethnic Lobbies and Their Influence: Some Conclusions

This survey of America's ethnic lobbies leads to several important conclusions about their impact on American foreign policy. First of all, ethnic groups matter. The Jewish lobby, the Cuban lobby, the Greek lobby, and, more recently, the Indian lobby have impacted American foreign policy in important ways. Their impact has primarily been tied to issues related to

US policy toward the countries of each lobby's origins. In this sense, the lobbies may not appear to have an effect on the overall conduct of American foreign policy. Yet, in fact, they do. Consider how America's close ties to Israel have affected its relationship with Arab countries and beyond. Similarly, the decision of the United States to tilt toward Greece or to tilt toward India has sometimes created difficulties with other countries in those countries' respective regions. In this sense, ethnic lobbies can impact American policy beyond the country of origin, since linkage politics operate more than ever in today's globalized world. The more vexing question is how much an ethnic lobby has shaped American policy toward a country or region, controlling for a variety of other factors.

Second, some lobbies are more influential on American foreign policy than others. This effectiveness is primarily due to a number of important group and organizational characteristics that we discussed throughout the chapter. The size of the ethnic community, the distribution of the group's population in particular congressional districts or states, and the group's political activism and involvement are important factors shaping an ethnic group's policy impact. Recall, for example, the size and involvement of the Jewish-American and the Greek-American communities compared to the Arab-American or Turkish-American communities. A high degree of motivation and commitment to a particular policy position, however, can often overcome an ethnic group's relative lack of size (e.g., the Armenian lobby). The ethnic group's organizational capacity and its skill in getting its message upward to policy makers and downward to its supporters are also important factors affecting its degree of policy influence. Note, for example, the organizational strength of the Jewish and the Indian lobbies as compared to that of the African-American, Mexican, and Eastern European lobbies.

Third, the type of policy sought by an ethnic lobby affects its success. Lobbies that seek to change American foreign policy in some important way (e.g., the Armenian lobby, the Greek lobby, or the Indian lobby) often have a bigger challenge than those lobbies that seek to reinforce current policy or the status quo (e.g., the Cuban lobby, the Jewish lobby, or even the Central and Eastern Europe lobbies).

Fourth, an ethnic lobby that forms a coalition with other ethnic lobbies will likely have more effect on policy. The Armenian lobby, for example, has been able to work with the Greek lobby to oppose Turkish interests, while the Turkish lobby for a time gained support from the Jewish lobby. In this sense, the limited capacity of one group is leveraged with the assistance of another. In the future, in fact, we are likely to see more and more ethnic groups cooperating with one another to accomplish their goals.

In large measure, the conclusions discussed so far could reasonably be made about any type of interest group—ethnic or otherwise—but ethnic groups possess a quality that makes them distinctive from other interest groups in one important way. That quality is the close personal identity that members of these ethnic groups feel toward the policy issues at hand. That is, the strong "identity politics" of ethnic group members, or, put differently, "the strong emotional bonds of large numbers of Americans to their cultural or ancestral homes," have been characterized as the "secret weapon" of these ethnic groups. Although these bonds can be beneficial to ethnic group members, they have also been criticized as having the potential to be carried to excess and thus prove "harmful to the national interest."[87] That is, do these groups come to believe that their ethnic interests are the same as the collective interests of the United States? In this sense, do ethnic lobbies ultimately distort American foreign policy in a way dangerous to the welfare of the United States as a whole?

Several years ago, noted political scientist Samuel Huntington advanced that argument. He contended that "ethnic interests are generally transnational or nonnational," they "promote the interests of people and entities outside the United States," and they thus erode the pursuance of the national interest.[88] The usual response is to argue that the national interest is not self-evident and that it is, in fact, the result of competition among competing interests, including ethnic interests.[89] At the same time, there is no doubt about the need to make certain that the ethnic lobbies continue to place their interests within the context of the collective interest of American foreign policy. Policy makers are aware of this dilemma, and, much as policy makers have learned to manage the impact of the media on foreign policy (the so-called "CNN effect"), they are increasingly capable of managing the effects of ethnic lobbying. Yet policy makers' management of these lobbies is far from complete. That is, these ethnic lobbies, often "experts" on a particular foreign policy issue, may combine with highly reputable reporters and media outlets to create what Bonardi and Keim describe as a "reputation cascade" for a "widely salient issue."[90] By this process, both the public and policy makers have lost their decision latitude on an issue—and, in this way, ethnic lobbies may continue to influence the direction of American foreign policy. In all, then, the number of ethnic groups, their increasing skill in lobbying Congress and the executive branch, their effectiveness in utilizing multiple media outlets, and their ability to influence public opinion make them a growing source of foreign policy influence today.

Notes

1. See the vote on "H.Res. 252: Affirmation of the United States Record on the Armenian Genocide, March 4, 2010, U.S. House of Representatives, Committee on Foreign Affairs," at http://hcfa.house.gov/hearing_notice.asp?id=1156&show=votes.

2. Three years earlier, the same resolution was introduced as H.R. 106 and was approved by the House Committee on Foreign Affairs by a vote of 27–21 on October 10, 2007. See http://thomas.loc.gov/cgi-bin/bdquery/z?d110:HE00106:@@@X for the summary of congressional action on this resolution.

3. Marilyn W. Thompson, "An Ex-Leader in Congress Is Now Turkey's Man in the Lobbies of Capitol Hill," *New York Times*, October 17, 2007, http://www.nytimes.com/2007/10/17/washington/17lobby.html.

4. Brian Knowlton, "A Changed U.S. House to Vote on Armenian Genocide," *New York Times*, March 3, 2010, http://www.nytimes.com/2010/03/04/us/04iht-genocide.html.

5. See "H. Res. 252 Narrowly Clears the House Foreign Affairs Committee," *Alaturka*, March 4, 2010, http://www.alaturkaonline.com/?p=2840/.

6. See James M. McCormick, *American Foreign Policy and Process*, 5th ed. (Boston: Wadsworth Cengage Learning, 2010): 490–91.

7. For the requirements of the Foreign Agents Registration Act, see http://www.fara.gov/ (a U.S. Department of Justice Web site).

8. See Charles McC. Mathias Jr., "Ethnic Groups and Foreign Policy," *Foreign Affairs* 59, no. 5 (1981): 975–98 for a discussion of these groups.

9. John J. Mearsheimer and Stephen M. Walt, *The Israel Lobby and U.S. Foreign Policy* (New York: Farrar, Straus & Giroux, 2007): 112.

10. See the AIPAC Web site at http://www.aipac.org/about_AIPAC/default.asp, where the site invites membership in the organization and to "join more than 100,000 pro-Israel activists online."

11. The American Israel Public Affairs Committee, "What is AIPAC?" http://www.aipac.org/about_AIPAC/26.asp/.

12. "What is AIPAC?" http://www.aipac.org/about_AIPAC/26.asp/.

13. See McCormick, *American Foreign Policy and Process*, 519.

14. See "AIPAC Achievments" at http://www.aipac.org/about_AIPAC/default.asp/.

15. McCormick, *American Foreign Policy and Process*, 519. One study in the 1970s found that Senate support for Israel averaged 84 percent. Although this level may have diminished somewhat over time, it undoubtedly remains remarkable.

16. Tony Smith, *Foreign Attachments: The Power of Ethnic Groups in the Making of American Foreign Policy* (Cambridge, MA: Harvard University Press, 2000): 86.

17. Smith, *Foreign Attachments*, 88.

18. For a more complete statement of the factors that facilitate ethnic interest group success, see Patrick J. Haney and Walt Vanderbush, "The Role of Ethnic Interest Groups in U.S. Foreign Policy: The Case of the Cuban American National Foundation," *International Studies Quarterly* 43, no. 2 (1999): 341–61. Aside from the ones already mentioned, Haney and Vanderbush point to the "*salience and resonance of the message*" of the group, promoting policies "that the government already favors" and "*mutually supportive relationships*" between themselves and policymakers." Emphasis in original.

19. Center for Responsive Politics, "Pro-Israel: Long-Term Contributions Trends," http://www.opensecrets.org/industries/totals.php?cycle=2010&ind=Q05.

20. The listing of speakers for the 2010 AIPAC Policy Conference is from the AIPAC Web site at http://www.aipac.org/PC2010/stories/pcdaily_aipac_hosts_its_largest_policy_conference_ever.asp.

21. Mathias, "Ethnic Groups and Foreign Policy," 978.

22. Lydia Saad, "Support for Israel in U.S. at 63%, Near Record High," *Gallup*, February 24, 2010, http://www.gallup.com/poll/126155/Support-Israel-Near-Record-High.aspx.

23. McCormick, *American Foreign Policy and Process*, 520.
24. See the mission statement of the Arab American Institute at http://www.aaiusa.org/about/14/our-mission/.
25. See Lydia Saad, "In U.S. Canada Places First in Image Contest; Iran Last," *Gallup*, February 19, 2010, http://www.gallup.com/poll/126116/Canada-Places-First-Image-Contest-Iran-Last.aspx; Saad, "Support for Israel in U.S. at 63%, Near Record High."
26. Quoted in Christopher Madison, "Arab-American Lobby Fights Rearguard Battle to Influence U.S. Mideast Policy," *National Journal* (August 31, 1985): 1936.
27. See Mearsheimer and Walt, *The Israel Lobby and U.S. Foreign Policy*, and their earlier article "The Israel Lobby," *London Review of Books* 28, no. 6, (2006): 3–12, http://www.lrb.co.uk/v28/n06/john-mearsheimer/the-israel-lobby/.
28. Mearsheimer and Walt, *The Israel Lobby and U.S. Foreign Policy*, 13.
29. See, for example, the July/August 2006 issue of *Foreign Policy* magazine for a number of critiques of the article. Also see Walter Russell Mead, "Jerusalem Syndrome: Decoding the Israel Lobby," *Foreign Affairs* 86, no. 6 (2007): 160–68.
30. Dan Fleshler, *Transforming America's Israel Lobby: The Limits of its Power and the Potential for Change* (Washington, DC: Potomac Books, 2009).
31. Telephone interview with a J Street staffer, June 29, 2010.
32. See the J Street Web site at "About Us" at http://www.jstreet.org/about/about-us/.
33. Telephone interview with a J Street staffer, June 29, 2010.
34. John Newhouse, "Diplomacy, Inc.: The Influence of Lobbies on U.S. Foreign Policy," *Foreign Affairs* 88 (May/June 2009): 81.
35. Patrick J. Haney and Walt Vanderbush, "The Helms-Burton Act: Congress and Cuba Policy," in *Contemporary Cases in U.S. Foreign Policy: From Terrorism to Trade*, 3rd ed., ed. Ralph G. Carter (Washington, DC: CQ Press, 2008): 285. For a comprehensive summary of the development of CANF, see Haney and Vanderbush, "The Role of Ethnic Interest Groups in U.S. Foreign Policy," especially 346–58.
36. See The Cuban American National Foundation Web site at http://www.canf.org/about/about-us/.
37. On these provisions, see Haney and Vanderbush, "The Helms-Burton Act: Congress and Cuba Policy," 289–90 and 294. The effectiveness of these titles is in question for differing reasons. The legislation also contained a provision allowing for a presidential waiver on the enforcement of Title III, which presidents have routinely used, and Title IV has apparently been used sparingly.
38. Haney and Vanderbush, "The Helms-Burton Act: Congress and Cuba Policy," 287 and 289.
39. See CANF White Paper—2003, "Recommendations for the Immediate Implementation of a U.S.-Cuba Policy under the 'Four Promises' Doctrine," http://www.canf.org/index.php?src=gendocs&ref=CANFWhitePaper2003.
40. See "Cuban American" at http://www.answers.com/topic/cuban-american/, for the estimate of Cuban-Americans in the United States (based upon the 2000 census).
41. Dick Kirschten, "From the K Street Corridor," *National Journal*, July 17, 1993: 1815.
42. Philip Brenner, Patrick J. Haney, and Walter Vanderbush, "Intermestic Interests and U.S. Policy toward Cuba," in *The Domestic Sources of American Foreign Policy: Insights and Evidence*, 5th ed., eds. Eugene R. Wittkopf and James M. McCormick (Lanham, MD: Rowman & Littlefield, 2008): 70–71; and Kirk Nielsen, "Cuba Libre?" *Miller-McCune* 1 (June-July 2008): 46–55, http://www.miller-mccune.com/politics/cuba-libre-4540/.

43. Patrick J. Haney, "Why Do We Still Have an Embargo of Cuba?" in *Contemporary Cases in U.S. Foreign Policy*, 4th ed., ed. Ralph G. Carter (Washington, DC: CQ Press, 2011): 342–43.

44. Brenner, Haney, and Vanderbush, "Intermestic Interests and U.S. Policy toward Cuba"; Nielsen, "Cuba Libre?."

45. See the American Hellenic Institute Web site for the information in this paragraph at http://www.ahiworld.org/.

46. See the American Hellenic Institute's Web site at http://www.ahiworld.org/membership.html.

47. Mathias, "Ethnic Groups and Foreign Policy," 988.

48. The list of AHI's stated achievements is taken from its Web site at http://www.ahiworld.org/about_ahi.html#whoweare/. The list of congressional legislation of interest to this lobby is available there as well.

49. For the lower estimate, see Table 52 of the U.S. Census Bureau, *Statistical Abstract of the United States 2010*, http://www.census.gov/compendia/statab/2010/2010edition.html. The data are for 2007. For the higher estimate, see U.S. Department of State, "Background Note: Greece," November 23, 2010, http://www.state.gov/r/pa/ei/bgn/3395.htm.

50. Mathias, "Ethnic Groups and Foreign Policy," 990.

51. See the "Report on Hellenic Issues" prepared by Rep. Carolyn Maloney at http://maloney.house.gov/documents/hellenic/20100218%20HELLENIC%20REPORT_111.pdf. This report lists the current membership of the Caucus.

52. Turkish Coalition of America, "TCA Welcomes 100th Member of the Turkish Caucus," October 16, 2009, http://www.turkishcoalition.org/TCA_welcomes_101609.html.

53. Thompson, "An Ex-Leader in Congress Is Now Turkey's Man in the Lobbies of Capitol Hill."

54. Alexander M. Haig, Jr., Henry A. Kissinger, George P. Schultz, James A. Baker III, Lawrence S. Eagleburger, Warren Christopher, Madeleine K. Albright, Colin L. Powell, "Former Secretaries of State and Defense Object to H.Res. 106," http://www.tc-america.org/forsec.pdf. The quoted passages are from the letter by the former secretaries of defense.

55. See U.S. Department of State, "Background Note: Armenia," November 17, 2010, http://www.state.gov/r/pa/ei/bgn/5275.htm.

56. See the Armenian National Committee of America Web site at http://www.anca.org/ancaprofile.php.

57. Jim Nichol, *Armenia, Azerbaijan, and Georgia: Political Developments and Implications for U.S. Interests* (Washington, DC: Congressional Research Service, Library of Congress, 2009): 27 and 35.

58. See Section 907 of P.L. 102–511 for the first quote and Nichol, *Armenia, Azerbaijan, and Georgia*, 20 for the second one. The presidential waivers are also included here.

59. Michael Barone and Richard E. Cohen, *The Almanac of American Politics, 2004: The Senators, the Representatives, and the Governors; Their Records and Election Results, Their States and Districts* (Washington, DC: National Journal, 2003): 241.

60. See the Armenian National Committee of America Web site at http://www.anca.org/ancaprofile.php for these links.

61. See Armenian Assembly of America, "Congressional Caucus on Armenian Issues," http://www.aaainc.org/index.php?id=39/.

62. Differing estimates exist regarding the number of Americans of Mexican descent. According to Table DP-1, Profile of General Demographic Characteristics: 2000 from the U.S. Census Bureau, Census 2000, the estimated size of the Mexican-American population is 20.6 million. See U.S. Census Bureau, *Profiles of General Demographic Characteristics 2000* (Washington, DC: May 2001), http://www.census.gov/prod/cen2000/doc/ProfilesTD.pdf. Another estimate puts the total at 30.7 million. See http://en.wikipedia.org/wiki/Mexican_American/ for this number.

63. Rodolfo de la Garza, "Introduction," in *Latinos and U.S. Foreign Policy: Representing the "Homeland?"* eds. Rodolfo O. de la Garza and Harry P. Pachon (Lanham, MD: Rowman & Littlefield, 2000): 9.

64. Peter Hakim and Carlos A. Rosales, "The Latino Foreign Policy Lobby," in *Latinos and U.S. Foreign Policy*, 133.

65. Smith, *Foreign Attachments*, 116 and 75, respectively, for the quoted passages.

66. Smith, *Foreign Attachments*, 73.

67. Mathias, "Ethnic Groups and Foreign Policy," 984–87. He discusses this organization and the considerable effect that it had on American foreign policy at the height of the Cold War.

68. Central and East European Coalition Web site at http://ceecoalition.org/ (site discontinued) listed the CEEC's member organizations, goals, mission, and principles. The quoted passage is from the "Mission and Principles" page.

69. Central and East European Coalition Web site at http://ceecoalition.org/ (site discontinued).

70. Position papers found at Central and East European Coalition Web site at http://ceecoalition.org/ (site discontinued).

71. From "Who We Are" at Central and East European Coalition, http://ceecoalition.org/ (site discontinued).

72. TransAfrica Forum, "Policy Overview," http://www.transafricaforum.org/policy-overview/.

73. These examples are taken from McCormick, *American Foreign Policy and Process*, 515–16.

74. See McCormick, *American Foreign Policy and Process*, 516, for these examples as well.

75. TransAfrica Forum, "Our History," http://www.transafricaforum.org/about-us/our-history/.

76. See U.S. Census Bureau, "The Asian Population: 2000" (Washington, DC: U.S. Department of Commerce, February 2002): 9, http://www.census.gov/prod/2002pubs/c2kbr01–16.pdf for the first set of figures and U.S. India Political Action Committee, "Indian-Americans: Demographic Information," http://www.usinpac.com/Census-2000/demographic-info.html.

77. Newhouse, "Diplomacy, Inc.," 81.

78. On the development of Indian-American lobby, see the excellent summary and analysis by Jason A. Kirk, "Indian-Americans and U.S.-India Nuclear Agreement: Consolidation of an Ethnic Lobby?" *Foreign Policy Analysis* 4, no. 3 (2008): 275–300, especially 287–92.

79. See the "About AIPAC," "Events," "Issues," and "Information Center" tabs at http://www.aipac.org/about_AIPAC/default.asp.

80. The list of members in the House Caucus in the 111th Congress is available at http://www.usindiafriendship.net/congress1/housecaucus/members.htm, and the discussion of the creation of the Senate Caucus is at http://www.usindiafriendship.net/congress1/senatecaucus/senatecaucus.htm.

81. See http://www.usinpac.com/Communities/Partner-Organizations/partner-organi
zation.html for a discussion of this program.
82. US India Political Action Committee, "Indian-Americans: Demographic Information," at http://www.usinpac.com/Census-2000/demographic-info.html.
83. Newhouse, "Diplomacy, Inc.," 81–82.
84. Kirk, "Indian-Americans and U.S.-India Nuclear Agreement," 286 for population
data on this community and 285–88 for the generational change.
85. Fareed Zakaria, *The Post-American World* (New York: W. W. Norton, 2008).
86. Kirk, "Indian-Americans and U.S.-India Nuclear Agreement," 292, 293, and 297,
with the quotations taken from p. 297. Emphasis in original.
87. For these arguments and quotations, see Mathias, "Ethnic Groups and Foreign
Policy," 996–97.
88. Samuel P. Huntington, "The Erosion of American National Interests," in *The Domestic Sources of American Foreign Policy,* 4th ed., eds. Wittkopf and McCormick (Lanham,
MD: Rowman & Littlefield, 2004): 63.
89. See James M. Lindsay, "Getting Uncle Sam's Ear: Will Ethnic Lobbies Cramp
America's Foreign Policy Style?" *Brookings* (Winter 2002), http://www.brookings
.edu/articles/2002/winter_diplomacy_lindsay.aspx.
90. See Jean-Philippe Bonardi and Gerald D. Keim, "Corporate Political Strategies for
Widely Salient Issues," *Academy of Management Review* 30 (September 2005): 555–76.
I am indebted to Raymond Hudon for bringing this article and this argument to my
attention.

15

The Allure of Reform

The Increasing Demand for Health Care Lobbying, from Clinton's Task Force to Obama's Big [Expletive] Deal

Timothy M. LaPira

"This is a big [expletive] deal," declared Vice President Biden to President Obama after introducing him to a crowd of supporters at the health care reform law signing ceremony at the White House on March 23, 2010. The "hot mic" moment, broadcast on live television, was intended as private praise for the young president from the elder vice president who had witnessed many failed attempts to reform the health care system in his nearly four decades as a US senator. Instead, the very public exchange went viral on YouTube and nearly eclipsed the news of the actual bill signing as the top story of the day. In a sign of the White House's excitement over shepherding such monumental health policy legislation into law, press secretary Robert Gibbs forewent embarrassment later that day when he Tweeted, "And yes, Mr. Vice President, you're right. . . ." Indeed, he was.

Regardless of whether they believe it is a remarkable leap forward or a treacherous encroachment of government power, most observers would at least agree that the law is an enormous change to the health policy status quo.[1] The Patient Protection and Affordable Care Act of 2010, and the corresponding Health Care and Education Reconciliation Act of 2010, represent a break from the mold since the Reagan era. The social policy consequence of the conservative movement's rhetoric of reduced government and personal responsibility has been a widening gap between rich and poor,[2] whereas the Obama health law promises to provide billions of dollars in health care subsidies to low- and middle-income families. The law extends coverage to more than 30 million Americans for whom health insurance was unaffordable and, as a consequence, for whom adequate health care was unattainable. And it fundamentally restructures how the fastest-growing sector of the American economy will deliver its products and services. The Obama reform law will directly impact the health care needs of more people than any health policy change enacted since the Great Society.

It is the most ambitious expansion of private sector health care coverage for the lower and middle classes since President Harry Truman originally championed the idea of "compulsory care."[3]

Though these benchmarks in the development of health policy are undeniable, "Obamacare" remains controversial. Pundits and politicians on the left see the law as an unsuitable compromise that falls short of the universal coverage ideal, and conservative political elites have promised to repeal, defund, constitutionally challenge, or otherwise obstruct the Patient Protection Act's key elements as they go into effect. Even if the social and economic repercussions of the health care law are diminished as it is implemented in the years after its inception, the fact that comprehensive health reform overcame political resistance and institutional barriers to become law is itself significant. And despite the criticism that it failed to codify universal health coverage through a single-payer system, as in many other advanced economies, or through the less-direct-government-involvement "public option," its passage still represents an enormous shift in how millions of Americans will receive and pay for their health care needs.

What's So Big about the Big [Expletive] Deal?

The fact that the Patient Protection Act represents such a substantial change in social *policy* is not necessarily what makes it such a big deal for interest group *politics*. The biggest obstacle to health care reform was the loose and informal—and potentially unstable—alliance of entrenched interests that supported the status quo. For ages, doctors resisted a change in how they conducted the business end of their practices, health insurers defied attempts to regulate how they managed financial risk (such as withholding coverage from those with preexisting conditions), and pharmaceutical and medical device companies pushed back on government attempts to curtail skyrocketing prices on drugs and medical equipment prescribed by doctors.

This fact did not escape the last president who attempted reform. On the day he created the Task Force on National Health Care Reform and appointed then First Lady Hillary Rodham Clinton to chair it, President Clinton declared:

> We will no doubt be criticized by some for undertaking something much too ambitious. But as I said in my inaugural address, we are going to have to make some tough choices. In the months ahead, powerful lobbies and special interests will attempt to derail our efforts. We may make those people angry, but we're determined to come up with the best possible solution for America.[4]

Clinton's indignant platitude against "powerful lobbies and special interests" was prescient, as his health care proposal would die in the Senate the following year. Many observers blamed the failure on "Harry and Louise," the average, middle-class Americans portrayed by actors in a series of television advertisements discussing the overreach of government involvement proposed by Clinton's reform plan.[5] Though few Americans actually saw the issue ads funded by the Health Insurance Association of America (now known as America's Health Insurance Plans, or AHIP), Harry and Louise became symbols of the ruthless lobbying and public relations campaign by entrenched corporate interests that ultimately doomed the Clinton health care reform effort to the legislative dustbin.

Why were the dominant health policy interests unable to replicate that show of power and influence seventeen years after defeating Clinton? Or, why was Obama successful in overcoming these entrenched interests when Clinton was not? The alignment of political forces that led to legislative failure during Clinton's health reform efforts were essentially the same as those for Obama: the president had high approval ratings after handily winning the office in light of a crumbling economy, and Democrats were enjoying the increasingly rare opportunity of governing with a unified government. And, more importantly for students of interest group politics, the health care reform debate's major stakeholders remained the same: physicians, nurses, and other health care providers and their employing institutions like hospitals, clinics, and nursing homes; health insurance companies; and pharmaceutical, biotechnology, and medical device manufacturers. Each of these groups' idiosyncratic economic stakes in health care policy did not miraculously change in the seventeen years between Clinton's and Obama's attempts at reform. If the "powerful lobbies and special interests" remained the same, however, what *did* change?

This essay explores the interest group politics behind this epic policy achievement from two perspectives. First, I begin with the simple observation that the number of groups with an interest in health policy has greatly expanded over time. Adopting an agenda-setting approach to interest group mobilization, I argue that this growth is as much a function of the government indirectly arousing interest or seeking out information and expertise as it is the self-interested motivations of groups seeking to influence or monitor government activity. Interest group mobilization is mutually beneficial to groups and government, so the mobilization of interest organizations is most likely to occur when the government makes an issue relevant to them a priority.

I show that not only did the number of health-related interest groups increase when both presidents prioritized health care reform, but also that the diversity of interest groups engaged in lobbying activities increased. Additionally, I illustrate that the interest groups at the center of the Obamacare conflict represent only a tiny fraction of all interest organizations that lobbied during the law's legislative development. Thousands of organizations other than the major industry trade associations and corporations attempted to influence the outcome of the health care reform debate. And a large proportion of those did not come from the health, insurance, or pharmaceutical sectors of the economy.

Second, I speculate how this government agenda–induced expansion of health care lobbying changed the political context in which comprehensive reform was debated. Though the economic and political preferences of health care reform's major players were the same under both presidents, Obama appears to have benefited from what Robert Salisbury referred to as the interest group paradox: as more groups establish themselves in Washington, D.C., the less clout the relatively few dominant groups have.[6] Years of pent-up political pressure resulting from the increase in health-related interest groups led to a perception by entrenched interests that change was inevitable. So they decided they might as well see to it that change occurred on their terms.

Even though the institutional contexts under Clinton and Obama were observably similar, those interests with the most at stake found themselves in a very different interest group environment under Obama. The perception of inevitability was absent during Clinton's attempt. Thus, one reason behind the dramatic shift in the health policy status quo was that the interest group environment allowed Obama to cobble together a coalition of major stakeholders who were willing to accept some significant changes.

Government Activity and Interest Mobilization: Supply versus Demand Theories

At the heart of the health care reform debate were the facts that the health sector of the economy had grown enormously over the past three decades and that the cost for health services for both public and private consumers had increased at a pace far above inflation. The health care sector now approaches 17 percent of gross domestic product, which ranks the United States as the overwhelmingly largest spender among all thirty-four Organization for Economic Cooperation and Development countries.[7] Because health care represents such a large—and growing—segment of the economy, it should be no surprise that government involvement in health care has grown as well.

The observation that the size of government and the scope of the interest group population are linked has long been established, though interest group scholars have proposed different reasons why. Broadly speaking, two schools of thought address the correlation between the expansion of government and the interest group system. The first school of thought focuses on the potential supply of organized interests in the overall economy and society. Though there are competing explanations of how potential groups form and maintain themselves, this school of thought explores how significant events, organizational resources, and entrepreneurs stimulate otherwise disorganized groups to act collectively to resolve common problems.

In 1950, political scientist David Truman offered up the first supply-oriented theory.[8] He attempted to explain the tandem expansion of groups and government with his concept of disturbances, referring to inevitable changes in the equilibrium of interests in the economy and society. When some latent or disorganized group in society—such as farmers, workers, or women—experiences some event that is perceived as a threat to the status quo, that group becomes motivated to organize itself as a social movement or to establish a lobbying presence. By disrupting the status quo, disturbances lead otherwise disaggregated factions of citizens, professionals, identity groups, or even businesses that previously had little reason to organize to come together. These newly organized interests would then seek greater government involvement in corresponding economic and social affairs, thus expanding the size and scope of the government's jurisdiction.

Mancur Olson offered an alternative supply-oriented theory of group mobilization. In *The Logic of Collective Action*, he critiqued Truman's explanation by highlighting the fact that the ability to organize for political action inherently favors those groups with the resources to offer particularized benefits to members and potential members.[9] By attracting the contributions of a relatively few with some tangible, usually material, benefit unrelated to the group's lobbying objectives, an otherwise unorganized group could then transform the resources gained from that transaction into influencing public policy. Absent the particularized benefit, most people would free ride on the contributions of others. The dilemma, then, is that when nobody contributes—even if they are faced with a threat—the latent group lacks the organizational resources to spontaneously seek a solution to their shared problems. Simply put, the free-rider problem limits the supply of some groups, resulting in a distribution of organized interests that disproportionately favors the economically advantaged.[10] Though the ability of other interests to countermobilize may be inherently limited by the collective action dilemma, there is still ample evidence that political and economic threats have a good deal of influence on the likelihood that an otherwise latent group will organize to influence public policy.[11]

Another alternative supply-side theory highlights rent-seeking behavior, or the idea that companies, associations, unions, and nonmember institutions seek to extract direct economic benefits from the government.[12] Applying this concept specifically to interest mobilization, Salisbury contended that interest group entrepreneurs have an incentive to invest in the relatively low-cost act of organizing a new group or mobilizing existing groups in exchange for a relatively large government benefit.[13] In this exchange theory of interest group mobilization, benefits may be independent of any actual political or economic threat to prospective members or lobbying clients. That is, entrepreneurs artificially drum up a supply of groups with the potential for securing government contracts, direct subsidies, sympathetic tax codes, or favorable regulation from government. Government will grow at least in part in response to the efforts of lobbying entrepreneurs, even in the absence of disturbances and in spite of the collective action dilemma.

The second school of thought focuses on the demand for interest representation. Government demand theory reverses the causal direction of the link between the private sector and the government by looking at how the government itself encourages groups to mobilize for political action. Most obviously, the government can offer direct subsidies to latent groups or establish programs that force nongovernmental entities to organize for their implementation.[14] Yet tangible subsidies or clientilistic programs are not the only form of demand. Gray and Lowery first addressed this idea with their population ecology approach to interest mobilization.[15] They argued that interest group mobilization is density dependent, or that any system of organized interests' capacity to grow is intrinsically limited. Even if there was, in theory, an infinite supply of groups to compete against each other, they "share a common resource in that they all seek space on the public agenda."[16]

Government activity stimulates interest group activity by creating a demand for lobbying. As the government's priorities shift, so too do the interest group system's priorities. Leech and colleagues demonstrated that as the federal government increases its attention to an issue domain, so too do organized interests shift their lobbying efforts to that domain.[17] In a cross-sectional analysis of fifty-six distinct issue areas in Washington, D.C., they showed that the number of congressional hearings held on topics related to a domain increased the number of groups who reported lobbying on those issues. These results hold up when controlling for the independent effects of government spending, the availability of potential groups in related industries, and historical trends of lobbying activity within the domain.

Subsequent empirical studies have confirmed and expanded on these findings to suggest that legislative activities other than hearings have varying impacts on lobbying activities,[18] that federal government attention stimulates interest group activity at the state level,[19] and that policy domains traditionally prioritized by presidents rather than Congress actually divert lobbying attention from the legislature and increase the effect of congressional demand for lobbying in its own traditional domains.[20] Most importantly, the demand effect applies equally to those who support and oppose the status quo.[21]

One aspect of this body of empirical work that has yet to be fully fleshed out is the timing and sequence of the demand effect on lobbying.

In one notable exception, Lowery and colleagues explicitly tested whether government agendas are a leading, lagging, or extemporaneous cause of interest mobilization.[22] That is, the authors asked whether increased attention to an issue domain in one legislative session precedes, follows, or is simultaneous with increases in lobbying efforts. Using three successive legislative sessions in state capitals, they found that within-session changes in government agendas affect lobbying when controlling for changes in lobbying activities before and after the session. Even so, this relatively short window of time does not speak to the long-term dynamics of policy change and interest group mobilization, where changes are variable and dramatic rather than constant and incremental.

An alternative way to explore government demand for lobbying is to analyze interest mobilization over a long period in select domains as opposed to many domains in a relatively small window of time—in this case, the health policy domain.[23] There is no doubt that the findings from a longitudinal case study—especially one as politically idiosyncratic as health care—may not apply to other domains. But a long-term trend analysis of the relationship between the political prioritization of health policy and health care industry lobbying from before the Clinton Task Force through the present can shed some light on how previously entrenched groups went from defending the status quo to supporting Obama's health care law.

Data on Health Interest Mobilization and Lobbying

The challenge of empirically testing the government demand theory over a long period is not related to the theory itself but rather to the scant availability of detailed information on interest mobilization and lobbying activities over long periods of time. At the federal level, the most thorough information can be derived from reports filed in accordance with the Lobbying Disclosure Act (LDA) of 1995. The LDA requires organizations who meet certain spending thresholds (or, in cases of lobbying firms who have clients, income thresholds) to file reports periodically on their lobbying activities. These reports include information on the individual lobbyists who worked for a client, the issue areas in which they were active, the specific issues and legislative bills that they lobbied on, and the government agencies they contacted.[24] However, the LDA only began requiring lobbyists at the federal level to report their activities beginning in 1996. Because the Clinton Task force on health care reform dissolved a year before the LDA was enacted, it is impossible to directly compare health lobbying between the Clinton and Obama reform episodes at the ideal level of detail.

The alternative to using data disclosed under the LDA is to count the number of health-related interest organizations listed in the *Washington*

Representatives directory of federal lobbyists and policy advocates.[25] Much like a phone book, *Washington Representatives* is a commercial directory whose listings are self-selected, as opposed to LDA reports that are compelled by law. It is an ideal source to create a time series of organizations that have a stake in comprehensive health care reform because it has been published every year since the mid-1970s. There is significant overlap because the directory editors include all organizations that file LDA reports, though the directory also includes many organizations that do not meet LDA reporting thresholds. However, *Washington Representatives* only indicates an organization's "lobbying presence."[26] It does not provide details on an interest organization's lobbying activities, as does the LDA.

Given these data limitations, then, analyzing a link between the expansion of government activity in health policy and lobbying activities by health care interests over the roughly twenty-year period from Clinton to Obama needs to look first at the growth of health-related groups over time from *Washington Representatives*, then observe lobbying activities on Obama's efforts via detail from LDA reports. The *Washington Representatives* time series compiled for this essay is a count of the number of organizations that are listed in the directory's subject index under Medicine/Health Care/Mental Health, Pharmaceutical Industry, and Insurance Industry from the 1990 through 2009 editions.[27] The time series begins in the George H. W. Bush administration just prior to Clinton's health reform attempt and ends with the most recent edition available.

I selected these subject index categories because they correspond to the dominant stakeholders emphasized in group conflict narratives[28] about health care reform, so they are considered to be "health-related" interests. The Pharmaceutical and Insurance Industry subject headings remained constant for the entire time period. However, the directory editors changed health-related subject categories twice, in 1993 and 1999. To maintain consistency, I needed to collapse several subject categories from earlier editions—such as Health Care, Hospitals/Nursing Homes, and Mental Health—to match the "Medicine/Health Care/Mental Health" category in the 1999 through 2009 editions. I simply refer to these combined subject headings here as Health. The Health category includes hospitals, physician and provider organizations, professional medical associations, and other health-services organizations, as well as consumer and patient advocacy groups. Additionally, it is important to note that the Insurance Industry category includes firms, trade associations, and occupational associations representing the entire insurance market, of which health insurance is only one segment. I use these data to measure whether there were significant changes in the number of health-related organizations with a Washington, D.C., presence when both Clinton and Obama made reform a top priority.

I drew the LDA data from the Center for Responsive Politics' (CRP) lobbying database. CRP, a nonpartisan research organization in Washington that tracks money and politics at the federal level, organizes LDA reports and identifies the primary industrial-economic interests that each client represents. For instance, CRP identifies both the trade association PhRMA and the drug company Pfizer as belonging to the pharmaceutical-manufacturing industry in the health sector. By categorizing individual groups by their primary economic interest, I can aggregate them by economic interests and analyze patterns of lobbying activities across sectors.

CRP's lobbying database provided the source for two more data sets. The first is a time series of lobbying activities to augment the *Washington Representatives* time series of lobbying presence, and the second is a cross-sectional data set of all organizations that reported lobbying specifically on Obama's health care reform. The LDA requires organizations to self-select up to seventy-eight issue areas on which they lobbied. These issue areas represent lobbying activity in broad policy domains rather than on particular issues like health care reform. The data in this time series—derived from LDA reports filed from 1998 through 2009[29]—are annual counts of the number of clients reporting lobbying activities in the Health Issues (HCR), Medicare/Medicaid (MMM), and Medical Research & Clinical Labs (MED) issue areas. Thus, the time series broadly measures the level of attention of all organized interests—not simply those from the health sector of the economy—to all health-related issues from the end of Clinton's second term leading up to Obama's first.

Because the LDA requires lobbying organizations to report the specific bills on which they lobby, I composed a second LDA data set consisting of all groups active on the four major legislative health care reform vehicles in the 111th Congress. The 2009–10 LDA health care reform data set includes all organizations that mentioned lobbying on health care reform bills in the 111th Congress.[30] I identified a sample of 1,527 organizations that reported lobbying on health care reform at any time during all four quarters of 2009 and the first three quarters of 2010.[31]

In addition to CRP's economic categorization, I also categorized lobbying clients according to the type of formal organization that they adopt, such as a business firm, trade or professional association, labor union, or nonmember institution.[32] I use this information to analyze the diversity of groups that lobbied on health care reform in the 111th Congress.

Though no single source of data on interest group activities is available to directly compare health care mobilization and lobbying influence between Clinton and Obama, the empirical analyses that follow demonstrate that the story behind the health care reform conflict is a complex one in which government agendas drove lobbying activities across a large and diverse set of interests.

How Did Health Care Reform Affect the Interest Group System?

Over the nearly twenty years between the two attempts at comprehensive health care reform, a clear government demand pattern emerges among the health-related interests at the core of the debate. Figure 15.1(a) shows the number of health, pharmaceutical, and insurance organizations listed in the *Washington Representatives* directory from 1990—three years before Clinton took office—to 2009, when Obama declared health care reform to be a top domestic policy priority.

Figure 15.1(a)   Health, Insurance, and Pharmaceutical Organized Interests, 1990–2009

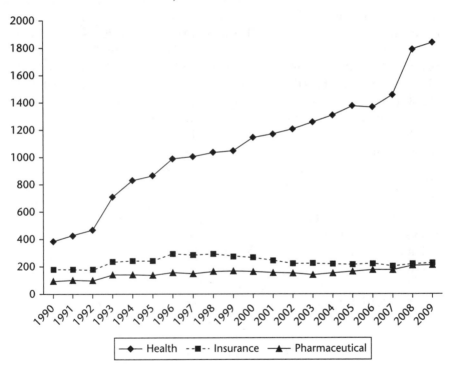

Source: Compiled by the author from annual editions of *Washington Representatives* (Washington, DC: Columbia Books).

Note: The data are counts of the number of clients listed in the selected subjects index under health-related categories, pharmaceutical industry, and insurance industry. For the 1990 through 1998 editions, several subject categories—such as health care, hospitals/nursing homes, and mental health—were collapsed to match the "Medicine/Health Care/Mental Health" category in the 1999 through 2009 editions, which is simply referred to here as Health.

The most striking feature is the sustained growth of health-related interests, which starkly contrasts with the relative stability of pharmaceutical and insurance interests. In 1990, there were as few as 384 health organizations with an established presence in Washington, D.C. By the time health care reform legislation was being developed in the 111th Congress, 1,837 health care groups were listed in *Washington Representatives* as having a lobbyist. This change represents a 378 percent net increase in health organizations. By comparison, the pharmaceutical industry roughly doubled, growing from 94 to 210 organizations. The insurance industry—which also includes non–health insurance firms that may not have any direct interest in health insurance regulation—grew only 26 percent. Clearly, the growth in the presence of health-related interests is lopsided compared to that of other stakeholders in health care reform.

Though the growth in health groups was dramatic compared to pharmaceutical and insurance interests, the year-to-year changes reveal that growth in all three industries came in predictable fits and starts. In Figure 15.1(b), the bars represent the annual changes in the Washington presence

Figure 15.1(b)   Weighted Annual Percentage Change in Number of Health, Insurance, and Pharmaceutical Organized Interests

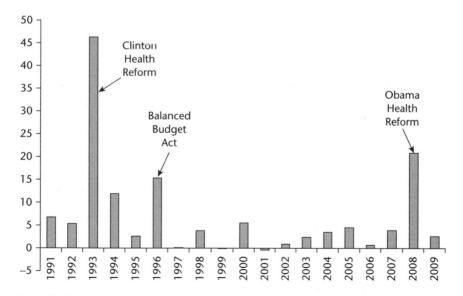

Source: Washington Representatives annual editions.

Note: Each bar represents the average percentage change from the previous year, weighted by the number of clients listed in the subjects index under health, insurance, and pharmaceutical categories.

of health, pharmaceutical, and insurance groups, weighted by the frequency of organizations in each category. That is, this graph represents the average annual percentage change in all three industries. Consistent with the government demand theory of interest mobilization, the largest annual percentage change increases occur on or about the presidential prioritization of health care reform. Of the net 1,453 new health groups with a Washington presence, 573 of them arrived in either 1993 or 2008. The largest change is in 1993 when President Clinton first proposed reform. Between 1992 and 1993 alone, the number of health groups increased by more than 50 percent, from 467 to 709 organizations. In 2008, a net of 332 health groups came to Washington.

It is inconceivable that these two spikes in the number of health groups were driven by a single disturbance in the health sector or by opportunistic interest group entrepreneurs. If so, year-to-year interest group expansions of this magnitude should be observed regularly, not intermittently and coincident with presidents' domestic policy priorities.

Proportionally, the growth of groups representing the pharmaceutical and insurance industries was comparable, though not quite as large. Respectively, groups representing these industries experienced 41 percent and 34 percent growth during the debate in the 104th Congress. By the time Clinton's proposal died in the Senate in 1994, there were 472 more health, pharmaceutical, and insurance organizations with a Washington presence than there were when he won office in 1992. This increase is remarkable in light of the fact that Clinton's proposal failed. The status quo prevailed. The only thing that happened was that Clinton made reforming health care the top domestic issue of his first administration.

A similar pattern is observed during the Obama health reform episode, with the largest increase occurring in 2008. Though he was still a candidate for office in 2008, Obama made health care reform a central theme of his campaign. This prompted the 110th Congress—under control of the Democrats for the first time since Republicans had become the majority during Clinton's first midterm election—to begin seriously developing the comprehensive health care reform legislation advocated by their party's nominee. From the time that the Democrats took the majority in the House in 2007 to the time Speaker Pelosi claimed credit for passing the first health care reform bill during Obama's administration in 2009, 470 new health organizations were listed in the *Washington Representatives* directory.

During this same time, though, only a combined thirty-nine new pharmaceutical and insurance groups established a presence. Though the specific year of the growth raises new questions about the timing and sequence of the agenda-setting effect for health interest mobilization in the short term, the approximate timing of these dramatic increases can unmistakably be linked to comprehensive health reform.

The other observable feature in the growth of health-related interests is that there is no comparable *decrease* when health care reform was not a major priority. This observation suggests that lobbying presence is "sticky," or that once a group establishes itself, it does not simply go away when the issue that drew it to Washington, D.C., drops off the agenda. With one exception, no year exhibits more than an average 10 percent net increase in the number of organizations with a presence. The only other instance when new groups significantly increased their presence in Washington coincides with the Balanced Budget Act (BBA) of 1997.

Though the BBA was passed as part of the annual reconciliation process in Congress to balance the government's books, it was most notable for those inside the Beltway because it reduced the Medicare reimbursement rate. That is, the BBA reduced the formula that the Medicare program used to calculate payments to hospitals, doctors, and nurse practitioners for the services they provide to the government insurance program's recipients. Not surprisingly, and perhaps consistent with a genuine disturbance, hospitals and practitioners opposed this threat to their revenue potential. Their mobilization in opposition to these changes is evident in the increase in health-related interests in 1996 when Medicare reform became a priority of Republicans in the House. As a consequence, there was a 14 percent increase in the number of health organizations and 13 percent rise in the number of pharmaceutical groups from 1995 to 1996.[33] Those reimbursement reductions were eliminated in the subsequent Congress.

The growth spurts during major health reform and relative stagnation in the intervening periods is even more telling when viewed in the context of the overall interest group system. Figure 15.2 illustrates the proportional effect of the expanded presence of health services groups.[34]

The proportion of pharmaceutical organizations remained constant, and the insurance industry actually declined slightly from 1991 to 2001. In contrast, health groups nearly doubled their share of the interest group population, from just over 5.4 percent before Clinton's reform efforts to 10 percent at the beginning of George W. Bush's first administration. These findings show that the sharp increase in the number of health groups over time illustrated in Figure 15.1 was not related to the normal expected growth across the universe of interests in Washington. Health care groups established a lobbying presence at an unusually higher rate than their cohorts. That growth can be attributed at least in part to identifiable shifts in the policy agenda.

These trends in Washington presence only look at those selected industries that can reasonably be expected to have a direct stake in the outcome of comprehensive health care reform. But, to fully examine the impact of policy agendas on interest mobilization, the government demand

Figure 15.2   Proportional Growth of Health, Pharmaceutical, and
Insurance Organized Interests

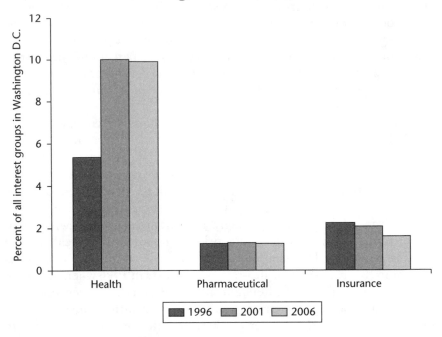

Source: Total counts of *Washington Representatives* data found in Schlozman (2010). Health, insurance, and pharmaceutical organizations compiled by the author from annual editions of *Washington Representatives* (Washington, DC: Columbia Books).

Note: The data are counts of the number of clients listed in the selected subjects index under health-related categories, pharmaceutical industry, and insurance industry. Unlike organization-type coding schemes found in Schlozman and Tierney (1986), Baumgartner and Leech (2001), Schlozman (2010), organizations may be included in multiple selected subjects index categories in *Washington Representatives*, and these categories include for-profit corporations, associations, institutions, and other types of interest organizations.

effects must also be measured for those interests that may only have an indirect or ephemeral interest in the issue.

A second time series—one that uses LDA data and so unfortunately cannot capture the effects of Clinton's efforts—illustrates how interests of all kinds shifted their attention to health lobbying when reform became a top issue in the 110th Congress. This data set includes all organizations that filed LDA reports between 1998 and 2009, not just those selected from the health, pharmaceutical, and insurance industries. That is, these trends measure lobbying activity regardless of the primary industry that the groups occupied in the economy. Figure 15.3(a) plots the number of organizations who indicated on LDA reports that they conducted lobbying activities on

Figure 15.3(a)   Lobbying Activity in Health-Related Issue Areas, 1998–2009

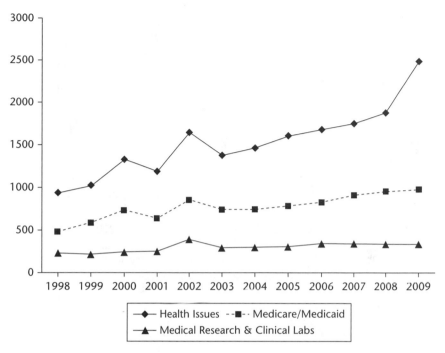

Source: CRP Lobbying Database.

Note: The data are counts of the number of clients reporting lobbying activities in the Health Issues (HCR), Medicare/Medicaid (MMM), and Medical Research & Clinical Labs (MED) issue areas.

the Health Issues (HCR), Medicare/Medicaid (MMM), and Medical Research & Clinical Labs (MED) issue areas.

All three issue areas experienced a growth in the number of active lobbying organizations, with HCR seeing the greatest expansion from 937 to 2,481 groups, a 165 percent change. The MMM and MED issue areas experienced growth rates of 101 percent and 45 percent, respectively.

Like the long-term trends in lobbying presence, the lion's share of these expansions can be attributed to easily identifiable instances of increased government attention to health issues. Figure 15.3(b) shows that the two spikes occurred during the development of the Medicare Prescription Drug, Improvement, and Modernization Act (MMA) of 2003 and at the beginning of comprehensive health reform legislation in 2008. The MMA expanded Medicare to cover prescription drugs, prompting an average growth across the three issue areas of 15 percent. This growth is noteworthy due to its contemporaneous nature with MMA, but it is overshadowed by

Figure 15.3(b)   Annual Percentage Change in Lobbying Activity in
Health-Related Issue Areas, 1998–2009

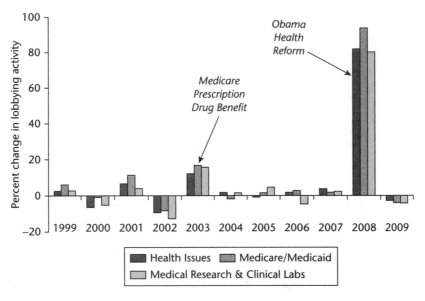

Source: CRP Lobbying Database.

Note: Each bar represents the percentage change from the previous year.

the expansion evident during comprehensive health reform. From 2007 to 2008 alone, the HCR issue area attracted 82 percent more lobbying organizations, MMM 94 percent more, and MED 81 percent more.

The upshot is that not only does presidential prioritization mobilize new groups with a direct stake in the issue to establish a presence in Washington, D.C., but it also attracts lobbying attention from organizations that might otherwise have little interest in the issue. These results suggest that government agendas not only increase the amount of lobbying overall but also increase the diversity of groups engaged in lobbying on key issues.

Who Lobbied on Health Care Reform?

Not only does highlighting health care reform lure new groups with health-related interests to come to Washington, D.C., but it also attracts the attention of groups from across the full set of organized interests who already have an established presence. Figure 15.4 compares the distribution of organized interests who reported lobbying on health care reform in the 111th Congress to two samples of the interest group population as a whole.

The Baumgartner and Leech[35] data are a sample of all 4,211 organizations who reported lobbying in 1996, the first year the LDA was in effect.

Figure 15.4 Comparison of Two LDA Samples with Lobbying on Major Health Reform Legislation in the 111th Congress

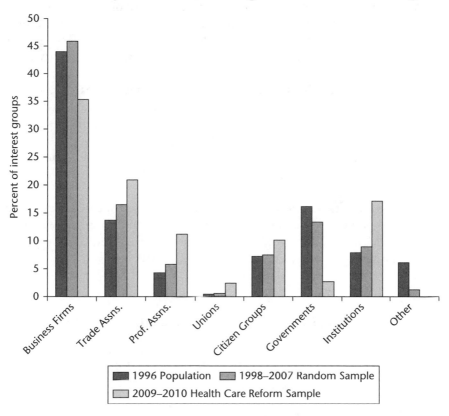

Sources: The 1996 Lobbying Disclosure Act (LDA) population data found in Baumgartner and Leech (2001, 1195); the 1998–2007 LDA sample and 2009–2010 Health Care Reform data sets as calculated by the author using the Center for Responsive Politics (CRP) Lobbying Database, available at http://www.opensecrets.org/lobby/index.php.

Note: This figure draws on three independently selected data sets. The Baumgartner and Leech data set includes the entire population of clients who reported lobbying under the LDA for the 1996 calendar year (*N* = 4,211 organizations). The 1998–2007 data set is a random sample of organizations that filed at least one LDA report during that time (*n* = 4,032). The 2009–2010 LDA health care reform data set includes all organizations that mentioned lobbying on at least one of the four major health care reform bills in the 111th Congress—H.R. 3200, H.R. 3590, H.R. 3962, and H.R. 4872 (*n* = 1,527 organizations).

Business firms, trade associations, and professional associations—which collectively represent "business" interests—represent 62 percent of the interest group population. The second data set—a random sample of 4,032 organizations that reported lobbying at least once between 1998 and 2007—shows a roughly similar pattern of business mobilization, suggesting a high degree of stability in the distribution of interests over time.

These population-level samples appear to be quite different from the roughly 1,500 organizations involved in the Obama health reform debate. The combined business interests represent 68 percent of the lobbying organizations that were active on health care, but there is a noticeable difference in the proportion of trade and professional associations. The greater number of these associations makes up for the reduced lobbying activity on the part of business firms.

Additionally, institutions are more likely to lobby on health care than their share of the interest group population would suggest. Institutions include hospitals and clinics, so it is not necessarily surprising to see that those interests exhibit more activity. In all, the set of organizations that chose to lobby on health care reform does not mirror the distribution of interest groups in the greater population. Actually, health care lobbying appears to be more diverse.

When cross-tabulated with CRP's economic interest categories, there appears to be even more variation among the types of interests who lobbied on health care. Table 15.1 shows the prevalence of different types of economic and political interests as defined by CRP.[36]

Table 15.1 Groups Lobbying on Major Health Reform Legislation in the 111th Congress

Organization Type	Economic / Political Interest (percent)					
	Health	FIRE	Ideological	Public	Multi-Sector	N
Business Firms	36	21	0	1	42	540
Trade Associations	43	13	2	5	37	320
Professional Associations	76	2	1	12	9	172
Unions	0	0	0	0	100	37
Citizen Groups	16	1	74	6	2	155
Government	2	0	0	93	5	41
Institutions	60	0	3	36	1	262
Overall Percentage	42	11	9	12	27	1,527

Source: CRP Lobbying Database.

Note: Cell entries are row frequency percentages of organizations that reported lobbying on at least one of the four major health care reform bills—H.R. 3200, H.R. 3590, H.R. 3962, and H.R. 4872. The economic/political interest categories are defined by CRP, which adapted the standard industrial codes in the 1980s to classify organizations. The acronym *FIRE* refers to the finance, insurance, and real estate industries. CRP's "public" category includes education, state/local governments, nonprofits, and religious organizations. The "multi-sector" category includes these CRP industries: agribusiness, communications/electronics, construction, defense, energy and natural resources, lawyers, transportation, miscellaneous business (including manufacturing, retail, tourism, and other services), and labor unions. Percentages may not sum to 100 due to rounding.

$\chi2$ (df = 24) = 58.3; p < 0.001.

For instance, three-fourths of the professional associations who lobbied on Obama's health proposal were from the health sector. Conversely professional associations represent only 2 percent of the groups attempting to influence health care reform in the financial services, insurance, and real estate (FIRE) sector. The health sector groups mostly represent physicians with various medical expertise, nurses and nurse practitioners, and other service providers. Yet, the AMA is only one of the 130 health sector professional associations. It's hard to argue that the AMA was the only voice representing doctors in the debate, meaning that group conflict descriptions likely overstate its influence in the negotiations.

The most revealing feature of Table 15.1 is not necessarily the idiosyncratic features of the health versus financial industries. Instead, roughly one in four groups that lobbied on Obama's health care proposals is primarily engaged in economic activities outside the health and financial sectors. That is, 27 percent of all active groups come from groups that do *not* have a primary interest in the health care or finance sectors of the economy. Excepting ideological groups and the public sector, the "multi-sector" category combines several industries that are not mentioned in the group conflict narratives for health care reform. Individually, each category represents an average of 3 percent of all active groups, though collectively they constitute the second-largest category of interests who actively lobbied on health care reform. This pattern is even more pronounced among for-profit business firms: 225 of the 540 identified businesses have primary economic interests other than health care or insurance.

A somewhat different picture emerges when the level of lobbying activity is measured. Under LDA guidelines, each organization may have multiple reports filed on its behalf during a single quarter. An organization self-files a spending report if it conducts in-house lobbying. If it also hires outside consultants, that firm-for-hire must submit a separate income report on behalf of the client. Each report may mention one or more of the four major health care bills. When summed, the "report-mentions" variable is the number of reports that mention any one of the four major health reform bills for each organization.[37] This measure reflects the best estimate of the amount of attention an individual organization gave to the issue.

Because the attention that interest groups give to a bill reflects the intensity of their interest in the legislation, uncovering patterns in the level of lobbying activity can tell us a great deal about the degree of interest group pluralism in the health care reform debate. Figure 15.5 lists the most active groups, or those that filed more than thirty-five LDA reports that mention health care reform.

The single most active organization—Blue Cross/Blue Shield, the largest health plan provider in the United States—actually reflects lobbying reports filed by its independently organized companies chartered at the

Figure 15.5   Most Active Organizations Lobbying on Major Health
Reform Legislation in the 111th Congress

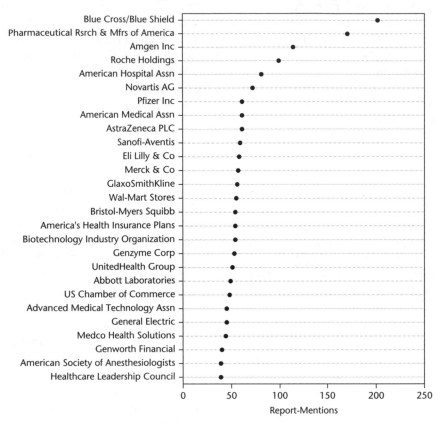

Source: CRP Lobbying Database.

Note: The data are "report-mentions," or the sum of the number of quarterly LDA reports filed by
or on behalf of a client that mention a major health care reform bill—H.R. 3200, H.R. 3590, H.R.
3962, and H.R. 4872.

state level, so the nearly 200 report-mentions is an artifact of its organizational form. Regardless, clearly this health insurance provider was a central
player in the development of the new health care law and devoted many
resources to influencing its outcome.

Among the other top groups are those major industry groups at the
center of the fray—PhRMA, AHIP, AMA—as well as the American Hospital Association, the Biotechnology Industry Organization, and the
Advanced Medical Technology Association. But also included among the
most active organizations are General Electric and Wal-Mart. These large
corporations have multiple political interests, and surely the structure of

government regulation of health care affects their internal human resources choices.[38] But they certainly do not represent health interests as commonly understood.

While these major players are not surprising, what is most revealing is that collectively, these most-active organizations actually account for less than 2 percent of all the organizations that lobbied on Obama's health care proposal. At the other extreme, 63 percent of the organizations mentioned health reform lobbying on five or fewer reports. Media accounts and the group-conflict story emphasize the lobbying activities of the most active groups, but they ignore the overwhelming majority of other groups who also attempted to influence the outcome of the health care debate. The only question remaining is whether groups at the top end of the lobbying activity scale roughly represent the same interests that are active at the lower end.

Interest Group Pluralism in the Health Care Debate

The observation that thousands of groups representing a large variety of interests actually lobbied on health care reform does not suggest that the pluralist ideal was achieved during the debate. In a theoretically ideal world—one where all interests are represented equally—we should expect to see equivalent levels of lobbying intensity across different types of organized interests.

I put this idea to a test by comparing report-mentions—my measure of lobbying attention—at equivalent levels for different types of organizations and for groups representing different political-economic interests. For instance, if the amount of lobbying attention is distributed equally, then the number of report-mentions among the most active business firms should be roughly equal to the number of report-mentions among the most active citizen groups and labor unions. This pattern should also be true when comparing health industry lobbying to public sector lobbying activity. To compare apples to apples, I arbitrarily selected different markers of lobbying activity levels by group type and interest at the 99th percentile (most active), 75th percentile (very active), 50th percentile (moderately active), and 25th percentile (less active). If lobbying attention is evenly balanced, then organizations would mention health care bills on the same number of reports across group type and interests.

The unequal distribution of lobbying attention across organization type is evident in Table 15.2. In the column on the far right-hand side, Table 15.2 shows that business firms and trade associations devoted more resources to lobbying on health care reform than did labor unions, citizen groups, government entities, and institutions. That is, business firms at the 99th percentile mentioned a health care bill sixty-one times on lobbying reports filed on their behalf, three times the number that institutions

Table 15.2   Lobbying Activity by Percentile across Organization Type (report-mentions)

	Less Active (25th Percentile)	Moderately Active (50th Percentile)	Very Active (75th Percentile)	Most Active (99th Percentile)
Business Firms	3	6	12	61
Trade Associations	4	7	12	54
Prof. Associations	4	6	10	39
Unions	3	7	10	37
Citizen Groups	3	5	7	26
Governments	2	4	6	13
Institutions	3	5	8	20

Source: CRP Lobbying Database.

Note: The data are "report-mentions," or the sum of the number of quarterly LDA reports filed by or on behalf of a client that mention a major health care reform bill—H.R. 3200, H.R. 3590, H.R. 3962, and H.R. 4872.

mentioned at an equivalent level of activity. The most attentive trade associations identified health care reform on fifty-four reports, and the most active professional associations referred to a health care bill on thirty-nine reports. By contrast, the most engaged state and local governments submitted only thirteen lobbying disclosure reports that mentioned health care reform. Clearly, the distribution of resources dedicated to lobbying on the Obama health care reform legislation favored corporations and industry groups over countervailing organizations like citizen groups and labor unions.

The pattern of health care reform lobbying activity becomes less distorted at lower levels. The distribution of lobbying resources at lower levels of activity is not as lopsided, but it is not exactly equal either. Business firms and trade associations at the "very active" level (75th percentile) mention health reform on twelve reports, compared to the eight reports filed by citizen groups and institutions in the same column in Table 15.2. At the lowest level of lobbying activity (25th percentile), the range between the most and least active was four reports, hardly a significant difference in the amount of resources dedicated to influencing major legislation.

A similar pattern across economic interest categories is displayed in Table 15.3. At the high end of lobbying activity, health care and financial services interests were three times as active as those representing the public sector. Health care sector groups at the highest level of activity (99th percentile) mentioned a reform bill on sixty-one reports. The most active FIRE groups mentioned it on fifty-four reports, whereas public sector groups at the equivalent level of attention mentioned it on only twenty reports. These stark differences begin to subside at the 75th percentile marker, with FIRE groups mentioning health care reform on thirteen reports

Table 15.3   Lobbying Activity by Percentile across Political-Economic Interest (report-mentions)

	Less Active (25th Percentile)	Moderately Active (50th Percentile)	Very Active (75th Percentile)	Most Active (99th Percentile)
Health	4	7	11	61
FIRE	3	6	13	54
Ideological	3	5	8	29
Public	1	4	6	20
Multi-Sector	2	5	9	37

Source: CRP Lobbying Database.

Note: The data are "report-mentions," or the sum of the number of quarterly LDA reports filed by or on behalf of a client that mention a major health care reform bill—H.R. 3200, H.R. 3590, H.R. 3962, and H.R. 4872.

compared to public sector groups reporting it just under half that with six mentions. The median (50th percentile) level of lobbying activity for all groups ranges from a high of seven reports among health groups to a low of four for those from the public sector of the economy.

All told, there appears to be both a great deal of diversity of groups in aggregate that lobbied on Obama's health care reform proposal, as well as an intense concentration of lobbying resources for the corporations and industry groups representing the economic sectors at the center of it all. There is little reason to expect all groups to be equally engaged in the debate. But uncovering these patterns of highly concentrated lobbying activities reveals that a select few interests maintained a distinct resource advantage over others in the debate.

Government Demand and Group Conflict over Health Care Reform

Government demand for lobbying is evident in the health care reform context. The long-term mobilization of interests generated by the allure of comprehensive health reform set the stage for a large, diverse set of groups to add their two cents to the debate. How did the long-term growth and diversification of interests in the health policy domain affect the policy outcome? The evidence put forth here does not address the particular positions that each group took on the various issues that arise during such broad debates as comprehensive health reform. So it is impossible to precisely measure how particular lobbying activities impacted policy outcomes.[39]

However, the growth in number and diversification of groups lobbying on health care suggests that Obama was aided by the fact that the groups that most resisted change over time had their influence diluted by others.

That is, Obama succeeded by taking advantage of the interest group paradox of "more groups, less clout" that was set into motion by Clinton's original efforts at reform. Fully aware of the danger of another Harry-and-Louise-style campaign against his policy objectives, Obama emerged as a different kind of policy entrepreneur who skillfully managed the negotiations among different stakeholders out of the public view.

To avoid the fate of his Democratic presidential predecessor, Obama adopted a strategy that many critics claimed would fail. Rather than micromanaging the finer points of health reform legislation, Obama publicly outlined broad principles and allowed congressional Democrats to negotiate the details. Though the Obama White House was involved in the development of legislative specifics behind closed doors, the hands-off approach in public allowed Obama to avoid direct blame for the often messy and complex details of legislative "sausage making" and gave him the wiggle room he needed to concede on points like the public option favored by the progressive wing of his party.

Using the apparent hands-off approach, Obama proceeded as if health care reform was a foregone conclusion. The process was just a matter of filling in the legislative details. This perception of inevitability was not lost on the major economic stakeholders. Obama first succeeded in winning over Karen Ignani, president and CEO of America's Health Insurance Plans (AHIP), the leading national trade association for the health insurance industry. In exchange for dropping opposition to the proposed law's restrictions on preexisting conditions, the top health insurance industry representative could promise her member-companies nearly 30 million new health insurance subscribers through the law's system of government-organized, state-based, private-sector insurance exchanges.[40]

Next Obama turned his attention to former representative-turned-Pharmaceutical Manufacturing and Research Association (PhRMA) president and CEO Billy Tauzin. Obama leveraged his momentum with AHIP by promising Tauzin that previously uninsured and underinsured patients would now be able to afford pharmaceutical blockbusters like Lipitor, Advair, and Plavix. In exchange, Obama extracted Tauzin's pledge to limit drug costs in the plan to $80 billion over ten years.[41] These deals were capped off with the not-so-subtle reappearance of Harry and Louise in new issue ads underwritten by PhRMA; they now touted support for Obama's reform efforts. Obama completed the deal by promising to stop planned Medicare payment cuts, winning over the formidable American Medical Association (AMA), which for decades had resisted reform on behalf of physicians.[42]

With all three major stakeholders placated, the only obstacle remaining was getting the bill through Congress. After enduring a summer of hyperbolic backlash organized by conservative groups in congressional districts around the country and the surprising Republican takeover of liberal stalwart Senator Ted Kennedy's seat in Massachusetts, there was a brief time where it appeared that reform was anything but inevitable. Yet with Democrats in control of the parliamentary reins in both the House and the Senate, the law was passed through a complex series of substantive and procedural maneuvers.

In the end, Obama could claim credit for shepherding through the most major overhaul of the health care system since the Great Society. Because Obama was able to mollify the pharmaceutical, health insurance, and health providers, Biden's assessment of Obama's signature social policy achievement was not just colorful. It was accurate.

Conclusion

Obama's brokerage of the group conflict succeeded where Clinton's had failed, but not necessarily because he exhibited superior political skill. Credit also should go to the interest group environment. The great irony for students of interest group politics is that both presidents had a remarkably similar impact on the number of health interests with a presence in Washington, D.C. By placing health care reform atop their agendas, both presidents helped to increase dramatically the presence of health-related groups in Washington. And, at least according to the available evidence of lobbying activities during the Obama episode, the president's domestic policy priorities also attracted groups that may or may not have had a primary, direct stake in the debate. Organized interests simply become active on an issue because the government is active on it, independently of the policy objective's success or failure.

Though the empirical work on the government agenda-setting effect on lobbying over long periods of time is in its early stages, the evidence I present here suggests that interest group mobilization is a consequence of, not simply a cause of, increased government activity. To be clear, the agenda-setting approach to interest mobilization does not rule out the fact that direct threats indeed motivate groups to react or that interest group entrepreneurs generate incentives to organize groups that might otherwise remain dormant. It simply recognizes that when governments prioritize some policy issues over others, the shift in attention has consequences for interest mobilization and lobbying strategy.

Industry giants like PhRMA, AHIP, and the AMA deserve much of the credit (or blame) for shaping the compromise that led to Obama's big deal. But so should the literally thousands of other interest groups that participated in the deliberations. Directly they certainly helped shape the content of the legislation, but indirectly they helped structure the political environment in which the legislation was crafted. These groups represented a wide variety of organizations and interests, and they should share in the responsibility for influencing the outcome.

Yet the diversity of active interest groups does not necessarily translate into pluralism in the health care debate. The existence of more groups does not mean that lobbying influence is distributed in a more just and democratically ideal way. Instead, as government agendas attract more and more groups, those groups with the most at stake tend to redouble their efforts to have their voices heard above the crowd. Government indeed creates a demand for advocacy. But only a select few have the resources to shout above the cacophony.

Notes

1. This account of the legislative development of health care reform draws on three thorough media and think-tank sources: The Henry J. Kaiser Family Foundation, "Summary of New Health Reform Law," June 18, 2010, http://www.kff.org/healthreform/8061.cfm; Marcia Clemmit, "Health Care Reform," *CQ Researcher* 20, no. 22 (2010): 505–28; Linda J. Blumberg and Karen Pollitz, "Health Insurance Exchanges: Organizing Health Insurance Marketplaces to Promote Health Reform Goals," *Timely Analysis of Immediate Health Policy Issues*, April 1, 2009, http://www.urban.org/publications/411877.html.

2. Larry M. Bartels, *Unequal Democracy: The Political Economy of the New Gilded Age* (New York: Russell Sage Foundation, 2008).

3. These points are intended to be objective descriptions about the perception of the law's impact when it was enacted, not necessarily the author's opinion. The interpretations of the social policy impact of the Obama health care reform law are drawn from Lawrence R. Jacobs and Theda Skocpol, "Hard Fought Legacy: Obama, Congressional Democrats, and the Struggle for Comprehensive Health Reform," paper prepared for working group on Obama's Agenda and the Dynamics of U.S. Politics (New York: Russell Sage Foundation, 2010), http://www.russellsage.org/sites/all/files/u4/Obama_Chapter%202_Health%20Reform.pdf; Jacob S. Hacker, "The Road to Somewhere: Why Health Reform Happened, or Why Political Scientists Who Write about Public Policy Shouldn't Assume They Know How to Shape It," *Perspectives on Politics* 8, no. 3 (2010): 861–76; Lawrence R. Jacobs, "What Health Reform Teaches Us About American Politics," *PS: Political Science & Politics* 43, no. 4 (2010): 619–23.

4. Clinton, William J., Statement from the White House, January 25, 1993. Available at http://www.ibiblio.org/darlene/task/.

5. Jacob S. Hacker, *The Road to Nowhere: The Genesis of President Clinton's Plan for Health Security* (Princeton, NJ: Princeton University Press, 1997). See also Richard Anderson and Richard L. Hall, "Issue Advertising and Legislative Advocacy in Health Politics," chap. 10 in this volume.

6. Robert H. Salisbury, "The Paradox of Interest Groups in Washington—More Groups, Less Clout," in *The New American Political System*, 2nd ed., ed. Anthony King (Washington, DC: AEI Press, 1990): 203–30.

7. Organization for Economic Cooperation and Development, *OECD Health Data 2010: Statistics and Indicators* (Washington, DC: Organization for Economic Cooperation and Development, 2010).

8. David B. Truman, *The Governmental Process: Political Interests and Public Opinion* (New York: Alfred A. Knopf, 1951); Jack L. Walker, "The Origins and Maintenance of Interest Groups in America," *American Political Science Review* 77, no. 2 (1993): 390–406; John Mark Hansen, "The Political Economy of Group Membership," *American Political Science Review* 79, no. 1 (1985): 79–96.

9. Mancur Olson, *The Logic of Collective Action: Public Goods and the Theory of Groups*, Harvard Economic Studies vol. 124 (Cambridge, MA: Harvard University Press, 1965).

10. E. E. Schattschneider, *The Semisovereign People: A Realist's View of Democracy in America* (New York: Holt, Rhinehart, and Winston, 1975); Kay Lehman Schlozman and John T. Tierney, "More of the Same: Washington Pressure Group Activity in a Decade of Change," *Journal of Politics* 45, no. 2 (1983): 351–77; Virginia Gray and David Lowery, *The Population Ecology of Interest Representation: Lobbying Communities in the American States* (Ann Arbor: University of Michigan Press, 1996); Frank R. Baumgartner and Beth L. Leech, "Interest Niches and Policy Bandwagons: Patterns of Interest Group Involvement in National Politics," *Journal of Politics* 63, no. 4 (2001): 1191–213.

11. John Mark Hansen, *Gaining Access: Congress and the Farm Lobby, 1919–1981* (Chicago: University of Chicago Press, 1991).

12. James M. Buchanan and Gordon Tullock, *The Calculus of Consent: Logical Foundations of Constitutional Democracy* (Ann Arbor: University of Michigan Press, 1962); Gordon Tullock, "The Welfare Costs of Tariffs, Monopolies, and Theft," *Western Economic Journal* 5, no. 3 (1967): 224–32; Anne Krueger, "The Political Economy of the Rent-Seeking Society," *American Economic Review* 64, no. 3 (1974): 291–303; Kevin B. Grier, Michael C. Munger, and Brian E. Roberts, "The Determinants of Industry Political Activity, 1978–1986," *American Political Science Review* 88, no. 4 (1994): 911–26.

13. Robert H. Salisbury, "An Exchange Theory of Interest Groups," *Midwest Journal of Political Science* 13, no. 1 (1969): 1–32; Scott Ainsworth and Itai Sined, "The Role of Lobbyists: Entrepreneurs with Two Audiences," *American Journal of Political Science* 37, no. 3 (1993): 834–66.

14. Truman, *The Governmental Process;* Walker, "The Origins and Maintenance of Interest Groups in America"; Theda Skocpol, *Protecting Soldiers and Mothers: The Political Origins of Social Policy in United States* (Cambridge, MA: Belknap Press of Harvard University Press, 1992).

15. Gray and Lowery, *The Population Ecology of Interest Representation.*

16. Gray and Lowery, *The Population Ecology of Interest Representation,* 65.

17. Beth L. Leech, Frank R. Baumgartner, Timothy M. LaPira, and Nicholas Semanko, "Drawing Lobbyists to Washington: Government Activity and the Demand for Advocacy," *Political Research Quarterly* 58, no. 1 (2005): 19–30; see also David Lowery, Virginia Gray, Matthew Fellowes, and Jennifer Anderson, "Living in the Moment: Lags, Leads, and the Links Between Legislative Agendas and Interest Advocacy," *Social Science Quarterly* 85, no. 2 (2004): 463–77.

18. Aaron Dusso, "Legislation, Political Context, and Interest Group Behavior," *Political Research Quarterly* 63, no. 1 (2008): 55–67.

19. Frank R. Baumgartner, Virginia Gray, and David Lowery, "Federal Policy Activity and the Mobilization of State Lobbying Organizations," *Political Research Quarterly* 62, no. 3 (2009): 552–67.

20. Frank R. Baumgartner, Heather A. Larsen-Price, Beth L. Leech, and Paul Rutledge, "Congressional and Presidential Effects on the Demand for Lobbying," *Political Research Quarterly* 64, no. 1 (2011): 3–16.

21. Frank R. Baumgartner, Jeffrey M. Berry, Marie Hojnacki, David C. Kimball, and Beth L. Leech, *Lobbying and Policy Change: Who Wins, Who Loses, and Why* (Chicago: University of Chicago Press, 2009).

22. Lowery, Gray, Fellowes, and Anderson, "Living in the Moment."

23. Lowery and Gray explicitly pointed to time series analysis as a fruitful way to improve the empirical study of lobbying activity and group mobilization. "Unfortunately, what is perhaps most notable about both the literatures on national and state interest systems is the sheer paucity of time series analyses of hypotheses about interest representation." See David Lowery and Virginia Gray, "The Comparative Advantage of State Interest Organization Research," in *The Oxford Handbook of American Political Parties and Interest Groups*, eds. L. Sandy Maisel and Jeffrey M. Berry (New York: Oxford University Press, 2010): 496. See also Lee Jared Drutman, "The Business of America is Lobbying: The Expansion of Corporate Political Activity and the Future of American Pluralism." PhD diss. University of California, Berkeley, 2010, http://www.leedrutman.com/uploads/2/3/0/1/2301208/lee_drutman_phd_dissertation.pdf. Drutman analyzed lobbying trends in select economic industries, including telecommunications, pharmaceuticals, financial services, and high tech.

24. The specific issues and government agencies data from LDA reports should be fruitful sources for better understanding interest group advocacy activities, but unfortunately the format in which the data are collected is seriously flawed. Not only is there little LDA guidance and compliance oversight, the specific-issues question is open-ended, so there is a great deal of variation in the level of detail. As for government agencies, individual members and committees of Congress are not included; rather, lobbyists need only indicate that they contacted the U.S. Senate and/or the U.S. House of Representatives, which hardly makes sense given the organization of Congress.

25. Kay Lehman Schlozman, "Who Sings in the Heavenly Chorus? The Shape of the Organized Interest System," in *The Oxford Handbook of American Political Parties and Interest Groups*, eds. L. Sandy Maisel and Jeffrey M. Berry. (New York: Oxford University Press, 2010).

26. Following Schlozman in"Who Sings in the Heavenly Chorus?" organizations listed in *Washington Representatives* are referred to as having a "presence" rather than as being engaged in lobbying activities.

27. The subject listings were not available for 2010 when this analysis was conducted.

28. Hacker, "The Road to Somewhere;" Jacobs, "What Health Reform Teaches Us about American Politics."

29. CRP uses the Senate Office of Public Records (SOPR) for their source of LDA data. SOPR did not begin making LDA data electronically available until 1998, and the full data set from 2010 was not complete at the time of this analysis.

30. This data set includes only those organizations that reported lobbying on health care reform bills as indicated by House legislative bill designations H.R. 3200, H.R. 3590, H.R. 3962, and H.R. 4872 (including punctuation variants such as "HR 3200"). This process likely does not include all organizations that engaged in some lobbying on health care reform in the 111th Congress, though there is little reason to believe that errors introduced by the open-ended format are biased toward any particular interest or organization.

31. Among other changes, the Honest Leadership and Open Government Act of 2007 amended the LDA to require reporting on a quarterly basis, rather than the semester

basis in the original 1995 law. The data were drawn from the CRP lobbying database in October 2010, before fourth-quarter 2010 reports were filed in February 2011.

32. The coding scheme is hierarchical to allow for aggregation. There are forty-two "organization-subtype" codes that correspond with the "group-type" codes used by Baumgartner and Leech in "Interest Niches and Policy Bandwagons."

33. The insurance industry demonstrates an even higher increase: 21 percent during 1996. This increase is most likely related to the financial deregulation legislation championed by House Republicans. Congress first turned its attention to repealing the Glass-Steagal Act, which prevented banks, securities firms, and insurance firms from operating under one roof. The new legislation, which came to be known as the Gramm-Leach-Bliley Financial Services Modernization Act, became law in 1999. Thus, this spike in the insurance industry is simply an artifact of the *Washington Representatives* subject index, which includes both health and non–health insurance firms.

34. The proportion of health, pharmaceutical, and insurance groups are calculated using the overall counts of organizations with a Washington, D.C., presence from a much more comprehensive *Washington Representatives* data set reported by Schlozman in "Who Sings in the Heavenly Chorus?" In that project, the researchers did not create a time series but rather complete cross-sectional data sets from selected years.

35. Baumgartner and Leech, "Interest Niches and Policy Bandwagons."

36. CRP adapted the U.S. Census Bureaus's standard industrial codes (SIC) in the 1980s to classify political donors' employers and political action committees by "industry," and it created several new codes to accommodate uniquely political categories for single-issue advocacy and ideological groups. The acronym *FIRE* refers to the finance, insurance, and real estate industries. CRP's "public" category includes education, state/local governments, nonprofits, and religious organizations. The "multi-sector" category includes these CRP industries: agribusiness, communications/electronics, construction, defense, energy and natural resources, lawyers, transportation, miscellaneous business (including manufacturing, retail, tourism, and other services), and labor unions.

37. Ideally, I would use lobbying expenditures to measure an organization's resource allocation. But because the LDA reporting system forces organizations to report the amount of money that they spend in the aggregate, it is not possible to know how much any organization spent on health care reform alone, or any other issue for that matter. Baumgartner and Leech demonstrated in "Interest Niches and Policy Bandwagons" that lobbying expenditures and counts of reports are very highly correlated. So at this level of analysis, the "report-mentions" variable should be a reliable measure of the level of resources that an organization commits to lobbying on any single issue.

38. See, for instance, Cathie Jo Martin, *Stuck in Neutral: Business and the Politics of Human Capital Investment Policy* (Princeton, NJ: Princeton University Press, 2000).

39. The LDA does not require lobbyists to state support for or opposition to the status quo for the issues that they lobby. See Baumgartner, Berry, Hojnacki, Kimball, and Leech, *Lobbying and Policy Change.*

40. Blumberg and Pollitz, "Health Insurance Exchanges."

41. This compromise was not without controversy, as Tauzin resigned shortly after reaching this agreement when PhRMA's larger member-companies disputed his

concessions. Duff Wilson and David Kirkpatrick, "Health Reform in Limbo, Top Drug Lobbyist Quits," *New York Times*, February 11, 2010, http://thecaucus.blogs .nytimes.com/2010/02/11/health-reform-in-limbo-top-drug-lobbyist-quits/.

42. Kim Geiger and Tom Hamburger, "AMA Does 180 on Health Care," *Chicago Tribune*, September 13, 2009, http://www.chicagotribune.com/news/chi-tc-nw-lobbying-ama-0912–0913sep13,0,7112379.story/.

IV. CONCLUSION

16

Stalemate Meets Uncertainty

Organized Interests in a Partisan Era

Allan J. Cigler and Burdett A. Loomis

In 1983, when we wrote the concluding chapter to the first edition of *Interest Group Politics*, we placed a great emphasis on representation as an avenue for understanding how organized interests behaved. We also harbored some thoughts that such understanding might well be central to the overall study of American politics. In the almost thirty years since then, we continue to see representation as highly important, but we have grown increasingly skeptical that organized interests, however important they may be, open up some coherent way to address American politics as a whole. As we noted several years ago, interest group politics is almost always a significant factor in analyzing politics and policy making in the United States, but rarely, if ever, is it central to some comprehensive understanding. Rather, focusing on organized interests complements our broader knowledge of political institutions, electoral politics, and the policy-making process, as well as our capacity to analyze them.

Organized interests often appear powerful—and as powerful explanatory forces—largely because we have a difficult time assessing their successes. Even careful, large-scale studies, such as Baumgartner et al.'s 2009 *Lobbying and Policy Change*, reach tentative and limited findings.[1] At the same time, membership organizations, corporations, unions, professional associations, and many other groups spend $5 to $6 billion[2] each year to lobby the Congress, the executive, independent agencies, and all the similar institutions within state governments. Beyond that, groups and corporations spend hundreds of millions, if not more, in litigation to protect their interests. In short, aggressively promoting one's interests is as American as apple pie. And there's the rub. As the number of organized interests and lobbyists grow, so does the likelihood that American policy making will tend toward stalemate, while its politics will grow more costly and acrimonious.

Since the New Deal, American government has produced a nonstop array of new and often complex policies, from weapons procurement for an expanding military establishment to extensive environmental and drug regulations to a Byzantine tax system. Although organized interests have often sought particular programs, new policies have regularly provided incentives for new groups to form, frequently focused on specific elements of these policies. For example, as the national government has intervened in health care over the past fifty years, the interest group community surrounding this issue area has grown larger and far more differentiated. Thus, even when overwhelming Democratic congressional majorities, in league with a Democratic president, enacted comprehensive health care reform, they did so with a package shaped in large part by such behemoths as the pharmaceutical and insurance industries, to say nothing of dozens of groups representing narrower, but still powerful, interests, such as physician-owned hospitals and rural health cooperatives.[3]

As American politics has become more polarized and partisan since the early 1980s,[4] organized interests have both complemented and resisted this trend. Such a dualism makes sense, in that groups need to work with those in power to further their interests, while at the same time remaining free agents in defending these same interests. In particular, with their highly aggressive "K Street Project" of the late 1990s on, congressional Republicans, later joined by the George W. Bush administration, sought to dictate hiring decisions by major Washington, D.C., lobbying firms and trade associations.[5] Despite some short-term success, K Street did not become an extension of the parties. To be sure, organized interests have always followed the election returns by adjusting their tactics and hiring in light of who holds power in Washington. Still, save for a relatively small number of party-linked organizations, such as labor unions with Democrats and some small-business groups with Republicans, most interests must work to shape policies with legislative committees, executive-branch offices, and regulatory agencies that are connected to, but not dependent on, partisan politics.

We need to address several interrelated trends when assessing the status and impact of organized interests as they perform their representational tasks:

1. The eighty-year growth of public policy, largely initiated by the federal government
2. The growth of organized interests at the national and state levels, which have combined to produce a large, dense superstructure of policies, rules, and regulations
3. The related growth of spending by organized interests on lobbying and electoral politics
4. The increasingly partisan and polarized nature of American politics as a part of the context of interest group politics and the emergence of social movements

In the end, groups affect representation at both the micro and macro levels. That is, individual groups and coalitions may well affect specific policies, such as tax laws, appropriations, or regulations. At the same time, the sum of group-based activities produces large-scale impacts that reduce the capacity of the political system to represent broad societal interests. For example, the successes by many interests to win favorable tax provisions help them create a highly complex tax code that reduces the overall efficiency of the economy.[6] Finally, both parties and groups must address issues of spending and governance raised by social movements from both the left and right, often articulated through non-traditional media, ranging from talk shows to blogs to social network sites.

The Interrelated Growth of Government and Organized Interests

The story of the interwoven growth of government entities and organized interests has been told often and well, perhaps most ably by Jonathan Rauch in *Demosclerosis* and *Government's End*.[7] Although he largely addresses the growth of organized interests and lobbying, the steady proliferation of federal programs—both in number and complexity—is interest groups' essential partner. However measured—by number of employees, expenditures, pages of laws and regulations—the US government has grown steadily since the New Deal era (see Figure 16.1). No single measure captures the overall growth; for example, federal employment may shrink while outside contracting soars.[8] Still, the growth of spending has been inexorable, as has the steady increase in rules and regulations that affect all Americans but the business community disproportionately.

Figure 16.1 Growth of Government Spending

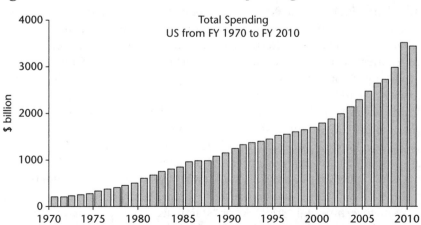

Source: http://www.usgovernmentspending.com/.

Note: This figure does not take into account inflation or GDP growth.

Within this context, groups of all stripes, but especially those representing myriad economic interests, from agribusiness to zookeepers, have sought to extract benefits from governmental programs, policies, and expenditures. Building on Mancur Olson and others, Rauch details the extent of "rent seeking"—broadly defined for groups as "lobbying the government for tax, spending or regulatory policies that benefit the lobbyists at the expense of taxpayers or consumers or some other rivals."[9] On occasion, the Congress has devised tactics to overcome this bias toward stasis, as with the military base-closing process, which requires an up-or-down vote on closing a substantial number of military facilities. The objective evidence of gross waste in keeping outdated facilities open virtually forced Congress's hand in devising a way to close bases, but this process stands out for its exceptional nature.

Even when major change does work its way through the American political system—as in the passage of the post-9/11 Patriot Act in 2002 or the passage of comprehensive health care reform in 2009–10 (see Chapter 10 by Hall and Anderson and Chapter 15 by LaPira), organized interests play major roles in shaping the nature of change. Indeed, the groups often place limitations on the extent of change (e.g., drug companies on health care reform) or use the opportunity for major change to insert various long-favored policies into comprehensive legislation, as with the Patriot Act's mélange of law enforcement groups' wish lists on wiretapping and other issues.

The question of whether groups' demands increase the size of government or whether the causal arrow largely runs in the opposite direction, from government programs and spending to the creation of more organized interests, while of theoretical significance, may be ultimately unimportant in assessing the thicket of relationships between an expanding government and a large, highly involved set of interest groups. Both spending and the number/activities of groups have grown steadily, and this does not account for the rise in the policy-oriented activities of institutions, such as corporations, universities, hospitals, cities, foundations, think tanks, and many others.

Despite some lingering debate over group formation—whether it is natural (David Truman) or fraught with organizational obstacles (Mancur Olson) or has some natural limits (Virginia Gray and David Lowery)—the growth of organized interests and governmental programs/regulations has produced a context in which organized interests and their lobbyist agents can prosper even when governmental policies do not.[10] This is especially true when it comes to assessing the overall impact of governmental policies at the national, state, and local levels. There is a temptation to think in terms of governmental "gridlock" or "stalemate," implying that policy making develops some kind of stasis in which little happens, save that new policies, spending, and regulations are piled upon old. But nothing could be further from the truth; there is continual action and often significant policy movement, at least within policy communities such as health, or transportation, or education. Indeed, orchestrating a host of actions among organized interests generates tremendous revenues and profits for lobbying firms and high salaries for many in-house corporate and trade association lobbyists.

Contemporary lobbying includes media relations, marketing, advertising, and public opinion research, to say nothing of the more traditional provision of information; all in all, it often becomes a most expensive business, especially on high-profile issues. Even on lesser issues, where there is often no serious competition, lobbyists profit from representing interests that depend on governmental decisions. Some past scholarship has viewed the relationships between organized interests and governmental actors, including legislators, administrators, and regulators, in terms of closed systems of "iron triangles" or "subgovernments."[11] Later work has broadened the analytical frame to talk more of more open policy communities and networks, in which the players are continually adjusting their levels of participation and their emphases on given policies.

Although there have been some notable triangular relationships that have dominated policy making, the community/network formulation fits well with the mutually beneficial linkages between a growing interest group population and the steady growth of governmental spending and regulation. These ties have developed across many different policy areas, albeit in distinct ways. While some corporations (General Electric) and trade associations (pharmaceuticals) lobby across many issue areas, from taxes to trade to subsidies, many remain active in a more limited policy domain, such as higher education spending, as Robert Kaiser has detailed in *So Damned Much Money*.[12] Moreover, as the economy changes and new economic giants (from Microsoft to Google, among others) enter the policy-political arena, the models of lobbying practices and communications strategies inform their actions, even as new methods, such as social networking, become established techniques.[13]

While Rauch and others emphasize the difficulties of group-based policy change and the tremendous overhang of well-established governmental policies, organized interests have steadily invested ever-increasing sums to lobby and to affect electoral outcomes. Indeed, even as partisanship has grown more powerful and the government-group nexus resists major change, organized interests have spent record amounts to influence the process.

The Growth of Spending on Lobbying and Campaigning

For most of American political history, good data on electioneering and lobbying were in short supply; after reporting reforms in the 1970s (campaign contributions) and the 1990s (lobbying expenditures), we have reasonably good, if incomplete, data. Still, with care, we can compare group-based campaign contributions and lobbying expenses across time. Here the findings are straightforward. Organized interests' spending on campaigns and lobbying has grown steadily. Over the 2009–10 election cycle, group-based expenditures totaled more than $10 billion. That sounds like a lot, but it bears noting that the annual federal budget stands at about $4 trillion, and the impacts of thousands of regulations and tax provisions may reflect even more targets for groups. Ten billion dollars spread over two years may well be a reasonable amount, given the scope and depth of governmental actions.

Lobbying

By most indicators, Washington-based lobbying has grown steadily over the past forty years (see Figures 16.2 aand 16.3). Unfortunately, the pre-1998 data are soft, at best. And there has been a modern professional lobbying corps in the capital since at least the FDR era. Still, the growth of lobbying expenditures in the 1999–2009 decade is remarkable; despite only modest inflation, reported expenditures more than doubled, and much actual spending—on unregulated grass-roots lobbying and social networking, among other things—went unreported, given the legal requirements.

   Likewise, the number of lobbyists has been seriously underestimated over the years, and this trend has accelerated in recent years, largely due to the Obama administration's well-publicized, if ineffective, attempts to limit the influence of lobbyists. As noted, those who engaged in grass-roots

Figure 16.2   Total Lobbying Spending

1998	$1.44 billion
1999	$1.44 billion
2000	$1.56 billion
2001	$1.64 billion
2002	$1.82 billion
2003	$2.04 billion
2004	$2.17 billion
2005	$2.43 billion
2006	$2.62 billion
2007	$2.85 billion
2008	$3.30 billion
2009	$3.49 billion
2010	$3.49 billion

Source: Center for Responsive Politics (OpenSecrets.org). Based on data from the Senate Office of Public Records. Data for the most recent year was downloaded on January 31, 2011.

Figure 16.3   Number of Registered Lobbyists*

Year	Number
1998	10,404
1999	12,943
2000	12,542
2001	11,845
2002	12,128
2003	12,924
2004	13,166
2005	14,075
2006	14,531
2007	14,885
2008	14,212
2009	13,721
2010	12,986

Source: Center for Responsive Politics (OpenSecrets.org). Based on data from the Senate Office of Public Records. Data for the most recent year was downloaded on January 31, 2011.

*The number of unique, registered lobbyists who have actively lobbied.

lobbying were excluded from registration requirements. And many policy strategists and lawyer/lobbyists who formally lobby only occasionally have chosen not to register with the Senate. That does not mean that, broadly speaking, they have ceased to act as lobbyists. The 13,000 or so registered lobbyists represent the top of the influence iceberg, with many other professionals (pollsters, media consultants) and support staff assisting them. Moreover, many ex-legislators, such as former senators Tom Daschle (D-SD) and Bob Dole (R-KS), have worked on the behalf of major clients without meeting the threshold for registration.

Overall, the lobbying establishment in Washington (to say nothing of state capitals), while perhaps not increasing in terms of registration, has continued to spend more money and communicate in more ways. This establishment continues to do well and perpetuate itself, and with good reason, given the range and detail of federal policies that affect all organized interests.

Campaigns: The Growth of Contributions and Direct Expenditures

Although lobbying expenditures have received increased attention from scholars, journalists, and other observers over the past fifteen years, they have regularly analyzed campaign funding since the Federal Election Commission began its reporting in 1972. For organized interests, lobbying offers a direct opportunity to affect policy outcomes, but participating in electoral politics constitutes a less direct, less certain arena for investments. Still, as Americans have become more partisan and more open to partisan change in Congress, the stakes in capturing the levers of power have grown far more important. For example, for forty years after the congressional election of 1954, Democrats controlled the House of Representatives, a fact not lost on the business community, especially after its members were reminded of this in the 1980s. Beginning with the shocking GOP victory in 1994, the House has shifted majority control three times (1994, 2006, 2010) in sixteen years. The Senate has been more volatile, with majority party status changing six times between 1980 and 2006. In short, almost every election in the modern era offers each major party the opportunity to win one or both chambers. Especially for the majority-based politics of the House, this creates great opportunities, as Speakers Nancy Pelosi (D-CA) and John Boehner (R-OH) have demonstrated in the 110th–112th Congresses (2007–2012).

Over the past forty years, the most important group-based trend in campaign funding has been the institutionalized presence of political action committees (PACs); in dollar amounts, PAC contributions rose from $50 million in the 1979–80 election cycle to $412 million in 2007–08.[14] Although once denigrated, PAC funding is now widely accepted, as it emphasizes groupings of small donors and transparency is the rule for both donations and PAC expenditures. If there is any powerful critique of PAC contributions, it is the overwhelming (75 to 80 percent) bias toward investing in incumbent lawmakers. For the most part, PACs reinforce the status quo of federal politics. This is less the case with much other group-based spending, which has grown increasingly large and partisan.

In the wake of the 2009–10 election cycle, groups can take advantage of a host of opportunities to affect electoral outcomes. Aside from the traditional means of PACs and direct contributions from individuals (union members, or doctors, or Google corporate executives, for example), organized interests can choose to spend directly on campaigns, using various channels ranging from purchasing advertisements, communicating directly with members, funding outside groups such as 527s and 501(c)(4)s with modest or no disclosure requirements. (See Chapter 7 by A. Cigler.) Much of the undisclosed funding, exemplified by $34 million spending through Karl Rove's American Crossroads (527) and Crossroads GPS (501)(c)(4) in 2009–10, may go to purchase ground-war resources (canvassing, direct mail, get-out-the-vote efforts) that are largely invisible. By and large, emboldened by Supreme Court decisions that have overthrown many limits on campaign spending, large and disproportionately conservative interests, at least as of the 2010 elections, have been advantaged in group-based electoral politics. Total spending by outside groups reached $400 million in 2010, an increase of almost 60 percent since the 2006 off-year election and an amount equal to all PAC contributions to candidates.[15] Not only has this kind of spending risen, its party-based orientation has also reinforced the broad trend toward partisan polarization in the electorate and within the Congress.

Organized Interests in a Partisan Era

Over the same past forty years that group spending on lobbying and elections has steadily grown, so too has partisan polarization in elections and legislative politics. The extent of electoral partisanship is debatable, but the trend is straightforward.[16] Even clearer is the rise in congressional partisanship, which has reached historic heights in the post-1994 era.[17] Although the Republicans' "K Street Project" did not achieve its goal of building partisan networks among groups and lobbyists, the legislative environment, on both sides of the Capitol, has become highly polarized.[18] For organized interests, such a context often means that their approach to electoral, legislative, and administrative politics must approximate a balancing act—making sure they can work with partisan majorities while protecting their own priorities, especially in terms of existing policy.

The bipartisan equilibrium of the "Textbook Congress" of the 1950s and 1960s has long been superseded by partisan majority building in the House and increased reliance on delaying tactics in the Senate. The nationalized elections of the post-2006 era have helped generate increased levels of spending by organized interests, who value the opportunity for change but also fear the lack of certainty produced by electoral swings and the related growth of ideologues within congressional parties, especially the GOP. Traditional organized interests, from the U.S. Chamber of Commerce to labor unions to multinational corporations to the largest membership organizations (e.g., AARP), must incorporate emerging social movements into their calculations and analyses; likewise, interest group scholars should address how movements like the tea party and MoveOn.org affect the stability of both group-based and partisan politics. In many ways, such movements, facilitated by social networking and fueled by small contributions, have become the wild cards of twenty-first-century politics.[19] Like many social movements, they may flame out, but they also reflect the capacity of sometimes inchoate interests to affect elections and substantive policy making.

In terms of group politics, broadly defined, the 2008 elections represented the ascendance of MoveOn.org, associated with liberals and Democrats, while those of 2010 witnessed the emergence of various tea party organizations and groupings. In large part, students of organized interests barely acknowledge the existence of party politics, to say nothing of party-linked social movements. More broadly, the overarching concept of "interest"—which helped frame analyses a century ago—has largely been ignored.[20] We have no desire to attempt to resurrect some revisionist group-based theory of politics, but we do think that placing broad interests within the context of American politics is worthwhile. In particular, we hark back to E. E. Schattschneider, the mid-twentieth-century scholar of political parties and organized interests, who fervently sought to develop strong, disciplined parties but who ultimately concluded that wealthy interests would prove more powerful than the nonideological parties of his era (1930s–1960s).[21] In *The Semisovereign People* (1960), Schattschneider famously stated, "The flaw in the pluralist heaven is that the heavenly chorus sings with a strong upper-class accent. Probably about 90 percent of the people cannot get into the pressure system."[22] This is demonstrably not true today, given the breadth of representation through organized interests, yet Schattschneider's overall conclusions ring true. Even if most people are represented, often by multiple groups, that does not mean this is done effectively at the top levels of decision making.

Sixty years after laying out his preferences in *Party Government*, Schattschneider's dream of strong, issue-based parties had been realized, yet the dominance of wealthy interests has grown much stronger.[23] In 1960, the top 1 percent of the population controlled about 31 percent of the national wealth (see Figure 16.4), and this fell to about 20 percent by 1980. Since then, this share has risen to about 35 percent, a figure exceeded in the past ninety years only by the decade of the 1920s.[24] To an extent, the partisan policies of Lyndon Johnson's Great Society and Ronald Reagan's conservative era contributed to these changes, but even a Democratic Congress over much of this period and a Democratic president in the 1990s did nothing to stem the post-1980 growth of wealth at the top. Likewise, the incomes of the wealthy reflect similar patterns, with their incomes in 2007 equaling (top 10 percent) or exceeding (top 1 percent) the levels of the Roaring Twenties.[25]

We are not arguing that organized interests, working at the behest of the wealthiest elements of American society, systematically produced these outcomes; the causes are varied and complex.[26] But as an overall interest, the wealthy have done disproportionately well, and the capacity of well-heeled interests to benefit from the extensive, expensive lobbying of investment banks, corporations, and tax specialists seems a reasonable inference. Moreover, although electoral influence is indirect and difficult to pin down, the large-scale investments in candidates from both parties have done wealthy individuals, corporations, investment banking firms, and others no harm—and probably a fair amount of economic good. Thus, even as organized interests do represent all sectors of society, including the poor and the neglected, this representation and its results scarcely produce equal access

Figure 16.4   Share of Wealth held by the Bottom 99 Percent and Top 1 Percent of US Population, 1922–2007

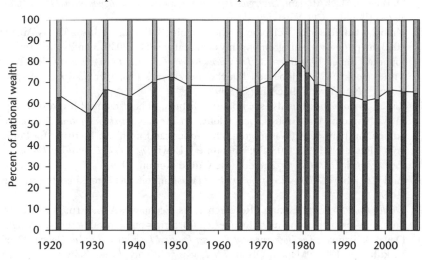

Source: E. N. Wolff, "Recent Trends in Household Wealth in the United States: Rising Debt and the Middle-Class Squeeze," Working Paper No. 502 (Annandale-on-Hudson, NY: Levy Economics Institute of Bard College, 2007).

or equal results. Moreover, although organized interests remain part of the story, they do not constitute the whole story of American politics. Rather, they operate within the contexts of our other institutions—the presidency, the Congress, the courts, the bureaucracy, the media, and elections, among others—to shape policies and be shaped by them, year to year, decade to decade.

Notes

1. Frank R. Baumgartner, Jeffrey M. Berry, Marie Hojnacki, David C. Kimball, and Beth L. Leech, *Lobbying and Policy Change: Who Wins, Who Loses, and Why* (Chicago: University of Chicago Press, 2009). More generally, see the conclusion to David Lowery and Holly Brasher's recent text, *Organized Interests and American Government* (New York: Waveland Press, 2011).
2. The official numbers come in at about $3.5 billion, but a tremendous amount of lobbying goes unreported. See Center for Responsive Politics, "Lobbying Database," http://www.opensecrets.org/lobby/index.php.
3. Among others, see Lawrence R. Jacobs and Theda Skocpol, *Health Care Reform and American Politics: What Everyone Needs to Know* (New York: Oxford University Press, 2010).

4. See, for example, Barbara Sinclair, *Party Wars: Polarization and the Politics of National Policy Making* (Norman: University of Oklahoma Press, 2006); Jeff Stonecash, Mark D. Brewer, Mack Mariani, *Diverging Parties: Social Change, Realignment, and Party Polarization* (Boulder, CO: Westview Press, 2002).

5. Nicholas Confessore, "Welcome to the Machine," *Washington Monthly,* July/August 2003, http://www.washingtonmonthly.com/features/2003/0307.confessore.html.

6. Jonathan Rauch, *Demosclerosis: The Silent Killer of American Government* (New York: Times Books, 1994); Jonathan Rauch, *Government's End: Why Washington Stopped Working* (New York: PublicAffairs, 1999).

7. Rauch, *Demosclerosis;* but also see Robert Salisbury, "The Paradox of Interest Groups in Washington: More Groups, Less Clout," in *The New American Political System,* 2nd ed., ed. Anthony King (Washington, DC: American Enterprise Institute for Public Policy Research, 1990): 203–30; Theodore J. Lowi, *The End of Liberalism: The Second Republic of the United States,* 2nd ed. (New York: Norton, 1979).

8. Paul C. Light, *The True Size of Government* (Washington, DC: Brookings Institution, 1999).

9. *The Economist,* "Rent-Seeking," Research Tools: Economics A–Z, http://www.economist.com/research/economics/alphabetic.cfm?term=randomwalk#rent-seeking/.

10. David B. Truman, *The Governmental Process: Political Interests and Public Opinion* (New York: Knopf, 1951); Mancur Olson, *The Logic of Collective Action: Public Goods and the Theory of Groups* (Cambridge, MA: Harvard University Press, 1965); Virginia Gray and David Lowery, *The Population Ecology of Interest Representation: Lobbying Communities in the American States* (Ann Arbor: University of Michigan Press, 2000).

11. See, for example, Gordon Adams. *The Politics of Defense Contracting: The Iron Triangle* (New Brunswick, NJ: Transaction Books, 1982).

12. Robert G. Kaiser, *So Damn Much Money: The Triumph of Lobbying and the Corrosion of American Government* (New York: Knopf, 2009).

13. See Michael Kinsley, "How Microsoft Learned the ABCs of D.C.," *Politico,* April 5, 2011, http://www.politico.com/news/stories/0411/52483_Page2.html.

14. Federal Election Commission, "Growth in PAC Financial Activity Slows," press release, http://www.fec.gov/press/press2009/20090415PAC/20090424PAC.shtml.

15. Danielle Kurtzleben, "Outside Spending Reached $400 Million in 2010 Election," *U.S. News and World Report,* November 9, 2010, http://www.usnews.com/news/articles/2010/11/09/outside-spending-reached-400-million-in-2010-election/.

16. Morris Fiorina, *Disconnect: The Breakdown of Representation in American Politics,* with Samuel J. Abrams (Norman: University of Oklahoma Press, 2009); Alan I. Abramowitz, *The Disappearing Center: Engaged Citizens, Polarization, and American Democracy* (New Haven, CT: Yale University Press, 2010).

17. For House, see Sinclair, *Party Wars;* for Senate, see Burdett Loomis, ed., *The U.S. Senate: From Deliberation to Dysfunction* (Washington, DC: CQ Press, 2011).

18. Ronald Brownstein, "Pulling Apart," *National Journal,* February 24, 2011, http://www.nationaljournal.com/magazine/congress-hits-new-peak-in-polarization-20110224/.

19. To be sure, many large donors/spenders, such as the Kochs, George Soros, et al., took part, but MoveOn.org raised almost $39 million in the 2007–08 cycle and less than $4 million of that total was in contributions of more than $200. See Center for Responsive Politics, "PACs: MoveOn.org," http://www.opensecrets.org/pacs/lookup2.php?cycle=2008&strID=C00341396.

20. Arthur F. Bentley, *The Process of Government* (Chicago: University of Chicago Press, 1908); Truman, *The Governmental Process*.
21. E. E. Schattschneider, *The Semisovereign People: A Realist's View of Democracy in America* (Hinsdale, IL: Dryden Press, 1975).
22. Schattschneider, *The Semisovereign People*, 34–35.
23. E. E. Schattschneider, *Party Government* (New York: Holt, Rinehart, and Winston, 1942).
24. G. William Domhoff, "Wealth, Income, and Power," updated January 2011, http://sociology.ucsc.edu/whorulesamerica/power/wealth.html.
25. Emmanuel Saez, "Striking It Richer: The Evolution of Top Incomes in the United States (Update with 2007 Estimates)," University of California, Department of Economics, August 5, 2009, http://escholarship.org/uc/item/8dp1f91x/.
26. Among others, see Larry Bartels, *Unequal Democracy: The Political Economy of the New Guilded Age* (Princeton, NJ: Princeton University Press, 2008).

Index

Note: page numbers followed by *f, t, b,* or n refer to figures, tables, boxes, and endnotes, respectively.